A SELECTED EDITION OF W. D. HOWELLS

Volume 29

Years of My Youth

AND

Three Essays

W. D. HOWELLS

Years of My Youth

AND

Three Essays

Introduction and Notes to the Text
by David J. Nordloh

Text Established by
David J. Nordloh

INDIANA UNIVERSITY PRESS

Bloomington and London

1975

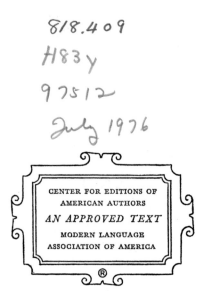

*Editorial expenses for this volume have been met in part by grants from
the National Endowment for the Humanities administered through the Center
for Editions of American Authors of the Modern Language Association.*

*Copyright © 1975 by Indiana University Press
and the Howells Edition Editorial Board*

*Library of Congress catalog card number: 78-166119
Standard Book Number: 0-253-36850-2*

Manufactured in the United States of America

Acknowledgments

FOR indispensable support in money and morale the editor of this volume and the Howells Edition Center gladly express their gratitude to John W. Ryan, President, and Lynne L. Merritt, Jr., Vice-President and Dean, Research and Advanced Studies, Indiana University. Gratitude is due as well to Herman B Wells and the Indiana University Foundation for the generous support provided for the production and printing of this volume. William White Howells and the heirs of W. D. Howells also deserve special acknowledgment for their gracious assistance and cooperation.

The editor could not have worked without the assistance of the student staff at the Howells Edition Center, especially Robert D. Schildgen, James P. Elliott and Ann Webster, or the continuing effort of Anthony Shipps of the Indiana University Library and Mrs. Gail Mathews and the staff of the Indiana University Interlibrary Loan Department.

Finally, the editor wishes to express his special thanks to those who gave so much of their time and thought to the work on this volume when it was being originally prepared as his doctoral dissertation at Indiana University, particularly his research committee—Edwin H. Cady, Ronald Gottesman, Philip B. Daghlian and Robert Dyer—Howells scholars George Arms, William M. Gibson and Louis J. Budd, and the staffs of the Houghton Library of Harvard University, the American Antiquarian Society and the Ohio Historical Society.

Contents

Illustration: Howells at age 79, by Underwood and Underwood,
from *The Outlook*, CXIV (29 November 1916), 705.
following page xxvii

Introduction

In November 1903, writing to longtime friend Thomas Sergeant Perry, Howells first raised the notion of writing that autobiography of which *Years of My Youth* represents the only completed part:

> I am writing an Easy Chair essay on autobiography apropos of Stoddard's and Trowbridge's in their contrasting unimportance, which I hope may interest you if you ever read it. I think I will write my own life, but these other minor authors have taught me that if I am to make a worthwhile book, I must tell of what I have been in the love of literature, rather than of what I have done. The way they whoop it up over their forgotten books, T. especially, is amusing.[1]

That Howells should think of writing his own life, at the end of a sixteen-year period during which he had written many things which could in one way or another qualify as autobiographical is, at first glance, difficult to understand. He had already published several reminiscences: "Year in a Log-Cabin, A Bit of Autobiography," first printed in 1887, a sketch of his family's stay at Eureka Mills on the Little Miami River in Ohio during that abortive communal experiment of 1850; *A Boy's Town*, serialized in *Harper's Young People* in 1890; the re-creation of the old-fashioned printing-shop in "The Country Printer" in May 1893; his life with books told in *My Literary Passions*, which ran for sixteen months in the *Ladies' Home Journal* beginning in December 1893; and the series of pieces, starting with "My First Visit to New England" in 1894, which culminated in

---

1. 22 November 1903; quoted in Richard Cary, "William Dean Howells to Thomas Sergeant Perry," *Colby Library Quarterly*, VIII (1968), 170–171.

Literary Friends and Acquaintance in 1900—the book about which he confessed to Thomas Bailey Aldrich in the midst of his final preparations, "In these days I seem to be all autobiography."[2]

The "Easy Chair" essay on autobiography,[3] which takes for its occasion the publication of Richard Henry Stoddard's *Recollections, Personal and Literary*, and J. T. Trowbridge's *Story of My Own Life*, emphasizes those qualities of the form most important to Howells as a realist, as the critic who would have literature emphasize "the smiling aspects of life": adherence to the average and the common, a generally optimistic attitude, and truth to the facts. Howells refers to autobiography as the most interesting and comprehensible of forms because it speaks to all men in all conditions: "The course of autobiography is . . . commonly not much above or below that of the ordinary lives of men. In fact, the greater part of the extraordinary lives of men keep the common mean, and perhaps that which fascinates us most in the self-portraiture of a distinguished man is the strong family likeness between his features and our own." Further, autobiography is to be preferred to any of the other confessional forms because of a general "cheerfulness" of effect resulting from the autobiographer's remaining perpetually alive on the page even when the book ends: "Biography suffers from the tragical close which involves the death of the protagonist, while autobiography is a melodrama which, whatever disaster it drags him through, at least brings him off alive." Moreover, the autobiographer can have an "impartiality and sincerity" which the biographer, who often must pay his respects to a family or public ideal or a grown or growing popular legend, cannot observe: "The autobiographer . . . may write of himself as he pleases, without fear of his wife and children, or his uncles and cousins; if he has any faults he may be trusted to deal with them in that tolerant spirit which more closely allies mercy than justice to wisdom."

---

2. 10 June 1900; quoted in *Life in Letters of William Dean Howells*, ed. Mildred Howells (Garden City, N.Y., 1928), II, 129.

3. "Editor's Easy Chair," *Harper's Monthly*, CVIII (1904), 478–482.

Finally, through these general considerations and through his specific criticism of the Stoddard and Trowbridge volumes runs a concern dominating all others: the function of the auto-biographer is to focus as fully as possible on himself, to reminisce about the persons and things around him only insofar as he must to tell his story:

> What we wish first and last and most of an autobiographer is himself, and this he cannot give us too freely or fully. We grudge the moments which he yields to others, except as they distinctly help to characterize him and explain him.

In view of these distinctions, then, no earlier piece could serve as the autobiography of W. D. Howells. "Year in a Log-Cabin," "The Country Printer," *A Boy's Town*, *My Literary Passions* and *Literary Friends and Acquaintance* were all studies of the worlds and literatures among which he lived rather than of his life; and they failed to tell of "what I have been in the love of literature, rather than of what I have done."

But the true autobiography he spoke of was long in coming. And the record of the preparation of it which went on during the next thirteen years is a story of changing plans and frustrated negotiations about publication, of a continuing search for infor-mation in the records of his personal and his public life, and of the struggle of a man with his own idea of himself.

Howells' next attempt at telling part of his life story again fell short of his definition of autobiography. In 1909 he began to write brief prefaces for each volume in the "Library Edition" of his works planned by Harper and Brothers, placing the books in the context of his life and career. He was at first enthusiastic about the project, writing to Frederick A. Duneka, Harper rep-resentative who handled Howells' general relations with the company, that "I am writing the 'Story of the Story' for a pref-ace to 'A Hazard of New Fortunes.' It goes so glibly that I am likely to have an unrequited passion for that kind of thing."[4]

---

4. 9 June 1909; quoted in Robert W. Walts, "William Dean Howells and His 'Library Edition'," *PBSA*, LII (1958), 288.

But soon he decided the idea would not work after all, and wrote to tell Duneka so:

> I have made a careful experiment of the type in an introduction to A Hazard of New Fortunes, and have convinced myself that I cannot write prefaces for the library edition, much as I would like to meet your wish in the matter. I believe I was right in wishing the volumes to go the public without any word of explanation or comment from me, because they are already most intimately full of me, and are their own explanation and comment.

But he softened the blow of his refusal with a postscript concession: "If it seems possible, when the edition is completed, to add a volume of Literary Autobiography, in which the story of my work as an author, rather that [sic] of my life shall be told, I may like to supply it. That would give the edition a novelty and distinction which the separate prefaces could not give."[5] Duneka, in reply, disagreed with Howells' opinion of the introductions, but conceded the point for the moment and continued:

> That is an interesting vista you opened when you say you might add a volume of literary autobiography which would tell the story of your work as an author. I wish this could be written and tell, not only of your work as an author, but also something of your life. Such a book should be written,—it is your sacred duty to write it and it should take its place with the four or five great lives that have enriched our literature.[6]

Howells took up the project in earnest. He wrote to his sister Aurelia, asking her to send all she could find of the old letters he had written to the family, and commented to his brother Joe a short while later on the experience of reading them through:

> It is cruel hard looking over them, and like delving in the

---

5. 19 June 1909. MS at American Antiquarian Society. Permission to quote from unpublished letters and papers written by Howells has been granted by William White Howells for the heirs of the Howells Estate. No republication may be made without this same permission.

6. 21 June 1909. Carbon of missing typescript letter at American Antiquarian Society.

tombs. I wish I was young enough to make material, literary material, out of the experience, but I recognize every day this part of my life is over. Things suggest themselves, but they don't grip me, and hold me to them as they used. Perhaps I may note something of the kind in the autobiography.[7]

But almost as suddenly as the idea of a full "literary autobiography" was raised, it seems to have disappeared from the center of Howells' attention. Instead in March 1910 he published, as one in a series of "turning-point" articles by famous people in *Harper's Bazar*, his story of that crucial decision in 1864 to try his hand in the competition of the literary East rather than to return to his native West.[8] In April he picked up another strand from his past, and wrote to Aurelia and Annie for information about it: "I am, after reflecting for 44 years, resuming my story of Eureka Mills, which I left off in 1866. I find the stuff very good, but my treatment of it loathsomely 'young.' I am bringing that up to date, however, and wish you girls would write out, no matter how vaguely, what you remember about our going to the Mills, and our life there."[9] And while he was at work on the fictional version of that story (which was published with the title *New Leaf Mills* in January 1913), six volumes of the "Library Edition," all with "Bibliographical" prefaces despite Howells' trepidation, were being released by Harper and Brothers.[10]

Then talk of autobiography began again. In November 1912, shortly after refusing Albert Bigelow Paine's kind offer to write a biography of him,[11] Howells advised Duneka that he was "blocking out and detailing in 'My Times and Places: an Auto-

---

7. 4 July 1909; *Life in Letters*, II, 267–268.
8. "The Turning Point of My Life," *Harper's Bazar*, XLIV (1910), 165–166.
9. 10 April 1910. Typed transcription at Harvard of missing letter. The manuscripts of these and all other letters cited are at Harvard unless otherwise noted. These materials are used by permission of the Harvard College Library.
10. The details concerning the six volumes of the edition, issued on 26 July 1911, are discussed in Walts, "William Dean Howells and His 'Library Edition' ''; several other prefaces had been prepared but did not appear: see George Arms, "Howells's Unpublished Prefaces," *NEQ*, XVII (1944), 580–591.
11. *Life in Letters*, II, 326.

biography.' "[12] The following March he was still making plans for the book, and asked Duneka for plenty of time to work on it, perhaps even till the following spring.[13] In the meantime, the illness of his daughter Mildred led to their plans for going abroad, though Howells appeased Duneka with the suggestion that during the trip he and she "could be talking autobiography in the form it seems to be taking with me."[14]

In December 1913, back in the United States, he was hard at work gathering information for the series of magazine-installment articles which he anticipated would eventually comprise the book. He wrote to the editors of the *Ohio State Journal* in Columbus to inquire about the history of the paper during his involvement with it in the late eighteen fifties and early sixties,[15] and advised Duneka that, following the divisions of the material he had indicated in the outline, "I am working at the paper on 'A State Capital Fifty Years Ago,' and I have some lively hopes of it's [sic] turning out worth while."[16] From this point to publication of *Years of My Youth*, Howells' letters are a record of the repeated changes of shape his material underwent, in response both to his publisher's demands and, more importantly, to his own mixed joy and sorrow with the whole process.

On 28 December he advised Duneka, "I have got on rather amazingly with my autobiographical study of Columbus, and there are moments when I do not blush for it. But I am going to

---

12. MS at American Antiquarian Society. The outline, represented by what seems to be Howells' original manuscript draft, is now in the Harper Collection at the Pierpont Morgan Library. For a transcription of it, see Appendix A to the present edition, pp. 253–257.

13. 29 March 1913. MS in George Arms' collection.

14. 1 June 1913. MS at American Antiquarian Society.

15. Howells corresponded regularly with Theodore T. Frankenberg of the *Journal* staff throughout this final period of preparation of the autobiography, requesting information and answering questions; Frankenberg in turn sent Howells clippings from the old *Journal* and whatever else he could learn about the pre-Civil War period in Columbus. The Martha Kinney Cooper Ohioana Library Association in Columbus has letters from Howells to Frankenberg dated 11, 24, 31 January, 7 February, 18 August, 27 September, and 6 November 1914; Frankenberg's letters to Howells are also in the Ohioana Library Association.

16. 14 December 1913. MS at American Antiquarian Society.

be very severe with it before I let you have it. Really it is at least an original way of looking at the subject and the author; at times the reader will not know which is which."[17] When he detailed the work to his son, John Mead Howells, two weeks later, however, that initial pleasure had begun to fade:

> I am working every day at the autobiog., with a general feeling that it is truck. I always supposed my Columbus life was most brilliant and joyous, but I can't seem to prove it, or that it was even important. I find largely that Tolstoy was right when in trying to furnish reminiscences for his biographer he declared that remembering was Hell: with the little brave and good you recall so much bad and base. However, I shall push on and get it all down, and then cut, cut, cut, until I make myself a respectable figure—somebody that the boys [John's sons] won't want to ignore when people speak of him. At present I feel that they may wish to change their names, or their last name, unless Fafa White [John's father-in-law, Horace White] makes out such a bad case for himself that mine shall seem better.[18]

And so the record continued in all its excruciating details, as Howells struggled with memories and the words for them. While Duneka offered reassurance,[19] Howells called upon his wife's cousin Laura Mitchell for help:

> Now, there is something I should like you to tell me. I have finished my Columbus history, but I have not been able to say anything about meeting Elinor, the vastly most important thing in my whole life. I haven't brought myself even to mention her, or so much as to say that here I met the one who became my wife. What shall I do? In his memoir my father barely noted the fact in regard to my mother, but they were most tenderly and beautifully attached, and from my own widowerhood, I know that he was always thinking of her. If I indulged my feel-

---

17. MS at American Antiquarian Society.
18. 12 January 1914; *Life in Letters*, II, 331.
19. 5 February 1914. Carbon of missing typescript letter at American Antiquarian Society.

ing, I should not say anything; that part of me is inexpressible. What do you think?[20]

By 15 April he was able to tell Duneka, "I have been pressed beyond anything I could have imagined with my reminiscences, in order to avoid repeating things already written, and to give the right form to the work. This has interfered with everything else, but at last I have nearly finished them, and I hope soon to show them to you." He went on in a postscript: "How do you like 'Years of my Youth' as a name for the reminiscences? There will be three papers."[21]

By early May 1914, Harper and Brothers had received and responded to the first installment of the long-proposed autobiography, and Howells was reacting plaintively to the suggestions his editors were making for it:

> It is my confession, it is a study of an old fashioned state capitol, it is the echo of a period. If much of either interest is left out it will be a hollow thing indeed. I say this frankly, feeling that I may be quite wrong, but so it seems to me, and I am by nature both editor and author, you know. I can pinch and pare, but to cut out pounds of flesh nearest my heart! Very likely the whole thing is a mistake; I don't say it isn't; but without the carefully painted background of time and place, it will be a lifeless portrait of me!
>
> You speak of "the book". Had you thought of publishing this apart from the rest of the autobiography, or don't you want any "rest"?[22]

Duneka replied that he did indeed want all that Howells was willing to write and explained, "I ventured to suggest certain deletions because the Magazine is such an ephemeral thing. Many men will buy one number and not the next, and an equal number of people will buy the second number and not the first. There is no continuity of background possible in a magazine."[23]

---

20. 9 February 1914; *Life in Letters*, II, 333.
21. 15 April 1914. MS in George Arms' collection.
22. 6 May 1914. MS in George Arms' collection.
23. 7 May 1914. Carbon of missing typescript letter in George Arms' collection.

Howells was sufficiently encouraged by Duneka's words to begin another of the sections outlined in his synopsis and to request more space in the magazine.[24] But the new episode, which he entitled "Hours of Childhood," also presented problems. He wrote to Aurelia about some of them: "At present I am working on my child life in Hamilton and Dayton, annoyed by having done so much of it already in my different books. Every now and then I reach into the emptiness where Joe was [Joe Howells had died in August 1912] and father was, and recover my balance with an effort" (25 May 1914). And when he sent the section to Duneka the next week, Howells showed his dissatisfaction with it and went on to make a specific proposal about the book which might result from his work:

> I hardly expected to be on time with the paper I am sending you by registered post today, and I am full of misgiving as to the wisdom of magazining it. Perhaps, after all, it will be best to begin at once with the Columbus episode, and let this begin a possible book to be made up of this paper, a reprint of *My Year in a Log Cabin*, a paper called *The Old Country Printer* and the Columbus chapters. Such a book would form a continuous autobiography up to the time I left Columbus; the rest we could "leave to God", as people used to do with their troubles.[25]

Duneka agreed that the piece was not quite right for the magazine, but that "in a book it is exactly as should be,"[26] and Howells replied with complete satisfaction:

> I am very glad indeed that you will not use my infant memoirs and pedigree in the magazine. The whole thing must be reshaped, and made the first part of the book, and we must begin with the Columbus episode in the monthly. At your convenience please return the copy of "Hours of Childhood." I have had several nightmares from it.[27]

---

24. 13 May 1914. MS at American Antiquarian Society.
25. 1 June 1914. MS in George Arms' collection.
26. 3 June 1914. Carbon of missing typescript letter in George Arms' collection.
27. 4 June 1914. MS at American Antiquarian Society.

When Duneka returned the paper Howells spent some time looking it over and admitted that, though he saw some way to make use of it, "For the most of these Hours of Childhood we will let sleeping dogs lie."[28]

On 23 June Howells was asking Duneka for proofs of the first of the three magazine installments to begin appearing in the September issue of *Harper's Monthly*.[29] Again he offered suggestions and continued his lament:

> If it is possible to return to the original title of my paper, I would like it to be called *In an Old-Time State Capital* instead of *Days of My Youth* as it now stands. I know that the last is the more taking name, but my first intention was to make the scene more important than the actors; (I wish I could have made it *all* scene) and the title now suggested would represent this intention. The much-cutting which the laws of space have exacted has hurt the proportions of the thing; I have not done it well; and I would like to save its face as much as possible. May I ask for early proofs of the remaining part, with your instructions as to how much cutting will be needed? Perhaps I can do better than I have done.[30]

There is a long silence in the extant letters, broken briefly in September by Howells' concern with the effect of the war growing in Europe on the book toward which he was working: "I suppose our poor little dirigible of an autobiography has fallen fluttering dead from the belligerent fire over yonder. Later I may want to talk of it."[31] In the meantime, "In an Old-Time State Capital," in three papers, ran in the September through November 1914 issues of *Harper's Monthly*.

Early the next year Howells wrote again to Thomas Sergeant Perry, with whom he had first raised the idea of writing the auto-

---

28. WDH to Duneka, 11 June 1914. MS at American Antiquarian Society.

29. MS at American Antiquarian Society.

30. WDH to Duneka, 12 July 1914. MS in George Arms' collection.

31. WDH to Duneka, 23 September 1914. MS in George Arms' collection. The "dirigible" is probably a reference to the German use of Zeppelins in the war and the preparation of defenses against them.

biography, to boast that "I have emancipated myself from my autobiography for the time, at least."[32] By March, however, his mind had returned to the book. He wrote Duneka proposing to get it ready for fall publication, and joked that fall would be as good a time as any for a book that wouldn't sell.[33] Duneka replied—

> We all think it would be a splendid notion to publish your "Old State Capital" this autumn. We need what we call a serious book to round out our list, and we could put special effort upon this volume in the expectation of selling it fairly well.
>
> I wish it were possible to achieve a better title than the one tentatively taken. The public is not interested in an "Old State Capital", but it is interested in anything associated with Mr. Howells. Can't you consider a more personal title?[34]

Howells responded quickly:

> Good! What do you think of—
> *Some Years of My Youth*
> in
> *An Old State-Capital*
> as a title?[35]

Two days later Duneka stated his agreement, and two days after that, 25 March 1915, Howells and Harper and Brothers formalized a contract for a book to be called *Some Days of My Youth in an Old State Capital*, on which Harper and Brothers agreed to pay Howells a 20% royalty.[36]

There was evidently little correspondence between author and publisher in the months that followed. On 29 April Howells forwarded a few pages of his book, "for business purposes," probably so that the printer could prepare sample text in type and the

32. 23 February 1915; quoted in Cary, "William Dean Howells to Thomas Sergeant Perry," p. 172.
33. 17 March 1915. MS at Brown University.
34. 19 March 1915.
35. 21 March 1915. MS at Brown University.
36. Contract at Harvard.

advertising department could have excerpts.[37] In June he asked Duneka to return what appears to have been some form of the "childhood" manuscript so that Howells could "make it the beginning of 'Years of my Youth' which you are to publish in the fall."[38] Finally, on 6 July, Duneka acknowledged receipt of the full manuscript.

Howells' relative silence during that two-and-a-half-month period is testimony to his struggle with his memories and his book. At one point, he asked Aurelia to help him recall that awful experience which he had never touched upon publicly before and which, even when he did relate it in *Years of My Youth*, he was still hesitant to explore:

> Do you, or does Annie, remember anything of that dreadful summer when I suffered from the fear of hydrophobia? Did father ever mention it in his later life to you? Just what summer was it? I think when I was about seventeen. . . . I think the episode is necessary to a full realization of my life.[39]

A month later he was complaining to Henry James: "I am doing my miserable memoirs, which really make me sick; but I promised to do them. I end them with going off to Venice. It is something awful and I wonder the more at the grace and ease with which you carry off your past in those two blithe books of yours."[40]

On 25 September 1915 Harper and Brothers began advertising the new year's crop of books, and *Some Years of My Youth* headed the list.[41] In the meantime Howells was trying to conclude his work on the autobiography, though with little success. The following April, still not satisfied with the shape or content of it, he appealed to Duneka:

---

37. WDH to Duneka, 29 April 1915. MS at Brown University. See A Note on the Manuscripts, p. 313ff., for a discussion of possible extant remnants of this stage of the text.

38. WDH to Duneka, 16 June 1915. MS at Brown University.

39. 23 May 1915.

40. 29 June 1915; *Life in Letters*, II, 350. The "two blithe books" are the two autobiographical works James had completed by this time: *A Small Boy and Others* (1913) and *Notes of a Son and Brother* (1914).

41. *Publishers' Weekly*, LXXXVIII (1915), 857.

If you bring out *Years of My Youth* in the autumn, that will be *three* books from me in the year, and I hope that to avoid this effect of pushing the public you will postpone the autobiography till next year. It is possible, if you can manage this that I may add a fourth part to it composed of that study of my old diary which you declined for the magazine, and of some other material which I have found, but I cannot promise this. What I wish to do now is to put the situation before you, and to beg you in view of its undesirability not to announce the book for this coming fall.[42]

But Harper and Brothers did not care to wait longer. The book was printed in a pre-publication run in June 1916, by which time Howells also managed to incorporate the diary materials he had spoken of.[43] On 23 September *Publishers' Weekly* carried the Harper fall list, this time headed by *Years of My Youth*, the title finally given the long-planned book.[44] Howells' search for and shaping of material were ended, not by the fulfillment of his ambition but by a publisher's deadline.

● Reviews of the book were few but generally appreciative, speaking with respect of Howells' place in American letters, praising *Years of My Youth* for its charm and noting its importance as a document of American history.[45] The *Independent* spoke of it as the "unpretentious record of the growing up of an Ohio

---

42. 3 April 1916. MS at the University of Rochester. The other two books were *The Daughter of the Storage*, published in April 1916, and *The Leatherwood God*, published in October 1916.

43. At pp. 61–67 in the present text; see also A Note on the Manuscripts, p. 329, for a discussion of an early manuscript of this section, entitled "The Real Diary of a Boy." With the exception of this addition, *Years of My Youth* was made essentially from the elements which Howells had enumerated for Duneka in June 1914—"Year in a Log-Cabin," "A Country Printer" and the "Columbus chapters," but with the addition of the "childhood" materials; see above, p. xix, and the Textual Commentary to the present edition, pp. 295–303.

44. *Publishers' Weekly*, XC (1916), 961.

45. *Years of My Youth* was reviewed in the following: Boston *Transcript*, 6 December 1916, p. 5; *Independent*, LXXXIX (22 January 1917), 153; *Literary Digest*, LIV (27 January 1917), 199, 202; New York *Times*, 3 December 1916, pp. 529, 539; *American Review of Reviews*, LV (January 1917), 99; *Spectator* (London), CXVII (30 December 1916), 834–835; Springfield *Republican*, 4 December 1916, p. 6; *Times Literary Supplement*, 7 December 1916, p. 585.

lad," and concluded it was "a book of real charm, and, as well, a valuable addition to our social history." The reviewer for the *Literary Digest* began with Renan's assertion "that the most interesting period in the life of distinguished men is their youth. . . . Intrinsically golden, that epoch of life hardly needs the adventitious aid of literary art to make it alluring to the reader." And, speaking of *Years of My Youth* in particular, he found the book perfect in every way: "When [the record of youth] exists for us complete, and has the charming mold of autobiography, there is little left to be desired in the way of literary interest." The reviewer for the New York *Times* referred to Howells' long and distinguished career and described *Years of My Youth* as "the story of a man's youth, told with a compelling charm from the ripe viewpoint of an age that has never lost touch with what is young and growing and beautiful"; he also pointed to the importance of the book as a cultural document, "full of the American spirit at its best and American accomplishment at its finest. . . ." The *Spectator* echoed the usual compliment by referring to it as "this delightful volume," but went on to find some degree of fault: "Mr. Howells writes of his memory as being 'perversely eclectic,' and he sometimes tantalizes us by his omissions; for instance, when he just alludes to an evening spent at the office of a paper he was connected with by Artemus Ward, whom, by the way, he is not afraid to describe as a 'unique genius.' But in the main his memory has served him singularly well." The review concludes that "Of the charm of the book it is difficult to speak in overpraise."

The reviewer for the *Times Literary Supplement*, proffering the most perceptive analysis, found *Years of My Youth* an important reflection upon Howells' civilized literary attitude and the career which had embodied it. He first scrutinized Howells' "realism," comparing it to that of Henry James:

> Both James and Howells have been what is vaguely termed "realists," but their attitude to reality was very dissimilar. Every careful reader of James is aware of the fact that, in spite

of his elaborate discretion, he shrank from probing none of the darkest secrets of the soul. Mr. Howells, on the other hand, has wilfully held his eyes averted from all the moral disease which leads to violent human action. His peculiarity as a novelist resides in his paradoxical relation to experience. No one has, within the sphere of his selection, kept closer than he to the formula of "naturalism" which Zola laid down. But he has restrained his attention from dwelling on anything unpleasant. He makes no secret of having done this on purpose.

Years of My Youth is thus the embodiment of the best American qualities, written by the finest of her authors: "At his great age he is the most dignified figure in the intellectual world of America, and rarely has a country produced a man of letters more consistently representative of her qualities."

Private reaction to the book was slight. The different members of his family expressed their pleasure with it, but there was little else—nor could there have very well been, since most of Howells' circle were gone, taken by death from the world in which he continued to live and write. After thirteen years of work he had to content himself with the respectful admiration of reviewers.

Clearly the writing of *Years of My Youth* had been a trial for Howells. The struggle to find material and to shape and make sense out of it and out of himself plagued his effort and overshadowed the joy he often took in the remembrance of the friends and pleasures of his youth. Despite his critical enthusiasm for the optimism and cheerfulness of autobiography, *Years of My Youth* is a book sobered by the knowledge of a life spent and not to be recovered. And it carries the scars of a personality which could not give itself so "freely or fully" as Howells believed the best autobiography should. The evidence of heavy revision in the surviving typescript and other working papers is one sign of Howells' grappling with the angels of memory and honesty.

He was conscious of his struggle, as the brief opening statements heading the four parts of the book reveal. At the beginning of Part IV he wrote concerning a man's remembrance of his youth that "In his own behalf, or to his honor and glory, he cannot recall the whole of his past, but if he is honest enough to intimate some of its facts he may be able to serve a later generation. His reminiscences even in that case, must be a tissue of egotism, and he will merit nothing from their altruistic effect" (page 153). And, most strikingly, at the beginning of Part III he confessed that man's "instinct of self-preservation will safeguard him from showing himself quite as he was," that the attempt to tell the truth will never result in the full truth: "No man, unless he puts on the mask of fiction, can show his real face or the will behind it" (page 110).

Outside the book, too, his later writings hinted his hard-found knowledge that autobiography is never that full record of a soul which he had imagined before attempting *Years of My Youth.* In an "Easy Chair" review of *The Education of Henry Adams* and two other current autobiographies, he made a new concession. He complained that Adams' record of his experience was far from complete. "But," he continued, "an autobiographer is always a privileged person, with inalienable rights to tell how much or how little he will, in what manner he will; and the reader is not his confessor with the right to impose a penance for an attitude which does not please him; the matter is always more vital than the manner."[46]

Yet, after all the pain, there remained the essential fascination which exploration of his life brought him. Despite his own statements that he would write no more about his life, that his daughter would carry on the project if anyone did, Howells was arranging with Harper in November 1916 for the publication of autobiographical papers on the Venetian period which followed upon the end of *Years of My Youth.* In August 1917 he reported to his sister Annie that he had written three such papers during the summer—they saw publication in *Harper's Monthly* in November 1918 and April and May 1919 as "Overland to Venice," "An Old Venetian Friend" and "A Young Venetian Friend."

---

46. "Editor's Easy Chair," *Harper's Monthly,* CXXXVIII (1919), 423.

And in March 1920, two months before his death, he was still at work, preparing an outline of the next section of his autobiography, which would include these essays, and writing in anticipation to the editor of *Harper's Monthly* that he had "blocked out the six papers of the new book, 'Years of My Middle Life.' "[47]

D. J. N.

---

47. WDH to Thomas B. Wells, 25 March 1920. MS in the Pierpont Morgan Library. The three essays are reprinted, with full textual apparatus, in the present edition. The transcription of a manuscript draft of the outline of "Years of My Middle Life," now at Harvard, appears in Appendix B, pp. 257–258.

Howells at age 79,
by Underwood and Underwood, from *The Outlook*,
CXIV (29 November 1916), 705.

Years of My Youth

AND

Three Essays

YEARS OF MY YOUTH

I

It is hard to know the child's own earliest recollections from the things it has been told of itself by those with whom its life began. They remember for it the past which it afterward seems to remember for itself; the wavering outline of its nature is shadowed against the background of family, and from this it imagines an individual existence which has not yet begun. The events then have the quality of things dreamt, not lived, and they remain of that impalpable and elusive quality in all the after years.

1

Of the facts which I must believe from the witness of others, is the fact that I was born on the 1st of March, 1837, at Martin's Ferry, Belmont County, Ohio. My father's name was William Cooper Howells, and my mother's was Mary Dean; they were married six years before my birth, and I was the second child in their family of eight. On my father's side my people were wholly Welsh, except his English grandmother, and on my mother's side wholly German, except her Irish father, of whom it is mainly known that he knew how to win my grandmother Elizabeth Dock away from her very loving family, where they dwelt in great Pennsylvania-German comfort and prosperity on their farm near Harrisburg, to share with him the hardships of the wild country over the westward mountains. She was the favorite of her brothers and sisters, and the best-beloved of her mother,

3

perhaps because she was the youngest; there is a shadowy legend that she went one evening to milk the cows, and did not return from following after her husband; but I cannot associate this romantic story with the aging grandmother whom I tenderly loved when a child, and whom I still fondly remember. She spoke with a strong German accent, and she had her Luther Bible, for she never read English. Sometimes she came to visit my home-sick mother after we went to live in southern Ohio; once I went with my mother to visit her in the little town where I was born, and of that visit I have the remembrance of her stopping me on the stairs, one morning when I had been out, and asking me in her German idiom and accent, "What fur a tay is it, child?"

I can reasonably suppose that it is because of the mixture of Welsh, German, and Irish in me that I feel myself so typically American, and that I am of the imaginative temperament which has enabled me all the conscious years of my life to see reality more iridescent and beautiful, or more lurid and terrible than any make-believe about reality. Among my father's people the first who left Wales was his great-grandfather. He established himself in London as a clock and watch maker, and I like to believe that it is his name which my tall clock, paneled in the lovely *chinoiserie* of Queen Anne's time, bears graven on its dial. Two sons followed him, and wrought at the same art, then almost a fine art, and one of them married in London and took his English wife back with him to Wales. His people were, so far as my actual knowledge goes, middle-class Welsh, but the family is of such a remote antiquity as in its present dotage not to know what part of Wales it came from. As to our lineage a Welsh clergyman, a few years ago, noting the identity of name, invited me to the fond conjecture of descent from Hywel Dda, or Howel the Good, who became king of Wales about the time of Alfred the Great. He codified the laws or rather the customs of his realm, and produced one of the most interesting books I have read, and I have finally preferred him as an ancestor because he was the first literary man of our name. There was a time when I leaned toward the delightful James Howell, who wrote the *Familiar Letters* and many books in verse and prose, and was of several shades of politics in the difficult days of Charles and Oliver; but I was forced to relinquish him because he was never married. My father, for his part, when once questioned as to our origin, answered that so far as he could make out we derived from a blacksmith, whom he considered a good sort of ancestor, but he could not name him, and he must have been, whatever his merit, a person of extreme obscurity.

There is no record of the time when my great-grandfather with his brothers went to London and fixed there as watchmakers. My tall clock, which bears our name on its dial, has no date, and I can only imagine their London epoch to have begun about the middle of the eighteenth century. Being Welsh, they were no doubt musical, and I like to cherish the tradition of singing and playing women in our line, and a somehow cousinship with the famous Parepa. But this is very uncertain; what is certain is that when my great-grandfather went back to Wales he fixed himself in the little town of Hay, where he began the manufacture of Welsh flannels, a fabric still esteemed for its many virtues, and greatly prospered. When I visited Hay in 1883 (my father always called it, after the old fashion, The Hay, which was the right version of its Norman name of La Haye), three of his mills were yet standing, and one of them was working, very modestly, on the sloping bank of the lovely river Wye. Another had sunk to be a stable, but the third, in the spirit of our New World lives, had become a bookstore and printing-office, a well-preserved stone edifice of four or five stories, such as there was not the like of, probably, in the whole of Wales when Hywel Dda was king. My great-grandfather was apparently an excellent business man, but I am afraid I must own (reluctantly, with my Celtic prejudice) that literature, or the love of it, came into our family with the English girl whom he married in London. She was, at least, a reader of the fiction of the day, if I may judge from the high-colored style of the now pathetically faded letter which she wrote to reproach a daughter who had made a runaway match and fled to America. So many people then used to make runaway matches; but when very late in the lives of these eloping lovers I once saw them, an old man and woman, at our house in Columbus, they hardly looked their youthful adventure, even to the fancy of a boy beginning to unrealize life. The reader may care to learn that they were the ancestors of Vaughan Kester, the very gifted young novelist, who came into popular recognition almost in the hour of his most untimely death, and of his brother Paul Kester, the playwright.

II

My great-grandfather became "a Friend by Convincement," as the Quakers called the Friends not born in their Society; but I do not know whether it was before or after his convincement that he sailed to Philadelphia with a stock of his Welsh flannels, which he sold to such advantage that a dramatic family tradition represents him wheeling the proceeds in a barrel of silver down the street to the vessel which brought him and which took him away. That was in the time of Washington's second Presidency, and Washington strongly advised his staying in the country and setting up his manufacture here; but he was prospering in Wales, and why should he come to America even at the suggestion of Washington? It is another family tradition that he complied so far as to purchase a vast acreage of land on the Potomac, including the site of our present capital, as some of his descendants in each generation have believed, without the means of expropriating the nation from its unlawful holdings. This would have been the more difficult as he never took a deed of his land, and he certainly never came back to America; yet he seems always to have been haunted by the allurement of it which my grandfather felt so potently that after twice visiting the country he came over a third time and cast his lot here.

He was already married, when with his young wife and my father a year old he sailed from London in 1808. Perhaps because they were chased by a French privateer, they speedily arrived in Boston after a voyage of only twenty-one days. In the memoir which my father wrote for his family, and which was published after his death, he tells that my grandmother formed the highest opinion of Boston, mainly, he surmises, from the very intelligent behavior of the young ladies in making a pet of her baby at the boarding-house where she stayed while her husband began going about wherever people wished his skill in setting up woolen-mills. The young ladies taught her little one to walk; and many years afterward, say fifty, when I saw her for the last time in a village of northwestern Ohio, she said "the Bostonians were very nice people," so faithfully had she cherished, through a thousand vicissitudes, the kind memory of that first sojourn in America.

I do not think she quite realized the pitch of greatness at which I had arrived in writing for the *Atlantic Monthly*, the renowned periodical then recently founded in Boston, or the fame of the poets whom I had met there the year before. I suspect that she was never of the literary taste of my English great-grandmother; but her father had been a school-teacher, and she had been carefully educated by the uncle and aunt to whom she was left at her parents' early death. They were Friends, but she never formally joined the Society, though worshipping with them; she was, like her husband, middle-class Welsh, and as long as they lived they both misplaced their aspirates. If I add that her maiden name was Thomas, and that her father's name was John Thomas, I think I have sufficiently attested her pure Cymric origin. So far as I know there was no mixture of Saxon blood on her side; but her people, like most of the border Welsh, spoke the languages of both races; and very late in my father's life, he mentioned casually, as old people will mention interesting things, that he remembered his father and mother speaking Welsh together. Of the two she remained the fonder of their native country, and in that last visit I paid her she said, after half a century of exile, "We do so and so at home, and you do so and so here." I can see her now, the gentlest of little Quaker ladies, with her white fichu crossed on her breast; and I hesitate attributing to her my immemorial knowledge that the Welsh were never conquered, but were tricked into union with the English by having one of their princes born, as it were surreptitiously, in Wales; it must have been my father who told me this and amused himself with my childish race-pride in the fact. She gave me an illustrated *Tour of Wales*, having among its steel-engravings the picture of a Norman castle where, by favor of a cousin who was the housekeeper, she had slept one night when a girl; but in America she had slept oftener in log-cabins, which my grandfather satisfied his devoted unworldliness in making his earthly tabernacles. She herself was not, I think, a devout person; she had her spiritual life in his, and followed his varying fortunes, from richer to poorer, with a tacit adherence to what he believed, whether the mild doctrine of Quakerism or the fervid Methodism for which he never quite relinquished it.

He seems to have come to America with money enough to lose a good deal in his removals from Boston to Poughkeepsie, from Poughkeepsie to New York City, from New York to Virginia, and from Virginia to eastern Ohio, where he ended in such adversity on his farm that he was glad to accept the charge of a woolen-mill in Steubenville. He knew the business thoroughly and he had set up mills for others in his various sojourns, following the line of least resistance among the Quaker settlements opened to him by the letters he had brought from Wales. He even went to the new capital, Washington, in a hope of manufacturing in Virginia held out to him by a nephew of President Madison, but it failed him to his heavy cost; and in Ohio, his farming experiments, which he renewed in a few years on giving up that mill at Steubenville, were alike disastrous. After more than enough of them he rested for a while in Wheeling, West Virginia, where my father met my mother, and they were married.

They then continued the family wanderings in his own search for the chance of earning a living in what seems to have been a very grudging country, even to industry so willing as his. He had now become a printer, and not that only, but a publisher, for he had already begun and ended the issue of a monthly magazine called *The Gleaner*, made up, as its name implied, chiefly of selections; his sister helped him as editor, and some old bound volumes of its few numbers show their joint work to have been done with good taste in the preferences of their day. He married upon the expectation of affluence from the publication of a work on *The Rise, Progress and Downfall of Aristocracy*, which almost immediately preceded the ruin of the enthusiastic author and of my father with him, if he indeed could have experienced further loss in his entire want of money. He did not lose heart, and he was presently living contentedly on three hundred dollars a year as foreman of a newspaper office in St. Clairville, Ohio. But his health gave way, and a little later, for the sake of the outdoor employment, he took up the trade of house-painter; and he was working at this in Wheeling when my grandfather Dean suggested his buying a lot and building a house in Martin's Ferry, just across the Ohio River. The lot must have been bought on credit, and he built mainly with his own capable hands a small brick house of one story and two rooms with a lean-to. In this house I was born, and my father and mother were very happy there; they never owned another house until their children helped them work and pay for it a quarter of a century afterward, though throughout this long time they made us a home inexpressibly dear to me still.

My father now began to read medicine, but during the course of a winter's lectures at Cincinnati (where he worked as a printer meanwhile), his health again gave way and he returned to Martin's Ferry. When I was three years old, my grandmother Dean's eldest brother, William Dock, came to visit her. He was the beloved patriarch of a family which I am glad to claim my kindred and was a best type of his Pennsylvania-German race. He had prospered on through a life of kindness and good deeds; he was so rich that he had driven in his own carriage from Harrisburg, over the mountains, and he now asked my father to drive with him across the state of Ohio. When they arrived in Dayton, my father went on by canal to Hamilton, where he found friends to help him buy the Whig newspaper which he had only just paid for when he sold it eight years later.

III

Of the first three years of my life which preceded this removal there is very little that I can honestly claim to remember. The things that I seem to remember are seeing from the window of our little house, when I woke one morning, a peach-tree in bloom; and again seeing from the steamboat which was carrying our family to Cincinnati, a man drowning in the river. But these visions, both of them very distinct, might very well have been the effect of hearing the things spoken of by my elders, though I am surest of the peach-tree in bloom as an authentic memory.

This time, so happy for my father and mother, was scarcely less happy because of its uncertainties. My young aunts lived with their now widowed mother not far from us; as the latest comer, I was in much request among them, of course; and my father was hardly less in favor with the whole family from his acceptable habit of finding a joke in everything. He supplied the place of son to my grandmother in the absence of my young uncles, then away most of their time on the river which they followed from the humblest beginnings on keel-boats to the proudest endings as pilots and captains and owners of steamboats. In those early days when they returned from the river they brought their earnings to their mother in gold coins, which they called Yellow Boys, and which she kept in a bowl in the cupboard, where I seem so vividly to have seen them, that I cannot quite believe I did not. These good sons were all Democrats except the youngest, but they finally became of my father's antislavery Whig faith in politics, and I believe they were as glad to have their home in a free state as my father's family, who had now left Wheeling, and were settled in southwestern Ohio.

There were not many slaves in Wheeling, but it was a sort of entrepôt where the negroes were collected and embarked for the plantations down the river, in their doom to the death-in-life of the far South. My grandfather Howells had, in the antislavery

tradition of his motherland, made himself so little desired among
his Virginian fellow-citizens that I have heard his removal from
Wheeling was distinctly favored by public sentiment; and afterward, on the farm he bought in Ohio, his fences and corn-cribs
suffered from the proslavery convictions of his neighbors. But
he was dwelling in safety and prosperity among the drugs and
books which were his merchandise in the store where I began to
remember him in my earliest days at Hamilton. He seemed to
me a very old man, and I noticed with the keen observance of a
child how the muscles sagged at the sides of his chin and how his
under lip, which I did not know I had inherited from him, pro-
jected. His clothes, which had long ceased to be drab in color,
were of a Quaker formality in cut; his black hat followed this
world's fashion in color, but was broad in the brim and very
low-crowned, which added somehow in my young sense to the
reproving sadness of his presence. He had black Welsh eyes and
was of the low stature of his race; my grandmother was blue-
eyed; she was little, too; but my aunt, their only surviving daughter, with his black eyes, was among their taller children. She was
born several years after their settlement in America, but she
loyally misused her aspirates as they did, and, never marrying,
was of a life-long devotion to them. They first lived over the
drug-store, after the fashion of shopkeepers in England; I am
aware of my grandfather soon afterward having a pretty house
and a large garden quite away from the store, but he always
lived more simply than his means obliged. Amidst the rude experiences of their backwoods years, the family had continued
gentle in their thoughts and tastes, though my grandfather
shared with poetry his passion for religion, and in my later boyhood when I had begun to print my verses, he wrote me a letter
solemnly praising them, but adjuring me to devote my gifts to
the service of my Maker, which I had so little notion of doing
in a selfish ideal of my own glory.

Most of his father's fortune had somehow gone to other sons,
but, whether rich or poor, their generation seemed to be of a
like religiosity. One of them lived in worldly state at Bristol be-

fore coming to America, and was probably of a piety not so insupportable as I found him in the memoir which he wrote of his
second wife, when I came to read it the other day. Him I never
saw, but from time to time there was one or other of his many
sons employed in my grandfather's store, whom I remember
blithe spirits, disposed to seize whatever chance of a joke life offered them, such as selling Young's *Night Thoughts* to a customer
who had whispered his wish for an improper book. Some of my
father's younger brothers were of a like cheerfulness with these
lively cousins, and of the same aptness for laughter. One was a
physician, another a dentist, another in a neighboring town a
druggist, another yet a speculative adventurer in the regions to
the southward: he came back from his commercial forays once
with so many half-dollars that when spread out they covered
the whole surface of our dining-table; but I am quite unable to
report what negotiation they were the spoil of. There was a far
cousin who was a painter, and left (possibly as a pledge of indebtedness) with my dentist uncle after a sojourn among us a
picture which I early prized as a masterpiece, and still remember as the charming head of a girl shadowed by the fan she held
over it. I never saw the painter, but I recall, from my father's
singing them, the lines of a "doleful ballad" which he left behind him as well as the picture:

> A thief will steal from you all that you havye,
> But an unfaithful lovyer will bring you to your grave.

The uncle who was a physician, when he left off the practice of
medicine about his eightieth year, took up the art of sculpture;
he may have always had a taste for it, and his knowledge of
anatomy would have helped qualify him for it. He modeled
from photographs a head of my father admirably like and full
of character, the really extraordinary witness of a gift latent till
then through a long life devoted to other things.

We children had our preference among these Howells uncles,
but we did not care for any of them so much as for our Dean
uncles, who now and then found their way up to Hamilton from

Cincinnati when their steamboats lay there in their trips from Pittsburg. They were all very jovial; and one of the younger among them could play the violin, not less acceptably because he played by ear and not by art. Of the youngest and best-loved I am lastingly aware in his coming late one night and of my creeping down-stairs from my sleep to sit in his lap and hear his talk with my father and mother, while his bursts of laughter agreeably shook my small person. I dare say these uncles used to bring us gifts from that steamboating world of theirs which seemed to us of a splendor not less than what I should now call oriental when we sometimes visited them at Cincinnati, and came away bulging in every pocket with the more portable of the dainties we had been feasting upon. In the most signal of these visits, as I once sat between my father and my Uncle William, for whom I was named, on the hurricane roof of his boat, he took a silver half-dollar from his pocket and put it warm in my hand, with a quizzical look into my eyes. The sight of such unexampled riches stopped my breath for the moment, but I made out to ask, "Is it for me?" and he nodded his head smilingly up and down; then, for my experience had hitherto been of fippenny-bits yielded by my father after long reasoning, I asked, "Is it good?" and remained puzzled to know why they laughed so together; it must have been years before I understood.

These uncles had grown up in a slave state, and they thought, without thinking, that slavery must be right; but once when an abolition lecturer was denied public hearing at Martin's Ferry, they said he should speak in their mother's house; and there, much unaware, I heard my first and last abolition lecture, barely escaping with my life, for one of the objections urged by the mob outside was a stone hurled through the window, where my mother sat with me in her arms. At my Uncle William's house in the years after the Civil War, my father and he began talking of old times, and he told how, when a boy on a keel-boat, tied up to a Mississippi shore, he had seen an overseer steal upon a black girl loitering at her work, and wind his blacksnake-whip round her body, naked except for the one cotton garment she wore. "When I heard that colored female screech," he said, and the old-fashioned word female, used for compassionate respectfulness, remains with me, "and saw her jump, I knew that there must be something wrong in slavery." Perhaps the sense of this had been in his mind when he determined with his brothers that the abolition lecturer should be heard in their mother's house.

She sometimes came to visit us in Hamilton, to break the homesick separations from her which my mother suffered through for so many years, and her visits were times of high holiday for us children. I should be interested now to know what she and my Welsh grandmother made of each other, but I believe they were good friends, though probably not mutually very intelligible. My mother's young sisters, who also came on welcome visits, were always joking with my father and helping my mother at her work; but I cannot suppose that there was much common ground between them and my grandfather's family except in their common Methodism. For me, I adored them; and if the truth must be told, though I had every reason to love my Welsh grandmother, I had a peculiar tenderness for my Pennsylvania-Dutch grandmother, with her German accent and her caressing ways. My grandfather, indeed, could have recognized no difference among heirs of equal complicity in Adam's sin; and in the situation such as it was, I lived blissfully unborn to all things of life outside of my home. I can recur to the time only as a dream of love and loving, and though I came out of it no longer a little child, but a boy struggling tooth and nail for my place among other boys, I must still recur to the ten or eleven years passed in Hamilton as the gladdest of all my years. They may have been even gladder than they now seem, because the incidents which embody happiness had then the novelty which such incidents lose from their recurrence; while the facts of unhappiness, no matter how often they repeat themselves, seem throughout life an unprecedented experience and impress themselves as vividly the last time as the first. I recall some occasions of grief and shame in that far past with unfailing distinctness, but the long spaces of blissful living which they interrupted hold few or no records which I can allege in proof of my belief that I was then, above every other when,

> Joyful and free from blame.

IV

Throughout those years at Hamilton I think of my father as absorbed in the mechanical and intellectual work of his newspaper. My earliest sense of him relates him as much to the types and the press as to the table where he wrote his editorials amidst the talk of the printers, or of the politicians who came to discuss public affairs with him. From a quaint pride, he did not like his printer's craft to be called a trade; he contended that it was a profession; he was interested in it, as the expression of his taste, and the exercise of his ingenuity and invention, and he could supply many deficiencies in its means and processes. He cut fonts of large type for job-work out of apple-wood in default of box or olive; he even made the graver's tools for carving the letters. Nothing pleased him better than to contrive a thing out of something it was not meant for, as making a penknife blade out of an old razor, or the like. He could do almost anything with his ready hand and his ingenious brain, while I have never been able to do anything with mine but write a few score books. But as for the printer's craft with me, it was simply my joy and pride from the first things I knew of it. I know when I could not read, for I recall supplying the text from my imagination for the pictures I found in books, but I do not know when I could not set type. My first attempt at literature was not written, but put up in type, and printed off by me. My father praised it, and this made me so proud that I showed it to one of those eminent Whig politicians always haunting the office. He made no comment on it, but asked me if I could spell baker. I spelled the word simple-heartedly, and it was years before I realized that he meant a hurt to my poor little childish vanity.

Very soon I could set type very well, and at ten years and onward till journalism became my university, the printing-office was mainly my school. Of course, like every sort of work with a boy, the work became irksome to me, and I would gladly have escaped from it to every sort of play, but it never ceased to have the charm it first had. Every part of the trade became familiar to me, and if I had not been so little I could at once have worked not only at case, but at press, as my brother did. I had my favorites among the printers, who knew me as the Old Man, because of the habitual gravity which was apt to be broken in me by bursts of wild hilarity; but I am not sure whether I liked better the conscience of the young journeyman who wished to hold me in the leash of his moral convictions, or the nature of my companion in laughter which seemed to have selected for him the fit name of Sim Haggett. This merrymaker was married, but so very presently in our acquaintance was widowed, that I can scarcely put any space between his mourning for his loss and his rejoicing in the first joke that followed it. There were three or four of the journeymen, with an apprentice, to do the work now reduced by many facilities to the competence of one or two. Some of them slept in a den opening from the printing-office, where I envied them the wild freedom unhampered by the conventions of sweeping, dusting, or bed-making; it was next to camping out.

The range of that young experience of mine transcends telling, but the bizarre mixture was pure delight to the boy I was, already beginning to take the impress of events and characters. Though I loved the art of printing so much, though my pride even more than my love was taken with it, as something beyond other boys, yet I loved my schools too. In their succession there seem to have been a good many of them, with a variety of teachers, whom I tried to make like me because I liked them. I was gifted in spelling, geography, and reading, but arithmetic was not for me. I could declaim long passages from the speeches of Corwin against the Mexican War, and of Chatham against the American War, and poems from our school readers, or from Campbell or Moore or Byron; but at the blackboard I was dumb. I bore fairly well the mockeries of boys, boldly bad, who played upon a certain simplicity of soul in me, and pretended, for instance, when I came out one night saying I was six years old, that I was a shameless boaster and liar. Swimming, hunting, fishing, foraging at every season, with the skating which the waters of the rivers and canals afforded, were my joy; I took my part in the races and the games, in football and in baseball, then in its feline infancy of Three Corner Cat, and though there was a family rule against fighting, I fought like the rest of the boys and took my defeats as heroically as I knew how; they were mostly defeats.

My world was full of boys, but it was also much haunted by ghosts or the fear of them. Death came early into it, the visible image in a negro babe, with the large red copper cents on its eyelids, which older boys brought me to see, then in the funeral of the dearly loved mate whom we school-fellows followed to his grave. I learned many things in my irregular schooling, and at home I was always reading when I was not playing. I will not pretend that I did not love playing best; life was an experiment which had to be tried in every way that presented itself, but outside of these practical requisitions there was a constant demand upon me from literature. As to the playing I will not speak at large here, for I have already said enough of it in *A Boy's Town*; and as to the reading, the curious must go for it to another book of mine called *My Literary Passions*. Perhaps there was already in my early literary preferences a bent toward the reality which my gift, if I may call it so, has since taken. I did not willingly read poetry, except such pieces as I memorized: little tragedies of the sad fate of orphan children, and the cruelties of large birds to small ones, which brought the lump into my throat, or the moralized song of didactic English writers of the eighteenth century, such as "Pity the sorrows of a poor old man." That piece I still partly know by heart; but history was what I liked best, and if I finally turned to fiction it seems to have been in the dearth of histories that merited reading after Goldsmith's Greece and Rome; except Irving's *Conquest of Granada*, I found none that I could read; but I had then read *Don Quixote* and *Gulliver's Travels*, and had heard my father reading aloud to my mother the poems of Scott and Moore. Since he seems not to have thought of any histories that would meet my taste, I fancy that I must have been mainly left to my own choice in that sort, though he told me of the other sorts of books which I read.

I should be interested to know now how the notion of authorship first crept into my mind, but I do not in the least know. I made verses, I even wrote plays in rhyme, but until I attempted an historical romance I had no sense of literature as an art. As an art which one might live by, as by a trade or a business, I had not the slightest conception of it. When I began my first and last historical romance, I did not imagine it as something to be read by others; and when the first chapters were shown without my knowing, I was angry and ashamed. If my father thought there was anything uncommon in my small performances, he did nothing to let me guess it unless I must count the instance of declaiming Hallock's *Marco Bozzaris* before a Swedenborgian minister who was passing the night at our house. Neither did my mother do anything to make me conscious, if she was herself conscious of anything out of the common in what I was trying. It was her sacred instinct to show no partiality among her children; my father's notion was of the use that could be combined with the pleasure of life, and perhaps if there had been anything different in my life, it would not have tended more to that union of use and pleasure which was his ideal.

Much in the environment was abhorrent to him, and he fought the local iniquities in his paper, the gambling, the drunkenness that marred the mainly moral and religious complexion of the place. In *A Boy's Town* I have studied with a fidelity which I could not emulate here the whole life of it as a boy sees life, and I must leave the reader who cares for such detail to find it there. But I wish again to declare the almost unrivaled fitness of the place to be the home of a boy, with its two branches of the Great Miami River and their freshets in spring, and their witchery at all seasons; with its Hydraulic Channels and Reservoirs, its stretch of the Miami Canal and the Canal Basin so fit for

swimming in summer and skating in winter. The mills and fac-
tories which harnessed the Hydraulic to their industries were of
resistless allure for the boys who frequented them when they
could pass the guard of "No Admittance" on their doors, or
when they were not foraging among the fields and woods in the
endless vacations of the schools. Some boys left school to work
in the mills, and when they could show the loss of a finger-joint
from the machinery they were prized as heroes. The Fourths of
July, the Christmases and Easters and May-Days, which were
apparently of greater frequency there and then than they apparently are anywhere now, seemed to alternate with each
other through the year, and the Saturdays spread over half
the week.

v

The experience of such things was that of the generalized
boy, and easy to recall, but the experience of the specialized
boy that I was cannot be distinctly recovered and cannot be
given in any order of time; the events are like dreams in their
achronic simultaneity. I ought to be able to remember when
fear first came into my life; but I cannot. I am aware of offering as a belated substitute for far earlier acquaintance with it
the awe which I dimly shared with the whole community at a
case of hydrophobia occurring there, and which was not les-
sened by hearing my father tell my mother of the victim's saying:
"I have made my peace with God; you may call in the doctors."
I doubt if she relished the involuntary satire as he did; his
humor, which made life easy for him, could not always have
been a comfort to her. Safe in the philosophy of Swedenborg,
which taught him that even those who ended in hell chose it
their portion because they were happiest in it, he viewed with
kindly amusement the religious tumults of the frequent revivals
about him. The question of salvation was far below that of the
annexation of Texas, or the ensuing war against Mexico, in his
regard; but these great events have long ago faded into national

history from my contemporary consciousness, while a tragical effect from his playfulness remains vivid in my childish memory. I have already used it in fiction, as my wont has been with so many of my experiences, but I will tell again how my mother and he were walking together in the twilight, with me, a very small boy, following, and my father held out to me behind his back a rose which I understood I was to throw at my mother and startle her.

My aim was unfortunately for me all too sure; the rose struck her head, and when she looked round and saw me offering to run away, she whirled on me and made me suffer for her fright in thinking my flower was a bat, while my father gravely entreated, "Mary, Mary!" She could not forgive me at once, and my heart remained sore, for my love of her was as passionate as the temper I had from her, but while it continued aching after I went to bed, she stole up-stairs to me and consoled me and told me how scared she had been, and hardly knew what she was doing; and all was well again between us.

I wish I could say how dear she was to me and to all her children. My eldest brother and she understood each other best, but each of us lived in the intelligence of her which her love created. She was always working for us, and yet, as I so tardily perceived, living for my father anxiously, fearfully, bravely, with absolute trust in his goodness and righteousness. While she listened to his reading at night, she sewed or knitted for us, or darned or mended the day's ravage in our clothes till, as a great indulgence, we fell asleep on the floor. If it was summer we fell asleep at her knees on the front door-step, where she had sat watching us at our play till we dropped worn out with it; or if it had been a day of wild excess she followed us to our beds early and washed our feet with her dear hands, and soothed them from the bruises of the summer-long shoelessness. She was not only the centre of home to me; she was home itself, and in the years before I made a home of my own, absence from her was the homesickness, or the fear of it, which was always haunting me. As for the quick temper (now so slow) I had from her, it showed itself once in a burst of reckless fury which had to be signalized in the family rule, so lenient otherwise, by a circumstantial whipping from my father. Another, from her, for going in swimming (as we always said for bathing) when directly forbidden, seems to complete the list of my formal punishments at their hands in a time when fathers and mothers were much more of Solomon's mind in such matters than now.

I never was punished in any sort at school where the frequent scourging of other boys, mostly boys whom I loved for something kind and sweet in them, filled me with anguish; and I have come to believe that a blow struck a child is far wickeder than any wickedness a child can do; that it depraves whoever strikes the blow, mother, or father, or teacher, and that it inexpressibly outrages the young life confided to the love of the race. I know that excuses will be found for it, and that the perpetrator of the outrage will try for consolation in thinking that the child quickly forgets, because its pathetic smiles so soon follow its pathetic tears; but the child does not forget; and no callousing from custom can undo the effect in its soul.

From the stress put upon behaving rather than believing in that home of mine we were made to feel that wicked words were of the quality of wicked deeds, and that when they came out of our mouths they depraved us, unless we took them back. I have not forgotten, with any detail of the time and place, a transgression of this sort which I was made to feel in its full significance. My mother had got supper, and my father was, as he often was, late for it, and while we waited impatiently for him, I came out with the shocking wish that he was dead. My mother instantly called me to account for it, and when my father came she felt bound to tell him what I had said. He could then have done no more than gravely give me the just measure of my offense; and his explanation and forgiveness were the sole event. I did not remain with an exaggerated sense of my sin, though in a child's helplessness I could not urge, if I had imagined urging, that my outburst was merely an aspiration for unbelated suppers, and was of the nature of prayers for rain, which good people sometimes put up regardless of consequences. With his Swedenborgian doctrine of degrees in sin, my father might have thought my wild words prompted by evil spirits, but he would have regarded them as qualitatively rather than quantitatively wicked, and would not have committed the dreadful wrong which elders do a child by giving it a sense of sinning far beyond its worst possible willing. As to conduct his teaching was sometimes of an inherited austerity, but where his own personality prevailed, there was no touch of Puritanism in it.

Our religious instruction at home was not very stated, though it was abundant, and it must have been because we children ourselves felt it unseemly not to go, like other children, to Sunday-school that we were allowed to satisfy our longing for conformity by going for a while to the Sunday-school of the Baptist church, apparently because it was the nearest. We got certain blue tickets and certain red ones for memorizing passages from the New Testament, but I remember much more distinctly the muscular twitching in the close-shaven purplish cheek of the teacher as he nervously listened with set teeth for the children's answers, than anything in our Scripture lessons. I had been received with three or four brothers and sisters into the Swedenborgian communion by a passing New Church minister, but there were no services of our recondite faith in Hamilton, and we shared in no public worship after my mother followed my father from the Methodist society. Out of curiosity and a solemn joy in its ceremonial, I sometimes went to the Catholic church, where my eyes clung fascinated to the life-large effigy of Christ bleeding on His cross against the eastern wall; but I have more present now the sense of walks in the woods on Sunday, with the whole family, and of the long, sweet afternoons so spent in them.

If we had no Sabbaths in our house, and not very recognizable Sundays, we were strictly forbidden to do anything that would seem to trifle with the scruples of others. We might not treat serious things unseriously; we were to swear not at all; and in the matter of bywords we were allowed very little range, though for the hardness of our hearts we were suffered to say such things as, "Oh, hang it!" or even, "Confound it all!" in extreme cases, such as failing to make the family pony open his mouth for bridling, or being bitten by the family rabbits, or butted over by the family goat. In such points of secular behavior we might be better or worse; but in matters of religious toleration the rule was inflexible; the faith of others was sacred, and it was from this early training, doubtless, that I was able in after life to regard the occasional bigotry of agnostic friends with toleration.

During the years of my later childhood, a few public events touched my consciousness. I was much concerned in the fortunes of the Whig party from the candidacy of Henry Clay in 1844 to the fusion of the antislavery Whigs with the Freesoil party after their bolt of the Taylor nomination in 1848, when I followed my father as far as a boy of eleven could go. He himself went so far as to sell his newspaper and take every risk for the future rather than support a slave-holding candidate who had been chosen for his vote-winning qualities as a victorious general in the Mexican War. I did not abhor that aggression so much as my father only because I could not understand how abhorrent it was; but it began to be a trouble to me from the first mention of the Annexation of Texas, a sufficiently dismaying mystery, and it afflicted me in early fixing my lot with the righteous minorities which I may have sometimes since been over-proud to be of. Besides such questions of national interest I was aware of other things, such as the French Revolution of 1848; but this must have been wholly through sympathy with my father's satisfaction in the flight of Louis Philippe and the election of the poet Lamartine to be the head of the provisional government. The notion of provisional I relegated to lasting baffle in its more familiar association with the stock of corn-meal and bran in the feed-stores, though I need but have asked in order to be told what it meant. The truth is I was preoccupied about that time with the affairs of High Olympus, as I imagined them from the mythology which I was reading, and with the politics of Rome and Athens, as I conceived them from

the ever-dear histories of Goldsmith. The exploits of the Ingenious Gentleman of La Mancha had much to do in distracting
me from the movement of events in Mexico, and at the same
time I was enlarging my knowledge of human events through
Gulliver's Travels and Poe's *Tales of the Grotesque and Arabesque.*

My father had not only explained to me the satire which
underlay *Gulliver's Travels*; he told me so much too indignantly
of De Foe's appropriation of Selkirk's narrative, that it long
kept me from reading *Robinson Crusoe*; but he was, as I have
divined more and more, my guide in that early reading which
widened with the years, though it kept itself preferably for a
long time to history and real narratives. He was of such a liberal mind that he scarcely restricted my own forays in literature,
and I think that sometimes he erred on that side; he may have
thought no harm could come to me from the literary filth which
I sometimes took into my mind, since it was in the nature of
sewage to purify itself. He gave me very little direct instruction,
and he did not insist on my going to school when I preferred
the printing-office. All the time, perhaps, I was getting such
schooling as came from the love of literature, which was the
daily walk and conversation of our very simple home, and somehow protected it from the sense of narrow means and the little
hope of larger. My father's income from his paper was scarcely
over a thousand dollars a year, but this sufficed for his family,
then of seven children, and he was of such a sensitive pride as to
money, that he would hardly ask for debts due him, much less
press for their payment; so that when he parted with his paper
he parted with the hope of much money owing him for legal
and even official advertising and for uncounted delinquent sub-
scriptions. Meanwhile he was earning this money by the work
of his head and hand; and though I must always love his memory for his proud delicacy, I cannot forget that this is not a
world where people dun themselves for the debts they owe.
What is to be said of such a man is that his mind is not on the
things that make for prosperity; but if we were in adversity we
never knew it by that name. My mother did the whole work of

her large household, and gave each of us the same care in health
and sickness, in sickness only making the sufferer feel that he
was her favorite; in any other case she would have felt such a
preference wicked. Sometimes she had a hired girl, as people
then and there called the sort of domestic that in New England
would have been called a help. But it must have been very seldom, for two girls alone left record of themselves: a Dutch girl
amusingly memorable with us children because she called her
shoes *skoes*, and claimed to have come to America in a *skip*;
and a native girl, who took charge of us when our mother was
on one of her homesick visits Up-the-River, and became lastingly abhorrent for the sort of insipid milk-gravy she made for
the beef-steak, and for the nightmare she seemed to have every
night, when she filled the house and made our blood run cold
with a sort of wild involuntary yodeling.

Apparently my mother's homesickness mounted from time
to time in an insupportable crisis; but perhaps she did not go
Up-the-River so often as it seemed. She always came back more
contented with the home which she herself was for us; once, as
my perversely eclectic memory records, it was chiefly because
one could burn wood in Hamilton, but had to burn coal at
Martin's Ferry, where everything was smutched by it. In my
old age, now, I praise Heaven for that home which I could not
know apart from her; and I wish I could recall her in the youth
which must have been hers when I began to be conscious of her
as a personality; I know that she had thick brown Irish hair and
blue eyes, and high German cheek-bones, and as a girl she would
have had such beauty as often goes with a certain irregularity
of feature; but to me before my teens she was, of course, a very
mature, if not elderly person, with whom I could not connect
any notion of looks except such as shone from her care and love.
Though her intellectual and spiritual life was in and from my
father, she kept always a certain native quality of speech and a
rich sense in words like that which marked her taste in soft
stuffs and bright colors. In the hard life of her childhood in the
backwoods she was sent to an academy in the nearest town, but

in the instant anguish of homesickness she walked ten miles back to the log-cabin where at night, as she would tell us, you could hear the wolves howling. She had an innate love of poetry; she could sing some of those songs of Burns and Moore which people sang then. I associate them with her voice in the late summer afternoons; for it was at night that she listened to my father's reading of poetry or fiction. When they were young, before and after their marriage, he kept a book, as people sometimes did in those days, where he wrote in the scrupulous handwriting destined to the deformity of over-use in later years, such poems of Byron or Cowper or Moore or Burns as seemed appropriate to their case, and such other verse as pleased his fancy. It is inscribed (for it still exists) *To Mary*, and with my inner sense I can hear him speaking to her by that sweet name, with the careful English enunciation which separated its syllables into Ma-ry.

VI

My mother was an honored guest on one or other of my uncles' boats whenever she went on her homesick visits Up-the-River, and sometimes we children must have gone with her. Later in my boyhood, when I was nine or ten years old, my father took me to Pittsburg and back, on the boat of the jolliest of those uncles, and it was then that I first fully realized the splendor of the world where their lives were passed. No doubt I have since seen nobler sights than the mile-long rank of the steamboats as they lay at the foot of the landings in the cities at either end of our voyage, but none of these excelling wonders remains like that. All the passenger-boats on the Ohio were then side-wheelers, and their lofty chimneys towering on either side of their pilot-houses were often crenelated at the top, with wire ropes between them supporting the effigies of such Indians as they were named for. From time to time one of the majestic craft pulled from the rank with the clangor of its mighty bell, and the mellow roar of its whistle, and stood out in the yellow stream, or

arrived in like state to find a place by the shore. The wide slope
of the landing was heaped with the merchandise putting off or
taking on the boats, amidst the wild and whirling curses of the
mates and the insensate rushes of the deck-hands staggering to
and fro under their burdens. The swarming drays came and
went with freight, and there were huckster carts of every sort;
peddlers, especially of oranges, escaped with their lives among
the hoofs and wheels, and through the din and turmoil passengers hurried aboard the boats, to repent at leisure their haste
in trusting the advertised hour of departure. It was never known
that any boat left on time, and I doubt if my uncle's boat, the
famous *New England No. 2*, was an exception to the rule, as my
father perfectly understood while he delayed on the wharf,
sampling a book-peddler's wares, or talking with this bystander
or that, while I waited for him on board in an anguish of fear
lest he should be left behind.

There was a measure of this suffering for me throughout the
voyage wherever the boat stopped, for his insatiable interest in
every aspect of nature and human nature urged him ashore and
kept him there till the last moment before the gang-plank was
drawn in. It was useless for him to argue with me that my uncle
would not allow him to be left, even if he should forget himself
so far as to be in any danger of that. I could not believe that a
disaster so dire should not befall us, and I suffered a mounting
misery till one day it mounted to frenzy. I do not know whether
there were other children on board, but except for the officers
of the boat, I was left mostly to myself, and I spent my time
dreamily watching the ever-changing shore, so lost in its wild
loveliness that once when I woke from my reverie the boat
seemed to have changed her course, and to be going down-
stream instead of up. It was in this crisis that I saw my father
descending the gang-plank, and while I was urging his return
in mute agony, a boat came up outside of us to wait for her
chance of landing. I looked and read on her wheel-house the
name *New England*, and then I abandoned hope. By what fell
necromancy I had been spirited from my uncle's boat to another

I could not guess, but I had no doubt that the thing had happened, and I was flying down from the hurricane roof to leap aboard that boat from the lowermost deck when I met my uncle coming as quietly up the gangway as if nothing had happened. He asked what was the matter, and I gasped out the fact; he did not laugh; he had pity on me and gravely explained, "That boat is the *New England*: this is the *New England No. 2*," and at these words I escaped with what was left of my reason.

I had been the prey of that obsession which every one has experienced when the place where one is disorients itself and west is east and north is south. Sometimes this happens by a sudden trick within the brain, but I lived four years in Columbus and as many in Venice without once being right as to the points of the compass in my nerves, though my wits were perfectly convinced. Once I was months in a place where I suffered from this obsession, when I found myself returning after a journey with the north and south quite where they should be; and, "Now," I exulted, "I will hold them to their duty." I kept my eyes firmly fixed upon the station, as the train approached; then, without my lifting my gaze, the north was back again in the place of the south, and the vain struggle was over. Only the other day I got out of a car going north in Fourth Avenue, and then saw it going on south; and it was only by noting which way the house numbers increased that I could right myself.

I suppose my father promised a reform that should appease my unreason, but whether he could deny himself those chances of general information I am not so sure; we may have both expected too much of each other. As I was already imaginably interested in things of the mind beyond my years, he often joined me in my perusal of the drifting landscape and made me look at this or that feature of it, but he afterward reported at home that he never could get anything from me but a brief "Yes, indeed," in response. That amused him, yet I do not think I should have disappointed him so much if I could have told him I was losing nothing, but that our point of view was different. The soul of a child is a secret to itself, and in its observance of life there is no foretelling what it shall loose or what it shall hold. I do not believe that anything which was of use to me was lost upon me, but what I chiefly remember now is my pleasure in the log-cabins in the woods on the shores, with the blue smoke curling on the morning or the evening air from their chimneys. My heart was taken with a yearning for the wilderness such as the coast-born boy feels for the sea; in the older West the woods called to us with a lure which it would have been rapture to obey; the inappeasable passion for their solitude drove the pioneer into the forest, and it was still in the air we breathed. But my lips were sealed, for the generations cannot utter themselves to each other till the strongest need of utterance is past.

I used to sit a good deal on the hurricane-deck or in the pilot-house, where there was often good talk among the pilots or the boat's officers, and where once I heard with fascination the old Scotch pilot, Tom Lindsay, telling of his own boyhood in the moors, and of the sheep lost in the drifting snows; that also had the charm of the wilderness; but I did not feel the sadness of his saying once, as we drifted past a row of crimson-headed whisky barrels on a wharf-boat, "Many a one of those old Red Eyes I've helped to empty," or imagine the far and deep reach of the words which remained with me. Somewhere in the officers' quarters I found a sea novel, which I read partly through, but I have not finished *The Cruise of the Midge*, to this day, though I believe that as sea novels go it merits reading. When I was not listening to the talk in the pilot-house, or looking at the hills drifting by, I was watching the white-jacketed black cabin-boys setting the tables for dinner in the long saloon of the boat. It was built, after a fashion which still holds in the Western boats, with a gradual lift of the stem and stern and a dip midway which somehow enhanced the charm of the perspective even to the eyes of a hungry boy. Dinner was at twelve, and the tables began to be set between ten and eleven, with a rhythmical movement of the negroes as they added each detail of plates and cups and knives and glasses, and placed the set dishes of quivering jelly at discrete intervals under the crystals of the chandeliers softly tinkling with the pulse of the engines. At last some more exalted order of waiters appeared with covered platters and spirit-lamps burning under them, and set them down before the places of the captain and his officers. Then the bell was sounded for the passengers; the waiters leaned forward between these when they were seated; at a signal from their chief they lifted the covers of the platters and vanished in a shining procession up the saloon, while each passenger fell upon the dishes nearest himself.

About the time I had become completely reconciled to the conditions of the voyage, which the unrivaled speed of the *New England No. 2* shortened to a three-days' run up the river, I woke one morning to find her lying at the Pittsburg landing, and when I had called my father to come and share my wonder at a stretch of boats as long as that at Cincinnati, and been mimicked by a cabin-boy for my unsophisticated amazement, nothing remained for me but to visit the houses of the aunts and uncles abounding in cousins. Of the homeward voyage nothing whatever is left in my memory; but I know we came back on the *New England No. 2,* though we must have left the boat and taken it again on a second trip at Wheeling, after a week spent with my mother's people at Martin's Ferry. My father wished me to see the glass-foundries and rolling-mills which interested him so much more than me; he could not get enough of those lurid industries which I was chiefly concerned in saving myself from. I feigned an interest in the processes out of regard for him, but Heaven knows I cared nothing for the drawing of wire or the making of nails, and only a very little for the blowing of the red, vitreous bubbles from the mouths of long steel pipes. With weariness I escaped from these wonders, but with no such misery as I eluded the affection of the poor mis-shapen, half-witted boy who took a fancy to me at the house of some old friends of my father where we had supper after the long day. With uncouth noises of welcome, and with arms and legs flying controllessly about, he followed me through a day that seemed endless. His family of kindly English folk, from the life-long habit of him, seemed unaware of anything strange, and I could not for shame and for fear of my father's reproach betray my suffering. The evening began unduly to fall, thick with the blackness of the coal smoke poured from the chimneys of those abhorred foundries, and there was a fatal moment when my father's friends urged him to stay the night and I thought he would consent. The dreams of childhood are oftenest evil, but mine holds record of few such nightmares as this.

VII

After my father sold his paper and was casting about for some other means of livelihood, there were occasional shadows cast by his anxieties in the bright air of my childhood. Again I doubt if any boy ever lived a gladder time than I lived in Hamilton, Butler County, Ohio: words that I write still when I try a new pen, because I learned to write them first, and love them yet. When we went to live in Dayton, where my father managed to make a sort of progressive purchase of a newspaper which he never quite paid for, our skies changed. It was after an interval of experiment in one sort and another, which amused his hopeful ingenuity, but ended in nothing, that he entered upon this long failure. The Dayton *Transcript* when he began with it was a tri-weekly, but he made it a daily, and this mistake infected the whole enterprise. It made harder work for us all than we had known before; and the printing-office, which had been my delight, became my oppression after the brief moment of public schooling which I somehow knew. But before the change from tri-weekly to daily in our paper, I had the unstinted advantage of a school of morals as it then appeared among us.

The self-sacrificing company of players who suffered for the drama through this first summer of our life in Dayton paid my father for their printing in promises which he willingly took at their face value, and in tickets which were promptly honored at the door. As nearly as I can make out, I was thus enabled to go every night to the theatre, in a passion for it which remains with me ardent still. I saw such plays of Shakespeare as "Macbeth" and "Othello," then the stage favorites, and "Richard III." and evermore "Richard III." I saw such other now quite forgotten favorites as Kotzebue's "Stranger" and Sheridan Knowles's "Wife," and such moving actions of unknown origin as "Barbarossa" and "The Miser of Marseilles," with many screaming farces such as helped fill every evening full with at least three plays. There was also at that time a native drama almost as acceptable to our public everywhere as "Uncle Tom's Cabin" afterward became. It seemed as if our public would never tire of "A Glance at New York," with its horribly vulgar stage conceptions of local character, Mose the fireman and Lize his girl, and Sikesy and their other companions, which drift up before me now like wraiths from the Pit, and its events of street-fighting and I dare say heroic rescues from burning buildings by the volunteer fire companies of the day. When it appeared that the public might tire of the play, the lively fancy of the theatre supplied a fresh attraction in it, and the character of Little Mose was added. How this must have been played by what awful young women eager to shine at any cost in their art, I shudder to think, and it is with "sick and scornful looks averse" that I turn from the remembrance of my own ambition to shine in that drama. My father instantly quenched the histrionic spark in me with loathing; but I cannot say whether this was before or after the failure of a dramatic attempt of his own which I witnessed, much mystified by the sense of some occult relation to it. Certainly I did not know that the melodrama which sacrificed his native to his adoptive patriotism in the action, and brought off the Americans victors over the British in a sea-fight, was his work; and probably it was the adaptation of some tale then much read. Very likely he trusted, in writing it, to the chance which he always expected to favor the amateur in taking up a musical instrument strange to him. He may even have dreamed of fortune from it; but after one performance of it the management seems to have gone back to such old public favorites as Shakespeare and Sheridan Knowles. Nothing was said of it in the family; I think some of the newspapers were not so silent; but I am not sure of this.

My father could, of course, be wiser for others than for himself; the public saved him from becoming a dramatist, but it was he who saved me from any remotest chance of becoming an actor, and later from acquiring the art of the prestidigitator. The only book which I can be sure of his taking from me was a manual professing to teach this art, which I had fallen in with. The days of those years in Dayton were in fact very different from the days in Hamilton when I was reaching out near and far to feed my fancy for fable and my famine for fact. I read no new books which now occur to me by name, though I still kept my interest in Greek mythology and gave something of my scanty leisure to a long poem in the quatrains of Gray's Elegy based upon some divine event of it. The course of the poem was lastingly arrested by a slight attack of the cholera which was then raging in the town and filling my soul with gloom. My dear mother thought it timely to speak with me of the other world; but so far from reconciling me to the thought of it, I suppose she could not have found a boy in all Dayton more unwilling to go to heaven. She was forced to drop her religious consolations and to assure me that she had not the least fear of my dying.

It was certainly not the fault of the place that we were, first and last, rather unhappy there. For one thing, we were used to the greater ease and simplicity of a small town like Hamilton, and Dayton was a small city with the manners and customs of cities in those days: that is, there was more society and less neighborhood, and neither my father nor my mother could have cared for society. They missed the wont of old friends; there were no such teas as she used to give her neighbors, with a quilting, still dimly visioned, at the vanishing-point of the perspective; our social life was almost wholly in our Sunday-evening visits to the house of my young aunt whose husband was my father's youngest brother. The pair were already in the shadow of their early death, and in the sorrow of losing their children one after another till one little cousin alone remained. I had not yet begun to make up romances about people in my mind, but this uncle and aunt were my types of worldly splendor in the setting of the lace curtains and hair-cloth chairs of their parlor, with her piano and his flute for other æsthetic grace. He was so much younger that he had a sort of filial relation to my father, and they were both very sweet to my mother, always lonely outside of her large family.

As usual, we lived in more than one house, but the first was very acceptable because of its nearness to the canal; the yard stretched behind it quite to the tow-path, with an unused stable between, which served us boys for circus-rehearsals, and for dressing after a plunge. As in a dream, I can still see my youngest brother rushing through this stable one day and calling out that he was going to jump into the canal, with me running after him and then dimly seeing him as he groped along the bottom, with me diving and saving him from drowning. Already, with the Hamilton facilities, I could hardly help being a good swimmer, and at Dayton I spent much of my leisure in the canal. Within the city limits we had to wear some sort of bathing-dress, and we preferred going with a crowd of other boys beyond the line where no such formality was expected of us. On the way to and fro we had to pass a soap-factory, where the boys employed in it swarmed out at sight of us stealing along under the canal bank, and in the strange outlawry of boyhood murderously stoned us, but somehow did not kill us. I do not know what boys we played with, but after we had paid the immemorial penalty of the stranger, and fought for our standing among them, the boys of our neighborhood were kind enough. One, whose father was a tobacconist, abetted our efforts to learn smoking by making cigars flavored with cinnamon-drops; I suppose these would have been of more actual advantage to me if I had learned to like smoking. When we went from his house to another, in what may have been a better quarter, we made no friends that I can remember, and we were never so gay. In fact, a sense of my father's adversity now began to penetrate to his older children, with the knowledge of our mother's unhappiness from it.

I am not following any chronological order here, and I should not be able to date my æsthetic devotion to a certain gas-burner in the window of a store under the printing-office. It was in the form of a calla-lily, with the flame forking from the tongue in its white cup; and I could never pass it, by day or night, without stopping to adore it. If I could be perfectly candid, I should still own my preference of it to the great painting of Adam and Eve by Dubuffe, then shown throughout our simple-hearted commonwealth. This had the double attraction of a religious interest and the awful novelty of the nude, for the first time seen by untraveled American eyes; the large canvas was lighted up so as to throw the life-size figures into strong relief, and the spectator strickenly studied them through a sort of pasteboard binocle supplied for the purpose. If that was the way our first parents looked before the Fall, and the Bible said it was, there was nothing to be urged against it; but many kind people must have suffered secret misgivings at a sight from which a boy might well shrink ashamed, with a feeling that the taste of Eden was improved by the Fall. I had no such joy in it as in the dramas which I witnessed in the same hall; as yet there was nothing in Dayton openly declared a theatre.

The town had many airs of a city, and there were even some policemen who wore a silver-plated star inside their coats for proof of their profession. There were water-works, and there was gas everywhere for such as would pay the charge for it. My father found the expense of piping the printing-office too great for his means, or else he preferred falling back upon his invention, and instead of the usual iron tubes he had the place fitted with tin tubes, at much less cost. Perhaps the cost was equalized in the end by the leaking of these tubes, which was so constant that we breathed gas by day as well as burned it by night. We burned it a good deal, for our tri-weekly was now changed to a daily, and a morning paper at that. Until eleven o'clock I helped put the telegraphic despatches (then a new and proud thing with us) into type, and between four and five o'clock in the morning I was up and carrying papers to our subscribers. The stress of my father's affairs must have been very sore for him to allow this, and I dare say it did not last long, but while it lasted it was suffering which must make me forever tender of those who overwork, especially the children who overwork. The suffering was such that when my brother, who had not gone to bed till much later, woke me after my five or six hours' sleep, I do not now know how I got myself together for going to the printing-office for the papers and making my rounds in the keen morning air. When Sunday came, and I could sleep as late as I liked, it was bliss such as I cannot tell to lie and rest, and rest, and rest! We were duteous children and willing; my brother knew of the heavy trouble hanging over us and I was aware of the hopeless burden of debt which our father was staggering under and my mother was carrying on her heart; and when I think of it, and of the wide-spread, never-ending struggle for life which it was and is the type of, I cannot but abhor the economic conditions which we still suppose an essential of civilization.

Lest these facts should make too vivid a call upon the reader's compassion, I find it advisable to remember here an instance of hard-heartedness in me which was worthier the adamantine conscience of some full-grown moralist than a boy of my age. There was a poor girl, whose misfortune was known to a number of families where she was employed as a seamstress, and the more carefully treated because of her misfortune. Among others my mother was glad to give her work; and she lived with us like one of ourselves, of course sitting at table with us and sharing in such family pleasures as we knew. She was the more to be pitied because her betrayer was a prominent man who bore none of the blame for their sin; but when her shame became known to me I began a persecution of the poor creature in the cause of social purity. I would not take a dish from her at table, or hand her one; I would not speak to her, if I could help it, or look at her; I left the room when she came into it; and I expressed by every cruelty short of words my righteous condemnation. I was, in fact, society incarnate in the attitude society takes toward such as she. Heaven knows how I came by such a devilish ideal of propriety, and I cannot remember how the matter quite ended, but I seem to remember a crisis, in which she begged my mother with tears to tell her why I treated her so; and I was put to bitter shame for it. It could not be explained to me how tragical her case was; I must have been thought too young for the explanation; but I doubt if any boy of twelve is too young for the right knowledge of such things; he already has the wrong.

My wish at times to learn some other business was indulged by a family council, and my uncle made a place for me in his drug-store, where, as long as the novelty lasted, I was happy in the experiments with chemicals permitted to me and a fellow-apprentice. Mainly we were busied in putting up essence of peppermint and paregoric and certain favorite medicinal herbs; and when the first Saturday evening came, my companion received his weekly wage over the counter, and I expected mine, but the bookkeeper smiled and said he would have to see my uncle about that; in the end, it appeared that by the convention with my father I was somehow not to draw any salary. Both my uncle and he treated the matter with something of the bookkeeper's smiling slight, and after an interval, now no longer appreciable, I found myself in the printing-office again. I was not sorry, and yet I had liked the drug business so far as I had gone in it, and I liked that old bookkeeper, though he paid me no money. How, after a life of varied experiences, he had lodged at last in the comfortable place he held I no longer know, if I ever knew. He had been at one time what would once have been called a merchant adventurer in various seas; and he had been wrecked on the Galapagos Islands, where he had feasted on the famous native turtle, now extinct, with a relish which he still smacked his lips in remembering.

This episode, which I cannot date, much antedated the period of my father's business failure, though his struggles against it must have already begun; they began, in fact, from the moment of his arrival in Dayton, and the freest and happiest hours we knew there were when the long strain ended in the inevitable break. Then there was an interval, I do not know how great, but perhaps of months, when there was a casting about for some means of living, and to this interval belongs somehow the employment of my brother and myself in a German printing-office, such as used to be found in every considerable Ohio town. I do not know what we did there, but I remember the kindly German printer-folk, and the merry times we had with them, in the smoke of their pipes and the warmth of their stove heated red against the autumnal cold. I explore my memory in vain for proof that my father had some job-printing interest in this German office, but I remember my interest in the German type and its difference from the English. I was yet far from any interest in the German poetry which afterward became one of my passions, and there is no one now left alive whom I can ask whether the whole incident was fact, or not, rather, the sort of dream which all the past becomes when we try to question it.

What I am distinctly aware of, through a sense of rather sullen autumnal weather, is that a plan for our going into the country evolved itself in full detail between my father and uncle. My uncle was to supply the capital for the venture, and was finally, with two other uncles, to join my father on a milling privilege which they had bought at a point on the Little Miami River, where all the families were to be settled. In the mean time my father was to have charge of a grist-mill and sawmill on the property till they could be turned into a paper-mill and a sort of communal settlement of suitable people could be gathered. He had never run a sawmill or a grist-mill, much less evoked a paper-mill from them; but neither had he ever gathered a community of choice spirits for the enjoyment of a social form which enthusiasts like Robert Owen had dreamed into being, and then non-being, in the Middle West in those or somewhat earlier days. What was definite and palpable in the matter was that he must do something, and that he had the heart and hope for the experiment.

VIII

I have told the story of this venture in a little book called *My Year in a Log Cabin*, printed twenty-odd years ago, and I cannot do better now than let it rehearse itself here from those pages, with such slight change or none as insists. For my father, whose boyhood had been passed in the new country, where pioneer customs and traditions were still rife, it was like renewing the wild romance of those days to take up once more the life in a log-cabin interrupted by many years' sojourn in matter-of-fact dwellings of frame and brick. It was the fond dream of his boys to realize the trials and privations which he had painted for them in rosy hues, and even if the only clap-boarded dwelling at the mills had not been occupied by the miller, we should have disdained it for the log-cabin which we made our home till we could build a new house.

Our cabin stood close upon the road, but behind it broadened a corn-field of eighty acres. They still built log-cabins for dwellings in that region, at the time, but ours must have been nearly half a century old when we went into it. It had been recently vacated by an old poor-white Virginian couple who had long occupied it, and we decided that it needed some repairs, to make it habitable even for a family inured to hardship by dauntless imaginations, and accustomed to retrospective discomforts of every kind.

So, before the family all came out to it, a deputation of adventurers put it in what rude order they could. They glazed the narrow windows, they relaid the rotten floor, they touched (too sketchily, as it afterward appeared,) the broken roof, and they papered the walls of the ground-floor rooms. Perhaps it was my father's love of literature which inspired him to choose newspapers for this purpose; at any rate, he did so, and the effect, as I remember, had its decorative qualities. He had used a barrel of papers from the nearest post-office, where they had been refused by people to whom they had been experimentally sent by the publishers, and the whole first page was taken up by a

story, which broke off in the middle of a sentence at the foot of
the last column, and tantalized us forever with fruitless conjecture as to the fate of the hero and heroine.

The cabin, rude as it was, was not without its sophistications,
its concessions to the spirit of modern luxury. The logs it was
built of had not been left rounded, as they grew, but had been
squared in a saw-mill, and the crevices between them had not
been chinked with moss, and daubed with clay, in true backwoods fashion, but plastered with mortar, and the chimney, instead of being a structure of clay-covered sticks, was laid in
courses of stone. Within, however, it was all that could be desired by the most romantic of pioneering families. It was six
feet wide and a yard deep, its cavernous maw would easily
swallow a back-log eighteen inches through, and we piled in
front the sticks of hickory cord-wood as high as we liked. We
made perfect trial of it, when we came out to put the cabin in
readiness for the family, and when the hickory had dropped into
a mass of tinkling, snapping, bristling embers, we laid our
rashers of bacon and our slices of steak upon them, and tasted
the flavors of the wildwood in the captured juices. At night we
laid our mattresses on the sweet, new oak plank of the floor,
and slept hard—in every sense.

In due time the whole family took up its abode in the cabin.
The household furniture had been brought out and bestowed in
its scanty space, the bookcase had been set up, and the unbound
books left easily accessible in barrels. There remained some of
our possessions to follow, chief of which was the cow; for in those
simple days people kept cows in town, and it fell to me to help
my father drive ours out to her future home. We got on famously,
talking of the wayside things so beautiful in the autumnal day,
panoplied in the savage splendor of its painted leaves, and of
the books and authors so dear to the boy who limped bare-
footed by his father's side, with his eye on the cow, and his mind
on Cervantes and Shakespeare. But the cow was very slow—far
slower than the boy's thoughts—and it had fallen night and was
already thick dark when we had made the twelve miles, and

stood under the white-limbed phantasmal sycamores beside the tail-race of the grist-mill, and questioned how we should get across with our charge. We did not know how deep the water was, but we knew it was very cold, and we would rather not wade it. The only thing to do seemed to be for one of us to run up to the saw-mill, cross the head-race there, and come back to receive the cow on the other side of the tail-race. But the boy could not bring himself either to go or to stay.

The kind-hearted father urged, but he would not compel; you cannot well use force with a boy when you have been talking literature and philosophy for half a day with him. We could see the lights in the cabin cheerfully twinkling, and we shouted to those within, but no one heard us. We called and called in vain. Nothing but the cold rush of the tail-race, the dry rustle of the sycamore leaves, and the homesick lowing of the cow, replied. We determined to drive her across, and pursue her with sticks and stones through the darkness beyond, and then run at the top of our speed to the saw-mill, and get back to take her in custody again. We carried out our part of the plan perfectly, but the cow had not entered into it with intelligence or sympathy. When we reached the other side of the tail-race again, she was nowhere to be found, and no appeals of Boss or Suky or Subose availed. She must have instantly turned, and retraced, in the darkness which seemed to have swallowed her up, the weary steps of the day, for she was found at her old home in town the next morning. At any rate, she had abandoned the father to the conversation of his son, for the time being, and the son had nothing to say.

I do not remember now just how it was that we came by the different "animals of the horse kind," as my father called them, which we housed in an old log-stable not far from our cabin. They must have been a temporary supply, until a team worthy our new, sky-blue wagon could be found. One of them was a colossal sorrel, inexorably hide-bound, whose barrel, as horse men call the body, showed every hoop upon it. He had a feeble, foolish whimper of a voice, and we nicknamed him "Baby."

His companion was a dun mare, who had what my father at once called an italic foot, in recognition of the emphatic slant at which she carried it when upon her unwilling travels. Then there was a small, self-opinionated gray pony, which was of no service conjecturable after this lapse of time. We boys rode him barebacked, and he used to draw a buggy, which he finally ran away with. I suppose we found him useful in the representation of some of the Indian fights which we were always dramatizing, and I dare say he may have served our turn as an Arab charger, when the Moors of Granada made one of their sallies upon the camp of the Spaniards, and discharged their javelins into it; their javelins were the long, admirably straight and slender iron-weeds that grew by the river. This menagerie was constantly breaking bounds, and wandering off; and was chiefly employed in hunting itself up, its different members taking turns in remaining in the pasture or stable, to be ridden after those that had strayed into the woods.

The origin of a large and eloquent flock of geese is lost in an equal obscurity. I recall their possession simply as an accomplished fact, and I associate their desolate cries with the windy dark of rainy November nights, so that they must, at least, have come into our hands after the horses. They were fenced into a clayey area next the cabin for safe-keeping, where, perpetually waddling about in a majestic disoccupation, they patted the damp ground down to the hardness and smoothness of a brickyard. Throughout the day they conversed tranquilly together, but by night they woke, goose after goose, to send forth a long clarion alarm, blending in a general concert at last, to assure one another of their safety. We must have intended to pluck them in the spring, but they stole their nests early in March, and entered upon the nurture of their young before we could prevent it; and it would then have been barbarous to pluck these mothers of families.

We had got some pigs from our old Virginian predecessors, and these kept as far as they could the domestic habits in which that affectionate couple had indulged them. They would willingly have shared our fireside with us, humble as it was, but, being repelled, they took up their quarters on cold nights at the warm base of the chimney without, where we could hear them, as long as we kept awake, disputing the places next to the stones. All this was horrible to my mother, whose housewifely instincts were perpetually offended by the rude conditions of our life, and who justly regarded it as a return to a state which, if poetic, was also not far from barbarous. But boys take every natural thing as naturally as savages, and we never thought our pigs were other than amusing. In that country pigs were called to their feed with long cries of "Pig, pig, pooee, poe-e-e!" but ours were taught to come at a whistle, and, on hearing it, would single themselves out from the neighbors' pigs, and come rushing from all quarters to the scattered corn with an intelligence we were proud of.

IX

As long as the fall weather lasted, and well through the mild winter of that latitude, our chief recreation, where all our novel duties were delightful, was hunting with the long smooth-bore shot-gun, which had descended laterally from one of our uncles, and supplied the needs of the whole family of boys in the chase. Never less than two of us went out with it at once, and generally there were three. This enabled us to beat up the game over a wide extent of country, and while the eldest did the shooting, left the others to rush upon him, as soon as he fired, with tumultuous cries of "Did you hit it? Did you hit it?" We fell upon the wounded squirrels which we brought down, on rare occasions, and put them to death with what I must now call a sickening ferocity. If, sometimes, the fool dog, the weak-minded Newfoundland pup we were rearing, rushed upon the game first, and the squirrel avenged his death upon the dog's nose, that was pure gain, and the squirrel had the applause of his other enemies. Yet we were none of us cruel; we never wantonly killed things that could not be eaten; we should have thought it sacrilege to shoot a robin or a turtle-dove, but we were willing to be amused, and these were the chances of war.

The woods were full of squirrels, which especially abounded in the woods-pastures, as we called the lovely dells where the greater part of the timber was thinned out to let the cattle range and graze. They were of all sorts, gray and black, and even big, red fox-squirrels, a variety I now suppose extinct. When the spring opened we hunted them in the poplar woods, whither they resorted in countless numbers for the sweetness in the cups of the tulip-tree blossoms. I recall with a thrill one memorable morning in such woods—early, after an overnight rain, when the vistas hung full of a delicate mist that the sun pierced to kindle a million fires in the drops still pendulous from leaf and twig. I can smell the tulip blossoms and the odor of the tree-bark yet, and the fresh, strong fragrance of the leafy mould under my bare feet; and I can hear the rush of the squirrels on the bark of the trunks, or the swish of their long, plunging leaps from bough to bough in the air-tops.

In a region where the corn-fields and wheat-fields were often fifty and sixty acres in extent, there was a plenty of quail, but I remember only one victim to my gun. We set figure-four traps to catch them; but they were shrewder arithmeticians than we, and solved these problems without harm to themselves. When they began to mate, and the air was full of their soft, amorous whistling, we searched for their nests, and had better luck, though we were forbidden to rob the nests when we found them; and in June, when a pretty little mother strutted across the lanes at the head of her tiny brood, we had to content ourselves with the near spectacle of her cunning counterfeit of disability at sight of us, fluttering and tumbling in the dust till her chicks could hide themselves. We had read of that trick, and were not deceived, but we were charmed the same.

It is a trick that all birds know, and I had it played upon me by the mother snipe and mother wild-duck that haunted our dam, as well as by the quail. With the snipe, once, I had a fancy to see how far the mother would carry the ruse, and so ran after

her, but in doing this I trod on one of her young, a soft, gray
mite, not distinguishable from the gray pebbles where it ran. I
took it tenderly up in my hand, and it is a pang to me yet to
think how it gasped once and died. A boy is a strange mixture—
as the man who comes after him is. I should not have minded
knocking over that whole brood of snipes with my gun, if I
could; but this poor little death was somehow very personal in
its appeal.

I had no such regrets concerning the young wild ducks, which,
indeed, I had no such grievous accident with. I left their mother
to flounder and flutter away as she would, and took to the swamp
where her young sought refuge from me. There I spent half-a-
day wading about in waters that were often up to my waist, and
full of ugly possibilities of mud-turtles and water-snakes, trying
to put my hand on one of the ducklings. They rose everywhere
else, and dived again after a breath of air, but at last one of them
came up in my very grasp. It did not struggle, but how its wild
heart sounded against my hand! I carried it home to show it
and boast of my capture, and then I took it back to its native
swamp. It dived instantly, and I hope it found its bereaved
family somewhere under the water.

The centre of our life in the cabin was, of course, the fire-
place, whose hugeness and whose mighty fires remained a wonder with us. There was a crane in the chimney and dangling
pot-hooks, and until the cooking-stove could be set up in an adjoining shed, the cooking had to be done on the hearth, and the
bread baked in a Dutch oven in the hot ashes. We had always
heard of this operation, which was a necessity of early days; and
nothing else, perhaps, realized them so vividly for us as the loaf
laid in the iron-lidded skillet, which was then covered with ashes
and heaped with coals.

I am not certain that the bread tasted any better for the historical romance of its experience, or that the cornmeal, mixed
warm from the mill and baked on an oak plank set up before
the fire, had merits beyond the hoe-cake of art; but I think there
can be no doubt that new corn grated from the cob while still

in the milk, and then moulded and put in like manner to brown
in the glow of such embers, would still have the sweetness that
was incomparable then. When the maple sap started in February, we tried the scheme we had cherished all winter of making
with it tea, which should be in a manner self-sugared. But the
scheme was a failure; we spoiled the sap without sweetening
the tea.

We sat up late before the big fire, at night, our faces burning
in the glow, and our backs and feet freezing in the draft that
swept in from the imperfectly closing door, and then we boys
climbed to our bed in the loft. We reached it by a ladder, which
we should have been glad to pull up after us, as a protection
against Indians in the pioneer fashion; but, with the advancement of modern luxury, the ladder had been nailed to the floor.
When we were once aloft, however, we were in a domain sacred
to the past. The rude floor rattled and wavered loosely under
our tread, and the window in the gable stood open or shut at
its own will. There were cracks in the shingles, through which
we could see the stars, when there were stars, and which, when
the first snow came, let the flakes sift in upon the floor.

Our barrels of paper-covered books were stowed away in that
loft, and, overhauling them one day, I found a paper copy of
the poems of a certain Henry W. Longfellow, then wholly unknown to me; and while the old grist-mill, whistling and wheez-
ing to itself, made a vague music in my ears, my soul was filled
with this new, strange sweetness. I read the "Spanish Student,"
there, and the "Coplas de Manrique," and the solemn and ever-
beautiful "Voices of the Night." There were other books in those
barrels, but these spirited me again to Spain, where I had already been with Irving, and led me to attack fitfully the old
Spanish grammar which had been knocking about our house
ever since my father bought it from a soldier of the Mexican War.

But neither these nor any other books made me discontented
with the boy's world about me. They made it a little more popu-
lous with visionary shapes, but that was well, and there was
room for them all. It was not darkened with cares, and the duties

of it were not many. By this time we older boys had our axes, and believed ourselves to be clearing a piece of woods which covered a hill belonging to the milling property. The timber was black-walnut and oak and hickory, and I cannot think we made much inroad in it; but we must have felled some of the trees, for I remember helping to cut them into saw-logs with the cross-cut saw, and the rapture we had in starting our logs from the brow of the hill, and watching their whirling rush to the bottom. We experimented, as boys will, and we felled one large hickory with the saw, instead of the axe, and scarcely escaped with our lives, when it suddenly split near the bark, and the butt shot out between us. I preferred buckeye and sycamore trees for my own axe; they were of no use when felled, but they chopped so easily.

They grew abundantly on the island which formed another feature of our oddly distributed property. This island was by far its most fascinating feature, and for us boys it had the charm and mystery which have in every land and age endeared islands to the heart of man. It was not naturally an island, but had been made so by the mill races bringing the water from the dam, and emptying into the river again below the mills. It was flat, and half under water in every spring freshet, but it had precious areas grown up to tall iron weeds, which, withering and hardening in the frost, supplied us with the darts for our Indian fights. The island was always our battle-ground, and it resounded in the long afternoons with the war-cries of the encountering tribes. We had a book in those days called *Western Adventure*, which was made up of tales of pioneer and frontier life, and we were constantly reading ourselves back into that life. This book, and Howe's *Collections for the History of Ohio*, were full of stories of the backwoodsmen and warriors who had made our State a battle-ground for nearly fifty years, and our life in the log-cabin gave new zest to the tales of "Simon Kenton, the Pioneer," and "Simon Girty, the Renegade;" of the captivity of Crawford and his death at the stake; of the massacre of the Moravian Indians at Gnadenhütten; of the defeat of St. Clair and the victory of

Wayne; of a hundred other wild and bloody incidents of our annals. We read of them at night till we were afraid to go up the ladder to the ambuscade of savages in our loft, but we fought them over by day with undaunted spirit. With our native romance I sometimes mingled from my own reading a strain of old-world poetry, and "Hamet el Zegri" and the "Unknown Spanish Knight," encountered in the Vega before Granada on our island, while Adam Poe and the Indian chief Bigfoot were taking breath from their deadly struggle in the waters of the Ohio.

x

When the spring opened we broke up the sod on a more fertile part of the island, and planted a garden there beside our field of corn. We planted long rows of sweet potatoes, and a splendid profusion of melons, which duly came up with their empty seed-shells fitted like helmets over their heads, and were mostly laid low the next day by the cut-worms which swarmed in the upturned sod. But the sweet potatoes had better luck. Better luck I did not think it, then; their rows seemed interminable to a boy set to clear them of purslane with his hoe; though I do not now imagine they were necessarily a day's journey in length. Neither could the corn-field beside them have been very vast; but again reluctant boyhood has a different scale for the measurement of such things, and, perhaps, now if I were set to hill it up, I might think differently about its size.

I dare say it was not well-cared for, but an inexhaustible wealth of ears came into the milk just at the right moment for our enjoyment. We had then begun to build our new house, and for this we were now kiln-drying the green oak flooring-boards. We had built a long skeleton hut, and had set the boards upright all round it and roofed it with them, and in the middle of it we had set a huge old cast-iron stove, in which we kept a roaring fire. The fire had to be watched night and day, and it often took all the boys of the neighborhood to watch it, and to turn the boards. It must have been cruelly hot in that kiln; but I remember nothing of that; I remember only the luxury of the green corn, spitted on the points of long sticks and roasted in the red-hot stove; we must almost have roasted our own heads at the same time. But I suppose that if the heat within the kiln or without ever became intolerable, we escaped from it and from our light, summer clothing, reduced to a Greek simplicity, in a delicious plunge in the river. We had our choice of the shallows, where the long ripple was warmed through and through by the sun in which it sparkled, or the swimming-hole, whose depths were almost as tepid, but were here and there interwoven with mysterious cool undercurrents.

We believed that there were snapping-turtles and water-snakes in our swimming holes, though we never saw any. There were some fish in the river, chiefly suckers and catfish in the spring, when the water was high and turbid, and in summer the bream that we call sunfish in the West, and there was a superstition, never verified by us, of bass. We did not care much for fishing, though of course that had its turn in the pleasures of our rolling year. There were crawfish, both hard shell and soft, to be had at small risk, and mussels in plenty. Their shells furnished us the material for many rings zealously begun and never finished; we did not see why they did not produce pearls; but perhaps they were all eaten up, before the pearl-disease could attack them, by the muskrats, before whose holes their shells were heaped.

Of skating on the river, I think, we had none. The winter often passed in our latitude without making ice enough for that sport, and there could not have been much sledding, either. We read, enviously enough, in Peter Parley's *First Book of History*, of the coasting on Boston Common, and we made some weak-kneed sleds (whose imbecile runners flattened helplessly under them) when the light snows began to come; but we never had any real coasting, as our elders never had any real sleighing in the jumpers they made by splitting a hickory sapling for runners, and mounting any sort of rude box upon them. They might have used sleighs in the mud, however; that was a foot deep on most of the roads, and lasted all winter. For a little while some of us went two miles away through the woods to school; but there was not much to be taught a reading family like ours in that log-hut, and I suppose it was not thought worth while to keep us at it. No impression of it remains to me, except the wild, lonesome cooing of the turtle-doves when they began to nest in the neighboring oaks.

Our new house got on slowly. The log-cabin had not become pleasanter with the advance of the summer, and we looked forward to our occupation of the new house with an eagerness which even in us boys must have had some sense of present discomfort at the bottom of it. The frame was of oak, and my father decided to have the house weather-boarded and shingled with black-walnut, which was so much cheaper than pine, and which, left in its natural state, he thought would be agreeable in color. It appeared to me a palace. I spent all the leisure I had from swimming and Indian-fighting and reading, in watching the carpenter work, and hearing him talk; his talk was not the wisest, but he thought very well of it himself, and I had so far lapsed from civilization that I stood in secret awe of him, because he came from town—from the little village, namely, two miles away.

I try to give merely a child's memories of our life, which were nearly all delightful, but it must have been hard for my elders, and for my mother especially, who could get no help, or only briefly and fitfully, in the work that fell to her. Now and then a New Church minister, of those who used to visit us in town, passed a Sunday with us in the cabin, and that was a rare time of mental and spiritual refreshment for her. Otherwise, my father read us a service out of the book of worship, or a chapter from the *Heavenly Arcana*; and week-day nights, while the long evenings lasted, he read poetry to us—Scott, or Moore, or Thomson, or some of the more didactic poets.

In the summer evenings, after her long, hard day's work was done, my mother sometimes strolled out upon the island with my father, and loitered on the bank to look at her boys in the river. One such evening I recall, and how sad our gay voices were in the dim, dewy air. My father had built a flat boat, which we kept on the smooth waters of our dam, and on Sunday afternoons the whole family went out in it. We rowed far up, till we struck a current from the mill above us, and then let the boat drift slowly down again. It does not now seem very exciting, but then to a boy whose sense was open to every intimation of beauty, the silence that sang in our ears, the stillness of the dam where the low uplands and the fringing sycamores, and every rush and grass-blade by the brink, perfectly glassed themselves, with the vast, blue sky overhead, were full of mystery, of divine promise and holy awe.

I recollect the complex effect of these Sunday afternoons as if they were all one sharp event; I recall in like manner the starry summer nights, and there is one of these nights that remains single and peerless in my memory. My brother and I had been sent on an errand to some neighbor's—for a bag of potatoes or a joint of meat; it does not matter—and we had been somehow belated, so that it was well after twilight when we started home, and the round moon was high when we stopped to rest in a piece of the lovely open woodland of that region, where the trees stood in a park-like freedom from underbrush, and the grass grew dense and rich among them. We took the pole, on which we had slung the bag, from our shoulders, and sat down on an old long-fallen log, and listened to the densely interwoven monotonies of the innumerable katydids, in which the air seemed clothed as with a mesh of sound. The shadows fell black from the trees upon the smooth sward, but every other place was full of the tender light in which all forms were rounded and softened; the moon hung tranced in the sky. We scarcely spoke in the shining solitude, the solitude which for once had no terrors for the childish fancy, but was only beautiful. This perfect beauty seemed not only to liberate me from the fear which is the prevailing mood of childhood, but to lift my soul nearer and nearer to the soul of all things in an exquisite sympathy. Such moments never pass; they are ineffaceable; their rapture immortalizes; from them we know that whatever perishes there is something in us that cannot die, that divinely regrets, divinely hopes.

XI

Our log-cabin stood only a stone's cast from the gray, old, weather-tinted grist-mill, whose voice was music for us by night and by day, so that on Sundays, when the water was shut off from the great tub-wheels in its basement, it was as if the world had gone deaf and dumb. A soft sibilance prevailed by day over the dull, hoarse murmur of the machinery; but late at night, when the water gathered that mysterious force which the darkness gives it, the voice of the mill had something weird in it, like a human moan.

It was in all ways a place which I did not care to explore alone. It was very well, with a company of boys, to tumble and wrestle in the vast bins full of tawny wheat, or to climb the slippery stairs to the cooling-floor in the loft, whither the little pockets of the elevators carried the meal warm from the burrs, and the blades of the wheel up there, worn smooth by years of use, spread it out in an ever-widening circle, and caressed it with a thousand repetitions of their revolution. But the heavy rush of the water upon the wheels in the dim, humid basement, the angry whirr of the millstones under the hoppers, the high windows, powdered and darkened with the floating meal, the vague corners festooned with flour-laden cobwebs, the jolting and shaking of the bolting-cloths, had all a potentiality of terror in them that was not a pleasure to the boy's sensitive nerves. Ghosts, against all reason and experience, were but too probably waiting their chance to waylay unwary steps there, whenever two feet ventured alone into the mill, and Indians, of course, made it their ambush.

With the saw-mill it was another matter. That was always an affair of the broad day. It began work, and quitted work like a Christian, and did not keep the grist-mill's unnatural hours. Yet it had its fine moments, when the upright-saw lunged through the heavy oak log and gave out the sweet smell of the bruised, woody fibres, or then when the circular-saw wailed through the length of the lath we were making for the new house, and freed itself with a sharp cry, and purred softly till the wood touched it again, and it broke again into its shrill lament. The warm saw-dust in the pits below was almost as friendly to bare feet as the warm meal; and it was splendid to rush down the ways on the cars that brought up the logs, or carried away the lumber.

It was in the early part of the second winter that it was justly thought fit I should leave these delights, and go to earn some money in a printing-office in X——, when the foreman of the printing-office appeared one day at our cabin, and asked if I could come to take the place of a delinquent hand. There was no question with any one but myself but I must go. For me, a terrible homesickness fell instantly upon me—a homesickness that already, in the mere prospect of absence, pierced my heart, and filled my throat.

The foreman wanted me to go back with him in his buggy, but a day's grace was granted me, and then my older brother took me to X——, where he was to meet my father at the rail-road station on his return from Cincinnati. It had been snow-ing, in the soft, Southern Ohio fashion, but the clouds had broken away, and the evening fell in a clear sky, apple-green along the horizon, as we drove on. This color of the sky must always be associated for me with the despair which then filled my soul, and which I was constantly swallowing down with great gulps. We joked, and got some miserable laughter out of the efforts of the horse to free himself from the snow that balled in his hoofs, but I suffered all the time an anguish of homesickness that now seems incredible. I had every fact of the cabin life before me; what each of the children was doing, especially the younger ones, and what, above all, my mother was doing, and how she was looking; and I saw the wretched little phantasm of myself moving about among them.

The editor to whom my brother delivered me over could not conceive of me as tragedy; he received me as if I were the merest commonplace, and delivered me in turn to the good man with whom I was to board. There were half-a-dozen school-girls boarding there, too, and their gayety, when they came in, added to my desolation. The man said supper was about ready, and he reckoned I would get something to eat if I looked out for myself. Upon reflection, I answered that I thought I did not want any supper, and that I must go to find my brother, whom I had to tell something. I found him at the station, and told him I was going home with him. He tried to reason with me, or rather with my frenzy of homesickness; and I agreed to leave the question open till my father came; but in my own mind it was closed.

My father suggested, however, something that had not occurred to either of us: we should both stay. This seemed possible for me; but not at that boarding-house, not within the sound of the laughter of those girls! We went to the hotel, where we had beef-steak and ham and eggs and hot biscuit every morning for breakfast, and where we paid two dollars apiece for the week we stayed. At the end of this time the editor had found another hand, and we went home, where I was welcomed as from a year's absence.

Again I was called to suffer a like trial, the chief trial of my boyhood, but it came in a milder form, and was lightened to me not only by the experience of survival from it, but by kindly circumstance. This time I went to Dayton, where my young uncle somehow learned the misery I was in, and bade me come and stay with him, while I remained in the town. I was very fond of him, and of the gentle creature, his wife, but for all that, I was homesick still. I fell asleep with the radiant image of our log-cabin before my eyes, and I woke with my heart like lead in my breast.

I did not see how I could get through the day, and I began it with miserable tears. I had found that by drinking a great deal of water at my meals, I could keep down the sobs for the time being, and I practised this device to the surprise and alarm of my relatives, who were troubled at the spectacle of my unnatural thirst. But I could not wholly hide my suffering, and I suppose that after a while the sight of it became intolerable. At any rate, a blessed evening came when I returned from my work and found my brother waiting for me at my uncle's house; and the next morning we set out for home in the keen, silent dark before the November dawn.

We were both mounted on the italic-footed mare, I behind my brother, with my arms round him to keep on better, and so we rode out of the sleeping town, and into the lifting shadow of the woods. They might have swarmed with ghosts, or Indians; I should not have cared; I was going home. By-and-by, as we rode on, the birds began to call one another from their dreams; the quails whistled from the stubble fields, and the crows clamored from the decaying tops of the girdled trees in the deadening. The squirrels raced along the fence-rails, and in the woods, they stopped half-way up the boles to bark at us; the jays strutted down the shelving branches to offer us a passing insult and defiance.

Sometimes, at a little clearing, we came to a log-cabin; the blue smoke curled from its chimney, and through the closed door came the low hum of a spinning-wheel. The red and yellow leaves, heavy with the cold dew, dripped round us; I was profoundly at peace, and the homesick will understand how it was that I was as if saved from death. At last we crossed the tail-race from the island, and turned up, not at the old log-cabin, but at the front door of the new house. The family had flitted during my absence, and now they all burst out upon me in exultant welcome, and my mother caught me to her heart. Doubtless she knew that it would have been better for me to have conquered myself; but my defeat was dearer to her than my triumph could have been. She made me her honored guest; I had the best place at the table, the tenderest bit of steak, the richest cup of her golden coffee; and all that day I was "company."

It was a great day, which I must have spent chiefly in admiring the new house. It was so very new, yet, as not to be plastered; they had not been able to wait for that; but it was beautifully lathed in all its partitions, and the closely-fitted floors were a marvel of carpentering. I roamed through the rooms, and up and down the stairs, and freshly admired the familiar outside of the house as if it were as novel as the interior, where open wood-fires blazed upon the hearths, and threw a pleasant light of home upon the latticed walls.

I must have gone through the old log-cabin to see how it looked without us, but I have no recollection of ever entering its door again, so soon had it ceased to be part of my life. We remained in the new house, as we continued to call it, for two or three months, and then the changes of business which had been taking place without the knowledge of us children called us away from that roof, too, and we left the Mills and the pleasant country that had grown so dear, to take up our abode in city streets again. We went to live in the ordinary brick house of our civilization, but we had grown so accustomed, with the quick and facile adaptation of children, to living in a house which was merely lathed, that we distinguished this last dwelling from the new house as a "plastered house."

Some of our playmates of the neighborhood walked part of the way to X—— with us boys, the snowy morning when we turned our backs on the new house to take the train in that town. A shadow of the gloom in which our spirits were steeped passes over me again, but chiefly I remember our difficulties in getting our young Newfoundland dog away with us; and our subsequent embarrassments with him on the train, where he sat up and barked out of the window at the passing objects, and finally became seasick, blot all other memories of that journey from my mind.

II

IF IN a child's first years the things which it apparently remembers are really the suggestions of its elders, it begins soon to repay the debt, and repays it more and more fully until its memory touches the history of all whom it has known. Through the whole time when a boy is becoming a man his autobiography can scarcely be kept from becoming the record of his family and his world. He finds himself so constantly reflected in the personality of those about him, so blent with it, that any attempt to study himself as a separate personality is impossible. His environment has become his life, and his hope of a recognizable self-portrait must lie in his frank acceptance of the condition that he can make himself truly seen chiefly in what he remembers to have seen of his environment.

I

We were now going from the country to Columbus, where my father, after several vain attempts to find an opening elsewhere as editor or even as practical printer, had found congenial occupation at least for the winter; and the reader who likes to date a small event by a great one may care to know that we arrived in the capital of Ohio about the time that Louis Kossuth arrived in the capital of the United States. In the most impressive exile ever known he came from Hungary, then trampled under foot by the armies of Austria and Russia, and had been greeted with a frenzy of enthusiasm in New York as the prophet and envoy of a free republic in present difficulties, but destined

57

to a glorious future. At Washington he had been received by both Houses of Congress with national honors which might well have seemed to him national promises of help against the despotisms joined in crushing the Magyar revolt; we had just passed a law providing for the arrest of slaves escaping from their owners in the South, and we were feeling free to encourage the cause of liberty throughout the world.

Kossuth easily deceived himself in us, and he went hopefully about the country, trying to float an issue of Hungarian bonds on our sympathetic tears, and in his wonderful English making appeals full of tact and eloquence, which went to the hearts if not the pockets of his hearers. Among the other state capitals he duly came to Columbus, where I heard him from the steps of the unfinished State House. I hung on the words of the picturesque black-bearded, black-haired, black-eyed man, in the braided coat of the Magyars, and the hat with an ostrich plume up the side which set a fashion among us, and I believed with all my soul that in a certain event we might find the despotisms of the Old World banded against us, and "would yet see Cossacks," as I thrilled to hear Kossuth say. In those days we world-patriots put the traitor Görgy, who surrendered the Hungarian army to the Austrians and Russians, beside our own Benedict Arnold; but what afterwards became of him I do not know. I know that Kossuth went disappointed back to Europe and dwelt a more and more peaceful newspaper correspondent in Turin till the turn of fortune's wheel would have dropped him, somehow politically tolerable to Austria, back in his native country. But he would not return; he died in Turin; and a few years ago in Carlsbad I fancied I had caught sight of his son at a café, but was told that I had seen the wrong man, who was much more revolutionary-looking than Kossuth's son, and more like Kossuth.

I adopted with his cause the Kossuth hat, as we called it, and wore it with the plume in it till the opinions of boys without plumes in their hats caused me to take the feather out. My father was of their mind about the feather, but otherwise we thought a great deal alike, and he was zealous to have me see the wonders of the capital. I visited the penitentiary and the lunatic, deaf and dumb, and blind asylums with him, though I think rather from his interest than mine; but I was willing enough to realize the consequence of Columbus as the capital of a sovereign American state, and I did what I could to meet his expectations. Together we made as thorough examination of the new State House as the workmen who had not yet finished it would allow, and he told me that it would cost, when done, a million dollars, a sum of such immensity that my young imagination shrank from grappling with it; but I am afraid that before the State House was done it may have cost more; certainly it must have cost much more with the incongruous enlargements which in later years spoiled its classic proportions. My father made me observe that it was built of Ohio limestone without, and later I saw that it was faced with Vermont and Tennessee marble within, where it was not stuccoed and frescoed; but as for the halls of legislation where the laws of Ohio were made and pro-vided, when I first witnessed the process, they were contained in a modest square edifice of brick which could not have cost a million dollars, or the twentieth part of them, by the boldest computation of the contractors. It was entirely modest as to the Hall of the House and the Senate Chamber, and I suppose that so were the state offices, wherever they were, unnoted by me. The State House, as much as I knew of it from a single visit to the Hall of Representatives, was of a very simple interior heated from two vast hearths where fires of cord-wood logs were blaz-ing high. There were rows of legislators sitting at their desks, and probably one of them was on his feet, speaking; I recall dimly a presiding officer, but my main affair was to breathe as softly as I could and get away as soon as possible from my father's side where he sat reporting the proceedings for the *Ohio State Journal*, then the Whig and later the Republican organ.

II

Nobody cares now for the details, or even the main incidents of state legislation, but in that day people seemed to care so much that the newspapers at the capital found their account in following them, and as I learned later the papers at Cincinnati and Cleveland had correspondents at Columbus to let them know by letter what went on in the House and Senate. My father could make a very full and faithful report of the legislative proceedings in long-hand, and for this he was paid ten dollars a week. As I have told elsewhere, I worked on the same paper and had four dollars as compositor; my eldest brother became very provisionally clerk in a grocery-store where he had three dollars, and read the novels of Captain Maryatt in the intervals of custom. Our joint income enabled us to live comfortably in the little brick house, on a humble new street, which my father hired for ten dollars a month from a Welsh carpenter with a large family. No sense of our own Welsh origin could render this family interesting; I memorized some scraps of their Cymric as I overheard it across the fence, but we American children did not make acquaintance with the small Welsh folk, or with more than these few words of their language, which after several attempts at its grammar still remain my sole knowledge of it. On the other side lived a mild, dull German of some lowly employ, whom I remember for his asking us across the fence, one day, to lend him a leather cover. When by his patient repetition this construed itself as an envelope, we loved him for the pleasure it gave us, and at once made leather-cover the family name for envelope. Across the street dwelt an English family of such amiable intelligence that they admired some verses of mine which my father stole to their notice and which they put me to shame by praising before my face.

In my leisure from the printing-office I was in fact cultivating a sufficiently thankless muse in the imitation of Pope and Goldsmith, for in me, more than his other children, my father had divined and encouraged the love of poetry; but in reproducing his poets, as I constantly did, to his greater admiration than mine, I sometimes had a difficulty which I did not carry to him. There is no harm in now submitting it to the reader, who may have noted in his own case the serious disadvantage of writing about love when he had as yet had no experience of the passion. I did my best, and I suppose I did no worse than other poets of thirteen. But I fell back mostly upon inanimate nature, which I knew very well from the woods where I had hunted and the fields where I had hoed; to be honest, I never hoed so much as I hunted, and I never hunted very successfully. I now went many walks into the woods and fields about the town in my longing for the wider spaces I had known, and helped my sisters dig up the wild flowers which they brought home and planted in our yard. But I recall more distinctly than any other a Sunday walk which I took with my father across the Scioto to the forsaken town on the western bank of the river. Franklinton had been thought of as the capital before Columbus, and it has now been rehabilitated in an indefinitely greater prosperity than it ever enjoyed in its prime, but during my life in the city which so promptly won the capital away from it, Franklinton lay abandoned by nine-tenths of its inhabitants, and stretched over the plain in rows of small, empty brick dwellings. I have the impression of disused county buildings, but I am not sure of them; I heard (but in days when I did not much concern myself with such poor unliterary facts) that the notion of Franklinton as the capital was rejected because it was apt in spring-time to be flooded by the Scioto, and was at other seasons infested by malaria which the swarms of mosquitoes bore to every household. The people, mostly sallow women and children who still gaze at me from a few of the doorways and windows, looked as if their agues were of unfailing recurrence every other day of every week; though I suppose that in winter they were somewhat less punctual. I should like to believe that Franklinton was precious to me because of its suggestion of Goldsmith's *Deserted Village*, but I cannot claim that it bore any likeness to the hamlet of the poet's fancy, even in the day when I was hungering to resemble all life to literature; and I never made it the subject of my verse, though I think now it merited as much and more. Since that time I have seen other abandoned cities, notably Pompeii and Herculaneum, but Franklinton remains of a memorable pathos and of a forlornness all the more appreciable because it had become ruin and eld amidst the young, vigorous life of a new country.

In *My Literary Passions* I have made full mention of the books I was reading that winter of 1851–2; but I was rather surprised to find that in a boyish diary of the time, lately discovered in the chaos of a storage warehouse, none of my favorite authors was specified. I could trace them, indeed, in the varying style of the record, but the diarist seems to have been shy of naming them, for no reason that I can now imagine.

The diary is much more palpable than the emotions of the diarist, and is a large, flat volume of foolscap paper, bound in marbled boards, somewhat worn with use and stained with age. The paper within is ruled, which kept the diarist's hand from wandering, and the record fills somewhat less than a fourth of the pages; the rest are given to grammatical exercises in Spanish, which the diarist was presently beginning to study, but even these interrupt themselves, falter, and are finally lost in space. The volume looks quite its age of sixty years, for it begins in the closing months of 1851.

The diarist practised a different handwriting every day and wrote a style almost as varied. The script must have been imitated from the handwritings which he successively admired, and the literary manner from that which seemed to him most elegant in the authors he had latest read. He copies not only their style, but their mental poses, and is often sage beyond his years, which are fourteen verging upon fifteen. With all its variety of script, the spelling in the diary is uniformly of the correct sort which printers used to learn as part of their trade, but which is said to be now suffering a general decay through the use of typesetting machines. There are few grammatical errors in the diversified pages and the punctuation is accurate and intelligent.

Though there is little note or none of the diarist's reading, there is other witness that it had already begun to be of wide range and copious variety. Now and then there are hints of his familiarity with Goldsmith's Essays, and Dickens's novels which his father was reading aloud, and one Sunday it appears that when he was so loath to get up that he did not rise until eight o'clock he tells us: "I slipped into my clothes, made the fire in the sitting-room, wrapped father's cloak about me, and sat down to read the travels of Hommaire de Hell, a Frenchman who traveled in the Russian Empire in the year 1840." I do not care much now who M. Hommaire de Hell was or what he had to say of the Russian Empire in 1840, but I wish I could see that boy wrapped in his father's cloak, and losing himself in the Frenchman's page. Though I have the feeling that we were once familiarly acquainted, I am afraid the diarist would not know me if he looked up across the space of threescore years, though he might divine in me a kindred sense of the heaviness of the long Sunday hours which he confronts when he rises from his reading.

Throughout the yellowing pages there is evident striving, not to say straining, for a literary style, the most literary style possible, and the very first page commemorates a visit to the Lunatic Asylum in terms of a noble participial construction. "Passing up the broad graveled path to the door of the institution, we entered the office, and leaving our hats on the table we proceeded on our way. The first room we entered contained those who were nearly cured. There was in it no one but an old and a young man. The old man I did not notice much, but the young one attracted my attention. He paced the floor all the time, not taking the least notice of us; then we went up-stairs where the most unmanageable ones were kept. Here was a motley crew, some of them lying at full length on the floor, standing up and walking about, while crownless hats and dilapidated shirt-bosoms were the order of the day. In the midst of these terrible men, thoughtless as the brute and ferocious as the tiger, stood a small man (the assistant physician) whom they could have torn limb from limb in a moment. Here was a beautiful instance of the power of mind over brute force. He was reading poetry to them, and the men, totally bereft of reason, listening like little children to the sweet cadence of the verse." All this and more is in a fine script, so sloping that it is almost lying down, either from the exhausting emotions of the diarist or from a temporary ideal of elegance. But the very next day it braces itself for a new effort and it is not many days before it stands upright in a bold, vertical file.

The writer does not know any boys except in the printing-office, and these he knows only in a shrinking sort, not venturing to take part, except once, in their wild hilarity, and scarcely knowing their names, even the name of the boy whom he is afterward to associate himself with in their first venture with a volume of verse. His chief companionship is with his father, whom he goes long walks and holds long talks with, and it is his father who encourages him in his versifying and who presently steals into the print of the newspaper employing them both a poem on the premature warm weather which has invited the bluebirds and blackbirds into the northern March. At first the boy was in dismay at the sight of the poem, with the introductory editorial note customary in those days, but he hides this from his diary, where he confides his joy in finding his verses "copied into a New York paper, and also in the Cincinnati *Commercial*. I mean the piece on Winter."

But the poet kept on and wrote more and more, while the diarist wrote less and less. It is needless to follow him through the pieces which were mostly imitated from some favorite poet of the moment or more originally drawn from the scenes of life known to the author. One of these, painting an emigrant's farewell to the home he is leaving, tells how he stoops over—

> "And pats the good old house dog
> Who is lying on the floor."

The morning after the piece appeared, a fellow printer-boy seems to have quoted the line aloud for all to hear, and dramatized it by patting the author on the head, inwardly raging but helpless to resent the liberty. In fact, the poet did not well know how to manage the publicity now thrust upon him. He behaved indeed with such outrageous resentment at finding his first piece of verse in print that his father, who had smuggled it into the editor's hands, well-nigh renounced him and all his works. But not quite; he was too fond of both, and the boy and he were presently abetting each other in the endeavor for his poetic repute—so soon does the love of fame go to the strongest head.

As yet neither looked for his recognition in that sort of literature which the boy was ultimately to be best or most known in. He seems not to have read at this time much prose fiction, but he was reading Homer in Pope's translation, or rather he was reading the Odyssey; the Iliad he found tiresome and noisy; and if the whole truth must be told, as I have understood it, he liked *The Battle of the Frogs and Mice* best of all the Homeric poems. It was this which he imitated in a burlesque epic of *The Cat Fight*, studied from nature in the hostilities nightly raging on the back fences; but the only surviving poem of what may be called his classical period, as the poets of it understood Queen Anne's age, is a pastoral so exactly modeled upon the pastorals of the great Mr. Pope, that but for a faulty line here and there and the intrusion of a few live American birds among the stuffed songsters of those Augustan groves, I do not see how Mr. Pope could deny having written it. He might well have rejoiced in a follower who loved him so devotedly and so exactly reproduced his artificiality in heroic couplets studied from his own, with the same empty motive to the same unreal effect, as the surviving fragments of it will witness.

> "When fair Aurora kissed the purple East
> And dusky night the struggling day released,
> Two swains whom Phœbus waked from sleep's embrace
> Led forth their flocks to crop the dewy grass.
> While morning blushed upon the cheek of day
> Young Corydon began the rural lay.

> *Corydon.*

> "Now ceases Philomel her nightly strain,
> And trembling stars forsake the ethereal plain;
> Pale Luna fades and down the distant West
> Sadly and slowly lowers her rayless crest;

But yellow Phœbus pours his beams along
And linnets sport where Philomela sung.
Here robins chirp and joyful orioles sing
Where late the owlet flapped his noiseless wing;
Here the pale lily spreads its petals wide,
And snowy daisies deck the green hillside;
Here violets' bloom with waterflowers wreath,
And forest blossoms scent the Zephyr's breath.
Fit spot for song where Spring in every flower
Rich incense offers to the morning hour.
Then let us sing! The hour is meet for love,
The plain, the vale, the music-breathing grove;
Let gentle Daphnis judge the doubtful song,
And soft Æolus bear the notes along.
I stake my pipe with whose soft notes I while
The tedious hours, and my toil beguile;
Whose mellow voice gives joy serener charms,
And grief of half its bitterness disarms."

Here should enter some unnamed competitor, but apparently does not.

"And I, my dog, who guards by yonder brook
Two careless truants from his master's flock;
Who views his timid charge with jealous eyes
And every danger for their sake defies.
In cheerful day my helpmate and my pride,
At night my brave companion and my guide.
The morning flies: no more the song delay,
  For morning most delights the Sylvan Muse,
Ere modest twilight yields to flaming day,
  And fervid sunbeams drink the cooling dews
And wither half the freshness of the Spring."

Another nameless person, possibly the "gentle Daphnis," now speaks:

"Alternate, then, ye swains must answering sing.
By turns the planets circle round the sun
In even turns the changing seasons run;
Smooth-coming night enshrouds the passing day,
And morn returning smiles the night away."

And doubtless now it is Corydon who resumes:

"Inspire my song, ye tuneful nine, inspire!
And fill the shepherd's humble lay with fire.
Around your altar verdant bays I twine,
And palms I offer on your sacred shrine.
Since Julia smiles, let Julia fire my strain,
    And smooth the language of the lay of love
Till conscious music breathes o'er all the plain,
    And joyous echoes wake the silent grove."

I have no facts to support my conjecture, but I will hazard the belief that the winter of 1851–2 was largely given to producing and polishing this plaster-of-paris masterpiece. I might find it easy to make a mock of the lifeless cast—a "cold pastoral," indeed!—but it would be with a faint, or perhaps more than faint, heartache for the boy who strove so fervently to realize a false ideal of beauty in his work. It is my consolation that his soul was always in his work and that when he turned to other ideals and truer, because faithfuler to the life he knew, he put his soul into them, too.

III

In the *State Journal* office I had soon been changed from the newspaper to the book room, and was put to setting up the House bills and Senate bills. I am not ready to say that these potential laws, with their clattering repetitions of, "An Act entitled an Act to amend an Act," intensified my sense of Columbus as a capital, with the lawmaking machinery always grinding away in it; but the formula had its fascination, and I remained contented with my work, with no apprehension, from the frequent half-holidays offered me by the foreman, that there was ever to be an end of it. All at once, however, the legislature had adjourned and my father's engagement ended with the session. My employment somehow ceased with both, and though we children were now no longer so homesick for the country, and would have liked well enough to live on in Columbus, we were eager for the new home which he told us he had found for us in the Western Reserve. In his antislavery opinions he agreed better with the Ohio New-Englanders there than with the Ohio Virginians and Kentuckians whom we had hitherto lived amongst; we understood that he had got a share in the Freesoil newspaper in Ashtabula; and I can recall no wider interval between the adjournment of the legislature and our taking passage on the newly completed railroad to Cleveland than sufficed me for a hardy experiment in gardening among the obdurate clods and brickbats of our small back yard.

In the news-room of the *State Journal* office I had seen the first real poet of my personal knowledge in the figure of the young assistant editor who used to come in with proofs or copy for the foreman, but I cannot hope that the reader will recognize him in his true quality under the name of Florus B. Plympton, or will quite withhold the sophisticated smile of these days for the simple-hearted American parents of the past who could so christen an unconsenting infant. I dare say most of his verse was no worthier of his best than this name, but if here and there a reader has known the lovely lines of the poem called *In Summer when the Days were Long*, he will be glad to have me recall it with him, and do what I can to bring it back from dumb forgetfulness. I myself had not read that poem when I used to see the young editor in the news-room, and he had perhaps not yet written it; I believe I did not think any great things of other pieces which he printed in the *State Journal*; and it was in the book-room, where I was afterward transferred, that I all unwittingly met the truest poet of our Middle West, and one of the truest poets of any time or place. With the name of John J. Piatt I would gladly relate my own more memorably than in the *Poems of Two Friends*, long since promptly forgotten, where I joined him in our first literary venture. We are now old men, hard upon our eighties, but we were then boys of thirteen or fourteen, with no dream of our adventure in joint-authorship, and we had our boyish escapades in the long leisure of the spring afternoons of 1850, when we did not yet know each other even by the nature of poets which we shared.

I can see Piatt now, his blue eyes laughing to tears in our romps and scuffles, and I can hear the trickling mirth of his reluctant chuckle, distinct across the days of the years that have brought us so far. He was setting up House Bills and Senate Bills too, with whatever subjective effect, in the intervals of our frolic, but his head must have been involved in the sunny mists that wrapt mine round. My life, then, as always, was full of literature to bursting, the literature I read and the literature I wrote, for my father had already printed some of the verses I could not keep to myself; and it is not strange that I can recover from the time so few and so trivial events of more exoteric interest. My love indeed was primarily for my work at the printer's case, but that had its hours, as while I was distributing the type, when my fancy roamed the universe in every dramatization of a proud and triumphant future. In these reveries I was a man brilliantly accepted by the great world, but in my waking from them I was a boy, with a boy's fears and anxieties in conditions which might not have appalled a bolder nature. There was, for instance, the Medical College in State Street, where years later I was to dwell so joyously when it had become a boarding-house in a suspense of its scientific function, but whence now, after the early dark had fallen, ghosts swarmed from the dissecting-room, and pursued me on my way home well round the corner into Oak Street, where they delivered me over to another peril, unfailingly in wait for me. There an abominable cur, which had instinctively known of my approach several houses away, rushed from his gate to meet me. It might have been my wisest course to run from the ghosts, but flight would not avail me with this little beast, and when he sprang out with sudden yelpings and barkings, and meteoric flashings about my legs, I was driven to the folly of trying to beat him off with sticks and stones. After he had once found his way to my terror, which remained to me from having been bitten by a dog years before, and left me without a formula of right behavior with a dog attacking me, nothing could save me from him but my final escape from his fence, his street, his city; and this, more than anything else, consoled me for any sense of loss which I may have felt in leaving the state capital.

IV

My elder brother and I had several ideals in common quite apart from my own literary ideals. One of these was life in a village, as differenced from life in the country, or in any city, large or little; another was the lasting renunciation of the printing-business in every form. The last was an effect from the anxiety which we had shared with our father and mother in the long adversity, ending in the failure of his newspaper, from which we had escaped to the country. Once clear of that disaster, we meant never to see a press or a case of types again; and after our year of release from them in the country my brother had his hopes of learning the river and becoming a steamboat pilot, but failed in these, and so joined us in Columbus, where he had put off the evil day of his return to the printing-business a little longer. Meanwhile I had yielded to my fate and spent the whole winter in a printing-office; and now we were both going to take up our trade, so abhorrent in its memories, but going gladly because of the chances which it held out to my father at a time when there seemed no other chance in the world for him.

Yet we were about to fulfill our other ideal by going to live in a village. The paper which we were to help make my father make his by our work—for he had no money to buy it—was published in Ashtabula, now a rather obstreperous little city, full of industrial noise and grime, with a harbor emulous of the gigantic activities of the Cleveland lake-front, but it must even then have had a thousand people. Our ideal, therefore, was not perfectly realized till our office was transferred some ten miles inland to the county-seat, for whatever business and political reasons of the joint stock company which had now taken over the paper, with my father as editor. With its four hundred inhabitants less Jefferson was so much more than Ashtabula a village; and its young gayeties welcomed us and our little force of printers to a social liberty and equality which I long hoped some day to paint as a phase of American civilization worthy the most literal fidelity of fiction. But I shall now never do that, and I must be content to borrow from an earlier page some passages which uninventively record the real events and conditions of our enterprise.

In politics, the county was already overwhelmingly Freesoil, as the forerunner of the Republican party was then called; the Whigs had hardly gathered themselves together since the defeat of General Scott for the presidency; the Democrats, though dominant in State and Nation, and faithful to slavery at every election, did not greatly outnumber among us the zealots called Comeouters, who would not vote at all under a constitution recognizing the right of men to own men. Our paper was Freesoil, and its field was large among that vast majority of the people who believed that slavery would finally perish if kept out of the territories, and confined to the old Slave States.

The people of the county were mostly farmers, and of these nearly all were dairymen. The few manufactures were on a small scale, except perhaps the making of oars, which were shipped all over the world from the heart of the primeval forests densely wooding the vast levels of the region. The portable steam saw-mills dropped down on the borders of the woods have long since eaten their way through and through them, and devoured every stick of timber in most places, and drunk up the water-courses that the woods once kept full; but at that time half the land was in the shadow of those mighty poplars and hickories, elms and chestnuts, ashes and hemlocks; and the meadows that pastured the herds of red cattle were dotted with stumps as thick as harvest stubble. Now there are not even stumps; the woods are gone, and the water-courses are torrents in spring and beds of dry clay in summer. The meadows themselves have vanished, for it has been found that the strong yellow soil will produce more in grain than in milk. There is more money in the hands of the farmers there now, but half a century ago there was so much less that fifty dollars seldom passed through a farmer's hands in a year. Payment was made us in kind rather than in coin, and every sort of farm produce was legal tender at the printing-office. Wood was welcome in any quantity, for our huge box-stove consumed it with inappeasable voracity, and even then did not heat the wide low room which was at once editorial-room, composing-room, and press-room. Perhaps this was not so much the fault of the stove as of the building; in that cold lake-shore country the people dwelt in wooden structures almost as thin and flimsy as tents; and often in the first winter of our sojourn, the type froze solid with the water which the compositor put on it when he wished to distribute his case, placed near the window so as to get all the light there was, but getting all the cold there was, too. From time to time, the compositor's fingers became so stiff that blowing on them would not avail; he made many excursions between his stand and the stove; in severe weather, he practised the device of warming his whole case of types by the fire, and when they lost heat, warming it again.

The first floor of our office-building was used by a sash and blind factory; there was a machine-shop somewhere in it, and a mill for sawing out shingles; and it was better fitted to the exercise of these robust industries than to the requirements of our more delicate craft. Later, we had a more comfortable place, in a new wooden "business block," and for several years before I left it, the office was domiciled in an old dwelling-house, which we bought, and which we used without much change. It could never have been a very comfortable dwelling, and my associations with it are of a wintry cold, scarcely less polar than that we were inured to elsewhere. In fact, the climate of that region is rough and fierce; I know that there were lovely summers and lovelier autumns in my time there, full of sunsets of a strange, wild, melancholy splendor, I suppose from some atmospheric influence of the lake; but I think chiefly of the winters, so awful to us after the mild seasons of southern Ohio; the frosts of ten and twenty below; the village streets and the country roads drowned in snow, the consumptives in the thin houses, and the "slippin'," as the sleighing was called, that lasted from December to April with hardly a break. At first our family was housed on a farm a little way out, because there was no tenement to be had in the village, and my father and I used to walk to and from the office together in the morning and evening. I had taught myself to read Spanish, in my passion for *Don Quixote*, and I was now, at the age of fifteen, intending to write a life of Cervantes. The scheme occupied me a good deal in those bleak walks, and perhaps it was because my head was so hot with it that my feet were always very cold; but my father assured me that they would get warm as soon as my boots froze. If I have never yet written that life of Cervantes, on the other hand I have never been quite able to make it clear to myself why my feet should have got warm when my boots froze.

V

It may have been only a theory of his; it may have been a joke. He had a great many theories and a great many jokes, and together they always kept life interesting and sunshiny for him. With his serene temperament and his happy doubt of disaster in any form, he was singularly fitted to encounter the hardships of a country editor's lot. But for the moment, and for what now seems a long time after the removal of our paper to the county-seat, these seemed to have vanished. The printing-office was the centre of civic and social interest; it was frequented by visitors at all times, and on publication-day it was a scene of gayety that looks a little incredible in the retrospect. The place was as bare and rude as a printing-office seems always to be: the walls were splotched with ink and the floor littered with refuse newspapers; but lured by the novelty of the affair, and perhaps attracted by a natural curiosity to see what manner of strange men the printers were, the school-girls and young ladies of the village flocked in, and made it like a scene of comic opera, with their pretty dresses and faces, their eager chatter, and lively energy in folding the papers and addressing them to the subscribers, while our fellow-citizens of the place, like the bassos and baritones and

tenors of the chorus, stood about and looked on with faintly sarcastic faces. It would not do to think now of what sorrow life
and death have since wrought for all those happy young creatures, but I may recall without too much pathos the sensation
when some citizen volunteer relaxed from his gravity far enough
to relieve the regular mercenary at the crank of our huge power-
press wheel, amid the applause of the whole company.

We were very vain of that press, which replaced the hand-
press hitherto employed in printing the paper. This was of the
style and make of the hand-press which superseded the Ramage
press of Franklin's time; but it had been decided to signalize our
new departure by the purchase of a power-press of modern con-
trivance, and of a speed fitted to meet the demands of a subscrip-
tion list which might be indefinitely extended. A deputation of the
leading politicians accompanied the editor to New York, where
he went to choose the machine, and where he bought a second-
hand Adams press of the earliest pattern and patent. I do not
know, or at this date I would not undertake to say, just what
principle governed his selection of this superannuated veteran;
it seems not to have been very cheap; but possibly he had a
prescience of the disabilities which were to task his ingenuity to
the very last days of that press. Certainly no man of less gift and
skill could have coped with its infirmities, and I am sure that he
thoroughly enjoyed nursing it into such activity as carried it
hysterically through those far-off publication days. It had obscure functional disorders of various kinds, so that it would from
time to time cease to act, and would have to be doctored by the
hour before it would go on. There was probably some organic
trouble, too, for though it did not really fall to pieces on our
hands, it showed itself incapable of profiting by several improve-
ments which he invented, and could, no doubt, have successfully applied to the press if its constitution had not been under-
mined. It went with a crank set in a prodigious fly-wheel, which
revolved at a great rate, till it came to the moment of making
the impression, when the whole mechanism was seized with such
a reluctance as nothing but an heroic effort at the crank could

overcome. It finally made so great a draft upon our forces that it was decided to substitute steam for muscle in its operation, and we got a small engine, which could fully sympathize with the press in having seen better days. I do not know that there was anything the matter with the engine itself, but the boiler had some peculiarities which might well mystify the casual spectator. He could easily have satisfied himself that there was no danger of its blowing up, when he saw my brother feeding bran or corn-meal into its safety-valve, in order to fill up certain seams or fissures in it, which caused it to give out at the moments of the greatest reluctance in the press. But still, he must have had his misgivings of latent danger of some other kind, though nothing ever actually happened of a hurtful character. To this day, I do not know just where those seams or fissures were, but I think they were in the boiler-head, and that it was therefore suffering from a kind of chronic fracture of the skull. What is certain is that, somehow, the engine and the press did always get us through publication day, and not only with safety but often with credit; so that many years after, when I was at home, and my brother and I were looking over an old file of the paper, we found it much better printed than either of us expected; as well printed, in fact, as if it had been done on an old hand-press, instead of the steam-power press which it vaunted the use of. The wonder was that, under all the disadvantages, the paper was ever printed on our steam-power press at all; it was little short of miraculous that it was legibly printed, and altogether unaccountable that such impressions as we found in that file could come from it. Of course, they were not average impressions; they were the very best out of the whole edition, and were as creditable as the editorial make-up of the sheet.

VI

Upon the whole, our paper was an attempt at conscientious and self-respectful journalism; it addressed itself seriously to the minds of its readers; it sought to form their tastes and opinions.

I do not know how much it influenced them, if it influenced them at all, and as to any effect beyond the circle of its subscribers, that cannot be imagined, even in a fond retrospect. But since no good effort is altogether lost, I am sure that this endeavor must have had some tacit effect; and I am very sure that no one got harm from a sincerity of conviction that devoted itself to the highest interests of the reader, that appealed to nothing base, and flattered nothing foolish in him. It went from our home to the homes of the people in a very literal sense, for my father usually brought his exchanges from the office at the end of his day there, and made his selections or wrote his editorials while the household work went on around him, and his children gathered about the same lamp, with their books or their jokes; there were a good many of both.

Our county was the most characteristic of that remarkable group of counties in northern Ohio, called the Western Reserve, and forty years ago the population was almost purely New England in origin, either by direct settlement from Connecticut, or indirectly after the sojourn of a generation in New York State. We were ourselves from southern Ohio, where the life was then strongly tinged by the adjoining life of Kentucky and Virginia, and we found these transplanted Yankees cold and blunt in their manners; but we did not undervalue their virtues. They were very radical in every way, and hospitable to novelty of all kinds. I imagine that they tested more new religions and new patents than have been even heard of in less inquiring communities. When we came among them they had lately been swept by the fires of spiritualism, which had left behind a great deal of smoke and ashes where the inherited New England orthodoxy had been. They were temperate, hard-working, hard-thinking folks, who dwelt on their scattered farms, and came up to the County Fair once a year, when they were apt to visit the printing-office and pay for their papers. They thought it droll, as people of the simpler occupations are apt to think all the more complex arts, and one of them once went so far in expression of his humorous conception as to say, after a long stare at one of the compositors dodging and pecking at the type in his case, "Like an old hen pickin' up millet." This sort of silence, and this sort of comment, both exasperated the printers, who took their revenge as they could. They fed it full, once, when a country subscriber's horse, hitched before the office, crossed his hind legs and sat down in his harness like a tired man, and they proposed to go out and offer him a chair, to take him a glass of water, and ask him to come inside. Fate did not often give them such innings; they mostly had to create their chances of reprisal, but they did not mind that.

There was always a good deal of talk going on, but although we were very ardent politicians, our talk was not political. When it was not mere banter, it was mostly literary; we disputed about authors among ourselves, and with the village wits who dropped in, and liked to stand with their backs to our stove, and challenge opinion concerning Holmes and Poe, Irving and Macaulay, Pope and Byron, Dickens and Shakespeare. But it was Shakespeare who was oftenest on our tongues; indeed, the printing-office of former days had so much affinity with the theatre, that compositors and comedians were almost convertible. Religion entered a good deal into our discussions, which my father, the most tolerant of men, would not suffer to become irreverent. Part of his duty, as publisher of the paper, was to bear patiently with the type of farmer who thought he wished to discontinue his paper, and really wished to be talked into continuing it. I think he rather enjoyed letting such a subscriber talk himself out, and carrying him from point to point in his argument, always consenting that he knew best what he wanted to do, but skilfully persuading him at last that a home-paper was more suited to his needs than any city substitute. Once I could have given the heads of his reasoning, but they are gone from me now.

He was like all country editors then, and I dare say now, in being a printer as well as an editor, and he took a just share in the mechanical labors. These were formerly much more burdensome, for twice or thrice the present type-setting was then done in the country offices. In that time we had three journeymen at work and two or three girl-compositors, and commonly a boy-apprentice besides. The paper was richer in a personal quality, and the printing-office was unquestionably more of a school. After we began to take girl-apprentices it became coeducative, as far as they cared to profit by it; but I think it did not serve to widen their thoughts or quicken their wits as it did those of the boys. They looked to their craft as a living, not as a life, and they had no pride in it. They did not learn the whole trade, as the journeymen had done; but served only such apprenticeship as fitted them to set type; and their earnings were usually as great at the end of a month as at the end of a year.

VII

The printing-office had been my school from childhood so largely that I could almost say I had no other, but the time had come, even before this, when its opportunities did not satisfy the hunger which was always in me for knowledge convertible into such beauty as I imagined and wished to devote my life to. I was willing and glad to do my part in helping my father, but he recognized my right to help myself forward in the line of my own longing, and it was early arranged that I should have a certain measure of work to do, and when it was done I should be free for the day. My task was finished early in the afternoon, and then my consuming pleasures began when I had already done a man's work. I was studying four or five languages, blindly and blunderingly enough, but with a confidence at which I can even now hardly smile; I was attempting many things in verse and prose which I seldom carried to a definite close, and I was reading, reading, reading, right and left, hither and yon, wherever an author tempted me. I was not meaning to do less than the greatest things, or to know less than the most, but my criticism outran my performance and exacted of me an endeavor for the perfection which I found for ever beyond me. Far into the night I clung to my labored failures in rhyme while I listened for the ticking of the death-watch in the walls of my little study;

or if I had imagined, in my imitations of others' fiction, some character that the poet had devoted to an early death, I helplessly identified myself with that character, and expected his fate. It was the day when this world was much more intimate with the other world than it is now, and the spiritualism which had evoked its phenomena through most houses in the village had left them haunted by dread sounds, if not sights; but it was not yet the day when nervous prostration had got its name or was known in its nature. For me this malady came in the hypochondria which was misery not less real because at the end of the ends I knew it to be the exaggeration of an apprehension without ground in reality.

I have hesitated to make any record of this episode, but I think it essential to the study of my very morbid boyhood, and I hope some knowledge of it may be helpful to others in like suffering. Somehow as a child I had always had a terror of hydrophobia, perhaps from hearing talk of that poor man who had died of it in the town where we then lived, and when years afterwards I was, as I have told, bitten by a dog, my terror was the greater because I happened to find myself alone in the house when I ran home. I had heard of excising a snake-bite to keep the venom from spreading, and I would now have cut out the place with my knife, if I had known how. In the end I did nothing and when my father came home, he did not have the wound cauterized. He may have believed that anything which tended to fix my mind upon it would be bad, and perhaps I forgot it the sooner for his decision. I have not forgotten the make of the gloomy autumnal afternoon when the thing happened, or the moment when years afterwards certain unguarded words awoke the fear in me which as many more years were needed to allay. By some chance there was talk with our village doctor about hydrophobia, and the capricious way the poison of a dog's bite may work. "Works round in your system," he said, "for seven years or more, and then it breaks out and kills you." The words he let heedlessly fall fell into a mind prepared by ill-health for their deadly potency, and when the summer heat came I was helpless under it. Somehow I knew what the symptoms of the malady were, and I began to force it upon myself by watching for them. The splash of water anywhere was a sound I had to set my teeth against, lest the dreaded spasms should seize me; my fancy turned the scent of the forest fires burning round the village into the subjective odor of smoke which stifles the victim. I had no release from my obsession, except in the dreamless sleep which I fell into exhausted at night, or that little instant of waking in the morning, when I had not yet had time to gather my terrors about me, or to begin the frenzied stress of my effort to experience the thing I dreaded. There was no longer question of work for me, with hand or head. I could read, yes, but with the double consciousness in which my fear haunted every line and word without barring the sense from my perception. I read many novels, where the strong plot befriended me and formed a partial refuge, but I did not attempt escape in the poor boyish inventions, verse or prose, which I had fondly trusted might be literature. Instinct taught me that some sort of bodily fatigue was my safety; I spent the horrible days in the woods with a gun, or in the fields gathering wild berries, and walked to and from the distant places that I might tire myself the more. My father reasoned to the same effect for me, and helped me as best he could; of course I was released from my tasks in the printing-office, and he took me with him in driving about the country on political and business errands. We could not have spent many days in this way, when, as it seems, I woke one morning in a sort of crisis, and having put my fear to the test of water suddenly dashed from a doorway beside me and failed of the convulsion which I was always expecting, I began imperceptibly to get the better of my demon. My father's talk always distracted me somewhat, and that morning especially his disgust with the beefsteak fried in lard which the landlady gave us for breakfast at the country tavern where we had passed the night must even have amused me, as a touch of the comedy blent with the tragedy in the Shakespearian drama of life. But no doubt a more real help was his recurrence, as often as I chose, to his own

youthful suffering from hypochondria, and his constantly repeated assurance that I not only would not and could not have
hydrophobia from that out-dated dog-bite, but that I must also
soon cease to have hypochondria. I understood as well as he
that it was not the fear of that malady which I was suffering,
but the fear of the fear; that I was in no hallucination, no illusion as to the facts, but was helpless in the nervous prostration
which science, or our poor village medicine, was yet many years
from knowing or imagining. I have heard and read that sometimes people in their apprehension of the reality can bring on a
false hydrophobia and die of it in the agonies their fancy creates.
It may be so; but all that fear could do was done in me; and I
did not die.

I could not absolutely fix the moment when I began to find
my way out of the cloud of misery which lowered on my life,
but I think that it was when I had gathered a little strength in
my forced respite from work, and from the passing of the summer heat. It was as if the frost which people used to think put
an end to the poisonous miasm of the swamps, but really only
killed the insect sources of the malaria, had wrought a like sani-
tation in my fancy. My fear when it once lifted never quite over-
whelmed me again, but it was years before I could endure the
sight of the word which embodied it; I shut the book or threw
from me the paper where I found it in print; and even now, after
sixty years, I cannot bring myself to write it or speak it without
some such shutting of the heart as I knew at the sight or sound
of it in that dreadful time. The effect went deeper than I could
say without accusing myself of exaggeration for both good and
evil. In self-defense I learnt to practise a psychological juggle;
I came to deal with my own state of mind as another would deal
with it, and to combat my fears as if they were alien.

I cannot leave this confession without the further confession
that though I am always openly afraid of dogs, secretly I am
always fond of them; and it is only fair to add that they recipro-
cate my liking with even exaggerated affection. Dogs, especially
of any more ferocious type, make up to me in spite of my diffi-

dence; and at a hotel where we were once passing the summer the landlord's bulldog, ugliest and dreadest of his tribe, used to divine my intention of a drive and climb into my buggy, where he couched himself on my feet, with a confidence in my reciprocal tenderness which I was anxious not to dispel by the least movement.

VIII

As soon as my nerves regained something of their former tone, I renewed my struggle with those alien languages, using such weapons as I could fit my hand to. Notably there was a most comprehensive manual which, because it proposed instruction in so many languages, I called (from my father's invention or my own, for I had early learnt the trick of his drolling) a sixteen-bladed grammar. I wish now I could see that book, which did not include Greek or Hebrew or German, but abounded in examples of Latin, Italian, French, Spanish and probably Portuguese, and other tongues of that kinship, with literal versions of the texts. These versions falsified the native order of the words to the end that the English of them might proceed in the wonted way, and when I detected the imposition, I was the more offended because the right order of the words in those idioms was always perplexing me. The sixteen-bladed grammar was superseded by the ordinary school-books, Arnold's for Latin, and Anthon's for Greek, but the perplexities of one sort or other persisted. Such a very little instruction would have enlightened me; but who was to give it me? My father, perhaps, but he may not have known how, though in his own youth he had written an English grammar and more or less taught it, or he may have thought I would find it out for myself. He would have temperamentally trusted to that; he was always prouder than I of what I did unaided; he believed I could do everything without help. That was an error, but more than I ever could say do I owe to his taste in literature and the constant guidance up to a certain limit which he gave me. When I came back from the fields and woods with the sense of their beauty, and eager to turn it into literature, he guarded me against translating it in the terms of my English poets, with their larks and nightingales, their daisies and cowslips. He contended that our own birds and flowers were quite as good, besides being genuine; but he taught me to love the earlier English classics; and if I began to love the later classics, both English and American, and to be his guide in turn, this is only saying that each one is born of his generation. The time came early in our companionship when he thought fit to tell me that he regarded me as different from other boys of my age; and I had a very great and sweet happiness without alloy of vanity, from his serious and considered words. He did not say that he expected great things of me; though I had to check his fondness in offering my poor endeavors for the recognition of print, and I soon had the support of editors in this. But he justified himself and convinced me by once bringing to our house a kindly editor from a neighboring city whom he showed some of my things, and who carried away with him one of the minutely realistic sketches in which I had begun to practise such art as I have been able to carry farthest. When week after week the handsomely printed *Ohio Farmer* came with something in it, verse or prose, which I had done, I am not sure I had greater joy in it than my father, though now he thought it well to hide his joy as I always did mine.

All the while I was doing sketches and studies and poems for our own paper, which I put into type without first writing them, and short stories imitated from some favorite author of the moment with an art which I imagined must conceal itself from the reader. Once I carried Shakespeare beyond himself in a scene transferred from one of the histories, with such comedy characters as Pistol and Bardolph speaking the interchangeable prose and verse of his plays in adapting themselves to some local theme, which met with applause from the group of middle-aged cronies whom I most consorted with at the time. Once, also, I attempted a serial romance which, after a succession of several numbers, faltered and at last would not go on. I have told in another place how I had to force it to a tragic close without mercy for the heroine, hurried to an untimely death as the only means of getting her out of the way, and I will not repeat the miserable details here. It was a thing which could not meet with praise from any one, not even my father, though he did his best to comfort me in the strange disaster.

If my mother was the heart, he was the soul of our family life. In those young days when he did so much of his newspaper work at home he would always turn from it to take part in our evening jollity. He was gladly our equal in the jokes which followed around our table; and when he was stricken in his great age with the paralysis which he rallied from for a time, it was his joy to join his gray-haired children at the board in his wheeled chair and share in their laughing and making laugh. It seems to me that I can render him intelligible by saying that while my very religious-minded grandfather expected and humbly if fervently hoped to reach a heaven beyond this world by means of prayers and hymns and revivals and conversions, my not less religious-minded father lived for a heaven on earth in his beloved and loving home; a heaven of poetry and humor, and good-will and right thinking. He made it that sort of heaven for himself, and as he was the bravest man I have known because he never believed there was any danger, I think he must have felt himself as safe from sorrow in it as if he were in the world beyond this. When one of my younger brothers died, he was as if astonished that such a thing could be; it burst his innocent and beautiful dream; and afterwards when I first met him, I was aware of his clinging, a broken man, to what was left of it. Death struck again and again, and he shrank under the bewildering blows; but a sense of that inexpressible pathos of his first bereavement remains with me.

IX

The family scene that passed in that earlier time was not always as idyllic as I have painted it. With five brothers in it there was often the strife which is always openly or covertly between brothers. My elder brother, who was four years my elder, had changed from the whimsical tease and guardian angel of our childhood to the anxious taskmaster of our later boyhood requiring the same devotion in our common work that his conscience exacted of himself. I must say that for my own part I labored as faithfully as he, and I hotly resented his pressure. Hard words passed between us two, as blows, not very hard, had passed, while we were still children, between me and my younger brothers. But however light the blows were, they had to be disclaimed, and formal regret expressed, at my father's insistence. He would ascertain who struck the first blow, and when he had pronounced that wrong he would ask, "And you struck him back?" If the fact could not be denied, he went on to the further question, "Well, do two wrongs make a right?" Clearly they did not, and nothing remained but reluctant apology and reconciliation. Reason and civic morality were on his side, but I could not feel that justice was, and it seems to me yet that the primary offender was guiltier than the secondary.

Long ago, long before our youth was passed, utter forgiveness passed between my elder brother and me. The years since were years of such mutual affection as I could not exaggerate the sense of in tenderness and constancy, and the exchange of trust and honor. He came even in our youth to understand my aim in life, and feel what was always leading me on. He could not understand, perhaps, why poetry in literature should be so all in all with me, but he felt it in nature as keenly and deeply as I; and I have present now the experience of driving with him one September afternoon, (on some chase of the delinquent subscriber) when he owned by his few spare words the unity of the beautiful in everything as I spoke the melting lines of Tennyson:

> "Tears, idle tears, I know not what they mean.
> Tears from the depths of some divine despair
> Rise in the heart and gather to the eyes,
> In looking on the happy autumn-fields,
> And thinking of the days that are no more."

He had a grotesque humor which vented itself in jokes at the expense of my mother's implicit faith in everything he said, as when she wondered how the cow got into the garden, and he explained, "She pulled out the peg with her teeth and put it under her fore leg and just walked through the gate," and my mother answered, "Well, indeed, indeed, I believe she did, child." She had little humor of her own, but she had a childlike happiness in the humor of us others, though she would not suffer joking from any but him. She relied upon him in everything, but in some things she drew a sharp line between the duties of her boys and girls in the tradition of her Pennsylvania origin. Indoor work was for girls, and outdoor for boys, and we shared her slight for the Yankee men who went by our gate to the pasture with their milk-pails. That was woman's work though it was outdoor work; and though it was outdoor work to kill chickens for the table, none of us boys had the heart to cut their heads off because we could not bear to witness their post-mortem struggles; but my brother brought out his gun and shot them, and this pursuit of them as game in our barnyard got us over a difficulty otherwise insuperable. The solution of our scruple, which my father shared, must have amused him; but my brother took it seriously. His type of humor was in the praise which long afterward he gave a certain passage of my realistic fiction, when he said it was as natural as the toothache.

Throughout that earlier time my father's chief concern was first that very practical affair of making his paper pay for the office and the house, and then incidentally preventing the spread of slavery into the territories. He was willing enough, I fancy, to yield his silent partnership in my studies to the young printer who now, for no reason that I can remember, began to take an active share in them. I have told in *My Literary Passions* how J. W. and I read Cervantes and Shakespeare together; but I could not say just why or when we began to be boon companions in our self-conducted inquiries into Latin and Greek, and then into German, which presently replaced Spanish in my affections through the witchery of Heine. He had the definite purpose of making those languages help him to a professorship in a Western college, but if I had any clear purpose it was to possess myself of their literature. To know them except to read them I do not think I cared; I did not try to speak or write the modern tongues; to this day I could not frame a proper letter in Spanish, German, French, or Italian, but I have a literary sense of them all. I wished to taste the fruit of my study before I had climbed the tree where it grew, and in a manner I did begin to gather the fruit without the interposition of the tree. Without clear knowledge of their grammatical forms, I imitated their literary forms. I cast my poetry, such as it was, into the metres of the Spanish poets I was reading, and without instruction or direction I acquainted myself with much of their literary history. I once even knew from the archaic tragedy of her name who Iñez de Castro was; I do not know now.

My friendship with J. W. early became chief of the many friends of a life rich in friendships. He was like most of his craft in his eccentric comings and goings to and from our employ, when sometimes we had no work to give him, and sometimes he had none to give us. When he left us he always went to Wisconsin, where he had once lived; and when he came back from one of these absences he would bring with him bits of character which he gave for our joy in his quaint observance, such as that of the mother who complained of her daughter because "she didn't cultivate her featur's none; she just let 'em hing and wallop," or the schoolmistress who genteelly explained in the blackberry-patch where he found her, that she was "just out picking a few berries for tea-he-he-he," or the country bachelor who belatedly made up his mind to marry, and in his default of female acquaintance took his place on the top rail of a roadside fence, and called to the first woman who passed, "Say! You a married woman?" and then at the frightened answer, indignantly gasped out, "Yes, sir!" offered a mere "Oh!" for all apology and explanation, and let himself vanish by falling into the cornfield behind him.

J. W. literally made his home with us, for as if the burden of work for our own large family were not enough for my mother, we had always some of the printers, men or maids, to board. He entered into the spirit of our life; but it was recognized that he was peculiarly my friend, and we were left to our special comradeship. In that village nearly everybody played or sang, and in the summer nights the young people went about serenading one another's houses, under the moon which was then always full; and J. W. shared in every serenade where a tenor voice was welcome. At the printing-office, in the afternoon when the compositors were distributing their cases, he led the apprentice-girls in the songs which once filled the whole young world. The songs were often poverty-stricken enough in sentiment, and I suppose cheap and vulgar in music, but they were better than the silence that I should once have said had followed them. Yet only last winter in a hotel on the New Jersey coast, where there was some repairing in the corridor outside my room, the young painters and carpenters gathered at their lunch near my door, and after they had begun to joke they suddenly began to sing together as if it were still the habit for people of their lot to do so, in a world I had thought so hushed, except for its gramophones; and though I could not make out the words, the gentle music somehow saved them from seeming common. It went to my heart, and made me glad of life where youth still sang as it used to sing when I was young.

Sometimes the village serenaders came to me, and then I left my books and stumbled down to the gate, half-dazed, to find the faces I knew before they flashed away with gay shrieking and shouting; and J. W. among them, momentarily estranged from me, jealous in that world where we had our intimacy. My ambition was my barrier from the living world around me; I could not beat my way from it into that; it kept me absent and hampered me in the vain effort to be part of the reality I have always tried to portray. Though J. W. expected to make a more definite use of our studies, he seemed to understand me as well at least as I understood myself in my vaguer striving. I do not now remember reading him the things I was trying to write; or of his speaking to me of them. Perhaps my shyness, my pride, went so far as keeping them from him, though I kept from him so few of my vagaries in that region of hopes and fears where youth chiefly has its being.

The songs he had were as many as the stories, but there was one song, often on the tongues of the village serenaders, which was oftenest on his, and which echoes to me still from those serenades and those choral afternoons in the printing-office, and more distinctly yet from what we felt a midnight of wild adventure, when he sang it alone. We had gone to call together on two of our village girls at school fifteen miles away, and had set out in the flattering temperature of a January thaw; but when we started home, many hours into the dark, the wind had whipped round from the south to the north and had frozen the curdling slush into icy ruts under the runners of our sleigh. Our coats were such as had suited the thaw, but J. W. had a pair of thin cotton gloves for driving, while I had none. We took turns in driving at first, but as the way lengthened the cold strengthened and I cowered definitively under our buffalo robe, then the universal provision against the rigor of winter travel. For a while we shouted together in some drama of the situation, but by and by our fun froze at our lips, and then J. W. began to sing that song he used oftenest to sing:

> "Talk not to me of future bliss,
> Talk not to me of joys gone by!
> The happiest time is this!"

He kept the measure of the tune by beating on the robe above my head, first with one fist and then the other, as he passed the reins from hand to hand, and by pounding with both feet on the floor of the sleigh beside me. We lived through the suffering of that drive partly because he was twenty-two years old and I was eighteen, but partly also because we realized the irony of the song, with all the joke of it. Yet it was a long nightmare of misery, with a moment of supreme anguish, when we stopped at the last toll-gate, two miles from home, and the keeper came shuddering out with his red blot of a lantern. Then the song stopped for an instant, but seems to have begun again, and not ended till we sat with our feet in the oven of the kitchen stove at home, counting our adventure all gain. The memory of it brings before me again the face of my friend, with its beautiful regularity of feature, its pale blue eyes, its smooth, rich, girlish complexion, and its challenging, somewhat mocking smile. But the date when I saw him last in life is lost to me. He went to Wisconsin, as usual, but there was no wonted return; we kept each other present in the long letters which we wrote so long, but they faltered with time and ceased, and I can only make sure now that he got the professorship he aimed at in some seat of learning so modest that it has kept its name from me; and then, years after, that he went into the war for the Union and was killed.

x

I had now begun to be impatient of the village, and when it came to my last parting with J. W., which I did not know was the last, I felt the life very dull and narrow which I had once found so vivid and ample. There had come the radiant revelation of girlhood, and I had dwelt in the incredible paradise where we paired or were paired off each with some girl of his fancy or fancied fancy. There had been the ranging of the woods in autumn for chestnuts and in the spring for wintergreen; there had been the sleigh-rides to the other villages and the neighboring farms where there was young life waiting to welcome us through the drifting snows; there had been the dances at the taverns and the parties at the girls' houses with the games and the frolics, and the going home each with the chosen one at midnight and the long lingering at the gate; there had been the moonlight walks; there had been the debating societies and the spelling-matches; there had been the days of the County Fair and the Fourths-of-July, and the Christmases rehabilitated from Dickens; and there had been the impassioned interest of the easily guessed anonymous letters of St. Valentine's day. But

these things had passed, and with a certain disappointment suffered and yet prized there had come the sense of spent witchery
and a spell outworn, and I chose to revolt from it all and to pine
for a wider world and prouder pleasures. Distance in time and
space afterwards duly set the village I had wearied of in a truer
and kinder light, and I came to value it as the potential stuff of
such fiction as has never yet been written, and now never will
be by me. I came to see that it abounded in characteristics and
interests which differenced it from any other village, and I still
think the companionship to which I passed in the absences of
J. W. such as would make into the setting for as strange a story
as we could ask of reality in the days when we wished life to
surpass romance in strangeness.

I have told in *My Literary Passions* of the misanthropical Englishman who led in our Dickens-worship and played the organ
in the little Episcopal church, and built the organs for such country churches about as could afford to replace their moaning
melodions with them. I have said, I hope without too much
attempt to establish the fact, that he was also a house-painter,
and that in the long leisures of our summer days and winter
nights and in the throes of his perpetual dyspepsia he was the
inveterate antagonist in argument of the vivid Yankee who built
steam-engines among us, and had taught school, and turned
his quick head and hand to any art or trade which making an
easy living exacted of him. They both lavishly lent me their
books, and admitted me on equal terms to their intellectual enmity and amity, which was shared in some tacit way with a
clever New England trader in watches, clocks, and jewelry. He
came and went among us on visits more or less prolonged from
some Eastern centre of his commerce (my memory somehow
specifies Springfield, Massachusetts), and he had a shrewd smile
and kindly twinkling eye which represent him to me yet. He
seldom took part in the disputes nightly held at the drug-and-
book store; but not from want of spirit, when he had the boldness to deny some ferocious opinion exploded by the organ-
builder in an access of indigestion.

The disputes nearly always involved question of the existence of a God, which was thought improbable by both of the debaters, and the immortality of the soul, which was doubted, in spite of the spiritualism rife in every second house in the village, with manifestations by rappings, table-tippings, and oral and written messages from another world through psychics of either sex, but oftenest the young girls one met in the dances and sleigh-rides. The community was prevalently unreligious; there was an aging attendance at the Baptist and Methodist churches, but there was no stated service of the Congregationalists, though there was occasional preaching at their house and sometimes a lecture from an antislavery apostle, who wasted his doctrine on a community steeped in it already. Among many of the young people of the village the prevalent tone was irreverent to mocking in matters of religion; but their unlimited social freedom was without blame and without scandal, and if our villagers were not religious, they were, in a degree which I still think extraordinary, literary. Old and young they read and talked about books, and better books than people read and talk about now, as it seems to me, possibly because there were not so many bad ones; the English serials pirated into our magazines were followed and discussed, and any American author who made an effect in the East became promptly known in that small village of the Western Reserve. There were lawyers, of those abounding at every county-seat, who were fond of reading, and imparted their taste to the young men studying law in their offices. I might exaggerate the fact, but I do not think I have done so, or that I was much deceived as to a condition which reported itself, especially to me whose whole life was in books, through the sympathy I met in the village houses. I was always reading whatever came to hand, either with an instinct for what was good in my choice of books or with good fortune in my chance of them. Literature was so commonly accepted as a real interest, that I do not think I was accounted altogether queer in my devotion to it. To be sure, at an evening session in one of the dry-goods and grocery stores where question of me came up, it was decided that I would be nowhere in a horse-trade, but this was a rare instance of slight, and I do not believe that my disability would have been generally counted against me.

XI

Somewhere about this time I gave a month to the study of law in the office of the United States Senator dwelling among us. I have never regretted reading a first volume of Blackstone through, or not going on to the second; his frank declaration that the law was a jealous mistress and would brook no divided love, was upon reflection quite enough for one whose heart was given to a different muse. I was usually examined in this author by the Senator's nephew, my fellow-student, whom I examined in turn; but once, at least, the Senator himself catechized me, though he presently began to talk about the four great English quarterly reviews which I was known in the village for reading, and which it seemed he read too. No doubt he found me more perfect in them than in Blackstone; at least I felt that I did myself more credit in them. I have elsewhere spoken more fully of this episode of my life; but I speak of it again because I think that the commonly accepted Wade legend scarcely does justice to a man not only of great native power, but of wider cultivation than it recognizes, and I would like to do what I can to repair the injustice. He was famed in contemporary politics as Old Ben Wade before he had passed middle life, and he was supposed to stand up against the fierce proslavery leaders in Congress with an intrepidity even with their own. He had a strong, dark face, and a deep, raucous voice, with a defiant laugh, and these lent their support to the popular notion of him as a rude natural force unhelped by teaching, though he had taught himself in the days of his early struggle, as Lincoln and most public men of his time had done, and later had taught others as country schoolmaster. Farm-boy and cattle-drover and canal-digger, more had remained to him from schoolmaster and medical student, than from either of his other callings, and though he became part of our history without the help of great intellectual refinement, he was by no means without intellectual refinement, or without the ability to estimate the value of it in others. Naturally he might also underestimate it, and perhaps it was from an underestimate that he judged the oratory of such a man as Charles Sumner, to whom he told me he had said of a speech of his, "It's all very well, Sumner, but it has no bones in it."

Wade was supposed by his more ill-advised admirers to lend especial effect to his righteous convictions by a free flow of profanity, but I have to bear witness that I never heard any profanity from him, though profanity must have been the common parlance of the new country and the rude conditions he grew up in. He was personally a man of silent dignity, as we saw him in the village, going and coming at the post-office, for he seldom seemed to pass the gate of his house yard on any other errand, in the long summer vacations between the sessions of the many Congresses when he sojourned among us. I have the sense of him in a back room of the office which stood apart from his house, after the old-fashioned use of country lawyers' and doctors' offices; and I can be sure of his visiting the students in the front room only that once when he catechized me in Blackstone, but I cannot say whether I stood in awe of him as a great lawyer, or quite realized his importance as United States Senator from the State of Ohio for eighteen years. Historically it has been thought his misfortune to outlive the period when the political struggle with slavery passed into the Civil War, and to carry into that the spirit of the earlier time, with his fierce alienation from the patient policy of Lincoln, and his espousal of the exaggerations of the Reconstruction. But it would be easy to do injustice to this part of his valiant career, and not easy to do justice to that part of it where he stood with the very few in his defiance of the proslavery aggression.

Probably he would not have understood my forsaking the law, and I evaded the explanation he once sought of me when we met in the street, dreading the contempt which I might well have fancied in him. I wish now that, knowing him a little on his æsthetic side, I might have had the courage to tell him why I could not give my heart to that jealous mistress, being vowed almost from my first days to that other love which will have my fealty to the last. But in the helplessness of youth I could not even imagine doing this, and I had to remain in my dread of his contempt. Yet he may not have despised me, after all. It was known with what single-handed courage I was carrying on my struggle with the alien languages, and their number was naturally overstated. The general interest in my struggle was reflected in the offer of a farmer from another part of the county to be one of three or four who would see me through Harvard. It was good-will which, if it had ever materialized, my pride would have been fierce to refuse; but now I think of it without shame, and across the gulf which I would fain believe has some thither shore I should like to send that kind man the thanks which I fancy were never adequately expressed to him while he lived. It remains vaguely, from vague personal knowledge, that he was of Scotch birth and breeding; he had a good old Scotch name, and he lived on his prosperous farm in much more than the usual American state, with many books about him.

I went back not without shame, but also not without joy from the Senator's law-office to my father's printing-office, and I did not go to Harvard, or to any college or school thereafter. I still think that a pity, for I have never agreed with Lowell, who, when I deplored my want of schooling, generously instanced his own overweight of learning as an evil I had escaped. It still seems to me lamentable that I should have had to grope my way and so imperfectly find it where a little light from another's lamp would have instantly shown it. I still remain in depths of incredible ignorance as to some very common things; for at school I never got beyond long division in arithmetic, and after my self-discovery of grammar I should be unable to say, *in due piedi*, just what a preposition was, though I am aware of frequently using that part of speech, and, I hope, not incorrectly.

I did what I could to repair the defect of instruction, or rather I tried to make myself do it, for I had the nature of a boy to contend with, and did not love my work so much as I loved the effect of it. While I live I must regret that want of instruction, and the discipline which would have come with it, though Fortune, as if she would have flattered my vanity when she could bring her wheel round to it, bore me the offer of professorships in three of our greatest universities. In fact, when I thought of coming home from my consulship in Venice, ten years after my failure to achieve any sort of schooling, it had been my hope that I might get some sort of tutorship in a very modest college, and I wrote to Lowell about it, but he did not encourage me. Yet I was hardly fixed in the place which much better suited me as the assistant editor of the *Atlantic Monthly*, when one of the faculty came to me from Schenectady to offer me the sub-professorship of English in Union College, and no long time after I was sounded by the first educational authority in the country as to whether I would accept a like place in Washington University at St. Louis. It was twice as long after this that those three supreme invitations which I have boasted came to me. But I knew better than any one, unless it was Fortune herself, the ignorance I had hidden so long, and I forbore to risk a middling novelist on the chance of his turning out a poor professor, or none. In every case the offer was such as might well have allured me, but when, after a sleepless night of longing and fearing over that of Harvard which Lowell conveyed me with the promise, "You shall wear the gown that Ticknor wore, and Longfellow wore, and I wore," I had the strength to refuse it, he wrote me his approval of my decision. It was a decision that I have rejoiced in ever since, with the breathless gratitude, when I think of it, of one who has withheld himself from a step over the brink of a precipice.

The other allurements to a like doom were hardly less gratifying. What indeed could have been more gratifying, except the Harvard offer of the professorship of the languages of the south of Europe (with the privilege of two years' preparation in the Latin countries, whose tongues I had tampered with), than the offer of the English professorship in Yale? It was Lounsbury, now lately lost for ever to these skies, Lounsbury the fine scholar, the charming writer, the delightful wit, the critic unsurpassed in his kind, who came smiling with the kind eyes, dimmed almost to blindness on the field of Gettysburg in the forgotten soldiership of his youth, to do me this incredible honor. Later came the offer of the same chair in Johns Hopkins, twice repeated by the president of that university. When in my longing and my despair I asked, What was the nature of such a professorship, he answered, Whatever I chose to make it; and this still seems to me, however mistaken in my instance, the very measure of the wisest executive large-mindedness. President Gilman had written to me from New York, and had come to see me in London, and again written to me in Boston, and I could not do less than go down to Baltimore and look at the living body of the university and see what part in it I might become. A day sufficed; where so many men were busy with the work which they were so singularly qualified to do, I could not think of bringing my half-heartedness to an attempt for which all the common sense I had protested my unfitness, my entire unlikeness to the kind of man he had so magnanimously misimagined me. I turned from that shining opportunity of failure as I turned from the others, and if the reader thinks I have dwelt too vaingloriously upon them he shall have his revenge in the spectacle of my further endeavors not to be the stuff which professors are made of.

XII

I could have been spared from the printing-office for the study of the law, when I could not be spared from it otherwise, because I might soon begin to make my living by practising before justices of the peace in the pettifogging which was then part of the study in the country offices. My labor, which was worth as much as a journeyman compositor's, could not have been otherwise spared; much less could my father have afforded the expense of my schooling; and I cannot recall that I thought it an unjust hardship when it was decided after due family counsel that I could not be sent to an academy in a neighboring village. I had not the means of estimating my loss; but the event seemed to have remained a poignant regret with my brother, and in after years he lamented what he felt to have been an irreparable wrong done me: now he is dead, and it touches me to think he should have felt that, for I never blamed him, and I am glad he gave me the chance to tell him so. I may have shed some tears when first denied; I did shed a few very bitter ones when I once confessed the hope I had that the editor of the *Ohio Farmer* might give me some sort of literary employment at a sum I named, and he said, "He would never pay you three dollars a week in the world for that," and I had to own in anguish of soul that he was doubtless right. He worked every day of the week and far into every night to help my father earn the property we were all trying to pay for, and he rightfully came into the eventual ownership of the newspaper. By an irony of fate not wholly unkind he continued for half a century in the printing-business, once so utterly renounced. Then, after a few years of escape to a consular post in the tropics which he used to say was the one post which, if it had been whittled out of the whole universe, would have suited him best, he died, and lies buried in the village, the best-beloved man who ever lived there.

It was the day with us of self-denials which I cannot trust myself to tell in detail lest I should overtell them. I was willing to make a greater figure in dress than nature has ever abetted me in, but I still do not think it was from an excess of vanity that I once showed my father the condition of my hat, and left him to the logic of the fact. He whimsically verified it, and said, "Oh, get it half-soled," as if it had been a shoe; and we had our laugh together, but I got the new hat, which, after all, did not make me the dashing presence I might have hoped, though the vision of it on the storekeeper's counter always remained so distinct with me that in Seville, a few years ago, it seemed as if its ghost were haunting me in the Cordovese hats on all the heads I met. Like them it had a wide flat brim, and it narrowed slightly upward to the low flat crown of those hats which I now knew better than to buy.

But if we seem to have spared on dress, our table was of as unstinted abundance as it might be in a place where there was no market, except as the farmers brought us chickens and butter and vegetables and the small fruits of the pastures and clearings, where every sort of wild berries grew. The region had abounded in deer, and after we came to the village in 1852 venison was only three cents a pound. Once a black bear was chased from forest to forest across our land, but he did not wait to fix the market price of his meat; half the sky was often hidden with wild pigeons, and there was a summer when the gray squirrels swarmed through the streets in one of their mystical migrations from west to east. Such chances of game scarcely enriched our larder; and the salt-pork barrel was our constant reliance. This was a hardship, after the varied abundance of the larger places where we had lived, but we shared it with our fellow-villagers, and in this as in other conditions of our life we did not realize as deprivation what was the lot of the whole community. If we denied ourselves it was to meet the debts which would not be denied, and to possess ourselves of the roof over our heads and an ampler future in the ownership of our means of living. But I think we denied ourselves too much, and that we paid far beyond its moral worth for the house we were buying. To own the house she lived in had always been my mother's dream since her young married days when my father built the first little house where they dwelt together, and where I was born. In all the intervening quarter of a century they had lived in rented houses, and she could not help feeling that the rent they paid ought to have gone toward buying a house of their own. In this she was practically right, but now the house which we all worked so hard to buy belongs to strangers, and unless there is an effect of our self-denial in some other world, the purchase was as much waste as rent paid to a landlord. We were in fact always paying a certain rent in the interest on the notes which we slowly accumulated the money to meet, but my mother could not feel that the same, and I am glad she had her wish long before she died, and her last years were passed under a roof which she owned.

In time, but I do not know how long time, for such things did not interest me, though I was doing my share in helping pay off our debt, the promissory notes which my father had given for the purchase of our newspaper were taken up, and the newspaper was also our property. Nobody could molest us or make us afraid in its possession; and in my hope of other things it did not concern me that the title vested in his partnership with my brother, who had most justly earned his half, and who by an enterprise of his own finally established the family fortunes in undreamed-of prosperity. It was characteristic of my father that as long as their partnership existed there were no accounts between them; after my brother had a family of his own each drew from the common income at his wish or need, and when I came of sufficient worldly wisdom to realize the risks to their peace from this anomalous arrangement, I protested against it in vain. They agreed with me that it was precarious and in a way ridiculous, and that it certainly ought to cease, but as long as they continued together they remained partners on these terms. After my father withdrew, my brother took his own son into partnership, and when he came in his turn to retire, he contritely owned to me that they had not departed from the same old unbusinesslike community of ways and means, though he had promised me very earnestly many times to end it. While I am upon these matters it is a pleasure for me to record that when I came home from Venice with the manuscript of *Venetian Life* promised publication by a London house if I could find an American house to take half the proposed edition, and I confessed that I had very little hope of getting this taken in New York or Boston, my brother promptly offered to take it himself. He was then in that undreamed-of prosperity which I have mentioned, and though he had no expectation of becoming a book publisher, he was very willing to incur the risks involved. As all my world knows the book found an equally courageous friend in New York, and came out with the American imprint of Hurd & Houghton instead of Joseph A. Howells & Co.

It is not surprising to me that I cannot date the time of our acquiring the newspaper, free and clear, as the real estate phrase is, but I am certainly surprised and more pained that I cannot remember just when the house, endeared to us as home, became our very own. Its possession, as I have said, had been the poetry of my mother's hardworking, loving life, and no doubt she had watched with hope and fear the maturing of each of the notes for it, with the interest they bore, until the last was paid off. In my father's buoyant expectation of the best in everything, I do not think he had any misgiving of the event; my brother must have shared my mother's anxiety, but we younger children did not, and the great hour arrived without record in my consciousness. Years later, when I came back from long sojourn abroad, I found that the little ground-wren's nest, as it looks to me in the retrospect, had widened by half a dozen rooms without rising above its original story and a half. All round it the garden space was red and purple with the grapes which my father had induced, by his steady insistence, the neighboring farmers to plant; my mother and he were growing sweetly old in the keeping of the place, and certain wild furred and feathered things had come to share their home with them. Not only the dooryard trees which we boys had brought from the woods, had each its colony of birds, but in the eaves a family of flying-squirrels had nested. I do not know whether I can impart the sense of peace and security which seemed to have spread from the gentle household to them, but I am sure that my mother could not have realized a fonder vision of the home she had longed for through so many years.

XIII

I do not think my father so much cared for the ownership of his newspaper. He took our enterprise more easily than my elder brother, but that was temperamental in both, and one was no more devoted than the other. My companionship was far more

with my father, but before my intimacy with J. W. interrupted
this my studies had already ascertained the limits of his learning
in the regions where I was groping my way, and where the light
of my friend's greater knowledge now made him my guide. If
J. W. was more definite in his ambition of one day getting some
sort of college professorship than I in my plans of literary achieve-
ment, he could not have been more intense in his devotion to
what we were trying to do. I was studying those languages because I wished to possess myself of their literatures; still groping
my way in the dark, where a little light shed from larger learning would have helped me so much. The grammars and the text-
books could tell me what I wanted to know, but they did not
teach it; and I realize now as I could not then that self-taught is
half-taught. Yet I think my endeavor merited reward; if I
worked blindly, I worked hard; and in my attempts at fiction
or at verse where I could create the light by mere trituration, as
it were, I did not satisfy myself with less than final perfection
so far as I could imagine it. I loved form, I loved style, I loved
diction, and I strove for them all, rejecting my faultier ideals
when I discovered them, and cleaving to the truer. In some
things, the minor things, I was of wavering preference; I wrote
a different hand every other week, and if I have now an established handwriting it is more from disgust of change than from
preference. In the spirit of my endeavor there was no variable-
ness; always I strove for grace, for distinctness, for light; and
my soul detests obscurity still. That is perhaps why I am beating out my meaning here at the risk of beating it into thin air.

In the final judgment of my father's help and unhelp in my
endeavors, I should say that they were the measure of his possibility. For a man of his conditioning he had a wonderful outlook in many directions on life, but he was without perspective;
he could not see how my unaided efforts were driving to the
vanishing-point. He had been my instructor in many things beyond my young ken; he had an instinct for beauty and truth;
he loved the poetry which was the best in his youth, though he
did not deny me the belief that the poetry of mine was better

still; his gentle intelligence could follow me where his liking failed, and he modestly accepted my opinions. His interest had once been absorbed mostly, but not wholly, by the faith which he had imbibed from his reading of Swedenborg, but when I began to know him as a boy may know his elder, he was more and more concerned in the national struggle with the proslavery aggression. Politics had always been his main worldly interest and not only as to measures; he passionately favored certain men, because he liked the nature of them, as well as because he believed them right. It seems to me now that he took a personal interest in conventions and nominations, but I am not sure, for I myself took no interest whatever in them; their realities did not concern me so much as the least unrealities of fiction; and I can only make sure of my father's interest in the elections after the nominations. I suppose that he was not very skilled in practical politics, as log-rolling and wire-pulling have come to be called, though in a village which was the home of a United States Senator, a Congressional Representative, a State Senator, and a Legislative Representative, with the full corps of county office-holders, and a Common Pleas Judge, the science might well have forced itself upon his study. Many years after our coming to the Western Reserve he was sent to the State Senate by a war-majority larger than any majority which had yet returned a candidate, or yet has; but long before that he began to find his way beyond the local favor or disfavor, and was chosen one of the House clerks in the State Legislature. That must have been when I was eighteen years old, but he seems to have left our newspaper to my sole charge without misgiving, and fortunately no trouble came of his trust in me. I was then taking my civic and social opinions from the more Tory of the English quarterlies, but nobody knew what I meant by them; I did not know myself, and I did no harm with them.

In the mean time our Congressman was writing for us every week from Washington a letter full of politics far more intelligible to our readers than mine were to me. He was that Joshua R. Giddings, early one of the paladins of antislavery in a series of proslavery Congresses, where he represented and distinguished his district for twenty years after his resignation under a vote of censure and his overwhelming re-election. But in a fatal moment of that fatigue which comes to elderly people, he finally let fall an expression of indifference to office. The minor and meaner men of his party who were his enemies promptly seized the chance of defeating him for the nomination which was equivalent to an election in our district, and an inferior good man was named in his place. His friends would have had him contest the decision of the convention, but he would not, and he passed into private life, where he remained till the favor of Lincoln sought him out, and he died Consul-General to Canada after he had lived to write several books and to tell the story of the Civil War up to its penultimate year. Neither he nor Wade was of that Connecticut lineage which almost exclusively peopled the Western Reserve, and especially in Ashtabula County desired power and place to itself. Wade was from western Massachusetts, and Giddings was from western Pennsylvania, but in the new country where they met, they joined their forces as partners in the law, and remained together till politics separated them in the same cause. They still remained fellow-citizens of the little town where they spent the summer leisure of the Congressional adjournments, but without, somehow I imagine, seeing much of each other. Giddings was far more freely about the place, where his youth had been passed in the backwoods, and where he made himself familiarly at home. The very simplicity of the place seemed to comport with his statesman-like presence, his noble head, and his great Johnsonian face, when he came out of his large old-fashioned dwelling, sole rival of the Wade mansion; and he had no need to stoop in being fellow-citizen with the least of his constituents. For myself, I cannot recall any passage of words with him after a forgotten introduction, and I wish it had been otherwise. I wish now I could have known him even as a boy in his middle teens may know a man of his make; though he might not have said anything to me worth remembering, or inspired me to any expression worthier the event than that of a Louisianian whom long later I saw introduced to him in Columbus, at his own request. The Southerner stared at the giant bulk of the man who must have long embodied to his imagination a demoniacal enmity to his section, and could think of nothing better to say than, "Very pretty day, Mr. Giddings," and when Giddings had assented with, "Yes, sir, a fine day," the interview ended.

> "Giddings, far rougher names than thine have grown
> Smoother than honey on the lips of men,"

Lowell wrote in one of those magnanimous sonnets of his, when he bent from his orient height to the brave Westerner, and though it has not yet come quite to that honeyed utterance, the name cannot be forgotten when the story of our Civil War, with its far or near beginnings, is told.

XIV

That winter of my editorship wore away to the adjournment of the legislature and my father's return home, after J. W.'s withdrawal into the vague of Wisconsin. But now another beloved friend had come to us. He had learned his trade with us in southern Ohio, where he lived with our family like one of ourselves, as brotherly as if he had been of our blood. In those days he and I read the same books and dreamed the same dreams, but he was nearer my eldest brother in age, and was as much his companion as mine. After he left us to live the wander-years of the journeyman printer, we heard from him at different points where he rested, and when the Civil War began in Kansas, five years before it began in South Carolina, we knew of him fighting and writing on the Free State side. In this time, my brother made it his romance to promote a correspondence between H. G. and a young girl of the village, which ended in their engagement. It was taking too great a risk in every way, but they were fitly mated in their tastes, and their marriage was of such lasting attachment that when she survived him and lay suffering in her last sickness, she prayed every night that she might die before she woke and be with him in the everlasting morning. Romance for romance, I think their romance of the greatest pathos of any I have known, and it had phases of the highest tragedy. H. G. was among the first to volunteer for the great war, and quickly rose from the ranks to be captain, but somehow he incurred the enmity of a superior officer who was able to have him cashiered in dishonor from the army. The great war which we look back upon as hallowed by a singleness of patriotic purpose was marked by many private wrongs which were promptly revenged, or kept for ultimate vengeance, sometimes forgone at last through the wearing out of the hate which cherished them. I am glad to think this was so with H. G.; his memory is very dear to me, and our friendship was of a warmth of affection such as I did not know for J. W., though he had so much greater charm for me, and in the communion of our minds I was so much more intimate with him.

Earlier in his absence, I had grown more and more into intellectual companionship with the eldest of my sisters, who was only little more than a year younger than myself. We had gone to the village parties and dances and sleigh-rides together, but she was devoted to my mother and the helper in her work, and gave herself far less than I to the pleasures which had palled upon me; she may never have cared for them much; certainly not so much as for the household life. It is one of those unavailing regrets which gather upon us if we question memory as I am doing now, and try to deal honestly with the unsparing truth of its replies, that I ignored so long her willingness to be my companion in the things of the mind. With my mother it was a simple affair; I was bound to her in an affection which was as devoted throughout my youth as it had been in my childhood; she was herself the home which I suffered such longing for if I ever left it; and I am now, in my old age, humbly grateful for the things I was prompted to do in my love of her. I could not, without an effect of exaggeration unworthy of her dear memory, express my sense of her motherly perfection within the limits of her nature, which I would not now have had different through worldly experience or privilege. She had, like my father, the instinct of poetry; and over what was left of her day's work for the long evenings which we spent reading or talking or laughing together, while my father selected copy for his paper without losing the fun we all made, she was gay with the gayest of us. Often I had savagely absented myself from the rest, but when I came out of my little study, dazed with my work, after the younger children had gone to bed, I have the vision of her rolling her sewing together in her lap, and questioning me with her fond eyes what I was thinking of or had been trying to do.

I believe she did not ask; that was forbidden by my pride and shame. I did not read to any of them what I had been writing; they would not have been hard enough upon it to satisfy me, though if they had criticised it I should have been furious. In fact, I was not an amiable or at least a reasonable youth; it was laid upon me to try solitarily for the things I had no help in doing, and I seldom admitted any one to the results until that sister of mine somehow passed my ungracious reserves. I do not know just how this happened; but perhaps it was through our confiding to each other, brokenly, almost unspokenly, our discontent with the village limit of our lives. Within our home we had the great world, at least as we knew it in books, with us, but outside of it, our social experience dwindled to the measure of the place. I have tried to say how uncommon the place was intellectually, but we disabled it on that side because it did not realize the impossible dreams of that great world of wealth, of fashion, of haughtily and dazzlingly, blindingly brilliant society, which we did not inconveniently consider we were altogether unfit for. The reader may or may not find a pathos in our looking at the illustration on the front of a piece of tawdry sheet music, and wondering whether it would ever be our high fortune to mingle with a company of such superbly caparisoned people as we saw pictured there, playing and singing and listening.

Vanity so criminal as ours, might have been for a just punishment lastingly immured in that village which the primeval woods encircled like a prison wall; and yet almost at that moment, when we had so tardily discovered ourselves akin in our tastes, our hopes and despairs, we were nearer the end of our imprisonment than we could have imagined. Whether we were punished in our enlargement which we were both so near, I cannot say; my own life since that time has been such as some know and any may know who care, and of hers I may scarcely speak. After a few happy weeks, a few happy months of our common escape, she went back to those bounds where her duty lay; and when after many years she escaped from them again it was to circumstances where she was so willingly useful as to feel herself very happy. Her last dream, one of being usefuller yet to those dearest to her, ended in a nightmare of disappointment; but that too had wholly passed before she woke to the recompense which we try to believe that death shall bring to all who suffer here to no final good.

Now it was life full beyond our fondest expectations, if not our fancies of its possibilities, which lured us forward. We were making the most of our mutual interest in the books we were reading, and she was giving, as sisters give so far beyond the giving of brothers, her sympathy to me in what I was trying to write. It was some time since I had turned, upon the counsel of J. W., from Greek to German, I forget from just what reasoning, though I think it was because he said I could study Greek any time, and now we could study German together. I had gone so far with it that I was already reading Heine and trying to write like him, instead of reading my Spanish poets and trying to imitate them in their own meters. But there is scarcely any definite memory of my sister's literary companionship left me. I remember her coming to me once with the praise, which I shamefacedly refused, of the neighbor who had pointed to a row of Washington Irving's works in her house, and said that some day my books would fill a shelf like that. For the rest, I am dimly aware of our walking summer evenings down a certain westward way from our house, and of her helping me dream a literary future. If she had then a like ambition she kept it from me, and it was not till twenty years later that she sent me a play she had written, with village motives and village realities, treated with a frankness which I still had not the intelligence to value. The play never came to the stage, and in that farther time, it was the fruition of hopes which had not defined themselves, that when my father's scheme was realized, not only I, but she too, was to return to Columbus with him. It would be easy to pretend, and I can easily believe that we had always, at the bottom of our hearts, thought of Columbus with distinct longing; but I am not sure that there was more in our remembrance of it than a sense of its greatness as the State capital to give direction to our ambition for some experience of the world beyond our village. There was no part for her in our journalistic plan; probably the affair for her was an outing which she had won by her unselfish devotion to the duties of her narrow lot; but what I am sure of, and what I am glad of now, amidst my compunctions for not valuing her loving loyalty at its true worth, is that she did have this outing.

III

THROUGHOUT his later boyhood and into his earlier manhood
the youth is always striving away from his home and the things
of it. With whatever pain he suffers through the longing for
them, he must deny them; he must cleave to the world and the
things of it; that is his fate, that is the condition of all achieve-
ment and advancement for him. He will be many times ridiculous and sometimes contemptible, he will be mean and selfish
upon occasion; but he can scarcely otherwise be a man; the
great matter for him is to keep some place in his soul where he
shall be ashamed. Let him not be afraid of being too unsparing
in his memories; the instinct of self-preservation will safeguard
him from showing himself quite as he was. No man, unless he
puts on the mask of fiction, can show his real face or the will
behind it. For this reason the only real biographies are the
novels, and every novel if it is honest will be the autobiography
of the author and biography of the reader.

I

It was doubtless a time of intense emotion for our whole family when my sister and I set out for the State Capital with my
father on his return to his clerical duties at the meeting of the
legislature in 1856. If I cannot make sure that Columbus had
become with those of us old enough to idealize it, a sort of metropolis of the mind to which we should repair if we were good
enough, or failing that, if fortune were ever kind enough, I am
certain that my father's sojourn there, with his several visits to

us during the winter before, had kept the wonder of it warm in my heart. The books that he brought me at each return from the State Library, renewed in me the sense of a State Capital which he had tried to implant in me when we lived there, and my sister could not have dreamt of anything grander or gayer. Perhaps we both still saw ourselves there in scenes like that in the title-page of that piece of sheet-music; but anything so definite as this I cannot be sure of. What I can be sure of is the substantial nature and occasion of our going, so far as I was concerned. "We were to furnish," my father and I, as I have told in *My Literary Passions*, "a daily letter giving an account of the legislative proceedings, which I was mainly to write from material he helped me get together. The letters at once found favor with the editors who agreed to take them, and my father then withdrew from the work, after telling them who was doing it." My sister of course had no part in the enterprise, and for her our adventure was pure pleasure, the pleasure we both took in our escape from the village, and the pleasure I did not understand then that she had in witnessing my literary hopes and labors.

In like manner I am belatedly sensible of the interest which our dear H. G. took in our going, and the specific instructions which he gave me for my entry into the great world; as if he would realize in my prosperous future the triumphs which fortune had denied him in his past. He adjured me not to be abashed in any company, but face the proudest down and make audacity do the part of the courage I was lacking in. Especially, he would have me not distrust myself in such a social essential as dancing, which was a grace I was confessedly imperfect in, but to exhaust the opportunities of improving in it which the Saturday evening hops at our hotel would give me. He advised me not to dress poorly but go to the full length of Polonius's precept—

"Costly thy habit as thy purse can buy"—

though what advantages his own experience in these matters had won him, could not have been very signal. He knew my ambition in that way, and how it had been defeated by the friendly zeal of our home-tailor; and we both held that with the clothing-stores of High Street open to my money all I had to do was to fix my mind upon a given suit which would fit me as perfectly as the Jew said and then wear it away triumphantly apparelled for the highest circles. We did not know that the art of dressing well, or fashionably, comes from deep and earnest study, and that the instinct of it might well have been blunted in me by my Quaker descent, with that desire to shine rather in the Other World than in this which had become a passion with my grandfather.

No fact of my leaving home upon the occasion which I must have felt so tremendous remains with me. I cannot even say whether it was through the snow or the mud that we drove ten miles from the county-seat to the railroad station at Ashtabula; whatever the going it was over the warped and broken boards of the ancient plank-road which made any transit possible in that region of snow and mud, and remained till literally worn away even in the conception of the toll-taker. Without intervening event so far as my memory testifies or circumstance any more than if we had flown through the air, we were there in Columbus together, living in an old-fashioned hotel on the northward stretch of High Street, which was then the principal business street, and for anything I know is so yet. The hotel was important to the eye of our village strangeness, but it was perhaps temperamentally of the sort of comfortable taverns which the hotels had come to displace. My father had gone to live there because he knew it from our brief sojourn when we came to the city from the country five or six years before, and because it was better suited to his means; but one of the vividest impressions of his youth had been the building of the National Road, a work so monumental for the new country it traversed, and he poetically valued the Goodale House for facing upon this road, which in its course from Baltimore to St. Louis became High Street in Columbus.

Not even in this association could it be equaled with the Neil House, then the finest hotel in the West, without a peer even in

Cincinnati. Dickens, in his apparently unreasoned wanderings, paused in it over a day, and admired its finish in black walnut, the wood that came afterward to be so precious for the ugliest furniture ever made. All visitors of distinction sojourned there, and it was the resort of the great politicians who held their conclaves in its gloomy corridors and in its office and bar on the eve of nominating conventions or the approach of general elections. I have a vision, which may be too fond, of their sitting under its porches in tilted armchairs as the weather softened, canvassing the civic affairs which might not have been brought to a happy issue without them. But however misled I may be in this I cannot err in my vision of the stately conflagration which went up with the hotel one windless night, a mighty front of flame hooded with sombre smoke. I watched it with a vast crowd from the steps of the State House which it was worthier to face than any other edifice of the little city; but this was long after that winter of ours in the Goodale House, which I remember for the boundless abundance of its table and for those society events which on Saturday nights crowned the week.

I dare say they were not so fashionable as H. G. imagined them, or I with a heart too weak and feet too untutored ever to join in them, but the world was present in other sophistications in our pleasant hotel which I could not so easily shun. Chief of these was the tipping, which there first insisted on my acquaintance by many polite insinuations, and when I would have withdrawn became explicit. The kind colored waiter who used to cumber me with service at table as his anxieties mounted once took courage to whisper in my ear that he thought he would like to go to the theatre that evening, and it grieves me yet to think that I resented this freedom and denied him the quarter he suggested. Since then, life has been full of the experiences of tipping, always so odious, though apparently more rapacious than it really is, but I have never again been able to deny a tip, or to give so little as I would often like to give. I know that some better citizens, or wiser, than myself, punish the neglect or ingratitude of service by diminishing or withholding the tip, but I have never been able to perform this public-spirited duty, perhaps because, though I loathe tipping, I do not believe any fellow creature—

"As meek and mere a serving-man,"

as may be, would take a tip if he were paid a just wage, or any wage, without it.

But all these incidents and interests were far in the future of that brave and happy time when I was intending and attempting the conquest of the whole field of polite learning from so many sides, in the studies which as at home now went on far into the night. These even included an Icelandic grammar, for the reason that, as I had read, the metre of *Hiawatha* was derived from that literature, but I do not know that I got so far as to identify it. My reading, now entirely from the State Library, included all the novels of Bulwer which I was not ashamed to enjoy after my more distinguished pleasure in Thackeray; the critical authorities would not then have abashed me in it, as they would now. The other day I saw on my shelves the volume of *Percy's Reliques* which my sister and I read together that winter; and I was so constantly and devotedly reading Tennyson and Shakespeare that I cannot understand how I had time for an equal constancy and devotion to Heine. I saw how much he had profitted by the love of those English ballads which I was proud to share with him; and there were other German poets of his generation whose indebtedness to them I perceived and enjoyed. I was now in fact reading German to the entire neglect of Spanish; as for Latin and Greek I had no more time or relish for them than those cultivated gentlemen who believe they read some Latin or Greek author every day before breakfast.

II

The life and the letters continued on terms which I should not have known how to wish different. I had a desk appointed me on the floor of the Senate as good as any Senator's for my convenience as a reporter; and my father gave me notes of the proceedings in the House, so that I could make a fair report of each day's facts which we so early abandoned the pretense of his making. Every privilege and courtesy was shown the press, which sometimes I am afraid its correspondents accepted ungraciously. Either the first winter or the next one of them was expelled from the floor of the House for his overbold criticisms of some member, and I espoused his cause with quite outrageous zeal. I had, indeed, such a swollen ideal of the rights and duties of the press that I spared no severity in my censure of Senators I found misguided. I was, perhaps, not wholly fitted by my nineteen years to judge them, though this possibility did not occur to me at the time with its present force; but if I was not impressed with the dignity of the Senate, the dignity of the Senate Chamber was a lasting effect with me, as, in fact, that of the whole Capitol was. I seemed to share personally in it as I mounted the stately marble stairway from the noble rotunda or passed through the ample corridors from the Senate to the House where it needed not even a nod to the sergeant-at-arms to gain me access to the floor; a nonchalant glance was enough. But the grandeur of the interior, which I enjoyed with the whole legislative body, was not more wonderful than its climate, which I found tempered against the winter to a summer warmth by the air rushing from the furnaces in the basement through gratings in the walls and floors. These were for me the earliest word of the comfort that now pervades our whole well-warmed American world, but I had scarcely imagined them even from my father's report. How could I imagine them or fail to attribute to myself something like merit from them? I enjoyed, in fact, something like moral or civic ownership of the whole place, which I penetrated in every part on my journalistic business: the court-rooms, the agricultural department, the executive offices, and how do I know but the very room of the Governor himself? The library was of course my personal resort; as I have told, I was always getting books from it, and these books had a quality in coming from the State Library which intensified my sense of being of, as well as in, the capital of Ohio.

Whether the city itself shared my sense of its importance in the same measure I am not sure. There were reasons, however, why it might have done so. It was then what would be now a small city, say not above twenty thousand, and though it had already begun to busy itself with manufacturing and had two or three railroads centering in it, the industries and facilities which have now swollen its population to almost a quarter of a million were then in their beginning. Its political consciousness may have been the greater, therefore; it may indeed have been subjectively the sovereign city which I so objectively felt it. In that time, in fact, a state capital was both comparatively and positively of greater reality than it has been since. With the Civil War carried to its close in the reconstituted Union, the theory of State Rights forever vanished, and with this the dignity which once clothed the separate existence of the states. Their shadowy sovereignty had begun to wane in the antislavery North because it was the superstition of the proslavery South, yet I can remember a moment when there was much talk, though it never came to more than talk, of turning this superstition to a faith and applying it to the defeat of the Fugitive Slave Law. If it was once surmised that the decisions of the Ohio courts might nullify a law of the United States, I do not believe that this surmise ever increased the political consciousness of our state capital. It remained a steadily prospering town like other towns, till now perhaps it may not feel itself a capital at all. Perhaps it could be restored to something like the quality I valued in it by becoming the residence of envoys from the other state capitals, and sending a minister to each of these. I have the conviction that public-spirited citizens could be found to take such offices at very moderate salaries, and that their wives would be willing to aid in restoring the shadow of state sovereignty by leaving cards upon one another.

III

The winter of 1856–7 passed without my knowing more of the capital than its official world. Even the next year, when I began to make some acquaintance with the social world it was with an alien or adoptive phase of it, as I realize with tardy surprise. There were then so many Germans in Ohio that an edition of the laws had to be printed in their language, and there was a common feeling that we ought to know their language, if not their literature, which was really what I cared more to know. I carried my knowledge of it so far as to render a poem of my own into German verse which won the praise of my teacher; and I wish I could remember who he was, gentle, tobacco-smoked shade that he has long since become, or who the German editor of what *republikanische Zeitung* was that sometimes shared my instruction with him. There were also two blithe German youths who availed with me in the loan of Goethe's *Wahlverwandschaften*, and gave me some fencing lessons in their noonings. I forget what employ they were of, but their uncle was a watchmaker and jeweler, and my father got him to gold-plate his silver watch, or dye it, as he preferred to say. When the Civil War came he went into it and was killed; and many years afterward, in my love and honor of him, I turned his ghost into a loved and honored character in *A Hazard of New Fortunes*. He was a political refugee, of those German revolutionists who came to us after the revolts of 1848, and he still dwells venerable in my memory, with his noble, patriarchally bearded head.

But it all appears very fantastic in the retrospect, that Teutonic period of my self-culture, and I am not sure that one fact of it is more fantastic than another. Such was my zeal for everything German that I once lunched at one of the German beer-saloons which rather abounded in Columbus, on Swiss cheese with French mustard spread over it and a tall glass of lager beer, then much valued as a possible transition from the use of the strong waters more habitual with Americans than now; but it made me very sick, and I was obliged to forego it as an expression of my love for German poetry. To a little earlier period must have belonged the incident of my going to see "*Die Räuber*" of Schiller, which I endured with iron resolution from the beginning to the end. It was given, I believe, by amateurs, and I tried my best to imagine that I understood it as it went on, but probably I did not, though I would have been loath to own the fact to any of the few German families who then formed my whole acquaintance with society. I never afterward met them at American houses; the cleavage between the two races in everything but politics was absolute; though the Germans were largely antislavery, and this formed common ground for them and natives of like thinking who did not know them socially.

In those first winters my knowledge of American society was confined to the generalized hospitality of the large evening receptions which some of the leading citizens used to give the two Houses of the legislature, including the correspondents and reporters attached to them. I cannot say just how or when I began to divine that these occasions were not of the first fashion, though the hosts and hostesses might have been so. There were great suppers, mainly of oysters, to which our distance from the sea lent distinction, and ice-cream, and sometimes, if I may trust a faint reverberation from the past as of blown corks, champagne. There was also dancing, and when some large, old-fashioned house was not large enough, a wooden pavilion was improvised over the garden to give the waltzes and quadrilles verge enough. I recall my share in the suppers, if not in the dancing, but my deficiency was far more than made up by the excess of a friend, who must then have been hard upon sixty years of age, yet was of a charming gayety and an unimpaired youthfulness. He stood up in every quadrille and he danced to the end of the evening, with a demure smile on his comely, smooth-shaven, rosy face, and a light, mocking self-consciousness in his kind eyes, as if he would agree as to any incongruity the spectator might find in his performance. He was one of the clerks of the House, an old politician, and the editor of a leading Cleveland newspaper, which he chose to leave for the pleasures of the capital. From his experience of the system which he was part of he whimsically professed to believe that as great legislative wisdom could be assembled by knocking down every other man in a crowd and dragging him into the House or Senate as by the actual method of nomination and election. At times he would support the theory of a benevolent despotism, and advocate the establishment of what he called a one-man power as the ideal form of government. I owed him much in the discharge of duties which my finding the most important in the world must have amused him, and when he went back to his newspaper he left me to write the legislative letters for it.

This gentle reactionary was the antithesis of another very interesting man, known to his fellow-legislators as Citizen Corry, in recognition of his preference for the type of French Red Republicanism acquired in Paris during his stay through the academic republic of 1848–50. Such a residence would alone have given him a distinction which we can hardly realize in our time, but he was, besides, a man of great natural distinction, and of more cultivation than any of his fellow-legislators. He was one of the Representatives from Cincinnati, and when another Cincinnati Representative of his own party struck a member from the Western Reserve, Citizen Corry joined the Republicans in voting his expulsion. But he had already made a greater sensation, and created an expectation of the unexpected in all he did by proposing an amendment to the Constitution abolishing the system of dual chambers in the legislature, and retaining only the House of Representatives. I think that in Greece alone is this the actual parliamentary form, but I believe that it was in that short-lived French republic of 1848 that Corry saw its workings and conceived the notion of its superiority. Under the present system he held that the House was merely a committee at the bar of the Senate, and the Senate a committee at the bar of the House, with a great waste of time and public advantage through the working of a very clumsy machinery. His proposition was not taken seriously by the Ohio House of Representatives, but to my young enthusiasm it seemed convincing by its mere statement, and the arguments on the other side, to the effect that the delays which he censured gave time for useful reflection, appeared to me very fallacious. Citizen Corry was not re-elected to the next legislature, and his somewhat meteoric history did not include any other official apparition. But while he was passing through the orbit of my world I was fully aware of his vivid difference from the controlled and orderly planets, and he dazzled in me an imagination always too fondly seeking the bizarre and strange. I do not think I ever spoke with him, but I tingled to do so; I created him citizen of that fine and great world where I had so much of my own being in reveries that rapt me from the realities of the life about me.

IV

The first winter of my legislative correspondence began with a letter to my Cincinnati newspaper in which I described the public opening of the new State House. I remember the event vividly because I thought it signally important, and partly because, to relieve myself from the stress of the crowd passing through the doorways, I lifted my arms and was near having my breath crushed out. There were a ball and a banquet but somewhere, somehow, amidst the dancing and the feeding and smoking, I found a corner where I could write out my account of the affair and so escaped with my letter and my life.

Much as I might have wished to share socially, with such small splendor as might be, in this high occasion, the reporter's instinct was first with me. I was there as the representative of a great Cincinnati newspaper, and I cared more to please its management than to take any such part as I might in the festivity. My part was to look on and tell what I saw, and I must have done this in the manner of my most approved good masters, no doubt with satirically poetic touches from Heine and bits of worldly glitter from Thackeray. I should like to see that letter now, and I should like to know how I contrived to get it, more or less surreptitiously, into the hands of the express agent for delivery to my newspaper. In those days there was a good deal of talk, foolish talk, I am since aware, of having the post office superseded in its functions by the express companies. Now the talk and the fact are all the other way; but then the mail was slow and uncertain, and if my letter was of the nature of manuscript the express might safely carry it, and deliver it in time for the next day's paper. That was rightful and lawful enough, but there was a show of secrecy in the transaction which was not unpleasing to the enterprise of a young reporter.

My letters as they went on from day to day contented the managers of the *Gazette* so well that when the session of the legislature ended they gave me an invitation which might well have abused my modesty with a sense of merit. This invitation was to come and be their city editor, which then meant the local reporting, at a salary twice as great as that which I had been getting as their legislative correspondent. I do not know whose inspiration the offer was, but I should like to believe it was that of the envoy from the paper who made it in person, after perhaps more fully satisfying himself of my fitness. He is long since dead, but if he were still alive I hope he would not mind my describing him as of less stature than myself even, wearing the large round glasses which give certain near-sighted persons a staring look, and of speech low almost to whispering, so that I could not quite be sure that the incredible thing he was proposing was really expressed to me. I like to recall the personal fact of him because he was always my friend, and he would have found me another place on the paper if he could when I would not take the one he had offered. He did make room for me in his own department for as long as he could, or as I would stay, when I went down to Cincinnati to look the ground over, and he kept me his guest as far as sharing his room with me in the building where we worked together, and where I used to grope my way toward midnight up a stairway entirely black to his door. There I lighted the candle end which I found within and did what I could to sleep till he came, hours later, when the paper went to press. I have the belief that the place was never swept or dusted, and that this did not matter to the quiet, scholarly man, whose life was so wholly in his work that he did not care how he lived. He was buoyed up, above all other things, by the interest of journalism, which for those once abandoned to it is indeed a kind of enchantment. As I knew it then and afterward, it has always had far more of my honor and respect than those ignorant of it know how to render. One incident of it at this time so especially moved me that I will give it place in this wayward tale, though it is probably not more to the credit of the press than unnumbered others which others could cite. A miserable man came late one night to ask that a certain report which involved his good name, and with it the good name of a miserable woman, and the peace of their families, might be withheld. He came with legal counsel, and together they threshed the matter out with our editorial force upon the point whether we ought or ought not to spare him, our contention being that as a prominent citizen he was even less to be spared than a more unimportant person. Our professional conscience was apparently in that scruple; how it was overcome I do not remember, but at last we promised mercy and the report was suppressed.

It was one of the ironies of life that after the only suspected avenue to publicity had been successfully guarded, the whole fact should have cruelly come out in another paper the next morning. But I cannot feel even yet that the beauty of our merciful decision was marred by this mockery of fate, or that the cause of virtue was served by it, and I think that if I had been wiser than I was then I would have remained in the employ offered me, and learned in the school of reality the many lessons of human nature which it could have taught me. I did not remain, and perhaps I could not; it might have been the necessity of my morbid nerves to save themselves from abhorrent contacts; in any case, I renounced the opportunity offered me by that university of the streets and police stations, with its faculty of patrolmen and ward politicians and saloon-keepers. The newspaper office was not the capitol of Ohio; I was not by the fondest imputation a part of the State government, and I felt the difference keenly. I was always very homesick; I knew nobody in the city, and I had no companionship except that of my constant friend, whom I saw only in our hours of work. I had not even the poor social refuge of a boarding-house; I ate alone at a restaurant, where I used sadly to amuse myself with the waiters' versions of the orders which they called down a tube into the kitchen below. The one which cheered me most was that of a customer who always ordered a double portion of corn-cakes and was translated as requiring "Indians, six on a plate."

Nearly all the frequenters of this restaurant were men from their stores and offices, snatching a hasty midday meal, but a few were women, clerks and shop-girls of the sort who now so abound in our towns and cities, but then so little known. I was so altogether ignorant of life, that I thought shame of them to be boldly showing themselves in such a public place as a restaurant. I wonder what they would have thought, poor, blameless dears, of the misgivings in the soul of the censorious youth as he sat stealing glances of injurious conjecture at them while he overate himself with the food which was the only thing that could appease for a moment the hunger of his homesick heart. If I could not mercifully imagine them, how could I intelligently endure the ravings of the drunken woman which I heard one night in the police station where my abhorred duties took me for the detestable news of the place? I suppose it was this adventure, sole of its sort, which clinched my resolve to have no more to do with the money-chance offered to me in journalism. My longing was for the cleanly respectabilities, and I still cannot think that a bad thing, or if experience cannot have more than the goodly outside in life, that this is not well worth having. There was a relief, almost an atonement, or at least a consolation in being sent next day to report a sermon, in fulfillment of my friend's ideal of journalistic enterprise, and though that sermon has long since gone from me and was perhaps at the time not distinctly with me, still I have a sense of cleansing from the squalor of the station house in listening to it. If all my work could have been the reporting of sermons, with intervals of sketching the graduation ceremonies of young ladies' seminaries such as that where once a girl in garnet silk read an essay of perhaps no surpassing interest, but remained an enchanting vision, and the material of some future study in fiction: if it could have been these things, with nothing of police stations in it, I might

have tried longer to become a city editor. But as it was I decided my destiny in life differently.

v

I must not conceal the disappointment which my father delicately concealed when I returned and took up my old work in
the printing-office. He might well have counted on my help in
easing him of his load of debt from the salary I had forgone, but
there was no hint of this in the welcome given me in the home
where I was again so doubly at home with my books and manuscripts. Now and then my friend of the *Gazette* management
managed to have some sketch of mine accepted for it, and my
life went on in my sister's literary companionship on much the
same terms as before our venture into the world the winter before. My father's clerkship had ended with the adjournment of
the legislature in the spring, but in the autumn, when it grew
toward winter, I asked again for the correspondence of the
Gazette. I got this by favor of my friend, and then I had courage
to ask for that of the Cleveland *Herald*, which the interest of the
blithe sexagenarian sufficed to secure me, and returned to the
capital with no pretence that I was not now writing the letters
solely and entirely myself. But almost before my labors began,
my health quite broke under the strain of earlier over-study and
later over-work. I gave up my correspondence for both those
honored newspapers to my father, who wrote it till the close of
the session, and at his suggestion the letters of the *Gazette* fell
the next winter to the fit and eager hands of a young man who
had just then sold his country newspaper and had come to try
his fortune in the capital. His name was Whitelaw Reid, in the
retrospect a tall, graceful youth with an enviable black moustache and imperial, wearing his hair long in the Southern fashion, and carrying himself with the native ease which availed
him in a worldly progress uninterrupted to the end. He wrote
the legislative letters so acceptably that when the Civil War
broke out the *Gazette* people were glad to make him their corre-

spondent in the field, where he distinguished himself beyond any other war correspondent in the West, or the East, for what I knew. The world knows how riches and honors followed him all his days, and how when he died the greatest Empire sent his dust home to the greatest Republic in such a warship as the war correspondent of these years could not have dreamed of. From time to time we saw each other, but not often; he was about his business in the State House, and now I was about mine in the office of the *Ohio State Journal,* the organ of the Republican party, which had been newly financed and placed on a firm footing after rather prolonged pecuniary debility.

I was at home in the autumn, as I had been all the summer, eating my heart out, (as I would have said in those days), when the call to a place on the *Journal's* editorial staff incredibly, impossibly came, and I forgot my ills, and eagerly responded. I hardly know how to justify my inconsistency when I explain that this place was the same which I had rejected at twice the salary on the Cincinnati *Gazette.* Perhaps I accepted it now because I could no longer endure the disappointment and inaction of my life. Perhaps I hoped that in the smaller city the duties would not be so odious or so onerous; perhaps it was because I would have been glad to return to Columbus on any terms; in any case it fell out that the duties of the place were undertaken by another who doted on them, and quite different and far more congenial functions were assigned to me.

My chief was Henry D. Cooke, the successful editor and proprietor of a newspaper in northern Ohio, and brother of the banker Jay Cooke, once nationally noted in our finance, and himself afterwards governor of the District of Columbia: the easiest of easy gentlemen, formed for prosperity and leisure, with an instinct for the choice of subordinates qualified to do the journalistic work he soon began to relinquish in his preoccupation with the politics of the capital. I have had no sweeter friend in a life abounding in friends, and after fifty years I think of his memory with gratitude for counsels which availed me much when given and would avail me still if I should ever again be a youth of twenty-one, proposing to do and say the things I then proposed. He rarely blamed anything I did in the stirring and distracted period of our relation, but one morning he brought me a too graphic paragraph, about a long-forgotten homicide done by an injured husband, and said, "Never, *never* write anything you would be ashamed to read to a woman," and so made me lastingly ashamed of what I had done, and fearful of ever doing the like again, even in writing fiction. It seems not to be so now with our novelists, begun or beginning; they write many things they ought to be ashamed to read to women, or if they are of that sex, things they should be ashamed to read to men. But perhaps they *are* ashamed and only hold out writing so for art's sake; I cannot very well speak for them; but I am still very Victorian in my preference of decency.

Mr. Cooke must have been often of a divided mind about his assistants, or about their expression of the opinions which he reticently held in common with them. He was a thorough Republican; he undoubtedly believed that the time had come for calling black black, but his nature would have been to call it dark gray, at least for that day or for the next. He would have oftenest agreed with us in what we said of the proslavery party and partisans, North and South, though he held it not honesty to have it thus set down. He would have liked better the *milde Macht* of a Hahnemannian treatment, while we were blistering and cauterizing, and letting blood wherever we saw the chance, and there were every day chances enough. I had been made news editor and in the frequent intervals of our chief's abeyance, I made myself the lieutenant of the keen ironical spirit who mostly wrote our leaders but did not mind my dipping my pen in his ink when I could turn from the paste and scissors which were more strictly my means of expression. My work was to look through the exchange newspapers which flocked to us in every mail, and to choose from them any facts that could be presented to our readers as significant. I called my column or two, "News and Humors of the Mail," and I tried to give it an effect of originality by recasting many of the facts, or when I could not find a pretext for this, by offering the selected passages with applausive or derisive comment. We had French and Spanish and German exchanges, and I sometimes indulged a boyish vanity by prefacing a paragraph from these with such a sentence as, "We translate from the *Courrier des États Unis*," or "We find in *La Cronaca* of New York," or "We learn from the *Wachter am Erie*," as the case might be. Why I should have been suffered to do this without admonition from our chief, or sarcasm from my senior I do not know; perhaps the one thought it best to let youth have its head when the head was harmlessly turned; and perhaps the other was too much occupied with his own work to trouble himself with mine; but certainly if I had caught a contemporary in such folly I should have tried what unsparing burlesque could do to make him wiser.

The reader who has no follies to own will probably not think me wise in owning mine, but from time to time I must do so; there were so many. It is with no hope of repairing these follies now that I confess the pride I felt in the poor little Spanish, German and French which it had cost me so much to acquire unaided and unguided, and I was willing that my acquirements should shed lustre on the newspaper I loved, almost as much as I loved myself. I admired it even more, and I wished to do all that I could to make it admirable, even enviable, with others. I think now that I was not using one of the best means to do it; I only contend that it was one of the best I could think of then. If any contemporary had turned it against us, I hope I should have been willing to suffer personally for it, but I cannot now be sure.

VI

We aspired at least tacitly to a metropolitan character in our journalism; there were no topics of human interest which we counted alien to us anywhere in the range of politics, morals, literature or religion; and I was suffered my say. The writer who was more habitually and profitably suffered his say was,

I still think, a man of very uncommon qualities and abilities. He was a journalist who could rightly be called a publicist, earnest if things came to that, of a faithful conscience, and of a mocking skill in the chances pretty constantly furnished us by our contemporaries, especially some of our Southern contemporaries whom it was difficult to take as seriously as they took themselves. When they made some violent proclamation against the North, or wreaked themselves in some frenzy of proslavery ethics, we took our pleasure in shredding the text into small passages and tagging each of these with a note of open derision or ironical deprecation. We called it "firing the Southern heart," in a phrase much used at the time. It was not wise, it was not well, but it was undeniably amusing, and we carried it to any lengths that the very intermittent supervision of our nominal chief would allow. We may have supposed that it would help laugh away the madness of the South which few in the North believed more than a temporary insanity, but the uneasy honesty which always lurks somewhere in my heart to make me own my errors, must acquit my fellow-editor of the worst excesses in this sort, so mainly literary with me. He was not only a man of high journalistic quality, of clear insight, shrewd judgment, and sincere convictions, but I do not believe that in the American press of the time he was surpassed as a clear thinker and brilliant writer. All the days of journalism are yesterdays; and the name of Samuel R. Reed will mean nothing to these oblivious morrows, even in Ohio, but all the more I wish to do his memory such honor as I may. We were of course daily together in our work, and often in our walks on the Sundays which were as other days to his stedfast agnosticism. The word was not yet, but the thing has always been, and especially it always was in the older West, where bold surmise of the whence and whither of life often defied the authority of Faith, then much more imperative than now. Reed's favorite author, whom he read as critically as if he were not his favorite, was Shakespeare; but his far more constant reading was the Bible, especially the Old Testament. I could not say why he read it so much, but he may have felt in it the mystical power which commands the imagination of men and holds them in respectful contemplation of a self-sufficing theory of the universe such as nothing in science or philosophy affords. He quoted it for a peculiar joy in the fitness of its application to every circumstance; he quoted Dickens, as everybody did then; he quoted Shakespeare a great deal more both in his talking and in his writing; and later in his life, long after mine had parted from it, he amused the spare moments of his journalistic leisure by a study of Shakespeare's women whom he did not take at the generally accepted critical appraisement.

I am tempted out of the order of these confessions to follow him to the end which death put to the long kindness between us, and I recall with tenderness our last meeting near New York where he was hesitating whether to continue on his way to Europe. He had at last given up his work in Cincinnati where he had spent the many years after the few years we spent together in Columbus. He owned that he had worn himself out in that work, toiling incessantly through many homicidal Cincinnati summers, and he blamed himself for the sacrifice. He felt that he had turned from it too late; and in fact he died at sea soon after. He accepted his impending doom with the stoical calm which he always kept, and which I had once seen him keep so wonderfully after the war began, when a Southern Unionist, the formerly famous, now forgotten Parson Brownlow of Tennessee, came to reproach him for the part which he held that such writing as Reed's had borne in bringing on the strife. Reed suffered the good man's passion almost with compassion, and when Brownlow was gone he would not let me blame him, but said that he had played a noble part in the struggle to hold his region in the Union. He always kept a countenance of bland calm, lit by pale-blue eyes which gave no hint of the feeling within, and if I had not loved him so much and known him so well, I might have thought the habitual smile of his clean-shaven lip sometimes a little cruel. He let his full soft beard grow inordinately long, and he had a way of stroking it as he slightly smiled and crisply spoke; it was the only touch of quaintness in him at a time when beards were self-indulgently worn in many fantastic ways. He was the best-dressed man I knew, in fashions as little aged as possible in their transition from the East to the West, and he was of a carefulness in such minor morals as gloves and boots very uncommon in our somewhat slovenly ways.

After his liking for Shakespeare and Dickens he liked the Ingoldsby Legends, but he did not care for the poetry which I was constantly reading and trying to write. The effect of my endeavor as it appeared in the passionate or pessimistic verse which I contributed to Eastern periodicals must have amused him; but perhaps he tolerated me because, along with this po-etical effusiveness, in which I was grievously sensitive to any breath of sarcasm, I had a tooth as sharp as his own in our journalism. He was intelligently and I suppose scientifically fond of music, since he failed of no chance to hear the best, a chance rare in our city; and he held that the composition of grand opera was the highest feat of the human intellect, which was to me a stumbling-block and foolishness, though I liked dramatic singing, and indeed singing of all kinds. We came together in our fondness for the theatre, and after our evening's work was done he sometimes turned with me into the barn-like structure on State Street which served the pathetic need of the drama in Columbus at that day. The place was heated in the winter for its twenty or thirty frequenters by two huge cast-iron stoves, one on either side of the orchestra; stoves such as I have since seen in English cathedrals; but when the curtain rose the blast of freezing air that swept out upon us made us shiver for the players in their bare arms and necks and their thin hosiery and drapery. They were often such bad players that they merited their sufferings; the prompter audibly bore a very leading part in the performance as he still does in the Italian theatre; yet for all his efforts we one night saw Hamlet in two acts; it was, to be sure, a very cold night, of an air eagerer and nippinger than even that the ghost walked in at Elsinore, and we would not have had the play longer. Yet we often saw very well given some of the old English comedies which are now no longer well

or ill given; and between the acts, somewhere, a plain young
girl, in a modest modicum of stocking, represented the ballet by
dancing the Highland Fling, always the Highland Fling. Such
plays as "The Lady of Lyons" happened now and then, and
"The Daughter of the Regiment" must have been, at least partly,
sung. We did not lack the more darkling melodrama, and there
were heroic pieces which gave the leading actor opportunities
not lost upon him, however they failed of effect with the rest of
the cast. I remember how one night a robustuous periwig-pated
fellow ramped and roared up and down the stage, but left quite
cold a large group of the *dramatis personæ* which his magnilo-
quence was intended to convulse either with sympathy or an-
tipathy; and how Reed noted with mock-thoughtful recognition of the situation, "Can't excite those fellows off to the left,
any." I should not be able to say how killingly droll I found this.

VII

I suppose that every young man presently attempting journalism feels something of the pride and joy I felt when I began
it; though pride and joy are weak words for the passion I had
for the work. If my soul was more in my verse, I did not know
it, and I am sure my heart was as much in my more constant
labors. I could find time for poetry only in my brief noonings,
and at night after the last proofs had gone to the composing-
room, or I had come home from the theatre or from an evening
party, but the long day was a long delight to me over my desk
in the room next my senior. To come upon some inviting fact,
or some flattering chance for mischief in an exchange, above all
a Northern contemporary with Southern principles, and to take
this to him and talk it or laugh it over and leave it with him, or
bring it back and exploit it myself, was something that made
every day a heyday. We shunned personalities, then the stock
in trade of most newspaper wits; we meant to deal only with the
public character of men and things. It seems to have been all
pleasure as I tell it, but there was a great deal of duty in it too;

though if burlesquing the opposite opinions of our contemporaries happened to be a duty, so much the better. If it were to do again, I should not do it, or not so much; but at the time I cannot deny that I liked doing it. So, too, I liked to write cutting criticisms of the books which it was part of my work to review; and I still hope to be forgiven by the kindness which I sinned against without winning the authority as reviewer which I aimed at.

I had much better been at the theatre than writing some of the things I then wrote. But it may as well be owned here as anywhere that whatever might have been its value to me as a school of morals the theatre was not good society in Columbus then; and I was now in a way of being good society, and had been so for some time. The rehabilitation of our newspaper was coincident with the rise of the Republican party to the power which it held almost unbroken for fifty years. It had of course lost the presidential election in 1856, but its defeat left it in better case than an untimely victory might have done. Ohio had at any rate a Republican governor in a man afterwards of a prime national importance, and already known as a statesman-like politician well fitted by capacity and experience for that highest office which never ceased to be his aim while he lived. Salmon P. Chase had been a lawyer of the first standing in Cincinnati, where, although a Democrat, he had early distinguished himself by his services in behalf of friendless negroes. The revolt of the whole self-respecting North against the repeal of the Missouri Compromise swept him finally out of the Democracy into that provisional organization which loosely knew itself as the Anti-Nebraska party; but before he was chosen governor by it he had already served a term in the United States Senate, where with one other Freesoiler he held the balance of power in an otherwise evenly divided body. He was a large, handsome man, of a very Senatorial presence, and now in the full possession of his uncommon powers; a man of wealth and breeding, educated perhaps beyond any of the other presidential aspirants except Seward, versed in the world, and accustomed to ease and state; and he gave more dignity to his office, privately and publicly, than it had yet known among us. He lived in a pretty house of the Gothic make then much affected by our too eclectic architecture, with his brilliant young daughter at the head of it; for the governor was a widower.

He was naturally much interested in the new control of the Republican organ, and it would not be strange if he had taken some active part in its rehabilitation, but I do not know that he had. At any rate, he promptly made the editorial force welcome to his house, where Reed and I were asked to Thanksgiving dinner; Mr. Cooke had not yet brought his family to Columbus. Thanksgiving was not then observed on the present national terms; it was still the peculiar festival of New England, and in our capital its recognition was confined to families of New England origin; our Kentuckians and Virginians and Marylanders kept Christmas, though the custom of New Year's calls was domesticated among us with people of all derivations, and in due time suffered the lapse which it fell into in its native New York. Our governor was born in New Hampshire where his family name was already distinguished in public life; and he kept the Thanksgiving which he had probably not officially invited his fellow-citizens to commemorate. I suppose we had turkey for our dinner but I am surer of the manner than the make of the feast, for it was served with a formality new to my unworldly experience. The turkey was set before the governor, who carved it, and then it was brought to the guests by a shining black butler, instead of being passed from hand to hand among them, as I had always seen it done. That was, in fact, my first dinner in society.

The young editors were the only guests; and after dinner the family did not forbid itself the gayeties befitting its young people's years. We had charades, then much affected in society, and I believe the governor alone was not pressed into helping dramatize the riddle to be finally guessed as Canterbury Bell. I do not remember how the secret was kept to the end, or guessed from the successive parts. My fear and pride were put to a crucial test in the first dissyllable, which the girlish hostess assigned me, and nothing but the raillery glancing through the deep lashes of her brown eyes, which were very beautiful, could have brought me to the self-sacrifice involved. I lived through the delight and anguish of that supreme evening, and found myself, as it were almost immediately afterwards in society. It could not have been quite immediately, for when I called at the governor's soon after New Year's and he asked me if I had made many New Year's calls, I answered that I had not made any because I knew no one. Then he said, I might have called at *his* house; and I did not fail, on this kind reproach, to go to Miss Chase's next reception, where again she laughed at my supposed dignity in refusing to dance; she would not suppose my inability.

But before entering that field so flowery fair which society now seemed to open before me, perhaps I had better continue my recollections of a man whose public career has its peculiar pathos. It was his constant, his intense, his very just desire to be president; no man of his long time was fitter to be president, unless his ambition was a foible that unfitted him. He accepted not the first place but the second place in the administration of the man whose place as president he had so ardently longed to fill, and after he had resigned his governorship of Ohio, and gone to Washington as Secretary of the Treasury under Lincoln, I saw him there when I went to look after the facts of the consulship which had been offered me. His fellow Ohioans must have swarmed upon him in the eagerness for public service afterwards much noted in them, and I do not blame him for imagining that I had called upon him in the hope that he would urge my case upon the president. He said, rather eagerly, that he had no influence with the administration, (it likewise became Lincoln's own humorous complaint) quite before I had asked it, and was sorry that he could not help me; and when I thanked him and remarked that I believed the president's private secretaries Hay and Nicolay were interested in my affair, he said with visible relief, Oh well, then, I was in the best possible hands; as indeed it turned out. I had heard before that he had spoken to the president in my behalf, and he may very well have felt that he had done his best.

Four years later, and ten years after my first acquaintance with Chase, I went to call upon him at his hotel in New York, when I was lately returned from my consular post in Venice, and ventured to offer him my congratulations upon his accession to the chief-justiceship of the Supreme Court. He answered bluntly that it was not the sort of office he had aspired to, and intimated that it was a defeat of his real aspirations. He was not commonly a frank man, I believe, but perhaps he felt that he could be frank with the boy I must still have seemed even at twenty-eight, bringing the devotion he possibly over-imagined in me. Since then those words of his, which were the last I was to hear from him, have been of an increasing appeal with me; and if the Republicans had not had Lincoln I still think it was a pity they could not have had Chase. At the end, the Democrats would not have him.

VIII

Chase was of course *our* man for the 1860 nomination, and the political relations between him and our chief were close; but somehow I went more to other houses than to his, though I found myself apparently launched from it upon a social tide that bore me through all the doors of the amiable little city. I was often at the evening parties (we called them evening parties then) which his daughter gave, and one day the governor himself, as we met in the street, invited me to luncheon with him. I duly went and passed the shining butler's misgiving into the dining-room where I found the family at table with no vacant place among them. The governor had forgotten me! That was clear enough, but he was at once repentant, and I lunched with him, outwardly forgiving but inwardly resolved that it should be the last time I would come at his informal bidding. I have since forgotten much more serious engagements myself; I have not gone to dinners where I have promised over my own signature to go; but at twenty-one men are proud, and I was prouder then than I can yet find any reason for having been.

In our capital at that day we had rather the social facts than the social forms. We were invited to parties ceremoniously enough, but we did not find it necessary to answer whether we would come or not. Our hostess remained in doubt of us till we came or did not come; at least that was the case with young men; we never inquired whether it was so with young girls or not. But sometimes when a certain youth wished to go with a certain maiden he found out as delicately as he could whether she was invited, and if she was he begged her to let him go with her, and arrived with her in one of the lumbering two-horse hacks which supplied our cab-service, and which I see still bulking in the far perspective of the State Street corner of the State House yard. If you had courage so high or purse so full you had sent the young lady a flower which she wore to the party: preferably a white camellia which the German florist, known to our young world only as Joe, grew very successfully, and allowed you to choose from the tree. Why preferably a camellia I could not say after this lapse of time; perhaps because its cold, odorless purity expressed the unimpassioned emotion which oftenest inspired the gift and its acceptance. It was very simple, very pastoral; I do not know when Columbus outgrew this custom, which of course it did long ago.

Bringing a young lady to a party necessarily meant nothing but that you enjoyed the pleasure of bringing her. Very likely she found her mother there when she came with you, unmindful, the one and the other, that there was such a thing as chaperonage in a more fastidious or censorious world. It seems to me indeed that parties at the Columbus houses were never wanting in the elders whom our American society of girls and boys used to be accused of ignoring. They superabounded at the legislative receptions, but even at the affairs which my sophistication early distinguished from those perfunctory hospitalities there were mature people enough, both married and unmarried, who, though they had felt no charge concerning their daughters or nieces, found it agreeable to remain till the young ladies were ready to be seen home by their self-chosen escorts. A youth who danced so reluctantly as I, was rather often thrown upon these charitable elders for his entertainment, and I cannot remember ever failing of it. People, and by people I do not mean women only, read a good deal in that idyllic Columbus, and it was my delight to talk with any one who would about the new books or the old. The old books were known mostly to that number of professional men—lawyers, doctors, divines and scientists— which was disproportionately large in our capital; they were each cultivated in his own way, and in mine too or the better part of it, as I found. The young and the younger women read the current fiction and poetry at least enough to be asked whether they had read this thing or that; and there was a group of young men with whom I could share my sometimes aggressive interest in our favorite authors. I put the scale purposely low; I think that I could truthfully say that there was then no American community west of the Alleghanies which surpassed ours in the taste for such things. At the same time I must confess that it would be easy for such an exclusively literary spirit as I was to deceive himself, and to think that he always found what he may have oftener brought.

For a long time after the advent of our new journalism, the kind of writing which we practiced—light, sarcastic, a little cruel, with a preference for the foibles of our political enemies as themes—seemed to be the pleasure of good society, which in that serious yet hopeful time did not object to such conscience as we put into our mocking. Some who possibly trembled at our boldness darklingly comforted themselves for our persiflage by the good cause in which it frisked. When anything very daring came out in the afternoon, the young news-editor in his round of calls could hear the praise of it from charming readers in the evening, or he might be stopped in the street next day and told how good it was by the fathers, or brothers, or brothers-in-law, of those charming readers. It was more like the prompt acclaim the drama enjoys than the slow recognition of literature; but I, at least, was always trying to make my writing literature, and after fifty-odd years it may perhaps be safely owned that I had mainly a literary interest in the political aspects and events which I treated. I felt the ethical quality of the slavery question, and I had genuine convictions about it; but for practical politics I did not care; I wished only to understand enough of them to seize any chance for a shot at the other side which they might give. I had been in the midst of practical politics almost from my childhood; through my whole youth the din of meetings, of rallies, of conventions had been in my ears; but I was never at a meeting, a rally, or a convention; I have never yet heard a political speech to the end. For a future novelist, a realist, that was a pity, I think, but so it was.

In that day of lingering intolerance, intolerance which can scarcely be imagined in this day, and which scarcely stopped short of condemning the mild latitudinarianism of the *Autocrat of the Breakfast Table* as infidelity, every one but a few outright atheists was more or less devout. In Columbus everybody went to church; the different forms of Calvinism drew the most worshippers; our chief was decorously constant with his family at the Episcopal service; but Reed was frankly outside of all ecclesiastical allegiance; and I who no more than he attended any religious service believed myself of my father's Swedenborgian faith; at any rate I could make it my excuse for staying away from other churches, since there were none of mine. While I am about these possibly needless confidences I will own that sermons and lectures as well as speeches have mostly been wearisome to me, and that I have heard only as many of them as I must. Of the three, I prefer sermons; they interest me, they seem really to concern me; but I have been apt to get a suggestive thought from them and hide away with it in a corner of my consciousness and lose the rest. My absences under the few sermons which I then heard must have ended chiefly in the construction or the reconstruction of some scene in my fiction, or some turn of phrase in my verse. Naturally, under these circumstances, the maturer men whom I knew were oftener doctors of medicine than doctors of divinity; in fact I do not think I knew one clergyman. This was not because I was oftener sick than sorry; I was often sorry enough, and very sensible of my sins, though I took no established means of repenting them; but I have always found the conversation of physicians more interesting than that of most other men, even authors. I have known myself in times past to say that they were the saints of the earth, as far as we then had saints, but that was in the later Victorian period when people allowed themselves to say anything in honor of science. Now, it is already different; we have begun to have our doubts of doubt, and to believe that there is much more in faith than we once did; and I, within the present year, my seventy-ninth, have begun to go to church and to follow the sermon with much greater, or more unbroken attention, than I once could, perhaps because I no longer think so much in the terms of fiction, or meditate the muse as I much more used to do.

In those far days I thought prose fit mainly for every-day use in newspaper work. I was already beginning to print my verses in such of the honored Eastern periodicals as would take them: usually for nothing. I wrote for the *Saturday Press*, of New York, which ambitious youth everywhere were then eager to write for, and I wrote for the *Atlantic Monthly* oftener than I printed in it. I have told all this and more in *My Literary Passions* and I will not dwell here upon the whirl of æsthetic emotion in which I eddied round and round at that tumultuous period. In that book I have also sufficiently told the story of my first formal venture in the little volume of verse which I united with my friend John J. Piatt in offering to the world. But I may add here that it appeared just at Christmas time in 1859, from the press of a hopeful young publisher of Columbus who was making his experiment in the disquieting hour when no good thing was expected to come out of our Western Nazareth. We two were of the only four poets west of the Alleghanies who had yet been accepted by the *Atlantic*, and our publisher had the courage to make our book very pretty in print and binding. It was so pretty that I am afraid some readers liked it for its looks; one young lady said that I at least could have no trouble in choosing what Christmas presents I should make my friends. She was that very beautiful girl who easily bore the palm for beauty in Columbus, and I do not yet understand how I was able to reject her unprofessional suggestion with as much pride as if she had been plain. I gave my book to no one, in my haughty aversion from even the shadow of advertising, and most of my friends had their revenge, I suppose, in not buying it.

IX

I had begun now to know socially and intrinsically the little capital which I had known only politically and extrinsically during the two winters passed there as a legislative correspondent. I then consorted with the strangers whom their share in the government made sojourners, and who had little or no local quality to distinguish them from one another. I shared the generalized hospitalities offered them with that instinctive misgiving which I have rather more than hinted; and though I distinguished among them, and liked and valued certain of them, yet I had a painful sense of our common exteriority and impermanence. I cannot say that I ever expected to become part of the proper life of the city, and when suddenly I found myself in that life if not of it, I was very willing to find it charming. How charming it was compared with the life of other cities I had no means of knowing, but now after the experiences, not too exhaustive, of half a century I still feel it to have been charming, with the wilding grace proper to all the West in those days, and the refinement remembered from the varied culture (such culture as there was) of the East and South it derived from.

Not so many people in our town could have known me for my poetry as for my journalism, and I do not pretend that the sexes were equally divided in their recognition. I have intimated my fancy that with most men, men of affairs, men of the more serious callings, the face of the poet was saved by the audacity of the paragrapher. If I could be so sharp, so hard in my comment on the day's events, I could not be so soft as I seemed in those rhymes where I studied the manner of Heine, the manner of Tennyson, and posed in this or that dramatized personality. I cannot flatter myself that I did not seem odd sometimes to many of my fellow-citizens, though I hope that with some of the hardest-headed among them I was acceptable for qualities which recommend average men to one another. Some of that sort made friends with me; some even who were of an entirely diverse political thinking tolerated my mockeries of opinions which they supposed their principles. But neither my pleasure nor my pride was in such friendships. What I wished to do always and evermore was to think and dream and talk literature and literature only, whether in its form of prose or of verse, in fiction, or poetry, or criticism. I held it a higher happiness to stop at a street corner with a congenial young lawyer and enter upon a fond discussion of, say, De Quincey's essays, than to prove myself worthy the respect of any most eminent citizen who knew not or loved not De Quincey. But I held it far the highest happiness to call at some house where there were young girls waiting and willing to be called upon, and to join them in asking and saying whether we had read this or that late novel or current serial. It is as if we did nothing then but read late novels and current serials, which it was essential for us to know one another's minds upon down to the instant; other things might wait, but these things were pressing.

Of course there were some houses where such problems were of more immediate and persistent interest than other houses. Such a house was the ever dear house of the S. family, which made itself a home any hour of the day up to midnight for such youth as had once been adopted its sons. It was not only a literary house, it was even more a musical house, where there was both singing and playing, with interludes of laughing and joking in all forms of seemly mirth, with the whole family, till the little boys of it stumbled up the stairs half asleep. I could not play, but I was sometimes suffered by that large-hearted hospitality to try singing; and I could talk with the best. So, it was

my more than content in the lapses of the music to sit with the
young aunt (she seemed so mature in her later twenties to me
in my earliest) and exchange impressions of the books new and
old that we had been reading. We frequenters of the house held
her in that honor which is the best thing in the world for young
men to feel for some gentle and cultivated woman; I suppose
she was a charming person apart from her literary opinions; but
we did not think of her looks; we thought of her wise and just
words, her pure and clear mind.

It was the high noon of Tennyson and Thackeray and George
Eliot and Dickens and Charles Reade, whose books seemed following one another so rapidly. *The Newcomes* was passing as a
serial through *Harper's Magazine,* and we were reading that with
perhaps more pleasure than any of the other novels and with
the self-satisfaction in our pleasure which I have before this argued was Thackeray's most insidious effect with youth striving
to spurn the world it longed to shine in. We went about trying
to think who in the story was like whom in life, and our kind
hostess was reading it too and trying to think that too; but it
was not well for her to say what she thought in the case of the
handsomest and for several reasons, really, the first among us.
It appeared that she thought he was like Clive Newcome and
that we others were like those friends of his whom in the tale his
nature was shown subordinating. She said something like this to
someone, and when her saying came to us others we revolted in
a body. No, we would not have that theory of our relation to our
friend; and I do not know to what infuriate excess of not calling
for a week we carried our resentment. I do not know how after
the week, if it was so long, we began calling again; but I surmise it was through something said or done by that dear Miss A.,
which made it easy for her sister to modify her wounding theory
into a recognition of the proud equality which bound us friends
together.

We are all dead now, all save me and the youngest daughter
of the house, but as I think back we are all living again, and
others are living who are also dead. Among these is a young lady

visitor from a neighboring city, one of those beautiful creatures who render the Madonna faces of the painters credible, and of a prompt gayety which shared our wonted mirth in its own spirit. Her beauty might have dedicated her to any mysterious fate; beauty is often of such tragical affinition; but not her gayety; and yet the glad die too, and this glad creature within a year had gone to the doom which sent no whisper back to the hearts left life-long aching. Her father was appointed consul to a Mediterranean port, and she sailed with him in the ship which sailed with them both into eternity, unseen, unsignaled, as messageless as if it had been a mist swept from the face of the sea. But well a year before this time and a year after our first meeting in Columbus I saw her in Boston, in a house swept as wholly from the face of the earth as that ship from the face of the sea. I suppose the Courthouse in Boston is an edifice as substantial as it is plain, but for me, when I look at the place where it stands my vision pierces to the row of quiet dignified mansions which once lined that side of Somerset street, and in one of which I somehow knew that I should find with her uncle's family the beautiful creature already so unimaginably devoted to tragedy, to mystery, to the eternal baffle of surmise. It seemed that from often being there she knew the city, so enchanted and enchanting to me then, and she went about with me from one wonder of it to another; and it remains in the glimmer of that association, which no after custom could wholly eclipse. It was a moment of the glad young American life of other days which seems so impossible to after days and generations; and with the Common and its then uncaterpillared elms, with the Public Garden, just beginning in leaf and flower, with the stately dwellings which looked upon those pleasances in the streets long since abandoned to business, with the Public Library, the fine old Hancock House, and the Capitol as Bullfinch designed and left it, and the Athenæum as it used to be, and Faneuil Hall, swarming with memories for my young ardor, and the Old State House, unvisited by its manifold transformations,—the brave little city of the past is full contemporaneous again.

X

As I have said, all they of that Columbus house but one are gone. One of the little boys went before they were men, and then the other; the mother went long afterwards; the elder daughter, who had been the widow of our repudiated Clive Newcome, went longer afterwards yet; and then still later, finding myself once on a very mistaken lecturing-tour in Kansas, where our beloved Miss A. had lived many married years, I asked for her, hoping to see her, and heard that she had died the year before. But first of all, the father died, leaving me the memory of kindness which I hardly know how to touch aright. He was my physician as well as my friend, and saw me through the many maladies, real and unreal, of my ailing adolescence, but he would have no fee for curing me of either my pains or my fears. I had come to him first with my father, who somehow knew him before me, and it was as if he became another father to me. Often in those nights of singing and playing, of talking and joking, he would look in for a moment between patients to befriend our jollity; and when at last it came to my leaving Columbus, and going that far journey to Venice, whither I seemed bound as on a journey to another planet, he asked me one night into his little outside office by the State Street gate, and had me tell him what provision I had made for the chances before me. I told him, and then whether he thought it not enough in that war-time when the personal risks were doubled by the national risks, he said, "Well, I am not a rich man, or the son of a rich man, but if you think you need something more, I can let you have it." I had been keeping my misgivings to myself, but now I owned them and borrowed the two hundred dollars which he seemed to have there with him, as if in expectation of my need.

For a darker tint in the picture I have been painting of my past let me record here a fact which may commend itself for the younger reader's admonition; the old cannot profit by it, perhaps, though as long as we live we are in danger of forgetting kindness. When my family first came to Columbus we were much beholden to another family, poor like ourselves, which did everything but turn itself out of doors to let us have the little house we were to occupy, after them. They shared it with us till they could place themselves elsewhere; and my father and mother remained bound to them in willing gratitude. When I came back to the capital after my five years of exile in our village, I too remembered our common debt; but when the world began to smile upon me, I forgot the friends who had not forgotten me, till one day my father wished me to go with him to see them. The mother of the family received me with a sort of ironical surprise, and then her hurt getting the better, or the worse, of her irony, she said some things about my losing sight of humble friends in the perspectives opening so alluringly before me. I could not recall, if I would, just the things she said, but they scorched, and the place burns yet; and if I could go back and repair the neglect which she brought home to me, how willingly, after nearly sixty years, would I do it! But at the time I hardened my heart, and as I came away I tried to have my father say something in extenuation of the fault which I angrily tried to make a merit of; but with all his tenderness for me he would not or could not.

Perhaps he too thought that I had been a snob, a thing that I had not needed the instruction of Thackeray to teach me the nature of; but I hope I was not so bad as that; I hope there was nothing meaner in me than youth flattered out of remembrance of old kindness by the new kindness in which it basked. I will confess here that I have always loved the world, and the pleasures which other sages pretend are so vapid. If I could make society over, or make it over a little, so that it would be inclusive rather than exclusive, I believe I would still like to go into it, supposing it always sent a motor to fetch and carry me, and did not insist upon any sort of personal exertion from me. But when I was between twenty and twenty-three and lived in Columbus, I was willing to be at almost any trouble for it. All up and down the wide shady streets which ran from High eastward and were called Rich and Town and State and Broad, there were large pleasant houses of brick, with or without limestone facings, standing in lawns more ample or less, and showing through their trees the thrilling light of evening parties that burst with the music of dancing from every window. Or if this was not the case with every house, beautiful girls were waiting in every other to be called upon, beside the grates with their fires of soft coal, which no more discriminated between winter and summer than the dooryard trees which seem to have been full-foliaged the whole year round.

It may be that with the passage of time there began to be shadows in the picture otherwise too bright. It seems to me that in time the calls and balls may have begun to pall, and a subtle *Weltschmerz*, such as we had then, to pierce the heart; but scarcely any sense of that remains. What is certain is that the shadow of incredible disaster which was soon to fill the whole heaven, still lurked below the horizon, or if it showed itself there, took the form of retreating clouds which we had but to keep on laughing and singing in order to smile altogether out of sight. The slavery question which was not yet formidably a question of disunion was with most of the older men a question of politics, though with men like Dr. S. it was a question of ethics; with the younger men it was a partisan question, a difference between Democrats and Republicans; with me it was a question of emotions, of impassioned preoccupations, and in my newspaper work a question of copy, of material for joking, for firing the Southern heart. It might be brought home to us in some enforcement of the Fugitive Slave Law, as in the case of the mother who killed her children in Cincinnati rather than let them be taken back with her to Kentucky; or in the return of an escaping slave seized in our own railroad station; and there was at first the horror of revolted humanity and then the acquiescence of sickened patience. It was the law, it was the law; and the law was constitutional and must be obeyed till it was repealed. Looking back now to that law-abiding submission I can see that it was fine in its way, and I can see something pathetic in it as well as in the whole attitude of our people, the South and North confronted in that inexorable labyrinth, neither side quite meaning it or realizing it.

That was a very crucial moment indeed, but the crisis had come for us five or six years before when the case of some conscientious citizens arrested in the Western Reserve for violation of that abominable law came before Chief Justice Swann of the Ohio Supreme Court. It was hoped by the great majority of the Republican party and largely expected that Justice Swann's opinion would in whatever sort justify the offenders, and it was known that the Governor would support the decision with an armed force against the United States, which must logically attempt the execution of the law with their troops. Very probably the State of Ohio would have been beaten in such an event, but Justice Swann defeated the popular hope and expectation beforehand by confirming the judgment against those rightminded but wrong-headed friends of humanity. Ohio was spared the disaster which befell South Carolina five or six years later, and Justice Swann suffered the penalty of men whose judgment is different from the convictions of their contemporaries. From being one of the most honored leaders of his party, with the prospect of any highest place in its gift, he remained one of the most distinguished jurists of his time whose best reward came coldly from those who would not blame where they could not praise. In Ohio the judiciary is elective, and Judge Swann hastened the decision of the court before the meeting of the Republican State Convention, in order that his party might not unwittingly renominate him in the expectation of an opinion from him favorable to the good men of Ohio who had broken the bad law of the United States.

There is a legend cherished more for its dramatic possibility than for any intrinsic probability that when Lincoln appointed Noah L. Swayne justice of the Supreme Court of the United States he supposed that he was appointing Joseph Swann, and that he was misled by the similarity of the names, not very great either to ear or eye. Swayne was then one of the most eminent members of the Columbus bar, and though he lacked the juridical experience of Swann was entirely fit for the place he was called to fill. If such a mistake was made it was one which could well retrieve itself, but it seems a very idle fancy which has toyed with its occurrence. It would be altogether too nice in the face of its unlikelihood to inquire whether Lincoln might have wished to express a certain sympathy for the eminent jurist in the arrest of his public career which followed his decision. One would first have to establish the fact of such a feeling in him and prove that if he had it he would have been so careless of the jurist's name as to mistake another name for it. These are the things that happen in fiction where the novelist is hard driven by the exigencies of his plot, but cannot easily occur in sober history.

I met both of these prominent men, during my Columbus years, as an improminent young fellow-citizen might, Justice Swayne rather often, and Justice Swann at least once, in their own houses. On this sole occasion, which dimly remains with me, I was paying one of those evening calls which we youth were diligent in making at houses where there were young ladies; and after due introduction to the great jurist, I was aware of him withdrawn and darkling in the next room, not unkindly, but not sensibly contributing to the gayety of the time in me. That might have been after I was asked to a party at his house, which I was told by a lady versed in such mysteries, was the greatest distinction which society had to offer in our city, and I suppose from this fact that the popular blame for his momentous decision, even if it was of much force, did not follow him into more rarefied air.

XI

We young men of that time were mostly Republicans, but some of us were Democrats and some of us were Southerners or derivatively Southern. I have said how little society with us was affected by New England, even in such a custom as Thanksgiving, and I may go a little farther and say how it was characterized for good as well as for evil by the nearer South rather than the farther East, but more for good than for evil. Many people of

Southern origin among us had chosen a Northern home, because they would rather live in a Free State than a Slave State; they had not cast their sectional patriotism, but when it came to a question of which ideal should prevail, they preferred the Northern ideal. They derived from that South which antedated the invention of the cotton-gin, and which could take a leading part in keeping the Northwestern Territory free, with Ohio the first Free State born of that great mother of Free States. The younger generation of their blood were native Ohioans, and these were not distinguishable from the children of the New-Englanders and the Scotch-Irish Pennsylvanians by anything that I can remember. We had already begun to be Ohioans, with an accent of our own, and I suppose our manners were simpler and freer than those of the East, but the American manners were then everywhere simple and free, and are so yet, I believe, among ninety-nine hundred-thousandths of our ninety-nine millions. It seems to me now that the manners in Columbus were very good, then, among the young people. No one can say, what change the over-muchness of subsequent money may have made in them, but one likes to think the change if any is not for the better. There seems to have been greater pecuniary equality then than there is now; there was an evener sky-line, with scarcely a sky-scraping millionaire breaking it anywhere. Within what was recognized as society there was as much social as pecuniary equality; apparently one met the same people everywhere on that easily ascertained level above the people who worked for their living with their hands. These were excluded, as they always have been excluded from society in all times and places; so that if I had still been a compositor at the printer's case I could not have been received at any of the houses that welcomed me as a journalist, though that did not occur to me then and only just now occurs to me, as something strange and sad; something that forever belies our democracy, but is so fast and deep-rooted in the conditions which our plutocracy has kept from our ancestral monarchies and oligarchies and must keep as long as men live upon one another in the law of competition.

In one house there was more singing and playing, and in another more reading and talking. All the young ladies were beautiful, with the supremacy of that young lady whom it was our poetry to hold so beautiful that no other might contest it. As I believe the use still is in the South, we called them Miss Lilly, Miss Julia, Miss Sally, Miss Fanny, Miss Maggie, whether they were the older or the younger daughters of the family. We were always meeting them at parties, or failing that, or including that, we went to call upon them at their houses. We called in the evening and it was no strange thing for a young man to call every evening of the week, not at one house but at three or four. How, in the swift sequence of the parties, we managed so often to find the young ladies at home, remains one of the mysteries which age must leave youth to solve. Possibly in that sharply foreshortened perspective of the past the parties show of closer succession than they really were.

At most of the houses we saw only the young ladies; it was they whom we asked for; but there were other houses where the mothers of the family received with the daughters, and at one of these my welcome was immediately of a kindness and always of a conscience which it touches me to realize. I was taken at the best I meant as well as the best I was by the friend who was the exquisite spirit of the house, and made me at home in it. My world had been very small, and it has never since been the greatest, but I think yet, as I divined then, that she was of a social genius which would have made her in any great-worldlier capital the leader she was in ours where her supremacy in that sort was no more questioned than the incomparable loveliness of that most beautiful girl whom everyone worshipped. Her house expressed her, so that when her home finally changed to another the new house obeyed the magic of her taste, and put on the semblance of the first, with a conservatory breathing through it the odor of her flowers and the murmur of the dove that lived among them: herself a flower-like and bird-like presence, delicate, elegant, such as might have been fancied of some fine, old-world condition in a new-world reading of it. She lived to rule socially in a community which attested its gentleness by its allegiance to her, until she was past eighty, but when I knew her first she was too young to be titularly accepted as their mother by her stepdaughters and was known to them as their cousin, in what must have been her own convention; but I suppose she liked to be not less than sovereign among her equals. With me she was not only the kindest but the most candid of my friends; my literary journalism and later my literature may have been to her liking, but she never flattered me for them when, as I now know, too much praise had made me hungry for flattery. No young man such as I was then could have had a wiser and faithfuller friend, and I render her memory my tribute, after so many years from a gratitude which cannot be spoken. After so many years I cannot make out whether she accepted or merely suffered my extreme opinions in politics; though she was wholly Ohioan, her husband's family had close affiliations with the South; but hers was certainly a Republican house, as nearly all the houses I frequented were. What may have made her even anticipatively my friend, was our common acceptance of the Swedenborgian philosophy, which long, long afterwards, the last time I saw her, I spoke of as a philosophy. But then she rejected the notion with scorn; it might be a pleasant fancy, she said, but a philosophy, no; and I perceived that she had come the way of that agnosticism which the whole cultivated world had taken. Now I have heard that in her last years she went back to the faith which was perhaps more inherited than reasoned in both of us. But I am sure that it was at first a bond and that she was conscientiously true to this bond of a common spiritual tradition, when upon some public recognition of my work, she reminded me how according to Swedenborg every beautiful thing we said or did was by an influx from the divine. I submitted outwardly, but inwardly I rebelled: not that my conceit of the things I did was so very great; I believe I thought rather modestly of myself for doing them, and I always meant to do much better things; in fact I still have my masterpiece before me; but, poor things as they were, I wished to feel them wholly mine.

For a kindred reason I quite as altogether refused, and more explicitly, the theory of my old friend, Moncure D. Conway, as to the true function of the West in literature. He was then a young Unitarian minister, preaching at Cincinnati an ever-widening liberalism in religion, and publishing a slight monthly magazine named after *The Dial* of Emerson at Concord and too carefully studied from it. For this paler avatar of that transcendental messenger he had asked me for contributions, and so a friendship, which lasted throughout our lives, sprang up between us. When he once came to Columbus he came to lunch with me, and quite took my appetite away by propounding his theory that the West was to live its literature, especially its poetry, rather than write it, the East being still in that darkling period when it could not live its literature. I do not remember the arguments by which he supported his thesis; but proofs as of holy writ could not have persuaded me of it as far as I myself was concerned. My affair was to make poetry, let who would live it, and to make myself known by both the quality and quantity of my poetry. It is not clear to me now how I declared my position without immodesty, but somehow I declared it and so finally that Conway was very willing to carry away with him for his magazine a piece of rhyme which I had last made. He could the more willingly do this, because *The Dial* was one of those periodicals, commoner then than now, that paid rather in glory than in money; in fact it was not expected to pay anything in money, so that I doubly defeated him: I was not only not living my poetry, I was not even living by it.

IV

THE DAYS of the years when youth is finding its way into manhood are not those which have the most flattering memories. It is better with the autobiographer both before and after that time, though both the earlier and later times have much to offer that should keep him modest. But that interval is a space of blind struggle, relieved by moments of rest and shot with gleams of light, when the youth, if he is fortunate, gathers some inspiration for a worthier future. His experiences are vivid and so burnt into him that if he comes to speak of them it will require all his art to hide from himself that he has little to remember which he would not much rather forget. In his own behalf, or to his honor and glory, he cannot recall the whole of his past, but if he is honest enough to intimate some of its facts he may be able to serve a later generation. His reminiscences even in that case, must be a tissue of egotism, and he will merit nothing from their altruistic effect.

I

Journalism was not my ideal, but it was my passion, and I was passionately a journalist well after I began author. I tried to make my newspaper work literary, to give it form and distinction, and it seems to me that I did not always try in vain, but I had also the instinct of actuality, of trying to make my poetry speak for its time and place. For the most part, I really made it speak for the times and places I had read of; but while Lowell was keeping my

Heinesque verses among the *Atlantic* MSS. until he could make sure that they were not translations from Heine, I was working at a piece of realism which when he printed it in the magazine, our exchange newspapers lavishly reprinted. In that ingenuous time the copyright law hung loosely upon the journalistic consciousness and it was thought a friendly thing to reproduce whatever pleased the editorial fancy in the periodicals which would now frowningly forbid it, but with less wisdom than they then allowed it, as I think. I know that as its author, the currency of *The Pilot's Story* in our exchanges gave me a joy which I tried to hide from my senior in the next room; and I bore heroically the hurt I felt when some of the country papers printed my long, overrunning hexameters as prose. I had studied the verse not alone in Longfellow's "Evangeline," but in Kingsley's "Andromeda," and Goethe's "Hermann and Dorothea," while my story I had taken from a potentiality of our own life, and in the tragedy of the slave girl whose master gambles her away at *monte* on a Mississippi steamboat, and who flings herself into the river, I was at home with circumstance and scenery. I still do not think the thing was ill done, though now when I read it (I do not read it often) I long to bring it closer to the gait and speech of life. The popularity of the piece had its pains as well as pleasures, but the sharpest anguish I suffered was from an elocutionist who was proposing to recite it on the platform, and who came to me with it, to have me hear him read it. He did not give it with the music of my inner sense, but I praised him as well as I could till he came to the point where the slave girl accuses her master with the cry of—

> "Sold me! Sold me! Sold! And you promised to give me my freedom!",

when he said, "And here I think I will introduce a shriek." "A shriek?" I faltered. "Yes, don't you think it would fill the suspense that comes at the last word 'Sold!'? Something like this," and he gave a screech that made my blood run cold, not from the sensibility of the auditor, but the agony of the author.

"Oh, no!" I implored him, and he really seemed to imagine my suffering. He promised to spare me, but whether he had the self-denial to do so I never had the courage to inquire.

In the letters to my sister which I was so often writing in those Columbus years, I find record of the constant literary strivings which the reader shall find moving or amusing as he will. "I have sold to Smith of the Odd Fellows' Monthly at Cincinnati, that little story I read to you early last summer. I called it 'Not a Love Story'. He gave me six dollars for it; and he says that as soon as I have time to dress up that translation which B. rejected, he will buy that. At the rate of two dollars a page, it will bring me sixteen or eighteen dollars. 'Bobby',"—I suppose some sketch,—"is going the rounds of the country papers. The bookseller here told our local editor that it was enough to make anybody's reputation—that he and his family laughed prodigiously over it. . . . I have the assurance that I shall succeed, but at times I tremble lest something should happen to destroy my hopes. I think, though, that my adversity came first, and now it is prosperity lies before me. I am going to try a poem fit to be printed in the *Atlantic*. They pay Fullerton $25 a page. I can sell, now, just as much as I will write."

It was two years yet before that poem I was trying for the *Atlantic* was fit, and sold to the magazine for $25, though it was three pages long. I was glad of the pay, but the gain was nothing to the glory; and with the letter which Lowell wrote me about it in the pocket next my heart, and felt for to make sure of its presence, every night and morning and throughout the day, I was of the potentiality of immeasurable success. I should have been glad of earning more money, for there were certain things I wished to do for those at home, which I could not do on my salary of ten dollars a week, already beginning to be fitfully paid. Once, I find that I had not the money for the white gloves which it seems I expected myself to wear in compliance with usage at a certain party; and there were always questions of clothes. Dress coats were not requisite then and there; the young men wore frock coats for the evening, but I had ambitiously provided my-

self with the other sort upon the example of a friend who wore
his all day; I wore mine outdoors once by day, and then pre-
sciently dedicated it to evening calls. The women dressed beautifully, to my fond young taste; they floated in airy hoops; they
wore Spanish hats with drooping feathers in them, and were as
silken balloons walking, in the streets where men were apt to go
in unblacked boots and sloven coats and trousers. The West has
of course brushed up since, but in that easy-going day the Western man did not much trouble himself with new fashions or new
clothes.

II

Whether the currency of *The Pilot's Story*, and the *Atlantic* publication of my Heinesque poems added to my reputation in our
city I could not say. It was the belief of my senior on the newspaper, that our local recognition was enervating and that it had
better go no farther, but naturally I could not agree with a man
of his greater age and observation, and it is still a question with
me whether recognition hurts when one has done one's best. I
cannot recall that I ever tried to invite it; I hope not; but certainly I worked for it and hoped for it; and I doubt if any like experiment was ever received with more generous favor than ours
by a community which I had reasons for knowing was intelligent
if not critical. Our paper, if I may say it, was always good society, but after a while and inevitably, it became an old story, or at
least an older story than at first, though it never quite ceased to
be good society. There remained the literary interest, the æsthetic
interest for me, after the journalistic interest had waned; there
was always the occasion, or the occasion could always be made.
Passages in those old letters home remind me that we talked long
and late about *The Marble Faun*, one night at a certain house;
at another we talked about other books from nine o'clock on, I
imagine till midnight. At another, the young lady of the house
"sang about a hundred songs." At still another the girl-hostess
said, "You haven't asked me to sing to-night but I will sing,"

and then sang divinely, half the night away, for all I know. There was a young lady who liked German poetry, and could talk about Goethe's lyrics; and apparently everywhere there were the talking and the laughing and the singing which fill the world with bliss for youth.

Perhaps I sacrifice myself in vain by my effort to impart the sense of that past which faded so long ago; perhaps some readers will hold me cheap for the fondness which recurs to it and lingers in it. But I believe that I prize its memories because they seem so full of honor and worship for the girlhood and womanhood which consecrate it in my remembrance. Within this gross world of ours as it now is, women are still so conditioned that they can lead the life of another and a better world, and if they shall ever come to take their rightful share of the government of the world as men have made it, I believe they will bring that other and better world of theirs with them and indefinitely advance the millennium. I have the feeling of something like treason to the men I knew in that time, when I own that I preferred the society of women to theirs, but I console myself with the reflection that they would probably have said the same as to mine. Our companionship could hardly have chosen itself more to my liking. It was mainly of law-students, but there was here and there one engaged in business, who was of a like joking and laughing with the rest. We lived together in a picturesque edifice, Gothic and Tudor, which had been meant for a medical college, and had begun so, and then from some financial infirmity lapsed to a boarding-house for such young men as I knew, though we were not without the presence of a young married pair, now and then, and even a young lady, a teacher or the like, who made us welcome when we ended a round of evening calls outside by calling on them from room to room. In my boyhood days at Columbus I was sometimes hustled off the sidewalk by the medical students coming from the College, then in its first prosperity, and taking up the whole pavement as they swept forward with interlinked arms. This was at noontime, when they were scarcely less formidable than the specters which after dark swarmed from the dissecting-room, and challenged the boy to a trial of speed in escaping them. Now the students had long been gone from the College and I dwelt in its precincts with such other favorites of fortune as could afford to pay three dollars and a half a week for their board. The table was even superabundant, and the lodging was almost flatteringly comfortable, after experience of other places. I can only conjecture that the rooms we inhabited had been meant for the students or professors when the College was still a medical college. They were large, and to my untutored eye, at least, were handsome, and romantically lighted by windows of that blend of Tudor and Gothic which I have mentioned, but their architecture showed more on the outside than on the inside, and of course the pinnacles and towers of the edifice were more accessible to the eye without. It was the distinction of people who wished to be known for a correct taste to laugh at the architecture of the College, and perhaps they do so still, but I was never of these. For me it had, and it has, a charm which I think must have come from something like genius, if not quite genius, in the architect, to whose daring I would like to offer this belated praise. At any rate it was the abode of entire satisfaction to me in those happy years between 1857 and 1860, when I could not have wished other companionship than I had there.

There could have been no gayer table than we kept, where we made the most of one another's jokes, and were richly personal in them, as youth always is. The management was of the simplest, but not incompatible with dignity, for the landlord waited upon the table himself, and whoever the cook might be, the place was otherwise in the sole charge of an elderly maid, with a curious defect of speech, which kept her from answering, immediately or ultimately, any question or remark addressed to her. We valued her for this impediment because of the pathetic legend attaching to it, and we did not value her the less, but the more, because she was tall and lank and uncouth of face and figure though of a beauty in her absolute faithfulness to her duties and the kindness beyond them which she always showed. The legend was that in her younger if not fairer time she had been married, and when one day her husband, suddenly killed in an accident, was brought home to her, she tried to speak, but could not speak, and then ever afterwards could only speak after great stress, and must often fall dumb, and go away without speaking.

I do not know whether we really believed in this or not, but we behaved as if we did, and revered the silent heroine of the tragedy as if it were unquestionably true. What kept me from trying to make it into a poem, I cannot say, but I would like to think it was that I felt it above rather than below the verse of even the poet I meant to be. How many rooms she had charge of, I could as little say, but I am certain that there were two of us young men in each of them. My own roommate was a poet, even more actual than myself, though not meaning so much as I to be always a poet; he was reading law, and he meant to practice it, but he had contributed two poems to the *Atlantic Monthly*, before any of mine had been printed there. This might have been a cause of bitterness with me. His work was certainly good enough to be a cause of bitterness, and perhaps I was not jealous because I felt that it would be useless; I should like to believe I was not even jealous of him for being so largely in society before I was. Later, when we came in from our evening calls, we sometimes read to each other, out of what books I could not say now, but probably some poet's; certainly not our own verse: he was too wise for that and I too shy.

He was then reading law, and sometime in my middle years at Columbus he left us to begin his law practice farther West. In noticing his departure as a friendly journalist should, I obeyed his wish not to speak of him as a poet; that, he said, would injure him with his new public; but whether it would or not I am not sure; the Western community is sometimes curiously romantic, and does not undervalue a man for being out of the common in that way. What really happened with him was that being of a missionary family and of a clerical tradition, he left the law, in no great time, and studied divinity. It was a whole generation afterwards before I saw him again; and now his yellow hair and auburn beard of the early days were all one white, but his gentle eyes were of the old hazel, undimmed by the age that was creeping upon us both. He had followed me with generous remembrance and just criticism in my fiction; and again he made me a sort of professional reproach for dealing in my novels (notably in *A Modern Instance*) with ethical questions best left to the church, he thought. I thought he was wrong, but I am not sure that I so strenuously think so now; fiction has to tell a tale as well as evolve a moral, and either the character or the principle must suffer in that adjustment which life alone can effectively manage. I do not say ideally manage, for many of the adjustments of life seem to me cruel and mistaken. If it is in these cases that religion can best intervene, I suppose my old friend was right; at any rate, he knows now better than I, for he is where there is no manner of doubt, and I am still where there is every manner of doubt.

I believe, in the clerical foreshadowing of his future, perhaps, he was never of those wilder moments of our young companionship, when we roamed the night under the summer moon, or when we foregathered around the table in a booth at the chief restaurant, and over a spirit-lamp stewed the oysters larger and more delicious than any to be found now in the sea; or when in the quarter hours of digestion which we allowed ourselves after our one-o'clock dinner we stretched ourselves on the grass, often sunburnt brown, before the College and laughed the time away at anything which pretended itself a joke.

We Collegians were mostly Republicans as most of the people we knew were. A few young men in society were not, but they were not of our companionship, though we met them at the houses we frequented, and did not think the worse of them for being Democrats. In fact, there was no political rancor outside of the newspapers, and that was tempered with jocosity. Slavery had been since the beginning of the Nation, the heritage of the States from the Colonies, and it had been accepted as part of the order or disorder of things. We supposed that sometime, somehow, we should be rid of it, but we were not sanguine that it would be soon; and with so many things of pressing interest, the daily cares, the daily pleasures, the new books, the singing and laughing and talking in the pleasant houses, I could leave the question of slavery in abeyance, except as a matter of paragraphing. There had been as many warnings of calamity to come as ever a people had. There had been the breaking of solemn promises from the South to the North; there had been the bloody fights between the sections in Kansas and the treacheries of the national government; there had been the quarrels and insults and violences in Congress; there had been the arrests and rescues of fugitive slaves; there had been the growth of hostile opinion, on one side fierce and on the other hard, maturing on both sides in open hate. There had been all these portents, and yet when the bolt burst from the stormy sky and fell at Harper's Ferry we were as utterly amazed as if it had fallen from a heaven all blue.

III

. Only those who lived in that time can know the feeling which filled the hearts of those who beheld in John Brown the agent of the divine purpose of destroying slavery. Men are no longer so sure of God's hand in their affairs as they once were, but I think we are surer that He does not authorize evil that good may come, and that we can well believe the murders which Brown did as an act of war in Kansas had not His sanction. In the mad skurry which followed the incident of Harper's Ferry in 1859 some things were easily shuffled out of sight. Probably very few of those who applauded or palliated Brown's attempt knew that he had taken men from their wives and children and made his partizans chop them down that their death might strike terror into the proslavery invaders, while he forbore from some strange policy to slaughter them with his own hand. His record was not searched to this dreadful fact in my knowledge, either by the Democrats who tried to inculpate the Republicans for his invasion of Virginia, or by the Republicans who more or less disowned him. What his best friends could say and what most of them believed, was that he had been maddened by the murder of his sons in Kansas, and that his wild attempt was traceable to the wrongs he had suffered. His own dignity as he lay wounded and captive in the engine-house at Harper's Ferry where the volunteer counsel for the prosecution flocked upon him from every quarter, and questioned him and cross-questioned him, did the rest, and a sort of cult grew up which venerated him before his death. I myself was of that cult, as certain fervent verses would testify, if I here refused to do so. They were not such very bad verses, as verses, though they were technically faulty in places, but in the light which Mr. Oswald Villard's history of John Brown has finally cast upon that lurid passage of his life, I perceive that they were mistaken. He was not bloodier than most heroes, but he was not a martyr, except as he was willing to sacrifice himself along with others for a holy cause, and he was a saint only of the Old Testament sort of Samuel who hewed Agag in pieces before the Lord. But from first to last he was of the inevitable, and the Virginians could no more have saved themselves from putting him to death than he could have saved himself from venturing his life to free their slaves. Out of that business it seems to me now that they came with greater honor than their Northern friends and allies. The South has enough wrongs against the negroes to answer for in the past and in the present, but we cannot lay wholly to its charge the fate of the slave's champion; he was of the make of its own sons in his appeal to violence, and apparently the South understood him better than the North. There was then no evil too great for us to think or say of the Virginians, and yet after they could free him from the politicians, mainly Northern, who infested him in the first days of his captivity, to make political capital or newspaper copy out of him, the Virginians tried him fairly, as those unfair things called trials go, and they remained with a sort of respect for him which probably puzzled them. Long after, twenty-five years after, when I was in an ancient Virginia capital, it was my privilege to meet some of Governor Wise's family; and I noted in them this sort of retrospective respect for Brown; they were now of Republican politics, and I found that I was not nearly

Black Republican enough for them. But in the closing months of the year 1859 there was no man so abhorred and execrated by the so-called Black Republicans as Governor Wise.

Without going to the files of our own newspaper I cannot now say just how we treated the Harper's Ferry incident from first to last, but I am safe in saying that it was according to the temperament of each writer. Our chief, who wrote very well when he could detach his interest from the practical politics so absorbing in the capital of a State like Ohio, may have struck the key-note of our opinion in an able leader, and then left each of us to follow with such music as responded in us. My vague remembrance of the result is the daily succession of most penetrating, most amusing comments from my senior. The event offered him the opportunity of his life for that cold irony he excelled in, and which he knew how to use so effectively in behalf of a good cause; I do not believe it was ever employed in a bad one. The main contribution to the literature of the event from his junior that I can distinctly recall was that ode or that hymn to John Brown, for which I cannot yet be ashamed or sorry, however I must rue the facts that have forever spoilt my rapture in it. I have the sense of a pretty constant passing from the room where I was studying the exchanges for material, and trying to get my senior's laugh for something I had written, or staying for him to read me the article he had just begun or finished. It was a great time, though it was a dreadful time, so thick with forecast, if we had only known it, of the dreadfuller time to follow.

While I have been saying this I have been trying to think how much or little our community was shaken by an event that shows so tremendous in the retrospect, and it seems to me little rather than much. People knew the event was tremendous, but so had the battles in Kansas been, and so had the attack on Sumner in the Senate Chamber, and so had the arrests and rescues of the fugitive slaves. They were of the same texture, the same web which fate was weaving about us, and holding us faster, hour by hour and day by day while we felt ourselves as free as ever. There must have been talk pretty constant at first, but dying away without having really been violent talk among people who differed most about it. What I think is that most people were perhaps bewildered, and that waiting in their daze they did not say so much as people would now imagine their saying. Or it may be that my memory of the effect is a blur of so many impressions that it is impossible to detach any from the mass; but I do not think this probable. The fact probably is that people did not realize what had happened because they could not, because their long experience of enmity between the South and North had dulled them too much for a true sense of what had happened.

But I wrote home to my father my disappointment that his paper had not had something "violent" about the John Brown raid. My head, which abstractly passionate and concretely descriptive rhymes had once had wholly to themselves, was now filled with John Brown when it could be relieved of a news-editor's duty; I thought of him and him only, except when I was making those perpetual calls at those pleasant houses where the young ladies were singing or talking every night. I got some consolation from one of the delightful German editors whom I seemed to know in those days. He was a '48 man, and he carried in his leg a ball which some soldier of the king had planted there, one day, when my friend stood behind a barricade in Berlin. He told me, as I read in one of my old letters home, that he had been teaching his children the stories of Schiller, the good poet of freedom, of Robert Blum, the martyr of liberty, and of our John Brown. He says, "My liddle girl, ven I deached dem to her, she veeped."

But I cannot recall having spoken of Brown with my friend Dr. S. whom I was so apt to speak with of the changing aspects of the slavery question, though I remember very well his coldness to my enthusiasm for the young English poet Richard Realf, who was so grotesquely Secretary of State in the Republic Brown had dreamed out, but who had passed from Canada with his department before the incident at Harper's Ferry, and was in Texas at the time of it and of the immediately ensuing events. What affair of state brought him to Columbus, after the death of his leader and comrades, I did not understand, and I cannot understand yet how he could safely be there within easy reach of any United States Marshal, but he was no doubt much safer there than in Texas, and he stayed some days, mainly talking with me about himself as a poet rather than as a Secretary of State. He interested me, indeed, much more as a poet, for I already knew him as the author of some Kansas war lyrics, which I am not sure I should admire so much now as I did then. He was a charming youth, perhaps my senior by two years, and so about twenty-four, gentle mannered, sweet voiced, well dressed, and girlishly beautiful. I knew, as he was prompt and willing to tell me again, that he had been a protégé of Lady Byron's, and that while in her house he had fallen in love with a young kinswoman of hers, and was forced to leave it, for with all his gifts he was the son of an agricultural laborer, and for that reason no desirable match. Yet Lady Byron seemed to have remained fond of him; she had helped him to publish a volume of verse which he had called *Guesses at the Beautiful* (I envied him the title) and at parting she had given him a watch for a keepsake, and money to bring him to America. He showed me the watch, and I dare say the volume of poems, but I am not sure as to this, and I vouch for no particular of his story, which may very well have been wholly true. In the long walks and long talks we had together, when he cared more to speak of his literary than his military life, I cannot make out that he expected to help further in any attack upon the South. Apparently he shared the bewilderment which everyone was in, but he did not seem to be afraid or anxious for himself as part of the scheme that had so bloodily failed. He was not keeping himself secret, and he went on to Canada as safely as he had come from Texas, if indeed he went to Canada. While he was briefly with us a hapless girl, of those whom there is no hope for in this life, killed herself, and Realf went to the wicked house where she lay dead, out of some useless pathos, since she *was* dead. I reported the fact to my friend Dr. S., with a faltering tendency, I am afraid, to admire Realf for it, and the doctor said coldly: Yes, he had better kept away; his motive had already been scandalously construed. It was this world speaking at its best and wisest, but I am not sure that it altogether persuaded me.

IV

Realf's stay in Columbus must have been in that time of abeyance between Brown's capture and his death; but it must have been after the hanging at Charlestown that one night I was a particle of the crowd which seemed to fill the State House yard on its western front, dimly listening to the man whose figure was a blur against the pale stone. I knew that this man was that Abraham Lincoln who had met Stephen A. Douglas in the famous Illinois debates, and who was now on his way home to Illinois from his recognition in the East as a man of national importance. I could not well hear what he said, and I did not stay long; if I had heard perfectly, I might not, with my small pleasure in public speaking, have stayed long; and of that incident, and of the man whom history had already taken into her keeping, and tragedy was waiting to devote to eternal remembrance, I have only the vision of his figure against the pale stone, and the black crowd spread vaguely before him. Later I had a fuller sense of his historic quality, but still so slight, when he stood on the great stairway within the State House, and received the never-ending crowd which pushed upward, man and woman after man and woman, and took his hand, and tried to say something as fit as it was fond. That would have been when he was on the journey, which became a flight, to his inauguration as President at Washington. He had been elected President, and the North felt safe in his keeping, though the dangers that threatened the nation had only gathered denser upon it, and the strange anomaly which called itself the government had been constantly betraying itself to the hostility within it and without.

The people who pushed upward to seize the great hand held out to every one looked mostly like the country folk such as he had been of, and the best of him always was, and I could hear their hoarse or cracked voices as they hailed him, oftenest in affectionate joking, sometimes in fervent blessing; but for anything I could make out he answered nothing. He stood passive, submissive, with the harsh lines of his lower face set immovably, and his thick-lashed eyes sad above them, while he took the hands held up to him one after another, and shook them wearily, wearily. It was a warm day such as in late February, or earliest March, brings the summer up to southern Ohio before its time, and brings the birds with it for the delusion of a week or a fortnight; and as we walked out, my companion and I, we left a sweltering crowd within the State House, and straying slowly homeward suffered under a sun as hot as June's.

v

I do not say July's sun or August's, because I wish my reader to believe me, and any one who has known the July or August, or the September even, of southern Ohio has known something worse than tropical heat, if travelers tell the truth of the tropics; and no one could believe me if I said such heat ever came in February or March. There were whole fortnights of unbroken summer heat in Columbus, when the night scarcely brought relief from the day, and the swarming fly ceded, as Dante says, only to the swarming mosquito. Few people, even of those who might have gone, went away; none went away for the season, as the use is now, though it is still much more the use in the East than in the West. There were excursions, to the northern lakes, or to Niagara and down the St. Lawrence; there were even brief intervals of resort to Cape May; but the custom was for people to stay at home, to wear the thinnest clothes, and drink cooling drinks, and use fans, and try to sleep under mosquito bars, after sitting out on the front steps. That was where calls were oftenest paid and received, and as long as one was young the talk did not languish, though how one did when one was old, that is, thirty or forty, or along there, we who were young could not have imagined. There was no sea or any great water to send its cooling breath over the land which stretched from the Ohio River to Lake Erie with scarcely a heave of its vast level. We had not even the satisfaction of knowing that we were suffering from a heat-wave; the notion had not been invented by quarter of a century yet; we suffered ignorantly on and on, and did not intermit our occupations or our pleasures; some of us did not even carry umbrellas against the sun; these we reserved for the rain which could alone save us, for a few hours in a sudden dash, or for a day in the storm that washed the air clean of its heat.

The deluging which our streets got from these tempests was the only cleaning which I can recollect seeing them given. There was indeed a chain-gang which intermittently hoed about in the gutters, but could not be said to clean them, while it remained the opprobrium of our civilization. It was made up mostly of negroes, but there were some drink-sodden whites who dragged a lengthening chain over the dust, or hung the heavy ball which each wore over the hollows of their arms when urged to more rapid movement. Once I saw with a peculiar sense of our common infamy in the sight, a quite well-dressed young man, shackled with the rest, and hiding his face as best he could with eyes fastened on the ground as he scraped it. Somehow it was told me that he had been unjustly sentenced to this penalty, and the vision of his tragedy remains with me yet, as if I had acted his part in it. I dare say it was not an uncommon experience by which when I used to see some dreadful thing, or something disgracefully foolish, I became the chief actor in the spectacle; at least I am certain that I suffered with that hapless wretch as cruelly as if I had been in his place. Perhaps we are always meant to put ourselves in the place of those who are put, or who put themselves, to shame.

Municipal hygiene was then in its infantile, if not in its embryonic stage, and if there was any system of drainage in Columbus it must have been surface drainage, such as I saw in Baltimore twenty-five years later. After the rain the sun would begin again its daily round from east to west in a cloudless sky where by night the moon seemed to reflect its heat as well as its light. They must still have such summers in Columbus, and no doubt the greatest part of the people fight or faint through them as they do in our cities everywhere, but in those summers, even the good people, people good in the social sense, remained, and not merely the bad people who justly endured hardship because of their poverty. I had become accustomed to the more temperate climate of the Lake Shore, and I felt the heat as something like a personal grievance, but not the less I kept at work and kept at play like the rest. Once only I was offered the chance of escape for a few days, (it was in the John Brown year of 1859,) when I was commissioned to celebrate the attractions of a summer resort which had been opened a few hours away from the capital. I had heard much talk of the coolness of White Sulphur, as it was called, and I expected much more than I had heard, but I now got much more than I had expected.

There must have been a break in the heat when at some unearthly hour of the July morning I had taken the train which would leave me at White Sulphur, but in the sleep which youth can almost always fall into I was not sensible of it. I say fell into, but I slept upright as one did on the trains in those times, and when my train stopped at the station which as yet made no sign of being a station I stumbled down the car steps to a world white with frost in the July morning. My foot slid over the new planking of the platform as on ice, and on the way up to the new hotel the fences bristled with the glacial particles which bearded the limbs of the wayside trees, and the stubble of the wheat and fields, and the blades of the corn, and sparkled in the red of the early sun which was rising to complete the devastation. I was in those thinnest summer linens, with no provision of change against such an incredible caprice of the weather, and when I reached the hotel, there was no fire I could go to from the fresh, clean, thrillingly cold chamber with its white walls, and green lattice door, which I was shown into. No detail of the time remains with me, except what now seems to have been my day-long effort to keep warm by playing nine-pins with a Cincinnati journalist, much my senior, but as helpless as myself against the cold. There must have been breakfast and dinner and supper, with their momentary heat, but when I went to bed I found only the lightest summer provision of sheet and coverlet, and I was too meek to ask for blankets.

VI

What account I gave of the experience in print, I cannot say after the lapse of fifty-seven years, but no doubt I tried to make merry over it, with endeavor for the picturesque and dramatic. Through the whole of a life which I do not complain of for lasting so long, though I do not like being old, I have found that in my experiences, where everything was novel, some of the worst things were the things I would not have missed. It had not been strictly in the line of my duty as news-editor to make that excursion, but I dare say I did it gladly, for the reasons suggested. There were other reasons which were to make themselves apparent during the year: on my salary of ten dollars a week I could not afford to be very punctilious; and if I was suffered to stray into the leading columns of the editorial page I could not stand upon the dignity of the news editor if I was now and then invited to do a reporter's work. Besides, there were tremors of insecurity in my position, such as came from the bookkeeper's difficulty in sometimes finding the money for my weekly wage, which might well have alarmed me for the continued working of the economic machine. Like every man who depends upon the will or power of another man to give him work, I served a master, and though I served the kindest master in the world I could not help sharing his risks. It appeared that our newspaper had not been reestablished upon a foundation so firm but that it needed new capital to prop it, after something over a year, and then a business change took place which left me out. I was not altogether sorry, for about the same time my senior resigned and went to Cincinnati to cast in his fortunes as joint owner and editor with another paper. Without him, though I should have fearlessly undertaken the entire conduct of our journal, I should not have felt so much at home in it; for I did not know then as I have learned and said long since that a strong writer, when he leaves a newspaper, leaves a subtle force behind him which keeps him indefinitely present in it. But there was no question of my staying, and though my chief's wish to have me stay almost made it seem as if I were staying, I had to go, and I had to leave him my debtor in two hundred dollars. I hasten to say that the debt was fully paid in no very long time, but it seems to me that the world was managed much less on a cash basis in those days than in these; people did not expect to be paid their money as soon as they had earned it; the economic machine creaked and wabbled oftener, and had to be sprinkled with cool patience when the joints worked dry of oil. This may be my fancy, partly built from the fact that my father in his life of hard work was nearly life-long in debt, while others lived and died as many dollars in debt to him.

It must have been before this humiliating event, which I cannot exactly date, that I was asked to deliver the poem before the Ohio Editorial Convention which used annually to grace its meeting with some expression in verse. There must have been an opening prayer and an address, but I remember neither of these, and I should not be able to remember my poem, or any part of it, if it had not afterwards been printed in our newspaper, from which the kindness of a friend has rescued it for me. I have just read it over, not wholly with contempt, but not without compassion for those other editors who listened to it and could have followed its proud vaticinations but darkly. It appears that I then trusted the promises of a journalistic future which have not all been kept as yet, and that I cast my prophecies in a form and mood which I might have accused Tennyson of imitating if he had not been first with his "In Memoriam."

> The Men that make the vanished past
> So brave, the present time so base,
> And people, with their glorious race,
> The golden future, far and vast!—

All ages have been dark to these,
   The true Knights-Errant! who have done
   Their high achievements not alone
In the remoter centuries;

But ever to their dawn's dim eye,
   Blinded with nightlong sorcery,
   Warring with Shadows seemed to be,—
In victory, seemed to fall and die!

Noons glowed. The poet held each name
   In hushless music to the ear—
   Low for the thinking few to hear,
Loud for the noisy world's acclaim;

And pondering, one that turns the page
   Whereon their story hath been writ,
   Gathers a purer lore from it,
Than all the wisdom of the sage;—

A simple lore of trust and faith
   For life's fierce days of dust and heat,—
   To keep the heart of boyhood sweet
Through every passion, unto death—

To love and reverence his time,
   Not for its surface-growth of weeds,
   But for its goodly buried seeds,—
To hope, and weave a hopeful rhyme!

The vision does not seem very clear even to me now, and I suppose not many of those kind, hard-working country printers and busy city journalists recognized themselves in my forecast of the coming newspaper man. Yet I think there is something in the glowing fancy which is here reflected only in part, and I believe some graduate of our university courses of journalism may possibly do worse than keep my fond dream in mind. In this case, the yawning counting-room may not so soon engulf his high intentions, and keeping clear of that shining sepulchre of noble ideals for a while, he may thank me for my over-generous faith in him.

No one that I can recall specifically thanked me at the time of that editorial convention, though no doubt the usual resolutions thanking the orator and poet were passed. I should be glad to believe that at the ball which crowned our festival some kind woman-soul may have tried to feign a pleasure in my verse which no man-soul attempted; but I have only the memory of my fearful joy in the dance which I seem to have led. I went back to Columbus with such heart as I could, but in the dense foreshortening of the time's events I cannot find that of my own unhorsing from the shining procession of journalists figured in my poem.

I can only be sure that I *was* unhorsed, and then suddenly, to my great joy and even greater surprise, was caught up and given a new mount, with even larger pay. That is, I was now invited to become professional reader for the young publisher who had issued the *Poems of Two Friends,* and who, apparently inspired by the signal failure of that book, imagined establishing a general publishing business in our capital. He followed it with several very creditable books and he seems to have had the offer of many more manuscripts than he could handle. I have no doubt I dealt faithfully with these, and I know that he confided entirely in my judgment, for I was now twenty-three, without a doubt of my own as to my competence. There was one manuscript, offered by a lady who had lived some years in Chile, which I thought so interesting, though so formless, that I wrote it quite over and my friend published it, in a book which I should like to read again; but I have no hope of ever seeing it. He also published a very good Ohio version of Gautier's *Romance of a Mummy,* but our bravest venture was a book which the publisher himself had fancied doing, and which he had fancied my writing. This was the life of Abraham Lincoln, printed with his speeches in the same volume with the life and speeches of Hannibal Hamlin, who was nominated with him on the Presidential ticket at the Republican Convention in 1860. It was the expectation of my friend, the very just and reasonable expectation that I should go to Springfield, Illinois, and gather the material for the work from Lincoln himself, and from his friends and neighbors. But this part of the project was distasteful to me, was impossible; I felt that there was nothing of the interviewer in me, at a time when the interviewer was not yet known by name even to himself. Not the most prophetic soul of the time, not the wisest observer of events, could have divined my loss; and I was no seer. I would not go, and I missed the greatest chance of my life in its kind, though I am not sure I was wholly wrong, for I might not have been equal to that chance; I might not have seemed to the man, whom I would not go to see, the person to report him to the world in a campaign life. What we did was to commission a young law student of those I knew, to go to Springfield and get the material for me. When he brought it back, a sheaf of very admirable notes, but by no means great in quantity, I felt the charm of the material; the wild poetry of its reality was not unknown to me; I was at home with it, for I had known the belated backwoods of a certain region in Ohio; I had almost lived the pioneer life; and I wrote the little book with none of the reluctance I felt from studying its sources. I will not pretend that I had any prescience of the greatness, the tragical immortality that underlay the few simple, mostly humble facts brought to my hand. Those who see that unique historic figure in the retrospect will easily blame my youthful blindness, but those who only knew his life before he overtopped all the history of his time, will not be so ready to censure me for my want of forecast. As it was, I felt the inadequacy of my work, and I regretted it in the preface which owned its hasty performance.

There were several campaign lives of Lincoln which must have seemed better than mine to him; I cannot care now how it seemed to others; but what he thought of it I never knew. Within a few years I have heard that he annotated a copy of it, and that this copy is still somewhere extant in the West; but I am not certain that I should like to see it, much as my curiosity is concerning it. He might, he must, have said some things which could not console me for missing that great chance of my life when I was too young to know it. I saw him twice in Columbus, as I have told here already, and once in Washington as I have told elsewhere. That was when I came from the office of his private secretaries at the White House, secure of my appointment as Consul at Venice, and lingered wistfully as he crossed my way through the corridor. Within no very long time past my old friend Piatt (he of the *Poems of Two Friends*) has told me that Lincoln then meant me to speak to him, as I might very fitly have done, in thanking him for my appointment, and that he had followed me out from the secretaries' room to let me do so. He might have had some faint promptings of curiosity concerning the queer youth who had written that life of him from material which he would not come to him for in person. But without doubting my friend, I doubt the fact; neither Hay nor Nicolay ever mentioned the matter to me in our many talks of Lincoln; and I cannot flatter myself that I missed another greatest chance of my life. Rather, I imagine that he did not know who I was, or could in the least care, under the burdens which then weighed upon him. He might have suspected me an office-seeker without the courage to approach him, instead of the office-seeker whose hopes he had, very likely without vividly realizing it, crowned with joy. I blame myself for not speaking to him, of course, as I blame myself for not having gone to him instead of sending to him for the facts of his past; in any event, with my literary sense, I must have valued those facts; but if Lincoln had not been elected in 1860 he would not have been nominated again; and in that case should I now be reproaching myself so bitterly?

VII

Another fame so akin to Lincoln's in tragedy, and most worthy of mention in the story of his great time, is that of a State Senator of ours in the legislative session of 1860. James A. Garfield, of whose coming to read Tennyson to us one morning in the *Journal* office I have told in *My Literary Passions*, was then a very handsome young man of thirty, with a full-bearded handsome face, and a rich voice suited to reading "The Poet" in a way to win even reluctant editors from their work to listen. It is strange that I should have no recollection of meeting Garfield again in Columbus, or anywhere indeed, until nearly ten years later, when I stopped with my father over a night at his house in Hiram, Ohio, where we found him at home from Congress for the summer. I was then living in Cambridge, in the fullness of my content with my literary circumstance, and as we were sitting with the Garfield family on the veranda that overlooked their lawn I was beginning to speak of the famous poets I knew when Garfield stopped me with "Just a minute!" He ran down into the grassy space, first to one fence and then to the other at the sides, and waved a wild arm of invitation to the neighbors who were also sitting on their back porches. "Come over here!" he shouted. "He's telling about Holmes, and Longfellow, and Lowell, and Whittier!" and at his bidding dim forms began to mount the fences and follow him up to his veranda. "Now go on!" he called to me, when we were all seated, and I went on, while the whippoorwills whirred and whistled round, and the hours drew toward midnight. The neighbors must have been professors in the Eclectic Institute of Hiram where Garfield himself had once taught the ancient languages and literature; and I do not see how a sweeter homage could have been paid to the great renowns I was chanting so eagerly, and I still think it a pity my poets could not have somehow eavesdropped that beautiful devotion. Under the spell of those inarticulate voices the talk sank away from letters and the men of them, and began to be the expression of intimate and mystical experience; and I remember Garfield's telling how in the cool of a summer evening, such as this night had deepened from, he came with his command into a valley of the Kanawha; for he had quickly turned from laws to arms and this was in the beginning of the great war. He said that he noticed a number of men lying on the dewy meadow in different shapes of sleep, and for an instant, in the inveterate association of peace, he thought they were resting there after the fatigue of a long day's march. Suddenly it broke upon him that they were dead, and that they had been killed in the skirmish which had left the Unionist force victors. Then, he said, at the sight of these dead men whom other men had killed, something went out of him, the habit of his life-time, that never came back again: the sense of the sacredness of life, and the impossibility of destroying it. He let a silence follow on his solemn words, and in the leading of his confession he went on to say how the sense of the sacredness of other things of peace had gone out of some of the soldiers and never come back again. What was not their own could be made their own by the act of taking it; and he said we would all be surprised to know how often the property of others had been treated after the war as if it were the property of public enemies by the simple-hearted fellows who had carried the use of war in the enemy's country back into their own. "You would be surprised," he ended, "to know how many of those old soldiers, who fought bravely and lived according to the traditions of military necessity, are now in the penitentiary for horse-stealing."

Once again I memorably met Garfield in my father's house in Ashtabula County (the strong heart of his most Republican Congressional district) where he had come to see me about some passages in Lamon's *Life of Lincoln*, which was then in the hands of my Boston publishers, withheld in their doubt of the wisdom or propriety of including them. I think Garfield was then somewhat tempted by the dramatic effect these passages would have with the public, but he was not strenuous about it, and he yielded whatever authority he might have had in the matter to the misgiving of the publishers; in fact, I do not believe that if it had been left to him altogether he would have advised their appearance. I met him for the last time, in 1879, (when my wife and I were for a week the guests of President Hayes,) as he was coming with Mrs. Garfield on his arm from calling upon us at the White House. He stopped me and said, "I was thinking how much like your father you carried yourself," and I knew that he spoke from the affection which had been many years between them. I was yet too young to feel the resemblance, but how often in my later years I have felt and seen it! As we draw nearer to the door between this world and the next it is as if those who went before us returned to us out of it to claim us part of them.

VIII

I never had any report of the book's sales, but I believe my *Life of Lincoln* sold very well in the West, though in the East it was forestalled by the books of writers better known. In the quiet which followed with a business which is always tending to quiescence (if the mood of the trade when discouraging authors may be trusted) my young publisher suggested my taking $175 of my money, and going to Canada and New England and New York on a sort of roving commission for another work he had imagined. It was to be a subscription book reporting the state and describing the operation of the principal manufacturing industries, and he thought it an enterprise peculiarly suited to my powers. I did not think so, but I was eager to see the world, especially the world of Boston, and I gladly took my $175 and started, intending to do my best for the enterprise, though inwardly abhorring it. The best I could do was to try seeing the inner working of an iron foundry in Portland, where I was suspected of designs upon the proprietorial processes and refused admission; and I made no attempt to surprise the secrets of other manufacturers. But I saw Niagara Falls which did not withhold its glories from me in fear of the publicity which I gave them in my letters to the Cincinnati *Gazette*; and I saw the St. Lawrence River, and Montreal and Quebec, with the *habitant* villages round about them. I also saw the ocean at Portland (not so jealous of its mysteries as the iron foundry); I saw Boston and Cambridge, and Lowell and Holmes, and their publisher Fields; I saw New York and Walt Whitman, and the Hudson River. This has been fully told in my *Literary Friends and Acquaintance*, and need not be told again here; but what may be fittingly set down is that when I arrived home in Columbus I found the publishing business still quieter than I had left it and my friend with no enterprise in hand which I could help him bring to a successful or even unsuccessful issue. In fact he had nothing for me to do, in that hour of mounting political excitement, and this did not surprise me. Neither did it surprise me that my old chief of the *State Journal* should ask me to rejoin him, though it did greatly rejoice me. He was yet in that kind illusion of his that he was working too hard on the paper; he expressed his fear that in the demand made upon his time by public affairs he should not be able to give it the attention he would like, and he proposed that I should return to a wider field in it, on an increased wage; he also intimated that he should now be able to bring up my arrears of salary, and he quite presently did so.

Again I was at the work which I was always so happy in, and I found myself associated in it on equal terms with a man much nearer my own age than my former associate Reed was. My new fellow-journalist had come to our chief from his own region in northwestern Ohio; I do not know but from his old newspaper there. I cannot write the name of Samuel Price without emotion, so much did I rejoice in our relation to the paper and each other, with its daily incident and bizarre excitement, throughout the year we were together. I like to bring his looks before me; his long face with its deep vertical lines beside the mouth, his black hair and eyes, and smoky complexion; his air very grave mostly, but with an eager readiness to break into laughter. It seems to me now that our functions were not very sharply distinguished, though I must have had charge as before of the literary side of the work. We both wrote leading editorials, which our chief supervised and censored for a while and then let go as we wrote them, perhaps finding no great mischief in them. Reed remained the tradition of the office, and if I had formed myself somewhat on his mood and manner, Price now formed himself on mine; and somehow we carried the paper through the year without dishonor or disaster.

It was that year so memorable to me for having five poems published in the *Atlantic Monthly*, two of them in the same number, and I must have been strongly confirmed in my purpose of being a poet. Of course I knew too much of the world, and the literary world, to imagine that I could at once make a living by poetry, but I probably expected to live by some other work until my volumes of poetry should accumulate in sufficient number and sell in sufficient quantity to support me without the aid of prose. As yet I had no expectation of writing fiction; I had not recovered from the all-but-mortal blow dealt my hopes in the failure of that story which I had begun printing in my father's newspaper before I had imagined an ending for it, though I must for several years have been working in stolen moments at another story of village life, which I vainly offered to the *Atlantic Monthly* and the *Knickerbocker Magazine*, and after that for many years tried to get some publisher to bring out as a book. The manuscript must still somewhere exist, and I should not be surprised, if I ever found it, to find myself respecting it for a certain helpless reality in its dealing with the conditions I knew best when I began writing it. But it was still to be nearly ten years before I tried anything else of the sort, and even in *Their Wedding Journey*, which was my next attempt, I helped myself out with travel-adventure in carrying forward a slender thread of narrative. Every now and then, however, I wrote some sketch or study, which I printed in our newspaper, where also I printed pieces of verse, too careless or too slight to be hopefully offered for publication in the East.

IX

I was not only again at congenial work, but I was in the place that I loved best in the world, though as well as I can now visualize the town which had so great charm for me then I can find little beauty in it. High Street was the only street of commerce except for a few shops that had strayed down from it into Town Street, and the buildings which housed the commerce were not impressive, and certainly not beautiful. A few hotels, three or four, broke the line of stores; there was the famous restaurant of Ambos, and some Jewish clothiers; but above all,

besides a music and picture store, there was an excellent bookstore, where I supplied myself from a good stock of German
books, with Heine and Schiller and Uhland, and where one
could find all the new publications. The streets of dwellings
stretched from High Street to the right, over a practically interminable plain, and shorter streets on the left dropped to the
banks of the Scioto where a lower level emulated the inoffensive
unpicturesqueness of the other plain. A dusty bridge crossed the
river, where in the slack-water ordinarily drowsed a flock of
canal-boats which came and went on the Ohio Canal. Some old-
fashioned, dignified dwellings stood at the northern end of High
Street, with the country close beyond, but the houses which I
chiefly knew were on those other streets. I cannot say now
whether they added to the beauty of the avenues or not; I suppose that oftenest they did not embellish them architecturally,
though they were set in wide grounds among pleasant lawns and
gardens. The young caller knew best their parlors in winter and
their porches in summer; there was little or no lunching or dining
for any one except as a guest of pot-luck; and the provisioning
was mainly if not wholly from the great public market. Green
grocers' and butchers' shops there were none, but that public
market was of a sumptuous variety and abundance, as I can
testify from a visit paid it with a householding friend who drove
to it in his carriage, terribly long before breakfast, and provi-
sioned himself among the other fathers and the mothers who
thronged the place with their market-baskets. This was years
after my last years in Columbus, when I was a passing guest;
while I lived there I was citizen of a world that knew no such
household cares or joys.

On my return from my travels, though I was so glad to be
again in Columbus, I no longer gave myself up to society with
such abandon as before. I kept mostly to those two houses where
I was most intimate, and in my greater devotion to literature I
omitted to make the calls which were necessary to keep one in
society even in a place so unexacting as our capital. Somewhat
to my surprise, somewhat more to my pain, I found that society

knew how to make reprisals for such neglect; I heard of parties which I was not asked to, and though I might not have gone to them I suffered from not being asked. Only in one case did I regret my loss very keenly, and that was at a house where Lincoln's young private secretaries, Hay and Nicolay, passing through to Washington before the inauguration, had asked for me. They knew of me as the author of "The Pilot's Story" and my other poems in the *Atlantic Monthly*, as well as that campaign life of Lincoln which I should not have prided myself on so much; but I had been justly ignored by the hostess in her invitations, and they asked in vain. I fully shared after the fact any disappointment they may have felt, but I doubt if I was afterwards more constant in my social duties; I was intending more and more to devote myself to poetry, and with a hand freer than ever, if that were possible, in the newspaper, I was again feeling the charm of journalism, and was giving to it the nights which I used to give to calls and parties.

I did not go back to live in the College, but with Price I took a room and furnished it; we went together for our meals to the different restaurants, a sort of life more conformable to my notion of the life of the literary free-lance in New York. But let not the reader suppose from this large way of speaking that there were many restaurants in Columbus, or much choice in them. The best, the only really good one, was that of Ambos in High Street, where as I have said before we silvern youth resorted sometimes for the mid-night oyster, which in handsome half-dozens was brought us on chafing-dishes, to be stewed over spirit-lamps and flavored according to our taste with milk and butter. We cooked them for ourselves; but our rejected, or protested, Clive New-come was the most skilled in an oyster-stew, and we all emulated him as we sat at the marble table in one of the booths at the side of the room. In hot weather a claret-punch sometimes crowned the night with a fearful joy and there was something more than bacchanalian in having it brought with pieces of ice clucking in a pitcher borne by the mystical Antoine from the bar where he had mixed it: that Antoine whom we romanced as of strange experiences and recondite qualities, because he was of such impregnable silence, in his white apron, with his face white above it, damp with a perennial perspiration, which even in the hottest weather did not quite gather into drops. We each attempted stories of him, and somewhere yet I have among my manuscripts of that time a very affected study done in the spirit and manner of the last author I had been reading.

I suppose he was not really of any intrinsic interest, but if he had been of the greatest I could not have afforded, even on my increased salary, to resort to Ambos's for frequent observation of him. Ambos's was the luxury of high occasions, and Price and I went rather for our daily fare to the place of an Americanized German near our office, where the cooking was very good, and the food without stint in every variety, but where the management was of such an easy kind that the rats could sometimes be seen clambering over the wall of the storeroom beyond where we sat. There was not then the present feeling against those animals, which were respected as useful scavengers, and we were rather amused than revolted by them, being really still boys with boys' love of bizarre and ugly things. Once we had for our guest in that place the unique genius destined to so great fame as Artemus Ward; he shared our interest in the rats, and we joked away the time at a lunch of riotous abundance; I should say superabundance if we had found it too much. For a while also we ate at the house of a lady who set a table faultless to our taste, but imagined that the right way to eat pie was with a knife, and never gave a fork with it. Here for a while we had the company of the young Cincinnati *Gazette* correspondent Whitelaw Reid, joyful like ourselves under the cloud gathering over our happy world. One day, after the cloud had passed away in the thunder and lightning of the four years' Civil War, he came radiant to my little house at Cambridge with a piece of news which I found it as difficult to realize for fact in my sympathy with him as he could have wished. "Just think! Horace Greeley has asked me to be managing editor of the *Tribune*, and he offers me $6000 a year!" A great many years afterwards we met in a train coming from

Boston to New York, when he brought the talk round to the Spanish War, and, for whatever reason, to his part in the Treaty of Paris and the purchase of the Philippines. "*I* did that," he said. But I could not congratulate him upon this as I did upon his coming to the editorship of the *Tribune*, being of a different mind about the acquisition of the Philippines.

X

Sometime during that winter of 1860–61 Greeley himself paid us a visit in the *Journal* office and volunteered a lecture on our misconduct of the paper, which he found the cause of its often infirmity. We listened with the inward disrespect which youth feels for the uninvited censure of age, but with the outward patience due the famous journalist (of such dim fame already!) sitting on the corner of a table, with his soft hat and his long white coat on, and his quaint child-face, spectacled and framed in long white hair. He was not the imposing figure which one sees him in history, a man of large, rambling ambitions, but generous ideals, and of a final disappointment so tragical that it must devote him to a reverence which success could never have won him. I do not know what errand he was on in Columbus; very likely it was some political mission; but it was something to us that he had read the *Journal*, even with disapproval, and we did not dispute his judgments; if we were a little abashed by them we hardened our hearts against them, whatever they were, and kept on as before, for our consciences were as clear as our hearts were light. No one, at that time, really knew what to think or say, the wisest lived from day to day under the gathering cloud, which somehow they expected to break as other clouds in our history had broken; when the worst threatened we expected the best.

Price was not the companion of my walks so much as Reed had been; he was probably of frailer health than I noticed, for he died a few years later; and I had oftener the company of a young man who interested me more intensely. This was the great sculptor, J. Q. A. Ward, who had come to the capital of his native state in the hope of a legislative commission for a statue of Simon Kenton. It was a hope rather than a scheme, but we were near enough to the pioneer period for the members to be moved by the sight of the old Indian-Fighter in his hunting-shirt and squirrel-skin cap, whom every Ohio boy had heard of, and Ward was provisionally given a handsome room with a good light, in the State House, where he modeled I no longer know what figures, and perhaps an enlargement of his Kenton. There I used to visit him, trying to imagine something of art, then a world so wholly strange to me, and talking about New York and the æsthetic life of the metropolis. My hopes did not rise so high as Boston, but I thought if I were ever unhorsed again I might find myself on my feet in New York, though I felt keenly the difference between the places, greater then than now, when literary endeavor is diffused and equally commercialized everywhere. Ward seemed to live much to himself in Columbus, as he always did, but I saw a great deal of him, for in the community of youth we had no want of things to talk about; we could always talk about ourselves when there was nothing else. He was in the prime of his vigorous manhood, with a fine red beard, and a close-cropped head of red hair, like Michelangelo, and a flattened nose like the Florentine's, so that I rejoiced in him as the ideal of a sculptor. I still think him, for certain Greek qualities, the greatest of American sculptors; his Indian Hunter in Central Park must bear witness of our historic difference from other peoples as long as bronze shall last, and as no other sculpture can. But the Kenton was never to be eternized in bronze or marble for that niche in the rotunda of the capitol where Ward may have imagined it finding itself. The cloud thickened over us, and burst at last in the shot fired on Fort Sumter; the legislature appropriated a million dollars as the contribution of the state to the expenses of the war, and Ward's hopes vanished as utterly as if the bolt had smitten his plaster model into dust.

Before Ward, almost indeed with my first coming to Columbus, there had been another sculptor whom I was greatly interested to know. This was Thomas D. Jones, who had returned to Ohio from an attempt upon the jealous East, where he had suffered that want of appreciation which was apt, in a prevalent superstition of the West, to attend any æsthetic endeavor from our section. He frankly stood for the West, though I believe he was a Welshman by birth; but in spite of his pose he was a sculptor of real talent. He modeled a bust of Chase, admirable as a likeness, and of a very dignified simplicity. I do not know whether it was ever put in marble, but it was put in plaster very promptly and sold in many such replicas. The sculptor liked to be seen modeling it, and I can see him yet, stepping back a little from his work, and then advancing upon it with a sensitive twitching of his moustache and a black censorious frown. The governor must have posed in the pleasant room which Jones had in the Neil House where he lived, how I do not know, for he was threadbare poor; but in those days many good things seemed without price to the debtor class; and very likely the management liked to have him there, where his work attracted people. One day while I was in the room the governor came in and, not long after, a lady who appeared instinctively to time her arrival when it could be most largely impressive. As she was staying in the hotel, she wore nothing on her dewily disheveled hair, as it insists upon characterizing itself in the retrospect, and she had the effect of moving about on a stage. She had in fact just come up on some theatrical wave from her native Tennessee, and she had already sent her album of favorable notices to the *Journal* office with the appeal inscribed in a massive histrionic hand, "Anything but your silence, gentlemen!" She played a short engagement in Columbus, and then departed for the East and for the far grander capitals of the Old World, where she became universally famous as Ada Isaacs Menken, and finally by a stroke of her fearless imagination figured in print as the bride of the pugilist Heenan, then winning us the laurels of the ring away from English rivalry. I cannot recall, with all my passion for the theatre, that I saw her on any stage but that which for a moment she made of the sculptor's room.

Jones had been a friend from much earlier days, almost my earliest days in Columbus; it was he who took me to that German house, where I could scarcely gasp for the high excitement of finding myself with a lady who had known Heinrich Heine and could talk of him as if he were a human being. I had not become a hopeless drunkard from drinking the glass of eggnog which she gave me while she talked familiarly of him, and when after several years Jones took me to her house again she had the *savoir faire* quite to ignore the interval of neglect which I had suffered to elapse, and gave me a glass of eggnog again. It must have been in 1859 that Jones vanished from my life, but I must not let him take with him a friend whose thoughtfulness at an important moment I still feel.

This was a man who afterwards became known as the author of two curious books, entitled *Library Notes*, made up somewhat in the discursive fashion of Montaigne's essays, out of readings from his favorite authors. There was nothing original in them except the taste which guided their selection, but they distinctly gave the sort of pleasure he had in compiling them, and their readers will recall with affection the name of A. P. Russell. He was the Ohio Secretary of State when I knew him first, and he knew me as the stripling who was writing in his nonage the legislative letters of the Cincinnati *Gazette*; and he alone remembered me distinctly enough to commend me for a place on the staff of the *State Journal* when Mr. Cooke took control of it. After the war he spent several years in some financial service of the State in New York, vividly interested in the greatness of a city where, as he was fond of saying, a cannon-shot could be heard by eight hundred thousand people; six million people could hear it now if anything could make itself heard above the multitudinous noises that have multiplied themselves since. When his term of office ended he returned to Ohio, where he shunned cities great and small, and retired to the pleasant town where he was born, like an Italian to his *patria*, and there ended his peaceful, useful days. It was my good-fortune in almost the last of these days to write and tell him of my unforgotten gratitude for that essential kindness he had done me so long before, and to have a letter back from him the more touching because another's hand had written it; for Russell had become blind.

Probably he had tried to help Ward in his hope, which was hardly a scheme, for that appropriation from the legislature for his Simon Kenton. They always remained friends, and during Russell's stay in New York he probably saw more of Ward, so often sequestered with the horses for his equestrian groups, than most of his other friends. I who lived quarter of a century in the same city with him saw him seldom by that fault of social indolence, rather than indifference, which was always mine, and which grows upon one with the years. Once I went to dine with him in the little room off his great, yawning, equine studio, and to have him tell me of his life for use in a book of "Ohio Stories" I was writing; then some swift years afterwards I heard casually from another friend that Ward was sick. "Would he be out soon?" I asked. "I don't think he'll be out at all," I was answered, and I went the next day to see him. He was lying with his fine head on the pillow still like such a head of Michelangelo as the Florentine might have modeled of himself, and he smiled and held out his hand, and had me sit down. We talked long of old times, of old friends and enemies, (but not really enemies) and it was sweet to be with him so. He seemed so very like himself that it was hard to think him in danger, but he reminded us who were there that he was seventy-nine years old, and when we spoke about his getting well, and soon being out again, he smiled in the wisdom which the dying have from the world they are so near, and tenderly patient of us expressed his doubt. In a few days, before I could go again, I heard that he was dead.

XI

But in that winter of 1859–60, after Lincoln had been elected, Ward was still hopeful of an order from the state for his Simon Kenton, and I was hopeful of the poetic pre-eminence which I am still foregoing. I used such scraps of time as I could filch from the busy days and nights, and gave them to the verse which now seemed to come back from editors oftener than it once did. This hurt, but it did not kill, and I kept on at verse for years in the delusion that it was my calling and that I could make it my living. It was not until four or five years later that a more practical muse persuaded me my work belonged to her, and in the measureless leisure of my Venetian consulate I began to do the various things in prose which I have mostly been doing ever since, for fifty years past. Till then I had no real leisure, but was yet far from the days when anything less than a day seems too small a space to attempt anything in. That is the mood of age and of middle age, but youth seizes any handful of minutes and devotes them to some beginning or ending. It had been my habit ever since I took up journalism to use part of the hour I had for mid-day dinner in writing literature, and such hours of the night as were left me after my many calls or parties; and now I did not change, even under the stress of the tragical events crowding upon us all.

I phrase it so, but really I felt no stress, and I do not believe others felt it so much as the reader might think. As I look back upon it the whole state of affairs seems incredible, and to a generation remote from it must seem impossible. We had an entire section of the Republic openly seeking its dismemberment, and a government which permitted and even abetted the seizure of national property by its enemies and the devotion of its resources to its own destruction. With the worst coming, relentlessly, rapidly, audibly, visibly, no one apparently thought the worst would come; there had been so many threats of disunion before, and the measures now taken to effect it seemed only a more dramatic sort of threats. People's minds were confused by the facts which they could not accept as portents, and the North remained practically passive, while the South was passionately active; and yet not the whole South, for as yet Secession was not a condition, but merely a principle. There was a doubt with some in the North itself whether the right of disunion was not implied in the very act of union; there had long been a devoted minority who felt that disunion without slavery was better than union with slavery; and on both sides there arose sentimental cries, entreaties from the South that the North would yield its points of right and conscience, appeals from the North that the South would not secede until the nation had time to decide what it would do. The North would not allow itself to consider seriously of coercing the seceding States; and there was a party willing to bid them, with unavailing tears, "Erring sisters, go in peace," as if the seceding States, being thus delicately entreated, could not have the heart to go, even in peace. There were hysterical conferences of statesmen in and out of office, to arrange for mutual concessions which were to be all on the part of the Union, or if not that then to order its decent obsequies.

I cannot make out that our chief had any settled policy for the conduct of our paper; but nobody had a settled policy concerning public affairs. If his subordinates had any settled policy, it was to get what fun they could out of the sentimentalists, and if they had any fixed belief it was that if we had a war, peace must be made on the basis of disunion when the war was over. In our wisdom we doubted if the sections could ever live together in a union which they had fought for and against. But we did not say this in print, though as matters grew more hopeless, Price one day seized the occasion of declaring that the Constitution was a rope of sand. I do not remember what occasion he had for saying this, but it brought our chief actively back to the censorship; Price's position was somehow explained away, and we went on much as before, much as everybody else went on. I will not, in the confession of our youthful rashness, pretend that there were any journalists who seemed then or seem wiser now, or acted with greater forecast; and I am sure that we always spoke from our consciences, with a settled conviction that the South was wrong. We must have given rather an ironical welcome to a sufficiently muddled overture of the Tennessee legislature which during the winter sent a deputation of its members to visit our own Houses, and confer with them as to what might be done.

The incident now has its pathos, there was so much that was well meant in the attempt to mend our bad business with kind words and warm feelings, though then I was sensible only of its absurdity. I did not hear any of the speeches, but I remember seeing the Tennessee statesmen about the capitol for the different conferences held there and noting that some of them spoke with a negroid intonation and not with that Ohio accent which I believed the best in the English-speaking world. No doubt they parted with our own legislators affectionately, and returned home supported by the hope that they had really done something in a case where there was nothing to be done.

Their endeavor was respectable, but there was no change in the civic conditions except from bad to worse. In the social conditions, or the society conditions, everything was for the better, if indeed these could be bettered in Columbus. Of all the winters this was the gayest; society was kind again, after I had paid the penalty it exacted for my neglect, and I began to forget my purpose of living in air more absolutely literary. Again I began going the rounds of the friendly houses, but now, as if to win my fancy more utterly, there began to be a series of dances in a place and on conditions the most alluring. For a while after the functions of the medical school were suspended in the College where I had lodged, the large ward where the lectures were once given was turned into a gymnasium and fitted up with the usual gymnastic apparatus. I do not recall whether this was taken away or not, or was merely looped up and put aside for our dances, and I do not know how we came into possession of the place; in the retrospect, such things happen in youth, much as things happen in childhood, without apparent human agency; but at any rate we had this noble circus for our dances. There must have been some means of joining them, but it is now gone from me, and I know only that they were given under the fully sufficing chaperonage of a sole matron. There were two negro fiddlers, and the place was lighted by candles fixed along the wall; but memory does not serve me as to any sort of supper; probably there was none, except such as the young men, after they had seen the young ladies home from the dance, went up-town to make on the oysters of Ambos.

It is strange that within the time so dense with incident for us there should have been so few incidents now separately tangible, but there is one that vividly distinguishes itself from the others. In that past I counted any experience precious that seemed to parallel the things of fact with the things of fiction. Afterward, but long afterward, I learned to praise, perhaps too arrogantly praise, the things of fiction as they paralleled the things of fact, but as yet it was not so. I suppose the young are always like us as we of the College dances were then, but romance can rarely offer itself to youth of any time in the sort of reality which one night enriched us amid our mirth with a wild thrill of dismay at the shriek in a girl's voice of "Dead?" There was an instant halt in the music, and then a rush to the place where the cry had risen. Somebody had fainted, and when the fact could be verified, it was found that one of the blithest of our company had been struck down with word from home that her sister had fallen dead of heart failure. Then when we began to falter away from the poor child's withdrawal, suddenly another tumult stayed us; a young father, who had left his first-born with its mother in their rooms above while he came down for some turns in the waltz, could not believe that it was not his child that was dead, and he had to be pulled and pushed up-stairs into sight and sound of the little one roused from its sleep to convince him, before he could trust the truth.

Here was mingling of the tragic and the comic to the full admired effect of Shakespearian drama, but the mere circumstance of these æsthetic satisfactions would have been emotional wealth enough; and when I got home on such a night to my slumbering roommate Price I could give myself in glad abandon to the control of the poet whose psychic I then oftenest was, with some such result as I found in a tattered manuscript the other day. I think the poet could hardly have resented my masking in his wonted self-mocking, though I am afraid that he would have

shrunk from the antic German which I put on to the beat of
his music.

> "To-night there is dancing and fiddling
> In the high windowed hall
> Lighted with dim corpse-candles
> In bottles against the wall.

> "And the people talk of the weather,
> And say they think it will snow;
> And, without, the wind in the gables
> Moans wearily and low.

> " '*Sa ! Sa !*'—the dance of the Phantoms!
> The dim corpse-candles flare;
> On the whirl of the flying spectres
> The shuddering windows stare.

> " 'Oh, play us the silent Ghost-Waltz,
> Thou fiddling blackamoor!'
> He hears the ghostly summons,
> He sees the ghosts on the floor.

> "He plays the silent Ghost-Waltz
> And through the death-mute hall
> The voiceless echoes answer,
> In time the ghost-feet fall.

> "Und immer und immer schneller,
> Und wild wie der Winterwind
> Die beide College Gespenster
> Sie walzen sinnengeschwind.

> "They waltz to the open doorway,
> They waltz up the winding stair:
> 'Oh, gentle ghosts we are sneezing,
> We are taking cold in the air.' "

XII

Very likely those dances lasted through the winter, but I cannot be sure; I can only be sure that they summed up the raptures of the time, which was the most memorable of my whole life; for now I met her who was to be my wife. We were married the next year, and she became with her unerring artistic taste and conscience my constant impulse toward reality and sincerity in my work. She was the first to blame and the first to praise, as she was the first to read what I wrote. Forty-seven years we were together here, and then she died. But in that gayest time when we met it did not seem as if there could ever be an end of time for us, or any time less radiant. Though the country was drawing nearer and nearer the abyss where it plunged so soon, few thought it would make the plunge; many believed that when it would it could draw back from it, but doubtless that was never possible; there is a doom for nations as there is for men, and looking back upon our history I cannot see how we could have escaped. The slaveholders in the old Union were a few hundred thousand against many millions, but a force in them beyond their own control, incessantly sought to control the non-slaveholding majority. They did not brook question of their will from others; they brooked no self-question of it; however little they seemed at moments to demand, they never demanded less than that conscience itself should come to their help in making their evil our good. Having said that black was white, that wrong was right, they were vitally bound to compel the practical consent of humanity. It was what it had been aforetime and must be to aftertime; Lincoln did not deny them in terms different from Franklin's, but the case had gone farther. The hour had come when they would not be denied at all; slavery could never keep its promises; it could hardly stay even to threaten. Long before there had been dreams of ending it by buying the slaves, but the owners would not have sold their slaves, and now though the war against slavery tried to believe itself a war for the Union, when it came to full consciousness it knew itself a war for freedom; such freedom, lame and halt, as we have been able to keep for the negroes; a war for democracy, such democracy as we shall not have for ourselves until we have an economic democracy.

The prevision of the young writers on the *State Journal* was of no such reach as this retrospect. The best that could be said of them was that so far as they knew the right, they served it, and it is no bad thing to say of them that they met insolence with ridicule and hypocrisy with contempt. Still, as always before in those columns, they got their fun out of the opportunities which the situation offered, and they did not believe the worst was coming; that would excuse their levity, and it availed as much as gravity. I do not remember that we took counsel with any one as to what we said, or that we consulted much with each other. We did not think that the Union would be dissolved, but if it should be we did not think that its dissolution was the worst thing that could happen; and this was the mind of vastly more at that day than most at this day will believe; some of those who were of that mind then may not like to own it now. People have the habit of saying that only those who have lived through a certain period can realize it, but I doubt if even they can realize it. A civic agitation is like a battle; it covers a surface so large that only a part of it can be seen by any one spectator at any one moment. The fact seems to be that the most of human motives and actions must always remain obscure; history may do its best to record and reveal them, but it will strive in vain to give us a living sense of them, because no one ever had a living sense of them in their entirety.

At the period which I am trying to tell of, the hours passed and the days and weeks and months, bringing us forever nearer the catastrophe; but I could not truthfully say that their passing changed the general mood. The College group which I used to consort with had changed, and it was no longer so much to my liking; it had dwindled, and for me it chiefly remained in the companionship of one friend, whom I walked and talked with when I was not walking and talking with Price. This was that protested and rejected Clive Newcome of ours who in real life was James M. Comly, law student then, and then soldier, and then journalist. Of all the friends in whose contrast I have been trying to find myself, he was temperamentally the most unlike me, but a common literary bent inclined us to each other. In his room there was not only euchre for those who could not bear to waste in idleness the half hours before dinner or supper, but there were the latest fashions in such periodicals as the *Cornhill Magazine*, then so brand new, and the *Saturday Review*, equally new, with the great Thackeray stooping from his Jovian height in the monthly to blunt against the weekly, with its social and critical offensives, such bolts as calling it the *Superfine Review*. Comly was of much the same taste as myself in authors, but not so impassioned; he was not so multifarious a reader and not so inclusive of the poets, and in obedience to his legalist instincts he was of more conservative feeling in politics. We had never a moment of misgiving for each other, yet I had one bad moment over an *Atlantic* poem of mine fabling the author as a bird singing in a tree, and flatteringly but unintelligently listened to by the cattle beneath which the title of the piece typified as "The Poet's Friends." The conceit had overtempted me, but when I had realized it in print, with no sense meantime of its possible relevance, I felt the need of bringing myself to book with the friend I valued most, and urging how innocently literary, how most merely and entirely dramatic the situation was. I think my anxiety amused him, as it very well might, but I still draw a long breath of relief when I remember how perfectly he understood.

Our association was mostly in the walks we took in the winter twilights and the summer moonlights, walks long enough in the far-stretching Columbus streets to have encompassed the globe; but our talks were not nearly so long as the walks, walks in which there were reaches of reticence, when apparently it was enough for us to be walking together. Yet we must often have talked about the books we were reading, that is to say the novels, though seldom about public events, which is the stranger, or the less strange, because as a student of law he was of course a potential politician, and I was writing politics every day.

He was the last but one of the friends whom my youth was so rich in, for no reason more, perhaps, than that we were young together, though they were all older than I, and Comly was five or six years my senior. When I knew him first, with his tall, straight figure, his features of Greek fineness, his blue eyes, and his moustache thin and ashen blond, he was of a distinction fitting the soldier he became when the Civil War began, and he fought through the four years' struggle with such gallantry and efficiency that he came out of it with the rank of brigadier-general. He had broken with the law amid arms, and in due time he succeeded to the control of our newspaper where he kept on terms of his own the tradition of Reed, which Price and I had continued in our fashion, and made the paper an increasing power. But he had never been the vigorous strength he looked, and after certain years of overwork he accepted the appointment of minister to Hawaii. The rest and the mild climate renewed his health, and he came back to journalism under different conditions of place. But the strain was the same; he gave way under it again, and died a few years later.

XIII

I cannot make out why, having the friends and incentives I had in Columbus, I should have wished to go away, but more and more I did wish that. There was no reason for it except my belief that my work would be less acceptable if I remained in the West; that I should get on faster if I wrote in New York than if I wrote in Columbus. Somehow I fancied there would be more intellectual atmosphere for me in the great city, but I do not believe this now, and I cannot see how I could anywhere have had more intelligent sympathy. When I came home from Venice in 1865, and was looking about for some means of livelihood, I found that Lowell had a fancy for my returning to the West, and living my literary life in my own air if not on my own ground. He apparently thought the experiment would be interesting; and if I were again twenty-eight I should like to try it. I would indeed have been glad then of any humble place on a newspaper in the West; but the East more hospitably entreated me, and after a flattering venture in New York journalism I was asked to the place in Boston which of all others in the world was that I could most have desired.

In those Columbus days I was vaguely aware that if I went farther from home I should be homesick, for where I was, in that happy environment, I was sometimes almost intolerably home-sick. From my letters home, I find that I was vividly concerned in the affairs of those I had left there, striving and saving to pay for the printing-office and the house with so little help from me. I was still sometimes haunted by the hypochondria which had once blackened my waking hours with despair; I dare say I was always overworking, and bringing my fear upon me out of the exhaustion of my nerves. Perhaps I am confiding too much when I speak of this most real, most unreal misery, but if the confession of it will help any who suffer, especially in the solitude of youth which inexperience makes a prison-house, I shall not be ashamed of what some may impute to me for weakness. If one knows there is some one else who is suffering in his kind, then one can bear it better; and in this way, perhaps, men are enabled to go to their death in battle, where they die with thousands of others; in the multitudinous doom of the Last Day its judgments may not be so dreadful to the single culprit. Like every one who lives, I was a congeries of contradictions, willing to play with the fancies that came to me, but afraid of them if they stayed too late. Yet I did not lose much sleep from them; it is after youth is gone that we begin to lose sleep from care; while our years are few we indeed rise up with care, but it does not wake nightlong with us, as it does when our years are more.

I had a most cheerful companion in my colleague Price, who so loved to laugh and to make laugh. If he never made the calls or went to the parties to which I tempted him, apparently he found our own society sufficient, and in fact I could not wish for anything better myself than when, the day's work and the night's pleasure ended for me, we sat together in the editorial room, where our chief seldom molested us, and waited for the last telegraphic despatches before sending the paper to press. Sometimes we had the company of officials from the State House who came over to while away the hours, more haggard for them than for us, with the stories they told while we listened. They were often such stories as Lincoln liked, no doubt for the humorous human nature and racy character in them. Very likely he found a relief in them from the tragedy overhanging us all, but not molesting our young souls with the portents which the sad-eyed man of duty and of doom was aware of, or perhaps not yet aware of.

The strangest impression that the time has left with me is a sense of the patient ignorance which seemed to involve the whole North. Doubtless the South, or the more positive part of it, knew what it was about; but the North could only theorize and conjecture and wait while those who were in keeping of the nation were seeking its life. In the glare of the events that followed volcanically enough, it seems as if the North must have been of the single mind which it became when the shot fired on Fort Sumter woke it at last to the fact that the country was really in peril. But throughout the long suspense after Lincoln's election till his inauguration there was no settled purpose in the North to save the Union, much less to fight for it. People ate and slept for the most part tranquilly throughout; they married and gave in marriage; they followed their dead to the grave with no thought that the dead were well out of the world; they bought and sold, and got gain; what seemed the end could not be the end, because it had never come before.

After the war actually began, we could not feel that it had begun; we had the evidence of our senses, but not of our experiences; in most things it was too like peace to be really war. Neither of the great sections believed in the other, but the South which was solidified by the slaveholding caste had the advantage of believing in itself, and the North did not believe in itself till the fighting began. Then it believed too much and despised the enemy at its throat. Among the grotesque instances of our self-confidence I recall the consoling assurance of an old friend, a chief citizen and wise in his science, who said, as the hostile forces were approaching each other in Virginia, "Oh, they will run," and he meant the Southerners, as he lifted his fine head and blew a whiff from his pipe into the air. "As soon as they see we are in earnest they will run," but it was not from us that they ran; and the North was startled from its fallacy that sixty days would see the end of the rebellion, whose end no prophet had now the courage to forecast. We of the Ohio capital were a very political community, the most political in the whole State, in virtue of our being the capital, but none of the rumors of war had distracted us from our pleasures or affairs, at least so far as the eyes of youth could see. With our faith in the good ending, as if our national story were a tale that must end well, with whatever suspenses, or thrilling episodes, we had put the day's anxieties by and hopefully waited for the morrow's consolations. But when the fateful shot was fired at Fort Sumter, it was as if the echo had not died away when a great public meeting was held in response to the President's call for volunteers and the volunteering began with an effect of simultaneity which the foreshortening of past events always puts on to the retrospective eye. It seemed as if it were only the night before that we had listened to the young Patti, now so old, singing her sweetest in that hall, where the warlike appeals rang out, with words smiting like blows in that "Anvil Chorus" which between her songs had thrilled us with the belief that we were listening to the noblest as well as the newest music in the world.

I have sometimes thought that I would write a novel, with its scene in our capital at that supreme moment when the volunteering began, but I shall never do it, and without the mask of fiction one cannot give the living complexion of events. Instantly the town was inundated from all the towns of the State and from the farms between as with a tidal wave of youth; for most of those who flooded our streets were boys of eighteen and twenty, and they came in the wild hilarity of their young vision, singing by

day and by night one sad inconsequent song, that filled the whole
air, and that fills my sense yet as I think of them:

"Oh, nebber mind the weather but git ober double trouble,
    For we're bound for the happy land of Canaan."

They wore red shirts, as if the color of the Garibaldian war for
Union in Italy had flashed itself across the sea to be the hue of
our own war for Union. With interlinked arms they ranged up
and down, and pushed the willing citizens from the pavement,
and shouted the day and shouted the night away, with no care
but the fear that in the out-pour of their death-daring they might
not be gathered into the ranks filling up the quota of regiments
assigned to Ohio. The time had a sublimity which no other time
can know, unless some proportionate event shall again cause the
nation to stand up as one man, and the spectacle had a mystery
and an awe which I cannot hope to impart. I knew that these
boys, bursting from their fields and shops as for a holiday, were
just such boys as I had always known, and if I looked at any one
of them as they went swaggering and singing up and down I recognized him for what they were, but in their straggling ranks,
with their young faces flushed the red of their blouses and their
young eyes flaming, I beheld them transfigured. I do not pretend
that they were of the make of armies such as I had seen pictured
marching in serried ranks to battle, and falling in bloody wind-
rows on the smoke-rolled plain. All that belonged to

"Old, unhappy, far-off days,"

and not to the morrows in which I dwelt. But possibly if I had
written that forever-to-be-unwritten novel I might have plucked
out the heart of the moment and laid it throbbing before the
reader; and yet I might rather have been satisfied with the more
subjective riddle of one who looked on, and baffled himself with
question of the event.

Only two or three of the friends who had formed our College
group went to the war; of these my friend, Comly, had been one
of the earliest, and when I found him officer of the day at the first

camp of the volunteers, he gave me what time he could, but he was helplessly preoccupied, and the whole world I had known was estranged. One morning I met another friend, coming down the State House steps and smiling radiantly; he also was a law student, and he had just been made adjutant of a newly accepted regiment. Almost immediately afterward he was changed to the line, and at the end of the war, after winning its last important battle, John G. Mitchell came out with the rank of brigadier-general, to which the brevet of major-general could scarcely add distinction. By the chances which play with our relations in life I had not known him so well as some others. He was not of the college group; but after the war we came familiarly together in the friendship of the cousins who had become our wives. In that aftertime he once held me rapt with the stories of his soldier life, promising, or half-promising, to put them down for print, but never doing it, so that now they are lost to that record of personal experience of battle which forms so vital a part of our history. No stories of that life which I have read have seemed to me so frank, so full, so real, as those he told.

Our first camp was in our pretty Goodale Park, where I used to walk and talk with the sculptor Ward, and try the athletic feats in which he easily beat me. Now the pine sheds covered the long tables, spread with coffee and pork and beans, and the rude bunks filled with straw, and here and there a boy-volunteer frowzily drowsing in them. It was one of the many shapeless beginnings which were to end in the review of the hundred thousands of seasoned soldiers marching to their mustering out in Washington after four years of fire and blood. No one could imagine that any of these boys were to pass through that abyss, or that they would not come safely out. Even after the cruel disillusion of Manassas the superstition of quick work remained with the North, and the three years' quota of Ohio was filled almost as jubilantly as the three months' but not quite so jubilantly. Sons and brothers came with tears to replace fathers and brothers who had not returned from Manassas, and there was a funeral undertone in the shrilling of the fifes and the throbbing of the drums which was not so before. Life is like Hamlet and will oftentimes "put an antic disposition on," which I have never been one to refuse recognition, and now I must, with whatever effect from it, own a bit of its mockery. One of our reporters was a father whose son had been among the first to go, and word came that the boy had been killed at Manassas. I liked the father as I had liked the son, and the old man's grief moved me to such poor offer of consolation as verse could make. He was deeply touched, but the next day another word came that the boy was alive and well, and I could not leave my elegiacs with his father, who was apparently reluctant to renounce the glory of them, although so glad. But he gave them back, and I depersonalized them by removing the name of the young soldier, and finally printed them in the volume of poems which two or three people still buy every year.

XIV

It was a question now whether I could get the appointment of a consulate which I had already applied for, quite as much I believe upon the incentive of my fellow-citizens as from a very natural desire of my own. It seemed to be the universal feeling, after the election of Lincoln, that I who had written his life ought to have a consulate, as had happened with Hawthorne who had written the life of Franklin Pierce. It was thought a very fitting thing, and my fellow-citizens appeared willing I should have any consulate, but I, with constitutional unhopefulness, had fixed my mind upon that of Munich, as in the way to further study of the German language and literature, and this was the post I asked for in an application signed by every prominent Republican in the capital, from the governor down. The governor was now William Dennison, who afterward became Postmaster General, and who had always been my friend, rather in the measure of his charming good will than my merit, from my first coming to Columbus; Chase had already entered Lincoln's cabinet as Secretary of the Treasury. I had heard that he spoke personally to the President in my behalf, and urged my appointment upon him, with what commendation I do not know. But in spite of this backing, the President, with other things on his mind, did not respond in any way until some months had dragged by, when one day I received without warning an official envelope addressed to me as "Consul at Rome, now at Columbus, Ohio." Rome was not exactly Munich, and the local language and literature were not German, but I could not have expected the State Department to take cognizance of a tacit ideal of mine, and the consulate was at any rate a consulate, which perhaps most of my friends supposed was what I wanted. It was welcome enough, for I was again to be dropped from the high horse which I had been riding for nearly a year past; one of those changes in the *State Journal* which Greeley, in his unsolicited lecture, had imputed to it for unworthiness was at hand, and the gentleman who was buying a controlling share in it, might or might not wish to write the editorials himself. At any rate the Roman consulship was not to be declined without inquiry, but as there was no salary, and the consul was supposed to live upon the fees taken, I tried to find out how much the fees might annually come to. Meanwhile I was advised by prudence to accept the appointment provisionally; it would be easy to resign it if I could not afford to keep it; and I waited to see what the new proprietor meant to do.

Apparently he meant to be editor as well as proprietor, and Price and I must go, which we made ready to do as soon as the new proprietor came into his own. Three or four times in my life, I have suffered some such fate as I suffered then; but I never lost a place except through the misfortune of those who gave it me; then with whatever heart I could, I accepted the inevitable. At the worst, I was yet "Consul at Rome now at Columbus," and I had my determination to work. I was never hopeful, I was never courageous, but somehow I was dogged. I had no overweening belief in myself, and yet I thought, at the bottom of my soul, that I had in me the make of the thing I was bent on doing, the thing literature, the greatest thing in the world.

When our new proprietor arrived, Price and I disabled his superiority, probably on no very sufficient grounds, but he had the advantage in not wanting our help, and I decided to go to Washington and look personally into the facts of the Roman consulship. As perhaps some readers of this may know it ultimately turned into the Venetian consulship, but by just what friendly magic has been told with sufficient detail in a chapter of *Literary Friends and Acquaintance*, and need not be rehearsed here. As for Price he had nothing at all before him, but he was by no means uncheerful. We had certainly had a joyous though parlous year together; our jokes could not have been numbered in a season when the only excuse for joking was that it might as well be that as weeping, though probably we had our serious times, especially when we foreboded a fresh dismay in our chief at some escapade in derision or denunciation of the well-meaning patriots' efforts to hold the Union together with mucilage.

But the time came when all this tragical mirth was to end. We found that we did not dislike the new owner, and he liked us well enough, but he was eager to try his hand at our work, and some time early in August we quitted the familiar place. If there was any form of adieu with our gentle chief I do not remember it, and in fact my mind holds no detail of our parting except the last hour of it, when we found ourselves together at midnight in the long, gloomy barn then known as the Little Miami Depot, where we were to take our separate ways in the dark which hid us from each other forever. We walked up and down a long time, talking, talking, talking, laughing, promising each other to be faithful in letters, and wearing our souls out in the nothings which people say at such times with the vain endeavor to hold themselves together against the fate which is to sunder them in the voluntary death of parting. We heard the whistle of an approaching train, we shook hands, we said good-by, and then in a long wait repeated the nothings again and again. But my train on the Central Ohio was already there; and as Price obeyed the call to board his train for Cleveland, I mounted mine for Washington, and we never saw each other again. It is long since he died, and I who still survive him after fifty years offer his memory this vow of abiding affection. If somewhere we should somewhen meet, perhaps it will be with a fond smile for the time we were young and so glad together, with so little reason.

THE END

THREE ESSAYS

"OVERLAND TO VENICE"

IN other places I have already told how I went to Washington in the late summer of 1861 with the hope of reconciling my application for the consulship at Munich with my appointment to the consulship at Rome, and how, at the suggestion of President Lincoln's secretaries, John Nicolay and John Hay, I gladly compromised on the consulship at Venice. Then I went home to wait for my commission, not to Columbus, but to the village in northern Ohio where my family lived. I promptly sent the Treasury Department a bond securing the nation against my malfeasance in office, and then I began taking interminable walks in the woods and reading all the novels of Scott. But my mind was so little on these that no sense of them remained in it, and long afterward I had to repair the loss by reading the best of them over again. Meanwhile I tried to fit myself for the duties of a commercial office by resuming the study of arithmetic, which I had ignored as much as possible during the few years of my boyish schooling. I became so skilled in it that when I revisited Washington years later I was praised by one of the Treasury authorities for the uncommon accuracy of my accounts. Perhaps the Treasury authorities were never very attentive in my case; after forwarding my bond to them I lost hope of any voluntary acknowledgment, and wrote to ask them if it had been received. They answered to some such effect as "Oh! Oh yes! Been mislaid," and I decided that in presenting a new bond I had better go on to Washington and do it in person. This was what I did, and when I had made my office secure in every way I went to New York to take ship for the first stage of my land journey to Venice.

I had somehow decided already that when I had once crossed the Atlantic I should not like to sail from Marseilles to Genoa, and there take the train for Venice, but should rather go from Paris to Strassburg, to Stuttgart, to Munich, to Vienna, and so over the Simmering Pass to Trieste, which was then the only all-rail route to Italy; but how or when I divined the fact I should not like trying to say. I am certain only of New York as imperatively my starting-point, and there I am certain of nothing so much as seeing much and often our divine sculptor, as Vasari would have called him, Quincy Ward, whom I had known so well in Columbus. In New York he had a studio looking eastward over Union Square and down on a mild statue of General Worth, now lost to fame as a hero of the Mexican War. The Civil War, so actual in our defeats at the South, had somehow in New York not the pressure on the mind and soul that it had in Washington. In fact, everywhere in the North the sense of it was relieved by the cheerfulness of the national temperament. But it was evident in Ward and his work, which had a militant coloring in its devotion, for one thing, to the designing of sword-hilts. I remember also the figure of a soldier in some heroic attitude meant to express a higher emotion than the simple poetry of the John Rogers groups once so prevalent during the war and long afterward; and I recall Ward looking rather misgivingly, with his head on one side, at a tentative figure which he had modeled. I was so very little instructed in his art that I asked him whether the whole group it was designed for was to be in the nude; and he patiently explained, Oh no, but you always had to model your figures nude. I believe that this hero and the like of him never got so far as to have their clothes put on, though between my many visits to Ward's studio there were chances for it.

I saw so much more of Ward than of any one else during my wait of a week in New York before I sailed that he remains chiefly in my mind. He came down to the ship with me, and he was the only one I knew in the sparse ten or a dozen well-wishers who lingered in the November drizzle to wish the *City of Glasgow* a good voyage. There was indeed one other acquaintance whom I saw putting out after the ship in a small boat after she had left her dock, and whom I divined as our vice-consul for Civ ità Vecchia. The consulship at Rome had been given to the painter and critic, William J. Stillman, who wished to be consul at Venice that he might write a book about its art, but who was willing to take Rome when I got Venice in place of Munich. He needed a vice-consul; but whether he wished to have this particular painter (he was also a painter, and a very good one) for his vice-consul I am not sure. Years afterward in Rome he praised his art to me, but said that temperamentally he was of the nature of a pendulum which sways back and forth but never quite so far as to tick. In the event which was my last experience of him he attested the accuracy of this characterization, but when I first met him in New York I clung eagerly to his promise that if I would wait a week for him before sailing he would go with me by my chosen route to Venice, and then continue on to his own post.

The *City of Glasgow* was not a swift vessel; she was a fortnight in getting to Liverpool, but she now outspeeded the vice-consul in his small boat, though his boatman put forth a strength visibly frantic as long as his craft continued in sight. Before the distance of the dim afternoon swell swallowed it up I could not do less than my best to second his endeavor. As for the vice-consul, he sat, a black-cloaked bulk, in the stern of the boat, and he had no interest for me except as I ardently longed for his company across the unknown continent I was already too rapidly approaching. I hurried from one ship's officer to another, representing the case, but failing to interest any one till the friendly first mate pointed out the captain and bade me ask *him* to slow the ship. I did so, and urged that our pursuer was not only my friend, but that he was also the American vice-consul at Civ ità Vecchia. The captain turned with a Scotch ferocity upon me, and shrieked, "I wadn't stope ma ship for the Keeng!"

He was not a bad captain, or even a bad man, and, though I

dropped his acquaintance for the moment, I believe we afterward became friendly enough when I realized how preposterous my suggestion had been. He did not take the head of the table where the first-cabin people sat down at the compromise hour of four o'clock, and either dined or supped as they chose to think. This was the custom on all the boats of that date; but there was a high tea afterward, and you could keep on ordering something from the stewards as long as you remained awake. On the *City of Glasgow* the table stretched the whole length of the saloon; and on either hand the doors of the state-rooms opened flush from it, so that you could burst from your chair to your berth at the slightest warning. But that day nobody seemed to mind the rolling of the ship, which never ceased afterward for fourteen days and nights. It was not yet Thanksgiving, but we had turkey for dinner in affection for the land we were leaving, and plum pudding in honor of the land we hoped to reach, and some one had heartened the others in the belief that there was nothing like a full meal against seasickness. Eventually it was not the specific which some of us boasted it, but who lost faith in it first I could not say. I know that I was not the last, and that I found a seat by the rail in the cold wet of the wild night far pleasanter than the thought of the warm state-room which I could share at any moment with my roommate; he had already gone into it and he did not come out till the ship lay still in her dock at Liverpool, where he wavered forth, a pallid phantom of the sewing-machine agent he had entered. He was not a good travelling companion, but he had the worst of it, and I still have a compassionate regard for him.

The misery of seasickness in others may be joked away, but even when it has passed for one's self, and one's appetite has come back in all one's youthful voracity, the experience remains a loathsome memory, though long before the first week was over I could look without blenching at the long pendulum in the gangway describing a vast arc as the ship turned half over, hesitated whether not to capsize entirely and then reluctantly reeled back. "She's built of rolling timber," was the one joke of our one stewardess when she found a passenger contemplating the play of the pendulum; and in the event the *City of Glasgow* never did roll entirely over, but burned peacefully to the water's edge in Cork Harbor. I once thought I should have liked to see her burn, but I am not sure now.

A sea voyage sixty years ago was not the sea voyage of to-day, and the steamers were not the steamers, with their luxuries, which are almost comforts, accumulated upon the passengers; but the *City of Glasgow* performed the chief use of a ship, which is to get you to the end of your voyage in safety; and so, peace to her very damp ashes! Of the densely thronging experiences of that fortnight little abides with me. One day we saw, no great way off, a vast and very dirty-looking iceberg, and we believed that it chilled the water about us, as any of us could have proved from the bucket of it which some of the crew pulled up over the ship's side. I think there were at times whales spouting at safe removes, but I will not be sure there were, or not so sure as of the amusingness of a little man from Washington who suddenly developed tipsiness one day at dinner and held the carving-knife under the nose of the first mate and bade him "Smell that!" He was killingly funny in his widely ranging talk throughout the meal, and touched nearly every one with his glancing wit, which would sober at times to a philosophy of life as he had not very edifyingly known it. After many years he took his place in a sea novel of mine with much imaginary detail, rounded out from nature's sketch by my invention. I think he was only occasionally sober, after that first spree, and I do not associate him with the young commercial Englishmen who form in the retrospect a large part of our passengers, and who made the smoking-room at the stern of the ship their resort. They were hardened against our sea-cold by the habit of their land-cold at home, and were a kindly enough company at a time when there was so little kindness between their country and ours. I tried to get from them some knowledge of where and how to go in London for the brief stay I meant to make there, but they were not very useful in the matter. "One thing I can tell you," one of them said;

"you won't find things as cheap in London as in New York," and he offered in proof the fact that just before sailing he had lunched on an oyster stew for twelve and a half cents. America, he held, was the cheapest country in the world, and I had no premonition that it was soon to become the dearest. The talk in the smoking-room was not more profitable, as a general thing, than as a particular study of life, but I suppose it was no worse than most young men's talk at that day; what such talk is at this day I would not venture to say, but I believe it is decenter.

There must have been other passengers on the *City of Glasgow*, but I specifically remember only a friendly family from one of the many Newtons near Boston—a minister with his wife and her gentle, elderly sister. We saw much of one another in such weather as permitted us to sit on deck; I suspect they were a good deal seasick, but this did not make them sad; we had laughing as well as talking, and our talk was somewhat of books, but they were religious rather than literary, and before we parted the minister said he would like to give me a Bible, and he sent it to me at Venice, where I confided that I was going officially to be. The incident is more important to me than it can be to the reader; but I think, with lingering regret, that I never saw these friendly people again, though I was twenty-five years near one of the Newtons when I went to live in Cambridge. While I was now with them, in the shelter of their friendship, I could not feel that I had altogether left home, and was fortified against the homesickness I was always dreading rather than feeling.

There was no one else on board whom I could have engaged in the talk of books and authors, then almost my sole talk. The human element partakes in my remembrance of the monotony of the watery element that widened round me day after day, a sullen void without event or variety. Sea travel, even now with all the adventitious helps of modern invention, is wanting in social charm, and life on the *City of Glasgow* had even some advantages. There was, for one thing, no music, and one ate one's very good food without molestation from the wind and stringed instruments blaring and bewailing themselves from soup to coffee. There was not even a piano on board, as how should there have been with only that vast dining-saloon serving for all the uses of modern music-room, library, lounge, and parlors, large and small, which now invite the miserable leisure of the voyage. There was a good stretch of flush deck with much more space for walking up and down than most of the largest ships of our day afford. I must have walked up and down, but if with any one else it was in a companionship which has utterly perished from the mind.

I suppose that I read a good deal, but what books I cannot think. I conjecture rather unreliably that I read *Les Misérables*, then a very popular new novel, but I make sure only of the Italian grammar which I studied in order to meet the Venetians on their own water. I studied it rather faithfully, expecting to use what little German I had the use of until I had mastered sufficient Italian, not imagining how this would socially disadvantage me with them in their hatred of the Austrians. It was more to the purpose that I much more diligently perused the manual of instruction for Consuls which the State Department had provided me with; I really mastered this, so that I could have entered confidently upon the duties of my office before I reached Liverpool, if I had been of a mind to assume them. But I had early decided to keep my consular office to myself; between me and me I was proud enough of it, but I must journey and sojourn cheaply, and I did not wish my official quality to share the humility of my personal economies. I had no need for anxiety; nobody on the ship cared to penetrate my reserve, and when once we had landed in Liverpool we were all, to all recollection of mine, wiped off the map of life together. My gentle Newton friends vanished with the rest, and I suppose they are all dead now; nearly everybody is dead now. My consular dignity travelled incognito with me on my second-class ticket, and at London went with me for my stay at the Golden Cross Hotel, which I chose because, for one thing, I knew it was cheap, and for another because it was the hotel where David Copperfield stayed.

If I have told this before, the reader, knowing the fact from some one of my many books, must be patient. I do not believe I have told how I overheard, and could not help overhearing, the talk of a recreant American in the coffee-room who was denying his country to an Englishman because of the corruption of our suffrage in Rhode Island where he said the poorer voters notoriously sold their votes. He himself bought their votes, he said, and he did not seem to feel that he was a sharer in their guilt. The Englishman was not apparently much interested, except as most Englishmen wished, in those dark days of our Civil War, to think ill of us; and my youthfulness abashed me in the presence of the much older man who was defaming us. I would very willingly have defied the renegade for his proof, and I believe I should have declared that at least so far as concerned Ohio his words were false; for whole neighborhoods in Ohio had not yet trafficked in the suffrage; but much more possibly I said nothing. Though at twenty-four I still felt very young, I knew that it was with the pen, not the tongue, I was cunninger of fence. I have ever since taken out my indignation in wondering who, what, and why this renegade was, or how he hoped to profit by his exposure of our dishonor. Probably he was of that strange party of the perverse, which in every event is of the worse side; or may have thought that he acquired personal merit from our national ignominy. He remains an unknown quantity in the problem of my far past, and I can only be sure that he put me to shame before his English listener, and before the waiter who, in my first experience of his convention, was serving me my first English dinner "off the joint."

The incident is the only one of my stay in London which remains of special distinctness. Yet I must have done the accustomed sights. Westminster Abbey still looms spectral in that pale, wintry air, and I am sure of riding on an omnibus-top under Temple Bar, which was still so far from demolition that it might have been lifting a row of traitors' heads on its parapet; but I am more aware of the red December sunsets, rich and dim, hurrying on the night at four o'clock, and of the belated fashion of spring-bottoms in the trousers which a Jewish clothier in Holborn tried to sell me, when all the other world was wearing peg-tops. No doubt I could tease things from my reluctant memory; nothing was probably lost upon it; but it will not be entreated now for more. After eighty memory serves mainly to make life a burden to others by the repetition of things told before from it.

The fear of this makes me shy of saying how much I was indebted to the friendliness of the young English commercial travellers who bore me company by land and sea on my second-class way from London to Paris. At Boulogne and beyond their apt French smoothed many a difficult step for me, and I was glad, and I hope fitly grateful, for their help on the way to Paris and in the hotel, both good and cheap, which these amiable fellows there led me to. They were for the South in our Civil War, but not offensively; they suffered me my patriotism and they came to see me off at the station when I left Paris.

In the mean while I had advised with our consul in Paris about the best way of getting to Venice by land and had met with more kindly interest than practical knowledge. He confessed he was a salad-consul in recognizing my tender leaf and owned himself of an ignorance concerning the several routes of travel which his vice-consul did nothing to repair; but I suppose he would have known better how to choose for me when I introduced him to the American Academy some fifty years later, for by that time he was in his early nineties, while I was still in my first seventies. He read a very brilliant paper on an interview with Alexander Dumas, and with his strong, full voice and his most impressive bearing added to the unique value of an admirably critical, quietly humorous, characterization of the great mulatto romancer.

But we were yet far from that moment, and I had to rely upon the standard information of the time-tables in Bradshaw's Railway Guide rather than any instinctive knowledge of how to get where I wanted to go. I cannot understand why I should not have chosen to cross into Italy over the pass of Mont Cenis, instead of traversing the snowy breadth of Germany, to Vienna, and then descending over the Simmering Pass to Trieste and ultimately Venice. There is a turmoil of impressions, physical and spiritual, left of that experience, which I should seek in vain to detach from one another, and there remains a tangle of arrivals by night and departures by day at the heated and fetid stations, where I seem always to have been weighed down in soul and body by my two vast hand-bags among gobbling and gabbling phantasms of every age and sex in the waiting- and eating-rooms. There were no such things yet as the belated sleeping-cars of Europe; people propped themselves up in the cushioned seats of the first-class carriages and warmed themselves with the carpeted flasks of hot water under their feet; but second-class travel watched and shivered the long days and long nights through. I tried now and then to practise a colloquial German adopted from the German poets, and I rejoiced when I could translate to myself the phrases which I had caught from my fellow-wayfarers. It must have been when we were drawing into Stuttgart that a young girl called out at some answer to a question of hers, "*Ich danke schön,*" in tones which remained long in my sense like an echo out of Heine's *Reisebilder*. She was pretty, and graceful as well as gracious, but who or what she was the past keeps for one of its secrets: the past which was and remains so young.

It was the prelude to my joyous sojourn at the little Suabian capital in the almost constant company of the resident consul who was even younger than myself, for he was twenty-two years old, while I was twenty-four. But he was matured by two or three months' service at a post where there was nothing to do, and I had not yet begun to serve at another post where there was almost less than nothing to do. I went to find him directly after breakfast and I cannot recall any time spent apart from him, though there must have been solitary intervals of the sort. In that time I wished to see German life subjectively from Heine and objectively from Thackeray, who then almost equally formed my favorite reading, and I suppose I had not always my friend's company in their poetic and satirical points of view; but he made up to me for all loss by introducing me to the varied society of his fellow-foreigners at the resorts of their leisure. Among them was one of those English expatriates who used to abound in the continental countries, mainly from economical motives, and who in this instance had been giving his inventive genius to the perfection of a system for breaking the bank of Baden-Baden, then the great gambling centre of Germany. His system, as he explained it, was infallible, but I never heard that it brought ruin to the grand-ducal institution which it was meant to destroy, and it was probably only one of the many devices for the same purpose which failed to enrich their inventors. I wish now I could have known the history of this gentleman, for it could not have failed of those phases which Thackeray loved to deal with, in studies and short stories of the minor German capitals, as these used to be.

I cared more for the phases of the local life, more immediately transferable to the literature I was always meditating, though without any very fixed purpose. But to this day I do not know quite what to do with the incident of being generously caught up from the barber's chair, and hurried to the barber's window, that I might not miss the sight of the old king of Würtemberg, who was pottering by on the sidewalk after a fashion he had of wandering unattended through his capital. It was said, but perhaps not very credibly, that an American who struck up against the sovereign one afternoon in ignorance of his sacred majesty upbraided him for the encounter as one of those demented Dutchmen who could not see after four o'clock in the afternoon, anyway.

No doubt it was a story which was used to flatter our national vanity with every American tourist, and I had my crude pleasure of it, though now I do not think it so very amusing. But my sojourn in Stuttgart was not rich in suggestion, though I gave the place all possible occasions for it. The literary soul is always offering itself to the impressions of life, in the hope of using them sooner or later, and I still value for its youthful ingenuousness the share I took in an extra-consular action of my friend the local consul. I was afterward destined, in my own place, to use what judgment I could summon to the management of other abnormal phases of American citizenship, but I was not eager to anticipate them by advising what was best to be done in the case of an American boy who had run away from the school where his people had put him, and been retaken by the schoolmaster, and was now held against his will. He had managed somehow to make his appeal to the consul for protection, and my friend felt that it was an affair for his intervention. He did not conceal from himself or from me that he could not intervene officially, and I represented that I had still less the right to intervene, not being in any wise accredited to the government of Würtemberg; but he argued that it would strengthen his very shadowy authority in the matter if I would add another consular presence to his in the visit which he proposed making to the schoolmaster, and letting him realize that the United States, however distracted by civil strife, was not unmindful of the least of American boys. This boy, when we saw him in the presence of the schoolmaster, was not apparently afflicted by his plight, whatever it was, and the schoolmaster, though serious, did not seem severe. While the wholly officious inquiry went on I tried to engage one of the teachers present in a discussion of German poetry, more especially that of Uhland, and if I did not interest him very much, I at least eliminated myself from the case in hand. I believe the incident was closed by the boy's promise not to run away any more, but, however it was, the consular dignities parted amicably with the school authorities by shaking hands, and went their way glad of getting out of the affair so lightly.

After I left Stuttgart I stopped two days at Munich on my way to Vienna, but so effectlessly, so adventurelessly to all recollection, that I might as well not have stopped at all. It had now begun to be very wintry, and the sense of the snowy landscape remains with me a dreary vision of white, broken by breadths of black woodland. I was aware that the scene was richly storied from innumerable wars, and I suspected it of all manner of romance, but I was preoccupied in keeping as warm as I could in my unheated compartment, and in all the famous and beautiful cities which I passed through I made no longer stay than the halt of the train at their several stations. When I arrived one black morning in Vienna, I became the prey of a misadventure, which with a garnish of fiction I used a few years afterward, but in the confidence I have come to feel that the present generation does not know my literature as well as I do, I will venture to recall it here. I had trusted implicitly to Bradshaw's Railway Guide for all information a traveller needs, not only in crossing Europe, but when I read in it that the Kaiserin Elisabeth was the only hotel in Vienna serving a table d'hôte dinner, I chose it for mine. I had learned to prefer a table d'hôte to any other form of dinner, not only because it was better than any I could imagine from a bill of fare, but because I distrusted the usefulness of the vocabulary I had gathered from my reading of the German poetry for choosing among the strange dishes which must be presented to me. Neither the great Goethe nor the good Schiller, as Thackeray had taught me to call them, nor Uhland nor Heine himself could help me in such a case; but at a table d'hôte I should simply have to eat of the dishes that came, one after another, and not trouble myself to make a selection. The Kaiserin Elisabeth became my first and remained my last preference, therefore, and when the driver of the fiacre to which the porter had led my stumbling steps asked where I wished to be taken, I answered confidently (and a little indignantly, perhaps, as if he ought to have known without asking), "The Kaiserin Elisabeth," and he drove off without hesitation.

I fell asleep instantly in the comfortable bed which was given me at the hotel, and made up for so much of the time that I had lost during the night that it was nine o'clock in the morning before I woke to the delicious coffee and rolls of my breakfast. I did not try to vary their convention to something more American; I felt more than ever how wise I had been in choosing a hotel where I should not have to order a dinner of my choosing, and I readily complied with the portier's suggestion that I should have a guide to the American consulate, and such other places as I wished to visit.

In that simple day of a united North we consuls all knew one another politically if not personally, and I knew this consul at Vienna for a German-American from Illinois, high in the local esteem of the Republican party, and quite possibly a personal friend of Lincoln, who had given him his place. I found him in one of the great Viennese apartment-houses which, after much experience of different dwellings in many lands, still remains impressive in my remembrance. A gilded housemaster received me at the outer door, and after fit parley led me up the public staircase of the stately court to the consul's door and there left me to his instant hospitality. His hospitality was not only instant, but it was constant throughout the delightful day, and he showed me the sights of the very noble city, where I found none so distinctly memorable as the beautiful old church of St. Stephen, though I must have seen them all. The reader will please to reflect that the America of 1862 was far less historically and architecturally august than at present, and that I might very well have been impressed by the other monuments which I have now almost wholly forgotten. But it may well be forgiven me if after the church of St. Stephen there was nothing impressed me so much as the sight of the street police shoveling up the overnight snowfall into carts and then dumping it into the Danube. It was not till forty years later that Colonel Waring taught our White Wings to shovel up the snow in New York (where it used to be piously trusted to the rain and sun for its removal) and cart it off and dump it into the North and East rivers.

Our long day in Vienna was white and shining, and I suppose we walked the place pretty well over, for I cannot think of any driving, except to the imperial suburb of Leopoldstadt, which also I remember in no manner of detail, unless it was for the overweening grandeur of the palaces. We were often tired, and then we stopped at the cafés for a tall glass of the coffee which the Viennese call a *mélange*, and which I suppose they still have so unsurpassably, so unapproachably, delicious. Memory does not support me in the supposition of lunch or dinner, but there must have been both, and then it came to be night and we agreed that I had better go to my hotel and rest a while before taking the train for Trieste and Venice. My friend said he would go with me, for the Kaiserin Elisabeth was just a block or two away, and we went gayly on in an exchange of thanks and refusals of them, which ended when we confronted the portier at his lodge in the court of the hotel. He did not seem the portier whom I had left in the morning, but this did not trouble me, for he might very well have been an alternate; it was his evident surprise when I bade my friend good-by and proposed going to my room that impressed me. With all civility he explained that there must be some mistake, for he did not recognize me as a guest of the hotel. Was not this the Hotel Kaiserin Elisabeth? I demanded, with some indignation, and the portier answered in his French that it perfectly was. "Very well, then," I began, but suddenly the place began to look strange to me, though I had left it so carelessly in the morning, that I might very well have failed to note its distinctive features. I looked from the portier to my friend for explanation, and he explained to the portier that I had arrived late the night before, and had spent the day with him, and now I wished to pay my bill and take the midnight train for Trieste; the whole affair was quite regular, for I had bidden the driver of my fiacre take me to the Kaiserin Elisabeth and he had done so; the mistake, therefore, was the portier's. But the portier regretfully shook his head and maintained that no gentleman resembling me had passed the night at his house. He remained so firm in his position that we could do nothing better than ask, Where, then, had I stopped if I had not stopped there? The portier could not say, but he politely suggested several houses in the neighborhood where I might have stopped, and my friend led me away in my tacit grudge which I felt as from an indefinable injury at the hands of the portier. This grudge might well have mounted in my experience at the behavior of the successive portiers whose hotels we visited, if I had not been humbled by their refusal to recognize me. The consul patiently explained the circumstances of my arrival in the dark of the early morning, but none of them remembered these, and none of them remembered me, though I held myself up with what dignity I could for their scrutiny. I began to lose my courage, and I began to lose my temper, but, happily, the portiers were not persons with a keen sense of humor, and gave no sign of sharing my own feeling that the thing was a joke and might pass at any moment. Whatever my friend felt he remained outwardly serious, and I had not the heart to suggest that there *was* no Hotel Kaiserin Elisabeth, and never had been. When the list of hotels which the first portier of that supposititious hotel had given us was exhausted, my friend thought of others, and we did not stop till we had visited all these. Then he said, "Let us go and get a *mélange*," as if there might be inspiration in that, and we stopped at the next café, where we were welcomed to a table by a Viennese gentleman whom he knew. My friend introduced me, and then confessed the strange adventure which we had been pursuing. "Why," this heaven-sent acquaintance, who spoke English perfectly, said—"why don't you go to the police? The landlord of the hotel he did stop at had to send in the gentleman's passport, and of course they have his address." My friend struck his forehead. "I never thought of that!" he said and I began to feel an instant superiority to a consul who had failed in such an elementary branch of consular knowledge. But I forebore to patronize him, and went meekly away with him in the hope of rescue from my strange case. My friend was restored to his self-respect by the sympathetic politeness of the police, who would not regard the affair as at all out of the common; those rascally drivers of fiacres were constantly carrying strangers to hotels where the landlords were in league with them, they said; and I believe they offered to make an example of my landlord, but if they did I would not hear of it, and we hurried away to a hotel where the portier instantly knew me, and welcomed me like one whose feelings were relieved by the return of a wandering brother.

For my part I was only too glad to find myself anywhere, and I hurried my departure for the station, willing even to be driven there by the scamp who had brought me from it. But my day of anomalous experiences was not to end without another worthy of them. I bought my ticket for Venice for the price which Bradshaw had fixed for me, but when my train was well on the way I found, in counting up my expenses, that I was poorer than I should be by one of the pounds sterling which I had paid for my ticket. To be sure, we had to translate the English into Austrian money, and I cannot be certain whether it was by the guile or the error of the ticket-seller that he remained the richer.

I was at an end, however, of my misadventures, unless I am to number among them my suffering from the bowl of scalding vermicelli soup which I hurriedly consumed at some station the next day where the train afterward halted long enough to let me repent my haste at leisure. I do not know what station it was, and I remember nothing of the country which we traversed in our long journey, for the window of my carriage was so thickly painted with frost that only when the door was thrown open at the stoppages did I see anything out of it. In the defect of the hot-water cylinders, the thick fur coats of my fellow-travellers did nothing to temper the freezing air for me in my winter wear of the milder climate of central Ohio. After the actual lapse of time I could not say now how many sleepless, but not dreamless days and nights I passed in this misery, when suddenly, one day or night, I woke from whatever dream it was in the soft air of Trieste where I changed to the train for Venice. It was as if I woke in another world, when I woke from another dream on the shore where my overland journey to Venice ended, and I embarked in a gondola for my hotel in the City in the Sea.

"AN OLD VENETIAN FRIEND"

WE met first in the office of my predecessor who was holding my place and enjoying my pay for no fault of his during the pleasure of the Austrian government while I waited three months for its permission to act as American Consul at Venice. I was probably myself to blame for the delay by having reported myself as a journalist to the Austrian police, who then held Venice in a paternal embrace and may have had their misgivings as to what I might be going to write, or might already have written about the political situation in the last years of the Austrian domination in the Lombardo-Venetian kingdom when the patriotic feeling of the Italians was at the hottest; but in any case I had to wait.

In those days of the Demonstration, as the Venetians called their passive resistance, you knew men's opinions by the cut of their beards, and I might have inferred from a moustache worn with neither whiskers nor imperial that the gentleman whom the acting consul introduced in English was of a temperamental abeyance in his thinking, no doubt for good reasons. At the same time I perceived that he was not English when he said he was glad of my acquaintance, but I was very content to have him Italian, and we began somehow to be friends at once. We presently began to be companions, to be almost comrades, though he was then about fifty-six and I was still twenty-four years of age. His moustache was quite gray, and his gray hair was thinning toward baldness; his eyes were blue and kind, and his friendly face was of a comely fullness and a ripe bloom; when we stood up to shake hands we were of that equal height which short men like other men to be of. It is now many years since I saw him last and many more since I then saw him first, but if I should be so happy as to meet him in some other life, I should know as far as I could see him that it was Pastorelli.

That was not really his name, but I call him so because I propose to be very frank with some details of our friendship, and I think his memory has a right to the privacy of a pseudonym.

The traits which endeared him to me were not his alone but were the traits of the whole lovable Latin race, which, in spite of literary tradition, I found kind and simple if not always sincere. We began going about together at once, and I did not mind his largely seeking my company because I knew that he wished to practice his English with me. It was already very fair English, for he had lived several years in England, mostly at Liverpool, which he pronounced Liver*pull*, with a fine trill of the middle *r* and a strong stress of the last syllable. I do not know why he had chosen Liverpool for his English sojourn, but I think he valued it largely because he had got there a copy of Webster's Unabridged Dictionary, which, if he did not find one of the finest books in our language, he owned that he liked to read better than any other. In fact I think myself that it is very good reading, though I should not put it above Shakespeare or the Bible. I read Shakespeare more than the Bible, but it was apparently from an interest in my peculiarities as a Protestant that he said one day, "You read the Bible?" and I was forced to own how little, and he did not follow up the question. Possibly he meant to follow it up with others in satisfaction of a scruple against his intimacy with a heretic, for Pastorelli was not only of a tempered patriotism, but was a better catholic than some younger friends of mine, though these were good enough catholics too in strenuously denying anything like Protestantism.

He was not a Venetian of Venice, but of the province, and his "country" as he translated his *patria* and pronounced *cauntree*, was a small city not far from Padua. He had continued there in the profession of an apothecary until he saved enough to retire upon and now he had come to pass his winters in Venice, though he always went back to his town for the summer. Just what degree of civil condition he was of, I could not say, but apparently he was as much in good society as he wished; and he was always promising to have me go with him to the Countess N——, whose house he mostly frequented. I never actually went, and I have preferred to believe this was because my Italian was never facile enough to justify him in presenting me there, with the hope of my enjoyment. If this was the case, I do not blame him, for at some Italian houses which I was free of I found myself as uncomfortable as I must have made others.

I have often wondered since what the Countess N—— was like, whether young and gay, or austerely illustrious, putting her guests to a proof of their merit in rank or riches by her own quality of *grande dame*; but I am afraid I shall never know. I believe my friend's origin was middle class, but his savings were handsome enough to justify his admission to the house of a countess, though this would not have been so difficult in Venice as we might suppose. If this is largely conjectural, I knew that long before Pastorelli had bought a title from the Pope; for he told me his reception at the Vatican had cost him sixty scudi to the different servants who came to remind him of their services, and he gave me the impression that he thought his title not worth the money it had cost.

What I still like most in his memory is that it is sweet with a modest good sense, and that however quaint he was he was never absurd; if he was canny he never was stingy as I had duly reason to know. My acquaintance with him advanced rapidly to a friendship, which seemed to pass entirely to me from my predecessor. He was in fact merely one of the consul's pupils, for by the terms of his office our generous government allowed the consul to trade, and he justly construed this leave as permission to teach English. He had $750 a year, but I, when I came into his place at last, had $1500, with office rent, and the consular regulations forbade me to trade; so that if I had wished to keep his pupils I could not have done so. I ought to be ashamed to own that in those proud days of my youth I was ashamed of his teaching one of the waiters at the Caffè Florian: a gentle creature, intelligent and self-respectful who though he took my tip for the cup he brought me, accepted the two soldi amounting to one cent with a smile of meek dignity lingering with me yet. Now I hope I should not be ashamed of teaching him myself, though I am not sure; I am still very proud; and even before I got my exequatur, or permission to act from the Austrian government I had decided to remove our national eagle to a worthier perch than the casement of a simple though decent lodging in the Frezzeria, and I had the advice and guidance of my Pastorelli in the search for an apartment. His good will was greater than his taste in the matter, and he led me to many places which I was obliged to reject, some for instance because I must have passed through the kitchen or the bedroom to reach the parlor, which I meant for my office, and some because they were otherwise below the consular dignity. Such as these I pronounced too shabby, and Pastorelli caught at the word so that presently, whatever the fact might be, he stared about the rooms and then turned to me with a flare of his inquiring eyes, and the suggestion, "Too shobby! Hah, too shobby!"

In the end, when I was really as well as officially consul, I did not choose as wisely or as fitly as I could now wish; but before this I had proof that my friend was ready to serve me in a way where he was better fitted than in helping me house my eagle. I had received my *exequatur*, but was one day counting up my resources and wondering whether they would last till I could draw my first quarter's salary, when Pastorelli mastered the situation from his imperfect English and then shouted with a sort of generous indignation, "I will give you all the money you want!"

He meant that he would lend me the money, but he would not let me explain the difference. "Listen!" he hurried on to say, "Tell me how much, and I will go to the Countess N——'s, and get it out of my strongbox," and I cannot say now whether I was more touched by his generosity, or charmed by the literary quality of the fact that he was keeping his money at the house of his friend in the fashion dear and sacred to how many tales of Latin life. I liked the fact all the better because there was a tang of miserly suspicion in it, far from him personally, but proper to a race and age when the capitalist would not trust his savings to a bank, even after there were banks to trust them to. I perceived that the usage must still have been commoner than I had imagined, and the fact was the more precious to me because it was more a national than a personal effect with him. I would have liked to ask him all about it, and make him feel my pleasure in it; but of course that was not feasible, and I only tried to disclaim any stress of anxiety in owning that I would like to borrow fifty florins. He said nothing, as if he had not quite understood, but he did not let the day pass without coming to me again. Then, holding and withholding something in his left hand and waving his right forefinger before his face for the Italian emphasis of negation he said, as before, "Listen! Between friends there is no interest," and he may have studied an English correctness in his phrasing. "Here are twelve Austrian sovereigns, which I have taken out of my strong-box at the Countess N——'s. When you wish to return the money do not bring it in florins, but go to a money-changer's and buy twelve Austrian sovereigns and pay it back to me in them."

Then he opened his left hand and put the coins, very yellow and thin and broad one after another into my palm, which they entirely covered. I was richly aware that they were such broad pieces as abounded in old ballads, and they were almost as thin as leaves, like the coinage of fairy gold. I asked what they were, and he explained that they were an issue of money that had not been in circulation for a hundred years. He preferred to keep his savings in them, and said that I could always get them at a money-changer's; there was no hurry; keep them as long as I liked.

I was able to return them sooner than I expected, but it might well have been later, for in those days American consuls at Venice had difficulties in cashing their drafts, which were not owing to doubt of our national solvency, but to a disability which a former consul (long before my immediate predecessor in the rapid succession of former consuls) had put us under. He had overdrawn his account at his banker's, and had left town without making the banker good, and the banker had then obliged all American consuls to wait till the money came from London before cashing their drafts on our government. I submitted helplessly to conditions which I felt an indignity till I happened to mention them one day to a banker of the good Hebrew brotherhood of Blumenthals, who said that I must not stand that; their house would cash my drafts at sight; and after this I went to them, not without some regret at parting with the Brothers Schielin, whom I could not, after all, blame so much.

But this was when I had long repaid the loan, though never the kindness of my friend in Austrian sovereigns, which it is pleasant to remember I bought of a money-changer on the Rialto bridge. Pastorelli was staying on into the summer at Venice later than his wont was, I believe, and we saw each other well nigh every day, especially at the cafés which we frequented together. These were not the glittering cafés under the arcades of the Piazza San Marco, but those which every campo possessed one of as unfailingly as a church and a pharmacy: a very staid and self-respectful café with a modest spread of chairs and tables in front of it, and an aging Youth (they called the waiter *Youth*, or *Giovinotto*, in Venice,) who brought us a basket of cakes after pouring our little cups of black coffee. We always somehow chose the sponge-cake drops which the Venetians call lady-mouths and we lady-fingers, to dip into our coffee, and to this day I always taste that gentle past in their flavor, with the relish of our friendship. I think we did not talk much, but our talk was always in English, though I ought now to have been qualifying myself as rapidly as possible for an evening at the Countess N——'s, if indeed it was my want of Italian which disqualified me.

It was well that Pastorelli was staying on in town, for with the summer heat I fell into a low fever of some sort, as he discovered one day when he came to see me at my rooms, perhaps because he missed me at our cafés. I suggested a doctor, but he said, "If a doctor finds out you are a consul he will keep you in bed six months," and from his skill as a pharmacist in the past he prescribed for me himself and brought me the medicine at once from the apothecary in the campo where I lived. It must have been a nauseous draught, but when I took it without too much wincing he stooped over and kissed me on the forehead in reward of my courage. I duly recovered and still live to tell the tale, in spite of the mosquitoes which swarmed upon me so at night that I had to wear a hood of netting over my head and gloves on my hands to save myself from them. I could indeed have drugged them by burning the pastilles used in Venice, but then I must have shared their partial suffocation.

It was a peculiarity of my friend's study of English that the only English books which he seemed to have read besides Webster's Unabridged Dictionary were some little tales and sketches which an Italian had written in our language with the daring opportunity peculiar to the Latin races. One of these stories was an Eastern romance where the heroine was always spoken of as "a beautiful she-slave"; but I had not the heart to note the grotesquery to Pastorelli, who for all colloquial uses had such a good vocabulary. Our talk was mostly personal, and we had perhaps pretty well worn out our wonted topics when he went away early in September for the *villeggiatura* at his *cauntree*. By the time he came back to Venice I had been married, and though my American wife welcomed him with the hospitable intelligence inspired by my talk of him in my letters to her, we could not fall into our old familiarity. The strangeness may have been heightened by his finding me no longer in my rooms in the campo where we had last met, for I had now taken an apartment on the Grand Canal; but he soon came again, bringing his son, a nice boy, in his last school years, with him, and then he came with the Italian regularity to call upon us. Long after our mutual strangeness passed he wished us to come and visit him in his town where he was going to pass the summer. Our visit seemed to be an ideal which he had formed from his acquaintance with English life, and we imagined how at every point he tried to make it like a visit at an English country-house. He lived in a pretty villa among orchards and gardens on or as nearly on the terms of an English country gentleman as he could; and the points of his failure as we recognized them from our knowledge of English fiction rather than English fact were sweeter to us than an unbroken success could have been. A maiden sister lived with him as his house-keeper, and was probably charged with the fulfillment of his ideal; but the very first morning after our arrival when he came to our room he found that she had not sent up our breakfast. He seized a very sharp-voiced little hand-bell which he had provided for our convenience, and rang it fiercely, and then still ringing it he ran to the door and called out, "Anita! Anita!" The kind soul came flying with the boiled eggs he had ordered for us; but whether it was he or she who had imagined bringing them chilled icy cold we never knew. In other points the table was a Venetian version of the English fare which he imperfectly remembered, and we famished on the feast provided for us. We plotted how we might go for a walk, and buy a few cakes at a shop, but it was part of Pastorelli's hospitality never to leave us unaccompanied. At our last midday dinner the chief dish was a stew of calves' brains which the Venetians are so fond of, but we dissembled our loathing as we best could, building hopefully upon whatever dessert should follow. This came a deep platter of beautiful strawberries and we had all but hailed it with applause when our kind host caught up a caraffe of the inky wine of Conegliano which the Venetians drink, or then drank, and drenched the fruit with it. Then indeed we despaired, but when we escaped the same afternoon with our lives, we ordered such a supper at the Caffè Pedrocchi in Padua as had never been ordered for two persons before.

This seems very ungracious in the telling, but I could not give a just impression of how far Pastorelli's hospitality came short of his English ideal without it. There was nothing wanting to his kind intention and every moment of our stay was graced by some touch of it. Even his afternoon nap was not taken without the just defence which he made of his habit: "If I sleep, I sleep to myself; if I do not sleep to whom do I not sleep?"

It was evident in several ways that he was one of the chief men of his town. He was in fact the *podestà* or mayor of the place, and though he was of a temporizing patriotism it was clear that in spite of a beard cut to a moustache alone he was no *Austriacante* in any unworthy sense. Once in our walks he stopped abruptly and ran shouting violently towards a house with closed shutters something we did not understand till he explained, that if the householder kept his dwelling shut in that way as if it were unoccupied he was tacitly inviting the Austrian military to billet upon him as many troops as it would hold. He did not desist from his outcry till a frightened-looking woman came to a window, and after a moment ran about within, opening the whole house to the day. Then he walked off with us on his errand of showing what he called his Possessions, in lordlier terms than he might have used for his property if he had had his Unabridged Dictionary by him. They were several thrifty farms with good cottages on them, and he let me stop and talk with the tenants who seemed on friendly terms with him. Neither he nor they seemed to expect I should find it strange when on being questioned about their living one of them should say that he had meat at Christmas but no other time in the year. In fact I am not sure that I found it strange myself; it was long yet before I rebelled against the economical terms of this unjust world as cruelly provisional to call them no worse. My friend was the owner of these broad acres and those broad pieces in his strong-box at the Countess N——'s because he had started in life with advantages which these peasants had not enjoyed, and I might then have ascribed the difference to their demerit if I had come to think of it.

Pastorelli no longer visited us so often in Venice partly because he was there less and less. He was habituated to seeing us at Casa Falier, and it was after longer intervals that he called at the Palazzo Giustiniani when we crossed the Grand Canal to another apartment. When we crossed the Atlantic there was an interval of many years, well nigh twenty of them, in which at first we

exchanged letters, and so kept the forms of our friendship for a
while and then through my fault rather than his, let them lapse,
and we heard no more from each other than if we were both dead.
Then once again I was in Venice, and when I asked about
Pastorelli, no one could tell me of him, and I accepted a tacit
theory of my own that he was no longer living. He must have been
already in his sixties when we parted, and now he would at least
be eighty, if he had, very improbably, still survived to that age.
Now I am myself eighty, but then I was fifty-six, and I did not
see how Pastorelli could have lived so long. I let the days go, and
kept the thought of him down, as I recognize with a consciousness
more and more guilty. "Yes," I decided, "he must be eighty, he
must be dead," and I felt very sorry; but as I asked myself,
"What could I do?" I am making this confession, which I find
painful, because I would not have the reader think too well of
me; I cannot think at all well of myself in the retrospect, and yet
I believe there is something to be said for me because suddenly
I could bear no longer this Tito Melema like behavior of mine,
and wrote to Pastorelli at his *cauntree*. I said that we were to be in
Venice only a few days more, passing smoothly over the fact that
we had already been there several weeks; I begged him to come
to see us that my family might all see him; and I got back an
answer in his dear old, familiar angular hand as quickly as the
mail could bring it. "I have taken a bad cold," he began in
English, and then he went on to say in Italian, that he was old,
and could not conveniently leave home, but I was young, and a
great traveller, and I could easily come with my family to see
him. In my shame and despair I could only write to him again,
and protest the impossibility of going to him; we were leaving
Venice in a few days, and I entreated him to come at least to
Padua where we could have half an hour together in the wait
which my train would make there. I explained and excused and
defended myself for not having written to him sooner, as I have
been wishing to do now; but I got no answer to my letter; and
at Padua I could only waste the little long half hour, in the vain
hope that somehow before the train started the vision of Pastorelli

would yet appear to me; and if it had been his phantasm, the ghost I had imagined him, I should have been abjectly grateful though it had come only to reproach me, and then abandon me to my remorse.

My punishment was not to be more than I could bear. The next morning, one of the children was not well enough to let us continue our journey, and with a wild rapture, a sense of the divine mercy which I could not exaggerate, I took the first train back to Padua, and at Padua I took the swiftest *timonella*, (which was the likeness of an American buggy,) I could find, and drove away through the sweet-smelling hayfields to the *cauntree* of my dear old friend. Perhaps the reader may think I am overdoing all this, and that after twenty years I might not have felt myself guilty of such an enormity in having tried to ignore the debt of love I owed him as if it were something like a money debt that might be outlawed. But I do not think so, and I cling to the sense of my meanness with the humiliation that seems a sort of atonement. When the driver, who was also the owner, of my *timonella* found his way to my friend's home and drove rattling over the cobble-stones into the court, I looked up, and there in the gallery was the son whom I remembered a comely boy and now saw a handsome young gentleman looking down, and "Oh, Signor Howells!" he shouted and called to his father somewhere indoors that I was there, and came running to help me dismount. By that time Pastorelli himself had come to welcome me and my un-heeded explanations. It seemed enough for him that I was there, expectedly or unexpectedly, but he did not embrace me, as if that would not have been in keeping with the ideal of a retired English gentleman which he was otherwise imperfectly realizing in his deep-brimmed straw hat and summer linen suit. He did not look so very much older than when I saw him last though he was grayer, and he had visibly to work back into the past before he could get on the old terms with me. We walked out into his garden, and paced its parallelogram, while he made me observe his beautiful house, which was not the villa I remembered but visibly if not confessedly the finest house in his town; he must have gone deep into the strong-box which he used to keep at the Countess N——'s to buy it: fifty thousand francs, he said. He asked me all about myself, and said that I must be very rich to be travelling over Europe with my family as I was doing. He asked me if I had breakfasted, and I said, Yes, at Pedrocchi's in Padua; but from time to time he recurred to the question, always breaking from his Italian with the entreaty in English of "Hah! Have a beef-steak, have a beef-steak." He led me up into his library, and there he took down a map, and had me show him just how I had come from America, in the voyage which I had first made through one of our great lakes and down one of our great rivers from Toronto to the straits of Belle Isle, and so across the sea to Liver*pull*, as he still called it. He preferred to speak Italian, but from time to time when he forgot that I had break-fasted he recurred hospitably to "Hah, have a beef-steak; have a beef-steak." Again he recurred to the fact that I was now living by authorship, and mainly by writing romances, as he called them, but since I still denied myself the beefsteak, which I do not think he could have given me, he had up bottles of every kind of wine which he made from the grapes on his Possessions, and then when we had talked out, he called in his son, who came with his gentle young wife, and made them listen to his proud version of my wondrous tale. He showed them how I had sailed from fifteen hundred miles inland before I reached the sea, and told them that I gained forty thousand francs a year by writing romances. He had me tell them about my family and then pres-ently, somehow, the young father and mother brought out the photograph of the little child they had lost and showed it with trembling lips and swimming eyes. My dear old friend would not or could not look at them; he kept staring straightforward as if they were not there; but when they had gone away he said that the poor little mother was the daughter of one of the most his-torical houses of Venice; and if he was proud of this I do not blame him. The old apothecary who had made himself the first citizen of his *cauntree* would naturally, such being human nature, feel this his greatest distinction. I could only love him the more for his pride in it, and I wish I could think now of our friendship with as great reason to respect myself as him. I know it was his romantic interest in my language which first drew him to me, but that was an eccentricity which had its appeal to me through my own like affection for all Latin peoples. I liked being a bit of his poetry, a color of the enthusiasm which endeared Webster's Unabridged Dictionary to him, but I hope my pleasure in this has not had an undue effect in my memories of him. I knew very little about him except what I knew of him in our intercourse, though I was aware of a certain reluctance from him in some of my *italianissimi* friends which I think derived from the cut of his beard rather than any unpatriotic quality of what was at worst his discreet opportunism in the political situation. I believe he was a better Catholic than most Venetians, but his charity was a mantle that covered all my sins of heresy; he may have learnt in Liver*pull* a greater toleration even than seemed to prevail among all the Venetians I knew and that allowed me to flatter myself that several clergymen of my acquaintance were also my friends. But Pastorelli was my friend above all except a friend nearer my own age who was still more constantly my companion, and with whom I exchanged our language in a more equal use of English and Italian. Pastorelli wished always to speak English, and this suited my indolent humor, when the obligation to speak Italian with almost everyone else was stressful.

If we should somehow meet somewhere in those dateless and placeless eternities which it seems less and less fond to trust in as the little left of time goes by, I shall know him as far as I can see him, and I shall see him in the figure and fashion of the earlier eighteen sixties, and I shall confidently hail him in the language of our Unabridged Dictionary with the hope that its resources will enable me to excuse, if not justify, my demerits and defects to him. I cannot hope that his purged vision will fail to pierce the mixed motives which had so nearly lost me our last earthly meeting, but I am sure he will forgive them all, and will keep me in the kindness which never ceased on earth to make me feel him unsurpassed among the friends of my over-friended life.

"A YOUNG VENETIAN FRIEND"

I DO not know just how or when it was that I made the acquaintance of my friend Biondini, but it must have been a little later than my meeting with Pastorelli, though again it was at the office of my consular predecessor. My first sense of Biondini was of a tall youth of nineteen or twenty, swarthy, with an aquiline nose and pouted lips, and with large, rather startled black eyes, full of alert intelligence, and more and more a look of dissembled humor. He was at once recognizable as of *condizione civile*, from his speech and bearing, and in time it appeared that his father was a timber merchant who sent up into the mountains above Venice and cut the trees which he floated down into the lagoon, where many rafts of logs weltered until they were ready to be sawn into lumber. His rafts were never distinctively known to me, and I cannot say just why or how he became known; perhaps it was because he wished to see what the strange young consul was like who had become the constant friend of a son perhaps almost as strange to him. There must have been a strain of the same intellectual curiosity in the father which attracted his son, but he was of a rather theatrical presence, very different from the serious calm of Biondini; a friend of both once characterized him to me as a *commediante*, in the phrase which Pio VII. applied to Napoleon after an histrionic scene which the emperor enacted before the Pope. He played less the part of a father anxious to know the make of his son's friend than that of a man of the world who was in the joke of the odd youth and was willing to share it with another man of the world, but at the same time was a little daunted by his son's qualities and ideals. We met rather late in my acquaintance with Biondini, who took me to call on his mother, a most domestic, gentle little woman, smiling in the sunless propriety of a peculiarly Venetian apartment away somewhere in a modest campo, or on a narrow canal. They all gave me the sense of a family life very simple and kind, altogether unlike the operatic notion of Italian things which indeed I had very early begun to reject.

Before my knowledge of Biondini's family began my acquaintance had spread to friends of his whom I was glad to keep mine as long as I lived in Venice, and I have studied in an early sketch so fully that I need not do much more here. They were first the brilliant young girl, niece of an old advocate, and the advocate's elderly secretary who acted as her chaperon, and then her mother whom I came to know at home, after I had known her daughter in her evening walks on the Piazzetta. The advocate had been compromised in one of the demonstrations against the Austrians, and he lived in a retirement which was a sort of captivity for the vivid young creature, but she had learned how to liberate herself in the charge of the secretary, and hardly less of the secretary's friend, Biondini. He, on his part, knew how presently to let me join him in her company; the affair must have been very irregular, but nothing could have been more decorous, and evening after evening we walked together, she talking Italian poetry and Venetian patriotism, and the secretary keeping her literary and revolutionary vivacity in bounds. I was already engaged in marriage beyond the sea, and it was confessed for the Paronsina, or Little Mistress, as her guardian called her, that she was promised to a young advocate of the mainland somewhere, who never appeared on our scene; so that we could pace together in front of the secretary in the reciprocal propriety which Biondini helped doubly to assure. They were both there to help out my faltering understanding of her Italian, with Biondini to respond proudly to my appeals in English when I got beyond my depth. In this part he was of an ideal gravity and a delicate propriety which the secretary tried to characterize to me when he described him as a "white fly" in the blameless purity of his life. For himself he could early offer the warranty of his fiduciary employment, his advanced age, and his care of the Paronsina from her earliest childhood.

It was all very pretty, and the prettier because our association remained without romantic effect in real life. Eventually the Paronsina married, not the young advocate of the mainland, but, when Venice had become politically part of Italy, a Senator of the realm. By that time Biondini had long since gone to live in Verona, and he could only give my wife and me the Paronsina's address, but when I went to call for the sake of the friendship which had grown up between our families, I found her absent from Venice. In the earlier day, the day of her girlish spirit and beauty which the silence and solitude of her uncle's house could not eclipse, she must have had her share of the honor and affection of the society which knew her mother akin to the President of the Venetian republic of 1848; and she would have helped receive this society on those days of the week when a reluctant fire was kindled in the plaster stove and cups of black coffee were served with little cakes to dip into them. In the service of this hospitality I figure her brilliantly smiling with that somewhat arch beauty of hers which was of a northern irregularity rather than of the classic forms which we imagine Italian. In these repressed functions the Paronsina would avow her patriotic passion in the verse of the Italian poets which she knew by heart; but her mother was not so rigidly bound to the Demonstration (as the passive resistance of Austria was called) that she wished to keep the girl wholly from the joy of life, and she even suffered herself to be taken with her to the opera by the American consul and his wife one night; yes, even that, but upon the sworn condition that they should be allowed to remain strictly in the back of the box where they could not be seen, or so much as surmised by any one who would betray this infraction of the iron law of their mourning for Italy.

It seems to me that I have told all this before somewhere else;

but if one were not to repeat one's self at eighty one would say very little, and there would not be much use in living so long. The worst of it is that it seems rather far from Biondini and my business of remembering him, for he would not have been of the society which frequented the house of the Paronsina's mother in those functional days. He was associated with the Paronsina solely by his friendship with her uncle's secretary, who was decidedly more of his class than hers; he shook his head in self-respectful ignorance when I mentioned Pastorelli's great friend, the Countess N——; and I do not suppose he was ever at the opera, unless he went in the rear of the pit, where he would have stood throughout with the Italians, smoking the long black crooked cigars tubed with straws and known as Virginias, which were almost equivalent to a declaration of enmity to the Austrian officers who sat smoking in the orchestra chairs. For the comedy which was allowed even to the most ardent patriots, we frequented the vast old barn called the Teatro Malibran, after the great daughter of the great Garcia, and saw there the plays of Goldoni, and many more of the modern dramas which I was beginning to read under Biondini's direction. We were now in the full exchange of our respective languages, less in the grammatical study of them than in the colloquial use; and it was our theory that I could not hear too much Italian spoken, whether on or off the stage. Out of the past which keeps so many vital things hidden, I can still see him struggling to tell me in English what I had not understood in Italian from the stage, with a torment of straining eyes and writhing limbs and of a despairing final shrug, and the vain cry of "*Non so spiegarmi*," till our neighbors hissed us silent, after the custom of the Malibran with all disturbers of the peace.

We went out at six o'clock in the plain day of the summer afternoons, and straight home at nine. It seems now a very strange life, and I dare say it really was strange, and my prevailing melancholy in it was something which my friend was not slow to note. Biondini himself was mostly of a serious mood, and he was very much in earnest about learning English. That summer he added French to it and we studied the accidence and prosody of that language from such Italian as I was beginning to have in common with him, so that I acquired the Italian accent of it which is more the surprise than the pleasure of the French.

Meanwhile, I acquired from him also something of the Latin punctuality, so much greater than the Anglo-Saxon punctuality which I had supposed in myself, and I grew to have at least more fidelity to engagements, though never so much as he. If his race is more prone than ours to say the thing that is not, I am bound to declare that I have never known a more truthful soul than he, though in this, as in his purity of life, he may have been a white fly. He was of a right-mindedness which I never knew falter except once when he broke our tacit pact of sympathy in all humane causes by arguing that we of the North were wrong to confiscate the property of the South in slaves. At all other times he and all the other Venetians I knew were constant to our cause as one with their own; and I never knew how he came by his false reasoning on this point, but he yielded it to my indignation, and we forgot it together. In the modern Italian poets and romancers, especially those whose veiled or open meanings burned with patriotic fire, he was as deeply versed as the Paronsina herself, and our talk was largely of these in our interminable walks together from the Campo di Marte at one end of the city to the Public Gardens at the other. He lent me lavishly of his favorite historical novels, like D'Azeglio's *Nicolò de' Lapi*, and Grossi's *Marco Visconti*, and Cantù's *Vavassori Bresciani*, and Guerrazzi's *Isabella Orsini*. I like to recall the names because of my love for him who loved the books, and I would like to pretend that I read them with something of his own fervor; but I will be honester with my reader than I was with my friend: I never could have much pleasure of historical novels, even English ones, much less the Italian which were fashioned after Scott's, and formed then the only Italian fiction. In those years I was reading Dickens and shrieking with joy in his grotesquery, and I tried to make Biondini enjoy it, but I remember how he confessed, after trying *Our Mutual Friend*, the impossibility, for him,

of the humor that intoxicated me. I think that this really hurt
the classic sense of his race with something like a physical wound,
and gave him grave doubt of my mental, if not moral, worth.
I blamed the Italian fiction for its want of contemporaneity, but
now I must own that it was better form than the fables of
Dickensland where I invited Biondini to share my riot.

Our walks were oftenest in the narrow footways crooking from
one open space before a church to another, and they became in
after years the scene of the dreams in which I still frequent some
of them; but what remains of a waking memory of our walks is
mostly a sense of the hot, dry closes of the summer days in the
spread of some vast space before a nameless church, where the
ground is strewn with the shells of pumpkin-seeds, and the air is
rank with the smell of frying cakes, and the shrieking of the
venders is penetrated by the sharp clack of the women's wooden-
heeled slippers. There is also the perception of Biondini stooping
toward me from his greater height to make sure of the meaning
of my very tired Italian.

I do not recall his ever going to the Piazza San Marco with
me; as a very good Venetian he could not go there till the
Austrian band had stopped playing at night, and possibly he
could not have afforded his share of the expense; of course he
would not have allowed me to play the host; that would not have
been Italian usage. His father very likely restricted this good son
in his pleasures, though later he spent freely upon his education
at the University of Padua. I think that all the time I first knew
him he was preparing for Padua, and that it was his spare hours
that he gave to his studies with me. In those long summer-
evening rambles, when we were not talking of the Italian poets
and romancers, we were talking of Venice and its life, and I
believe he always told me true, so that if I had reported him
alone in my conjectures I should never have gone wrong, as I
think I did in certain matters.

Our friendship was in its mild heyday at the close of my first
year. When I began my second with the help of her who was to
be my best help in good things while she lived, Biondini was not

less than dismayed by his introduction to her on my return from England, where I had gone to meet her with her brother; for I had not told him or any one of the errand which was taking me from Venice. He could only gasp incoherently in Italian, till he managed to bring out in English, "Your sister?" "No; my wife." Then he gasped, and stared with all his eyes, till at last he broke into a helpless, irrelevant laugh in which we could all join.

In time he began coming to me again; but we never could habituate him to the mild hospitality we wished to have shown him. The traditions of his past forbade the comfort which people of our race have in breaking bread with one another. Once, when we did lure him to our table, he cut his steak into small cubes and then ate the cubes one by one till all were gone; we saw that the case was hopeless, and tormented him no more with our good-will. But we lived in greater and greater ease with one another; he became a house friend of such inclusiveness that after a year or so, when we went a journey to Rome and Naples and left our little one in charge of her uncle the sculptor, who came from Florence to be my vice-consul, Biondini joined him in the care of the baby and the consulate.

Eventually, in the succession of the consuls who were appointed after me, he was able to advise them in their duties, and became himself consul in everything but Presidential appointment. But now his most distinguished and exceptional function was the part he bore as interpreter between the sculptor and the beautiful Venetian girl who fell in love with each other in her going to and from the Piazza with her parents; and it must have been by Biondini's instruction in the Italian etiquette that when their feeling became unmistakable to themselves the sculptor wrote to her father and begged, if there were no previous engagement, that he might be allowed to offer himself to her. After that, when the father and mother took their evening walks to the Piazza, Biondini went before them with the lovers and helped construe them to each other in alternate English and Italian. He must also have been present at the family council which the uncle from Milan summoned to consider the question of their differing churches. At the close of this conference the sculptor afterward reported himself as having said in English, "Gentlemen, I don't know whether I've understood you exactly, but if you expect me to change my religion you are very much mistaken." This, as interpreted, might logically have ended the affair, and might well have done so, if the heroine had not used a heroine's right of falling sick and refusing to be comforted. The uncle from Milan, who had favored the match from the beginning, came again, and did not rest till, as I have heard, all the hierarchy of Venice, up to the Patriarch himself, were interested in the affair. I do not say that the reverend clergy actually intervened in the lovers' behalf, but it was somehow decided that since the church would not and could not join the lovers in marriage there was nothing for them to do but to go into the kingdom of Italy and be united there by the civil rite. This was what they did, and at Florence they were made man and wife by the syndic and lived there forty years in one of the happiest marriages that ever were. Twice or thrice they visited America, and on one of those visits the wife was almost converted at the Moody and Sankey revivals, but being saved from this the good Catholic and the good Protestant grew closer on other terms: he went to mass with her, though he was no more persuaded to be of her faith than she had been to be of his.

The time passed, and it appeared to the consul that he had better be thinking of a future which did not seem to lie in office-holding, though he might have remained in his place indefinitely through the succession of Republican presidents. The war was over, and, in the hope of finding his future in journalism or literature at home, he got leave of absence and returned provisionally. The tie of friendship with Biondini had not been severed or even weakened by his absence at Padua, where he had now been in the university for a year or more. Our train had scarcely halted there for the brief stay it made when Biondini burst into our carriage to bid us good-by. He brought flowers for my wife, and some sort of gift for our little daughter; for me, he had only an adieu impassioned beyond the friendship I had hitherto known in its Anglo-Saxon rather than its Latin phase—he threw his arms round my neck and kissed me.

The years passed in America, and Biondini visited us with letters faithfuller than our answers. He no longer lived in Venice, but in Verona, where he had got a professorship in a technical school, and seemed very happy. Then there came a cry for help, an appeal for our kindness in advising him how to come to America, and support himself in the city of Boston by teaching Italian; he wished to live with us, as we read his wish; and his letter filled us with despair for him, it seemed so little like him, so national, so unpersonal. After all, we said, he was of his emotional civilization, and not the calm, reasonable being he had always seemed. Of course the thing for us was to be kind, however cruel, and tell him that there was no popular interest in Italian literature in Boston, while teachers of the languages superabounded. We had to say that we could not receive him into our family, and we explained why.

Then came a cry of pain, of wounded pride. He had wished only to live *near* us, not *with* us, though he owned that the phrase —*presso di voi*—which he had used would bear either meaning. He submitted that we must be right about the Italian lessons, and he must give up the notion of coming; but he did not give us up; his letters continued, not so frequent as before, but in the old kindness which he never forgot, though they lapsed rather more into Italian from the English he used in them.

I do not remember just how or when we came to know the reason of that bitter urgency in his wish for expatriation; but we might have imagined the sole cause. It was not for twenty years, and not till we revisited Italy, that we learned it, after we had seen him again in Venice, where he came from Verona to welcome me and my family, and to be an affectionate cousin, or uncle, to our children as he was a younger brother to us, though older now in his serious and always rather formal regard. In the first of my acquaintance with him we used sometimes to talk of our different religions, if we might call our persuasions so. I knew that he seldom went to mass and never to confession, and he used to say in justification, "The church is good, the priests are bad," which was the position of so many men at Venice in those days. At the same time he denied the notion of anything like Protestantism, for the simple and sufficient reason that if it had been a wise and good thing the Italians and not the Germans would have found it out, and if they remained within the church it was because the church was the best place. But we did not often dispute about matters of faith, and I could never have imagined his opinions bringing a lifelong sorrow upon him. Yet so it was to be, and shortly before he wrote us that stressful letter he was to feel a supreme cause for it. He had fallen in love with a young lady of Padua, who returned his love, and they wished to marry. She was of a devout family, but her mother and she asked nothing of Biondini except that he should be reconciled to the church in one particular. It was not enough that he should say the church was good, whatever he said the priests were (I myself knew some of them who seemed angelic); it was not enough that he should go to mass—he consented to that—but they wanted him to go also to confession at least once a year, and this Biondini, perhaps with his poor opinion of priests, could not, or at least would not, do. The match was broken off, but so clingingly and longingly on both sides that he remained friends with the girl and her mother. He did not cease to visit them while he lived in Padua, or in Venice when he returned home, or in Verona when he went there. Every other Sunday he spent with them, and the conscience in their steadfast hearts kept them to the terms of marriage which made marriage impossible. The young lovers grew from their twenty years to their forty, and when we tarried a fortnight with Biondini in Verona they were lovers still.

We knew nothing of his affair then, and, for all we knew, we had him our old friend on the old terms. He had come first to see us in Venice, and then, when we stopped at Verona for our farewell to Italy, he met us at the station with a book in his hand for the child he had known in her babyhood but now a young girl with our hopes, rather than hers, radiant before her, for there seemed even then the prescience of our loss at her heart. The book was a wonderful Italian translation of "Romeo and Juliet" which he had bound up with the English for her, and entitled, from his own fancy in English, *A Girl's Guide to Verona*. It was constantly with us there, and while she lived it seemed always about, but now that she is lost (twenty-eight long years ago!) I hope it is lost, too. So many things that were joys are now pangs! But there was something rarely thought in this kind remembrance of his; and there was something charming in his conceit of Shakespeare's Italians as realistic portraitures of actual life in Verona. He held that people spoke there now as Shakespeare made them speak in his play, with the same gay and fond fancies, and I should be glad to think he was right.

He seems to have been with us all the time, except for those visits, as he called the calls, which he paid at the houses he frequented with punctilious reference to the days and hours established and carefully noted in the memorandum he carried. He seemed happy, at least to us in our ignorance of his constancy to his first and sole love. He said, to account for no longer living in Venice, "Verona is a small city, and everybody loves me," and I could well believe that everybody loved him. He seemed to know everybody and was always saluting people right and left in our walks, or at the cafés where we sat long in the warm May evenings at the ices, which he taught us frugally to order in half portions. Sometimes we had the company there of the Jewish friend whose modest silk warehouse Biondini made his address, or *ricapito*, after what seemed a local fashion, and got his letters there. This friend was a descendant of a Hebrew family which one of the fool Philips, III. or IV., had expelled from Spain, and he still kept the key of his ancestral house in the fancy, which could not be the hope, of return from exile. He accepted a portion of our friendship with Biondini in the eager fashion of his race, but Biondini would not let him overrun us. He would not let him call himself a silk manufacturer, for he said that to an American that would express something in a measure vastly out of scale with his modest business; and he did not ask him to join us at the café in the Piazza Brà, as it used to be called, lest he should be guilty of some *ebreata* or other. "If a beggar comes up, I give him a copper, but De C—— gives him a lump of the sugar which belongs to the café; and I call that an *ebreata*—a Jewishness!" All the same we liked this friend of his, who was of a cordiality not at all oppressive, and he liked our liking him.

Biondini said truly of himself that everybody loved him in Verona, where he seemed to know not only all his townsmen, but all the strangers within their gates who spoke English. He had taught De C—— as much of the language as he would learn, but this would not give him the practice he wanted, and he used to lie in wait for the English and American travellers, and help them out of their difficulties with his language. In this way he made many friends of these casual acquaintances, and I doubt if his kindness was ever rebuffed, for it must have been clear that he was a gentleman, however quaint his approach might be. It really kept his English bright, and this, after the adventurous pleasure, must have been the great matter with him.

He did not offer to go about with us, for he knew us bold and experienced travellers, who were almost as much at home in Italy as he; but he came every afternoon to see us in our beloved hotel beside the Adige, where the mills in the middle current outsang the swift stream, and stayed till his faithful note-book reminded him that he must "pay a visit" to this lady or that whose hour and day it was. He would not eat with us at the early dinner which we always prolonged through five portions of strawberries—the dry, hard little strawberries of the country which smelled so much better than they tasted; but though he would not eat with us he was glad to talk, sitting apart, and finding his pleasure in answering any question, especially of the children. "Ah, I will explain you that is a very curious thing," he would say, laying his finger sagaciously beside his nose, in a formula which the children promptly adopted, and which was never quite lost out of our family life. They loved him as much as we did, and he was gentle and equal with them all.

He might well have outlived me, who after twenty years am so imperfectly recording our friendship, laying hold upon this frail fact and that, and not despising any credible conjecture because I cannot verify it. No doubt when we meet Yonder we shall wonder together how I could have forgotten this thing and that which would have set our common history in the very light my earth-bound memory has failed to lend it. But I am less anxious for the incidents and the implications of our life than for the meaning which I hope his nature as I knew it will have for such readers as may cling to our old Northern superstition concerning the gentle people of the South. So many of us still think the Italians are rash as fire and false as water, and do not conceive of them as patient and faithful and just, but judge them all by the mongrel races of the Sicilies, or by the inventions of medieval fiction, not realizing that they are of a Christianity and a civility older than ours by centuries, which cannot have failed to beautify and purify their natures. But this has only tangentially to do with Biondini, who did not fail throughout our friendship in whatever stress I put upon it. When my book about Venice reached him he read it, and gently deplored the view I had taken of the morals of Venetian society, but said no more than that he wished I had gone further for my facts. In the later editions of *Venetian Life* (why *will* people call it "Venetian Days"?) I have expressed my grief for my error, but not sufficiently my gratitude to him for the faithfuller light which his constant instruction cast upon the place and the people, always with some glance of humor in it. He had a graphic wit which would glancingly portray a character or a condition, as when, after passing one day in Verona a friend who had married a rich American girl, he implied the husband's actual relation to her by twiddling his finger at the side of his hat to suggest the cockade of a footman.

After those brief days in Verona we came north through Milan and Bellinzona, all our hearts aching for the Italy we were leaving, which had been our first home, and which our children had retroactively made theirs through our talk of it, and now through the friend we were none of us to see again. His letters followed us for a while, and then we heard, after a lapse, that he had suffered a slight stroke of paralysis. I do not know whether he wrote me

of this, or whether some one else told me, but I am right in thinking that when one of my wife's sisters was afterward in Venice,
he went to find her there, and she saw him in the wheeled chair
which he went about in; he could not walk, he who had trodden
those narrow ways with me so often! I always have the vision of
him there, or, if the reader likes better, in Verona, the small city
where everybody loved him.

APPENDIX A:

"*My Times and Places. An Autobiography*"

[The outline of "My Times and Places. An Autobiography," referred to in the Introduction (see page 215), is reproduced here in its entirety. The manuscript, which is in the Harper Collection at the Pierpont Morgan Library, consists of five leaves of laid, watermarked paper, 5 in. x 8 in., inscribed in Howells' hand in black ink with some pencil revision on the recto only. It is reproduced below in a line-by-line transcription, with all deletions printed within angle brackets at the points where they occur in the manuscript. Pencilled materials are not distinguished from those in black ink here, overwritings have not been noted, and errors are printed without the use of *sic*. Printed by permission of the Morgan Library and Harper & Row, Publishers.]

MY TIMES AND PLACES.
An Autobiography.

I   *Wales and Pennsylvania.*
     Late 18th and early 19th centuries.
     Welsh and German ancestry,
     with English and Irish strains.
     Studies of Conditions and
     characters among my fathers
     and mother's people.

II   *Southern Ohio from 1837 to 1850.*
     Society, Religion, Politics.
     Boyhood. First Books. Play
     and playmates. Social
     and Domestic Conditions.

III *Connecticut Western Reserve* from
     1850 to 1857. A Transplanted

New England. The people,
their agnosticism and love
of reading. Absolute
social equality in Jefferson,
county seat of Ashtabula.
My reading and companion-
-ships. Young life; parties;
seranades; dances; fairs;
printing office; studies in
Spanish Latin, Greek,
German, French. Constant
literary aims. Friendships.
<and love affairs. > Essays
in journalism. Sojourns
in Columbus. Failing
health.

IV.	*Columbus a State Capital*
1857	of the old kind. Out-
1861	-look into the World of
——	Society. <Ar> Parties,
	calls, picnics, theatres Public
	Characters. On the
	verge of the Civil
	War. The winter before
	Sumter. The volunteering
	and first camps. My Life
<V>	of Lincoln. First
	contributions to the Atlantic
	eastern papers. Visit to
	Canada and <Bo>
	New England. <Meet
	with my wife>. Literary
	feeling in Columbus. Very
	cultivated Society. Seeking
<V>	a consulship

V.	*Italy on the Verge of Union.*
1861	Appointment to Venice

1865 and life there from Dec.
—— 1861 to July 1865. Voyage
out. First impressions of
London and Paris.
Journey by rail through
Vienna to Venice in mid-
-winter. Social and
political conditions at Venice.
Journeys into "free Italy"—
Milan. <Flor> <Ver> Journeys
in Venetia, to Verona,
Vicenza, Padua, etc.
Study of revolutionary
feeling. Marriage at
Paris, in 1862. Home-
-coming to Venice. House-
-keeping <C> in Casa
Falier and Palazzo
Giustiniani. Journeys to
Florence, Genoa, Na-
-ples, Rome.

VI. *America just after the*
1865 *Civil War.* Return on
—— Leave of Absence. No
prospect of immediate
employment. Resign my
office. Beating about
New York for a "basis"
on some paper. Finding
"basis" on The Nation.
Study of New York in 1865–6.
Invitation to go to Boston
as Ass't Editor Atlantic.

VII *Life in Cambridge.* The
1866 College turning University.
1878 College Society—Society
—— Generally—Intellectual

Tone—Boston from Cam-
-bridge. First acquaint-
-ances and friendships—
Conditions after the War—
Its traces.

VIII.　　*Removal to the Country.*
1882　　　Four Years of Work—Country
1883　　　life a mistake—First
——　　　 <f> visit to Europe <after>
　　　　　1882 since 1865. London
　　　　　and its charm. Winter
　　　　　in Florence and Siena.
　　　　　Venice revisited. London
　　　　　again. Return home in
　　　　　July 1883.

IX　　　　*Settlement in Boston.* Its
1883　　　charm for me. Society.
1888　　　Dinners, lunches, breakfast
——　　　 Interesting personalities
　　　　　of all Kinds. Devotion
　　　　　to Fiction. Invitation to
　　　　　place on Harpers. Resump-
　　　　　-tion of reviewing and
　　　　　essaying. Books.

X.　　　　Years of Drifting. Buffalo
1887　　　and its charming Society.
1890　　　New York. Back to
——　　　 Boston. Long summers
　　　　　in the Country of New
　　　　　<York>. England. Books.

XI　　　　Final Settlement in
1891　　　New York.

——

XII　　　*Travel Years.*

1898 <Rome> Carlsbad;
1912 Germany; San
——   Remo; Rome;
      Paris; London;
      Spain. Working all
      the time. Studies
      of <all> places visited.
      Their changes in
      forty five years.

APPENDIX B:

"Years of My Middle Life"

[The synopsis of "Years of My Middle Life," referred to in the Introduction (see page xxvii), is reproduced here in its entirety. The manuscript, which is in the Houghton Library at Harvard University, consists of a single sheet of 8½ in. x 11 in. wove, unwatermarked paper, folded along its shorter dimension. It is inscribed in black ink in Howells' hand on the two portions of one side of the sheet only. It is apparently a draft, containing a few deletions of false starts and misspellings (which are printed within angle brackets at the points where they occur in the manuscript). Errors are retained and are not accompanied by *sic*.]

YEARS OF MY MIDDLE LIFE.

I

Consular Service at Venice—Fitness and Unfitness—Marriage in Paris—Different Residences—Conception of Italian Character—Study of Modern Italian Literature—Question of prolonged Consular Service or return Home and resumption of journalism—Various Acquaintance among Italians—Limited Experience through Political

Conditions—Domestic Conditions—Travels through Italy—Excursions to cities in nearer regions—Decision to go Home after Lincoln's Death—Return through England—Trying to get "Venetian Life" published in London and failure—First Impressions of English character—Effect of English Unfriendliness <through> during the Civil War—Return to America at Boston, and first Defeat of <Literar> journalistic Hopes—Journalistic <H> Success in New York—New York journalists and Literati—Invitation to Boston and acceptance of Assistant Editorship of Atlantic Monthly—Settlement in Cambridge, where no rentable house was to be found, as now, <anywhere> because of left-over war conditions—Charles Eliot Norton joins with my wife's father in buying us a little house <—> in Sacramento Street— <Sell> I sell this house after four years at a profit of $40—Remove to Berkeley street where we live two years—Buy land from Professor Parsons on Concord Avenue and build a house where we meant to spend our lives, but spent six years—Bret Harte and his family came to us in Berkeley street, and we made our great first social essay in a party for them—In Concord Avenue my intimacy with Mark Twain began—John Hay and his wife visited us—W. <Waldof?> Waldorff Astor brought letter from Hay and lunched with us, and we went more and more into society, and came to know everybody in Cambridge—Longfellow came to supper to meet Garfield—Three or four years intimacy with Henry James when we walked daily together and read each other what we had written—I took all his stuff for the Atlantic except one "humorous" story—Bayard Taylor, the Stoddards, and all the young writers of both sexes occurred—Charles Dudley Warner—Mark Twain and his pastor blow in at one of our parties after a partial walk from Hartford to Cambridge—*Removal to Belmont in a house built for us by McKim, Mead and White*. These partners studied in their relation to this work.

Notes to the Text

Annotation is provided only where the information is not available in standard, one-volume reference works. Except as noted, the source of bibliographical information is William M. Gibson and George Arms, *A Bibliography of William Dean Howells* (New York, 1948). Two works frequently drawn upon are cited by short title: *Life in Letters of William Dean Howells*, ed. Mildred Howells (Garden City, N.Y., 1928), is cited as *Life in Letters*; and William Cooper Howells' *Recollections of Life in Ohio, from 1813 to 1847* (Cincinnati, 1895) as *Recollections*.

3.14   six years before my birth: William Cooper Howells (1807–1894) wed Mary Dean (1812–1868) on 10 July 1831.

3.14–15   the second child in their family of eight: the other Howells children were Joseph (1832–1912), Victoria (1838–1886), Samuel (1840–1908), Aurelia (1842–1931), Annie (1844–1938), John (1846–1864), and Henry (1852–1906).

4.19ff.   his great-grandfather: his name is not known, and Howells is probably in error: in a letter to his sister Aurelia of 9 August 1903 (*Life in Letters*, II, 176) he noted that the name of the maker on the clock, "George Howells," was that of his father's great-uncle.

4.22–23   Two sons followed him: there were three sons— George (?–?), William (?–?), and Thomas Howells (1750–1824); William was probably the one who returned to Wales (see 4.24–25 in the present text).

4.24   one of them married in London: Thomas Howells, William Dean Howells' great-grandfather, married Susannah Beesley (?–1820) on 5 September 1772.

4.30   Hywel Dda: or Howel Dda (?–950), was prince of Deheubarth (south central Wales) before 915, and king of Wales, or of the West Welsh, from 943 to 950.

5.9–10 my great-grandfather with his brothers went to London: according to William Cooper Howells' *Recollections* (page 1), only one brother, William, accompanied Thomas Howells to London.

5.16   Parepa: Euphrosyne Parepa-Rosa (*née* Parepa de Boyescu), a mid-nineteenth century soprano (1836–1874), was born in London.

5.32   the English girl: Susannah Beesley Howells; see Note to 4.24.

6.6–8   Vaughan Kester . . . . Paul Kester: Vaughan (1869–1911) and Paul Kester (1870–1933) were related to Howells through Harriet Howells, their great-grandmother and his great-aunt.

6.21ff. another family tradition: the story is also recounted in *Recollections*, page 5.

6.31   He was already married: Joseph Howells (1783–1858), one of the sons of Thomas Howells, married Anne Thomas (c.1785–1863) on 17 February 1805.

6.31–32 my father a year old: William Cooper Howells was born on 15 May 1807.

6.34–7.1 In the memoir which my father wrote: *Recollections*, which was published with W. D. Howells' help, but not until 1895, one year after William Cooper Howells' death.

7.2–3   he tells that my grandmother formed the highest opinion of Boston: *Recollections*, page 7.

7.8–9   I saw her for the last time in a village of northwestern Ohio: Bowling Green, where Anne Thomas Howells died; Howells' last visit was probably that made in September 1861, mentioned in his letters of the time.

7.15–16   the fame of the poets whom I had met there the year before: the story of his 1860 trip is told by Howells in "My First Visit to New England," *Literary Friends and Acquaintance*.

8.5   *Tour of Wales*: Howells' memory has probably provided him with a generalized title which could apply to any number of books, among them Defoe's *A Tour Through England and Wales*.

8.36   *The Gleaner*: William Cooper Howells describes the magazine, which was published for one year beginning December 1828 in Buffalo Creek, near Wheeling, in *Recollections*, pages 165–171.

9.1   his sister: Anne Cooper Howells (1809–1868).

9.5   *The Rise, Progress and Downfall of Aristocracy*: the title page notes that the book was published in Wheeling by "The author" (William Mathers) in 1831.

9.9ff.   he was presently living contentedly: Howells is wrong at several points about the sequence of events in his father's life. The details given by William Cooper Howells in his own *Recollections* (pages 172–193) are as follows: he went to St. Clairsville (not St. *Clairville*, as Howells records at 9.10–11) in August 1831 to work for the *Belmont Chronicle*, but quit the job after a one-year term and got temporary employment as printer in the office of Horton J. Howard in St. Clairsville; after a month there, he went to Mt. Pleasant, Ohio, to work on a monthly periodical called the *Repository*; after a year in that position he went back to Wheeling and, in the fall of 1833, had a job as pressman in a local firm until April 1834, when he went to Chillicothe, Ohio, to work for the *Scioto Gazette*; he gave up that job in turn, moved onto a farm in Chillicothe with his father in the spring of 1835, and worked at setting type while studying medicine on his own— until he got sick in December 1835 and could carry on neither task; but in March 1836 he was back at setting type to pay for his intended medical studies, this time working until the spring of 1836, when his health still failed to respond sufficiently and he decided to move to Martinsville near his father-in-law and get odd jobs at house-painting; by means of this work he managed to buy a lot there, build a house (the one in which William Dean Howells was born) and remain until the fall of 1839, when construction in the area had so fallen off that he could find little employment to support himself; finally, in the fall of 1839, he accompanied his mother's brother, William Dock, to Dayton, from there to join the rest of the family in Hamilton.

9.27   William Dock: 1793–1840(?).

9.35   the Whig newspaper: the Hamilton *Intelligencer*.

10.4ff.   The things that I seem to remember: both the peach-tree in bloom and the drowning incident are described in the first chapter of *A Boy's Town* (1890), "Earliest Experiences."

10.18–19   my young uncles: their names were apparently William Dean, Samuel Dean, and Alexander Dean.

10.29–31 my father's family, who had now left Wheeling, and were settled in southwestern Ohio: Howells' sentence is misleading in its suggestion that William Cooper Howells' family moved to that part of Ohio after he did; according to *Recollections*, pages 192–193, the family had preceded him.

11.18–19 my aunt, their only surviving daughter: besides Anne Cooper Howells there had been one other daughter, Harriet (1824–1829).

11.34ff. other sons: Joseph Howells had at least four brothers, but two died in infancy and a third at the age of 19, so only one can be imagined as having more than one wife—Henry Charles Howells (1784–1865), who William Dean Howells once said had 26 children.

12.8–9 Some of my father's younger brothers: William Cooper Howells had one older brother who died in infancy in 1806 and four others younger than he—Joseph Howells (1814–1896), the physician; Israel Howells (1820–1854), a dentist in Dayton, Ohio; Henry Howells (1816–1905), the druggist; and Thomas Howells (1811–1888), who is presumably the "speculative adventurer" William Dean Howells speaks of (at 12.12).

12.24–25 The lines are from some version of the folk ballad commonly entitled "The Wagoner's Lad" or "On Top of Old Smoky"; cf. Cecil J. Sharp, ed., *English Folk Songs from the Southern Appalachians* (London, 1932), II, 123.

13.27 their mother's house: the home of Elizabeth Dock Dean (c.1794–1842), wife of John Dean (?–?).

14.27–28 the ten or eleven years passed in Hamilton: the Howellses were actually in Hamilton from the spring of 1840 to May 1849.

15.3   Tennyson, "A Dream of Fair Women," l. 80.

15.26   My first attempt at literature: the piece has not been
              located in the extant files of the Hamilton *Intelligencer*.

16.13   Sim Haggett: the real or fictional person has not been
              identified.

17.30–31   "Pity the sorrows of a poor old man": Thomas Moss,
              "The Beggar," l. 1.

18.17   Hallock's *Marco Bozzaris*: Fitz-Greene *Halleck* (1790–
              1867), whose poem was first published in book form
              in *Alnwick Castle, with other poems* (1827).

20.3ff.   I have already used it in fiction: in chapter VIII of
              The Flight of Pony Baker (1902), "How Pony Baker
              Came Pretty Near Running Off With a Circus."

21.7   Solomon's mind: cf. Proverbs, especially chapter
              XIII, for the relations of parents and children.

28.22   a car going north in Fourth Avenue: Howells wrote a
              good part of *Years of My Youth* in New York City.

29.16   Tom Lindsay: he has not been identified.

29.24   *The Cruise of the Midge*: by Michael Scott (1789–1835);
              the novel was published in 1835.

31.15   we went to live in Dayton: William Cooper Howells
              bought the Dayton *Transcript* in May 1849.

32.4   Kotzebue's "Stranger": the play is an English trans-
              lation of *Menschenhass und Reue* (1789–1790) by August
              Friedrich Ferdinand von Kotzebue (1761–1819).

32.4–5   Sheridan Knowles's "Wife": "The Wife, a Tale of
              Mantua" (1833) by James Sheridan Knowles (1784–
              1862).

32.6   "Barbarossa": a very popular tragedy by John Brown (1715–1766), first performed on 17 December 1754 by David Garrick.

32.6   "The Miser of Marseilles": a play by this name, origin unknown, was being performed in New York in 1856.

32.11   "A Glance at New York": a play by Benjamin A. Baker, first produced in 1848 with the title "A Glance at New York in 1848"; it became the great success of the 1847–1848 New York season, and went through several revisions, including the addition of characters like Eliza Stebbens ("Lize"), Sykesy, and Little Mose.

32.21   "sick and scornful looks averse": Tennyson, "A Dream of Fair Women," l. 101.

32.25   a dramatic attempt of his own: William Cooper Howells' historical melodrama on the War of 1812; cf. Edwin H. Cady, *The Road to Realism* (Syracuse, 1956), page 32.

33.14   a long poem in the quatrains of Gray's Elegy: this early attempt has not been identified.

33.16   the cholera: newspaper reports indicate that an epidemic of cholera in Dayton, which resulted in more than two hundred deaths, occurred in the summer of 1849.

35.10   Dubuffe: Claude Marie *Dubufe* (1789–1864), painter of portraits, religious tableaux, and scenes from mythology.

37.31–32   the famous native turtle, now extinct: the Galapagos land-tortoise is still very much alive.

38.20–21   a plan for our going into the country: the family moved to Eureka Mills on the Little Miami River in October 1850; Howells made fictional material out of his family's experience in the utopian settlement in *New Leaf Mills* (1913).

39.2–3   *My Year in a Log Cabin*: published as a book in 1893 after first being printed in *Youth's Companion* in 1887.

44.7   red fox-squirrels: the fox squirrel (*sciurus niger*) is not extinct.

47.27   *Western Adventure*: *Sketches of Western Adventure* (1832) by John Alexander McClung (1804–1859).

47.30   Howe's *Collections for the History of Ohio*; first published in 1847 and often thereafter in new editions, by Henry Howe (1816–1893).

47.33ff.   the tales of "Simon Kenton, the Pioneer": this and the other incidents listed here by Howells are contained in Howe's *Collections for the History of Ohio*, and some of them in *Sketches of Western Adventure*.

48.6–7   "Hamet el Zegri" and the "Unknown Spanish Knight": both figures in Washington Irving's *A Chronicle of the Conquest of Granada* (1829).

48.8   Adam Poe and the Indian chief Bigfoot: Howe's *Collections for the History of Ohio* records the meeting of the famous Indian fighter Adam Poe with the Wyandot chief Bigfoot in combat near Fort Pitt on the Ohio in the summer of 1782 and Poe's killing of the Indian.

49.29   Peter Parley's *First Book of History*: this book (published in 1831) was one of more than a hundred books for children released under the name of Peter Parley, a pseudonym for Samuel Griswold Goodrich (1793–1860), who initiated the series.

50.31   *Heavenly Arcana*: a translation of Emmanuel Sweden-borg's *Arcana coelestia* (1785–1789).

53.11   a printing-office in X———: Xenia, Ohio.

54.21   Again I was called to suffer a like trial: Howells' calendar of the events of his first trip, to Xenia (see Note to 53.11), and his second, to Dayton, and of the events after that and until the trip to Columbus (57.15ff.) can just barely be fitted into the period between the family's move to Eureka Mills in late 1850 and the departure for Columbus in the winter of 1851; he indicates that he went to Xenia in the second fall, and to Dayton sometime afterward, re-turning with his brother in "the November dawn" (55.5), probably early in the month; after that they lived in the new house "for two or three months" (56.9–10) before going to Xenia again (56.19ff.) to catch the train for Columbus, arriving there at the end of December 1851 (see Note to 57.18–19ff.).

57.18–19ff.   the reader who likes to date a small event by a great one: Lajos Kossuth (1802–1894), Hungarian patriot who was a leader of the revolution of 1848–1849, was forced to leave Hungary after the invasion of Russian troops in late 1849, and spent several years attempting to get official support for the revolution in England and America; he arrived in the United States on 5 December and proceeded to Washington, where he spoke before Congress, on 30 December 1851.

58.13   he duly came to Columbus: Kossuth arrived on 4 February 1852.

58.29   I fancied I had caught sight of his son: Ferenc Kossuth (1841–1914), briefly president of the Hungarian Party of Independence.

59.5–6   the new State House: the structure, which took more than ten years to complete, was officially opened on 7 January 1857.

59.30–31   he sat reporting the proceedings for the *Ohio State Journal*: William Cooper Howells held the position until the legislature adjourned in March 1852.

60.6ff.   As I have told elsewhere: Howells recounts several details of the Columbus experience in chapter XXIII of *My Literary Passions* and in a slightly different version in "In an Old-Time State Capital."

61.2   poets of thirteen: 1 March 1852 was in fact Howells' fifteenth birthday; cf. 62.26 in the present text.

62.5   a boyish diary of the time: the diary, under the title "Diary and Spanish Exercises, 1850–59," is in the Houghton Library; the description of it which follows in the present text is derived from Howells' unpublished essay, "The Real Diary of a Boy" (see Introduction, page xxiii, and A Note on the Manuscripts, page 329). Howells' description of the diary as beginning in the "closing months of 1851" is accurate and the library title for it is wrong. Howells' quotations from it and references to material in it are essentially correct.

63.4   the travels of Hommaire de Hell: Ignace Xavier Morand Hommaire de Hell (1851–1883) wrote *Les Steppes de la mer Caspienne, la Caucase, la Crimée et la Russie méridionale* (1843–1844), first translated into English in 1847.

64.8   the name of the boy: John James Piatt (1835–1917), with whom Howells published *Poems of Two Friends* in 1860; see the present text at 68.28ff.

64.14 a poem on the premature warm weather: "[Old winter, loose thy hold on us.] For the Ohio State Journal," *Ohio State Journal*, 23 March 1852, page 2; the *Journal's* "customary editorial note" reads: "Thanks to our young friend for the following. There is as much *truth* as poetry in it, and a fair amount of both . . ." The poem was reprinted in the Cincinnati *Commercial*, 24 April 1852, page 4; the New York paper has not been identified.

64.27–28 "The Emigrant's Last Meal in the Old House," *Ohio State Journal*, 3 June 1852, page 1, ll. 23–24; the original version reads—

> "He pats the good old house dog
> Who lies upon the floor."

65.11 *The Battle of the Frogs and Mice*: the Greek poem *Batrachomuomachia* has been variously attributed to Homer, Aesop, and others; Pope did not translate it.

65.12 *The Cat Fight*: the poem, which does survive but has not been published, is in manuscript in the Houghton Library and is there entitled "Battle of the Cats."

65.14 the only surviving poem: the untitled manuscript of this poem, unpublished before *Years of My Youth*, is on a loose sheet in the boyhood diary at the Houghton Library; the present text is different in a great many details from that version.

67.13 "cold pastoral": Keats, "Ode on a Grecian Urn," l. 45.

68.5 no wider interval: the legislature adjourned at the end of March 1852 and the Howells family left for Ashtabula in July.

68.14   Florus B. Plympton: Florus Beardsley *Plimpton* (1830–
          1886), Ohio journalist, may have contributed to the
          Ohio State Journal, but is not known to have held an
          editorial position there. Howells offers as the title of
          Plimpton's poem (68.19–20) the first line of it; en-
          titled "Summer Days," it was collected posthumously
          in *Poems* (1886); the first date of publication is not
          known.

68.32–35 we were then boys of thirteen or fourteen . . . in the
          long leisure of the spring afternoons of 1850: given
          the chronology of other events, Howells is wrong on all
          counts; the period in question is the spring of 1852,
          and Howells, two years younger than Piatt, had turned
          fifteen on 1 March of that year; the error is pointed
          out in Cady, *The Road to Realism*, page 39n.

69.19   the Medical College in State Street: Starling Medical
          College; cf. the present text at 157.24ff.

70.24–25 The paper which we were to help make my father
          make his: the Ashtabula *Sentinel*.

70.30–31 our office was transferred some ten miles inland to the
          county-seat: the *Sentinel* offices were moved from Ash-
          tabula to Jefferson, Ohio, in January 1853.

71.4   an earlier page: the material which follows in the
          present text is derived from Howells' "The Country
          Printer"; see Textual Commentary, pages 300–301,
          for a description of the original text and the sections
          from it printed here.

71.13   Comeouters: abolitionists turned Christian Anar-
          chists.

74.10–11 the Ramage press: a hand press, made at first entirely
          of wood and later of iron, developed by Adam Ramage
          of Philadelphia and said to be the first press made in
          America.

74.16–17   a second-hand Adams press: invented by Isaac Adams (1802–1883) of Boston in about 1830, this press had a stationary platen to hold the paper and a bed which moved only vertically—down to allow the inking rollers to pass over the type on the bed, and up to the platen which held the paper to make the impression.

81.14–15   I could not absolutely fix the moment when I began to find my way out of the cloud of misery: at the time of writing *Years of My Youth* Howells had difficulty placing the date of the occurrence of his hypochondria; see his letter to his sister Aurelia of 23 May 1915 (MS at Harvard), quoted in the Introduction (page xxii). Cady (*The Road to Realism*, page 55n.) established the period as the spring of 1856.

82.23–24   the ordinary school-books, Arnold's for Latin, and Anthon's for Greek: Rev. Thomas Kerchever Arnold (1800–1853), *Henry's First Latin Book* (1839), which went through twenty-five editions by 1881; Charles Anthon (1797–1867), *A Grammar of the Greek Language* (1838).

83.19–20   week after week the handsomely printed *Ohio Farmer* came with something in it: at least six pieces by Howells have been identified in the *Ohio Farmer* for the years 1854–1860; the earliest, "Nightly Rain," printed in 1854, has not yet been located.

83.28   Once I carried Shakespeare beyond himself: "Our Emended Edition of Shakspeare" [sic], Ashtabula *Sentinel*, 24 August 1854, page 2.

83.33–34   I attempted a serial romance: "The Independent Candidate," Ashtabula *Sentinel*, 23, 30 November, 7, 21, 28 December 1854, 4, 11, 18 January 1855.

83.35   in another place: chapter XIV of *My Literary Passions*.

84.24   When one of my younger brothers died: Howells is
               probably referring to the death of his brother John in
               1864 at the age of 18.

85.32–36   Tennyson, "The Princess; a Medley," ll. 21–25.

86.31–32   I have told in *My Literary Passions* how J. W. and I read
               Cervantes and Shakespeare together: in chapters XIII
               and XIV of that book Howells recounts the interests in
               literature he shared with his friend, who is not identi-
               fied there; the friend is probably Jim Williams, whose
               name is given in Howells' boyhood diary.

87.14–15   Iñez de Castro: the daughter of a Castilian nobleman
               attached to the court of Alphonso IV of Portugal; a
               Prince Pedro married her secretly, but the king dis-
               covered the fact and had Iñez murdered; when Pedro
               himself took the throne in 1357, his first act was to
               avenge himself on his wife's murderers. The subject
               has been treated in various poems, including one by
               Camoens, and in a short drama by Landor.

89.24–26   The source of this quotation has not been located.

91.14–15   I have told in *My Literary Passions* of the misanthropical
               Englishman: in chapter XV and following of that
               book Howells describes, without naming, the man
               Mildred Howells (*Life in Letters*, I, 121) identifies as
               William Goodrich.

93.5–6   study of law: Howells spent May 1855 in the office of
               Benjamin Franklin Wade (1800–1878), U.S. Senator
               from Ohio from 1851 to 1869.

93.12   the Senator's nephew, my fellow-student: Decius S.
               Wade (1835–?), who was admitted to the bar in
               Jefferson in 1857, and was appointed chief-justice of
               the Montana Territory by President Grant in 1871.

93.14–15   the four great English quarterly reviews: *Edinburgh Review, Westminster Review, London Quarterly,* and *North British Review*; Howells describes the episode in chapters XVIII and XIX of *My Literary Passions*.

96.9   some sort of tutorship in a very modest college: in the Norton Papers at Harvard is a letter of 11 February 1865 from Howells in Venice to James Russell Lowell asking about the possibility of an appointment in a "diffident little college."

96.13–14   sub-professorship of English in Union College: Howells refused a professorship of rhetoric offered him there in 1868.

96.16–17   a like place in Washington University: the offer was made by William G. Eliot (1811–1887), president of Washington University from 1871 to 1887.

96.22–24   the offer . . . of Harvard: in 1886 Howells turned down the Smith Professorship at Harvard, which had been held by Longfellow and Lowell, among others.

96.36   Lounsbury: Thomas Raynesford Lounsbury (1838–1915), professor of English at Yale from 1871 to 1906.

97.6   the offer of the same chair in Johns Hopkins: in 1882 Howells declined the offer made by Daniel Coit Gilman (1831–1908), president of Johns Hopkins from 1875 to 1901.

98.19–20   a few years of escape to a consular post in the tropics: Joseph A. Howells was American consul to Turk's Island, British West Indies, from 1906 to 1911, one year before his death.

100.12   undreamed-of prosperity: Joseph Howells published very successful song-books designed for Union soldiers.

100.35 As all my world knows: the story of the publication of *Venetian Life* is detailed in chapter III of *Literary Friends and Acquaintance*, "Roundabout to Boston."

103.22–23 he was sent to the State Senate: William Cooper Howells was elected to a two-year term in 1864.

103.26 chosen one of the House clerks in the State Legislature: he served in the term beginning in the fall of 1856, when W. D. Howells was nineteen.

103.35–36 Joshua R. Giddings: Giddings (1795–1864) was a United States Representative from 1838 to 1859, and Consul-General to Canada from 1861 to 1864. The meaning of Howells' statement that Giddings' loss of the Congressional nomination in 1859 was the result of "an expression of indifference to office" (104.5) is not quite clear, but seems to be in essential agreement with the statement by his son-in-law, George W. Julian (*The Life of Joshua R. Giddings* [Chicago, 1892], page 241), that Giddings could not decide whether to run again but consented to be nominated, only to be defeated because no one worked in his behalf on the assumption that his reputation guaranteed victory.

105.8–9 Lowell, "Sonnet XXVI: To J. R. Giddings," ll. 1–2.

105.29 H. G.: Harvey Green (or Greene), mentioned in Howells' early diary and some later letters.

109.2–3 she sent me a play she had written: Howells encouraged all his sisters in their occasional literary endeavors; Victoria's play has not been identified.

111.10–11 as I have told in *My Literary Passions*: chapter XXIII, "Tennyson," pages 160–161; Howells' quotation is essentially accurate. The letters he speaks of were published in the Cincinnati *Gazette* from 7 January to 20 April 1857, although Howells may have stopped writing them about 31 March; see Gibson and Arms, *Bibliography*, pages 76–77.

111.32   *Hamlet*, I, iii, 70.

112.30–34   the National Road . . . became High Street in Colum-
                bus: the National Road followed Broad Street, the
                east-west thoroughfare, and not High Street, which
                stretched north-south, in Columbus. His father's re-
                membrance of the building of the road may refer to
                work on the project around Wheeling, to which point
                the road had been completed by 1818.

113.12   the stately conflagration: the Neil House of Howells'
                memory was destroyed in a fire on 6 November 1860,
                the day after the presidential election.

114.3   Tennyson, "Will Waterproof's Lyrical Monologue,"
                l. 151; the original reads: "As just and mere a serving-
                man . . ."

115.6–7   I espoused his cause with quite outrageous zeal:
                Howells wrote of the expulsion of the Cincinnati
                Commercial correspondent by a Mr. Andrews in his
                "Letter from Columbus," Cincinnati *Gazette*, 9 Feb-
                ruary 1857; an article with almost exactly the same
                contents, signed "Genug" (a name Howells used
                several times), appears in a "Letter from Columbus"
                in the Cleveland *Herald* of the same date.

115.32–33   as I have told, I was always getting books from it:
                chapter XXIII of *My Literary Passions*.

117.19   a loved and honored character in *A Hazard of New
                Fortunes*: Lindau. The name of the real man is not
                known, but he was only a partial inspiration for the
                fictional character.

119.5–6   he left me to write the legislative letters: the politician-
                editor's name is not known. The context of Howells'
                description here could mean that he began to write
                the legislative report for the Cleveland *Herald* during

the session of 1857, and not just that of 1858, as Gibson and Arms (*Bibliography of William Dean Howells*, page 79) indicate. Thus the series of articles entitled "Letter from Columbus" which appeared in the *Herald* beginning 7 January 1857 may be his; see also the Note to 115.6–7.

119.8   Citizen Corry: William Corry of Hamilton County, who served in the Ohio General Assembly in 1812, 1819, 1826, and 1856–1857.

120.9   The first winter of my legislative correspondence: actually, the description of "The State House Warming at Columbus" was Howells' second "letter" to the Cincinnati *Gazette* (8 January 1857, page 1); the first had appeared the day before.

121.12–13   the envoy from the paper who made it in person: probably Edmund B. Babb, for many years editor of the *Gazette*; Howells mentions his name in a letter to his brother Joe of 10 April 1857, reprinted in F. C. Marston, Jr., "An Early Howells Letter," *AL*, XVIII (1946), 163–164.

124.28   Whitelaw Reid: born 1837; correspondent for the Cincinnati *Gazette* and other papers for several years before 1860; in 1860 he was made city editor of the *Gazette*, which sent him to the front when the Civil War began; in 1868 he joined the staff of the New York *Tribune* as chief editorial writer, becoming managing editor in 1869; in 1888 he was made minister to France by President Harrison; he was a member of the peace commission in Paris in 1898, at the end of the Spanish-American War; he died in 1912 in London, where he had been ambassador since 1905.

125.26   Henry D. Cooke: 1825–1881; the firm of which he was a partner took over the *Ohio State Journal* on 28 April 1858.

126.23–24 the *milde Macht* of a Hahnemannian treatment: Christian Friedrich Samuel Hahnemann (1755–1843), German physician and founder of homeopathy, believed that drugs in much smaller doses than were generally used exerted their powers effectively; *milde Macht*—mild force.

126.34–35 "News and Humors of the Mail": Howells appears to have written this column from November 1858 to February 1860.

128.25 Samuel R. Reed: no information about him has been located outside Howells' account.

129.24 Parson Brownlow: William Gannaway Brownlow (1805–1877), newspaper editor, leader of the Union sympathizers in Tennessee, Governor of Tennessee, 1865–1869, member of the U. S. Senate, 1869–1875.

130.7 Ingoldsby Legends: a group of verse tales published in book form in 1840, written by Richard Harris Barham (1788–1845).

131.4 "The Lady of Lyons": "The Lady of Lyons; or, Love and Pride" (1838), by Sir Edward George Bulwer-Lytton (1803–1873); the play had its first New York performance in 1843.

131.5 "The Daughter of the Regiment": a translation of the Italian light opera *La Figlia del Reggimento* by Gaetano Donizetti (1797–1848), first performed in English in 1848.

132.23 Salmon P. Chase: 1808–1873; U. S. Senator from Ohio, 1849–1855; Governor of Ohio, 1855–1859; Secretary of the Treasury, 1861–1864. He did not resign the governorship of Ohio to take the Cabinet appointment (as Howells indicates at 134.22ff.), but did resign his senatorship to become Governor.

134.11–12   Miss Chase's next reception: Kate Chase Sprague (1840–1899) was hostess for her father during his term as Governor of Ohio and a social leader of Washington during his service there.

139.20   I wrote for the *Saturday Press*: Howells had thirteen items, twelve of them poems, published in the *Saturday Press* between 1859 and 1861.

139.22   I wrote for the *Atlantic Monthly*: he published seven pieces of poetry there in 1860–1861.

139.23   I have told all this and more in *My Literary Passions*: chapters XXIV–XXVII.

139.26–27   the story of my first formal venture: chapter XXVII, "Charles Reade"; the volume, *Poems of Two Friends*, was issued by Follett and Foster of Columbus, and the "hopeful young publisher" was Frank Foster of that firm.

139.33–34   the only four poets west of the Alleghanies who had yet been accepted by the *Atlantic*: in addition to Howells and Piatt, the others were Howells' Columbus roommate, Fullerton (see Note to 159.13), and Leonard Case (1820–1880) of Cleveland.

141.28   the S. Family: the family of Dr. Samuel M. Smith, who was professor of theory and practice and dean of the Starling Medical College in Columbus.

142.12   *The Newcomes*: Thackeray's novel, first released in England, ran in the United States in *Harper's Monthly* from November 1853 to October 1855, at least three years before the period at which Howells places it.

142.36–143.1   a young lady visitor: the only available information is that she was the daughter of one Mr. I. Thomas, who was appointed consul to Algiers in 1862 but never reached his post.

143.13   I saw her in Boston: perhaps during Howells' visit there in the summer of 1860, which is recounted in "My First Visit to New England," *Literary Friends and Acquaintance*, or during his second one just before departing for Venice in November 1861.

144.5–6   the widow of our repudiated Clive Newcome: Elizabeth Marion Smith married James M. Comly (identified by Howells at 196.2 in the present text) in 1863.

144.19–20   when at last it came to my leaving Columbus: although Howells here suggests that the borrowing of the two hundred dollars was carried on in Columbus, his letters of the period indicate that he requested the money in a letter addressed to Mrs. Smith (28 September 1861, MS at Ohio Historical Society) and that actually Smith gave him $150, for which Howells thanked him in a letter of 3 October 1861 (MS at Ohio Historical Society).

147.6   Chief Justice Swann: Joseph Rockwell *Swan* (1802–1884), Justice of the Ohio Supreme Court, 1855–1859, Chief-Justice, February–November 1859. Howells' references to the times of events are unclear here: that crisis which "had come for us five or six years before" (147.3–4) came in the case "Ex parte Bushnell" in 1859. The true story of Swan's (or his enemies') decision has never been adequately clarified: he may either have resigned from the office or been refused the nomination in 1859, and there was a popular story that he twice refused a place in the U. S. Supreme Court.

147.32   Noah L. Swayne: Noah *Haynes* Swayne (1804–1884), made Justice of the U. S. Supreme Court in 1862.

150.22–23   the exquisite spirit of the house: Mrs. Dr. Francis Carter; cf. *Life in Letters*, I, 18–20.

152.5 a slight monthly magazine: Conway (1832–1907) named his own magazine *The Dial: A Monthly for Literature, Philosophy and Religion*, and published it from January through December of 1860. Howells contributed four items before its demise: "Convention" and "A Poet" in the June issue, "Misanthropy" in September, and "[The moonlight is full of the fragrance]" in November.

154.10 *The Pilot's Story*: the poem was first published in the *Atlantic*, VI (September 1860), 323–325. The quotation from it (154.29–30) is line 65 of the poem.

155.6–21 "I have sold to Smith . . . .": the quotation is derived, with several interesting changes, from Howells' letter to his sister Victoria of 2 January 1859 (MS at Harvard); the significant portions of the original letter are as follows:

> I must tell you all my little triumphs. I have sold to Smith of the Odd-Fellow's Casket at Cincinnati, that little story you remember I read to you early last summer. I called it "Not a love story." He gives me six dollars for it; and he says that as soon as I have time to dress up that translation that Babb rejected, he will buy that. At the rate of two dollars a page, it will bring me sixteen or eighteen dollars. "Bobby" is going the rounds of the country papers. Aston, the bookseller here, told our local editor that it was enough to make anybody's reputation—that he and his family laughed prodigiously over it. Dear to me—O how unspeakably sweet are these little flattering speeches, and I cannot repeat them, I thank heaven! to those who will prize them equally. O, how genially I come out in this ray of sunlight, after being frozen up so many years in Jefferson. All my faculties expand, and the gloom leaves me, that haunted me forever. I have the assurance that I shall succeed, but, O God! sometimes, I tremble lest something should happen to destroy my hopes. I think, though, that my adversity came first, and now it is prosperity lies before me. I am going to try and get up a poem fit to be printed in the Atlantic. They pay Fullerton $25 a page. I can sell, now, just as much as I will write.

155.8–9 'Not a Love Story': published in the *Odd-Fellows Casket* [not *Monthly*], I (February 1859), 222–224.

155.12   'Bobby': published in the *Ohio State Journal*, 14 December 1858, page 1.

155.22–23   It was two years yet before that poem . . . sold to the magazine: "Andenken," *Atlantic*, V (January 1860), 100–102. Howells' sense of the sequence of publication of his various poems is not completely accurate.

156.29   Passages in those old letters home: see, for example, Howells' letter to his sister Victoria, written in April and May of 1859; *Life in Letters*, I, 18–20.

159.13   My own roommate was a poet: Artemas Thomas Fullerton (1834–1901), briefly Union Army chaplain and then Presbyterian minister in churches in Ohio and Washington, D.C.; according to the *Atlantic* index, he had actually published three poems there before Howells' first, "Andenken," in January 1860: "By the Dead" (I [1858], 595), "The Birth-Mark" (II [1858], 412), and "Two Years After" (III [1858], 548).

162.7   certain fervent verses: Howells' poem, "Old Brown," was printed in the Ashtabula *Sentinel*, 25 January 1860, page 1. Mildred Howells (*Life in Letters*, I, 25) indicates that the poem was published in the *Ohio State Journal* on 26 November 1859, but it has not been located there.

162.10–11   Mr. Oswald Villard's history of John Brown: *John Brown, 1800–1859; A Biography Fifty Years After* (Boston and New York, 1910); Howells reviewed the book in "John Brown after Fifty Years," *NAR*, CXCIII (1911), 26–34.

162.15–16   Samuel who hewed Agag in pieces: cf. I Samuel 15:33.

163.3   Governor Wise: Henry Alexander Wise (1806–1876), Governor of Virginia from 1856 to 1860, who quelled Brown's raid on Harper's Ferry.

164.25   Robert Blum, the martyr of liberty: Blum (1807–1848) was a prominent leader of the liberal party in the German revolution of 1848, one of a deputation sent to Vienna with the address of the parliamentary opposition; on the capture of that city he was arrested and shot.

164.31   Richard Realf: Realf (1834–1878) published his volume of verse in 1852 with the help of Harriet Martineau, Samuel Rogers, and Lady Byron, the literary set of Brighton; after being sent to stay with Lady Byron's nephew at Leicestershire, he had an affair with a girl of the family and was dismissed from the house. His father sent him to a sister in Maryland; he found his way to John Brown's "convention" in Canada in 1858; when the Civil War began he enlisted in an Illinois regiment; he spent the last part of his life as a newspaperman.

166.5–6   that time of abeyance between Brown's capture and his death: Brown was captured on 18 October and executed on 2 December 1859.

166.6–11   it must have been after the hanging at Charlestown that one night I was . . . listening to . . . . Abraham Lincoln: Howells must actually have seen Lincoln a full month before Brown's capture, on 16 September 1859, when Lincoln made his only visit to Columbus before the election; he was not returning from the East (where he traveled in February and March 1860), but was on a special trip to Ohio cities.

166.26   on the journey . . . to his inauguration: Lincoln stayed over in Columbus on 13 and 14 February 1861.

167.21–22   the swarming fly ceded, as Dante says, only to the swarming mosquito: *Divina Commedia*, "Inferno," XXVI, 28: "come la mosca cede a la zanzara . . ."

169.13   White Sulphur: Howells' article on the visit, "A Day at White Sulphur," appeared in the *Ohio State Journal*, 6 July 1859, page 2.

171.18–19   I was asked to deliver the poem before the Ohio Editorial Convention: his poem, "The Coming," was first published in the *Ohio State Journal* on 23 January 1860, page 4. Only a portion of it is reproduced in the present text.

171.24   the kindness of a friend: the text of the poem was sent to Howells by Theodore T. Frankenberg (1877–1958), who worked on the staff of the *Ohio State Journal* from 1903 to 1916. Howells corresponded with Frankenberg about details of the Columbus period (cf. Introduction, page xvi, footnote 15).

173.24   one manuscript: Follett, Foster and Company published *Three Years in Chile*, "By a Lady of Ohio" (Mrs. George B. Merwin), sometime after 15 September 1861, and thus *after* Howells' trip to the East (see 178.7ff.).

173.29   Gautier's *Romance of a Mummy*: a translation of *Le roman de la momie*, by Théophile Gautier (1811–1872). The exact date of publication is not known, but a review of the book, entitled "Romance of the Mummy," probably written by Howells, appeared in the *Ohio State Journal* on 2 July 1860, page 2.

173.32   the life of Abraham Lincoln: *Lives and Speeches of Abraham Lincoln and Hannibal Hamlin*, published by Follett, Foster and Company sometime in June 1860.

174.12–13   a young law student: John Quay Howard.

174.32   I have heard that he annotated a copy of it: in the summer of 1860 Lincoln made corrections in a copy of the book owned by Samuel C. Parks, at Parks' request; a facsimile of this copy was published by the Abraham Lincoln Association (Springfield, 1938) and the Indiana University Press (Bloomington, 1960).

175.1–3   I saw him . . . as I have told elsewhere: "First Impressions of Literary New York," *Literary Friends and Acquaintance*.

175.31–33   James A. Garfield, of whose coming to read Tennyson . . . I have told in *My Literary Passions*: chapter XXVII, "Charles Reade."

176.4   nearly ten years later: in a letter to his wife dated 4 June 1871 (MS at Harvard), Howells mentions spending the previous evening with Garfield and several members of the Hiram faculty.

176.21   the Eclectic Institute of Hiram: now Hiram College; Garfield was a student there from 1851 to 1854, then held the Institute's chair of Latin and Greek in 1855, and was principal from 1856 to 1859.

176.31   Kanawha: the opposing armies met in this part of Virginia several times during the course of the war; Garfield was probably present during the encounters of June and August 1864, and not early in the war.

177.22   Lamon's *Life of Lincoln*: the book, by Ward Hill Lamon (1828–1893), was published in 1872 by J. R. Osgood and Company, Howells' Boston publisher at that period.

178.24–25   my letters to the Cincinnati *Gazette*: seven letters with the general title "Glimpses of Summer Travel" were published between 21 July and 9 August 1860; Howells also reported this trip for the *Ohio State Journal* in seven more letters entitled "En passant" from 23 July to 7 August 1860.

178.30–31   This has been fully told in my *Literary Friends and Acquaintance*: "My First Visit to New England."

179.18 Samuel Price: when Price (?–1870) and Howells parted (see page 205 of this text), Price went to Cleveland, which may have been his home; he later studied law, and then was associated from 1862 until his death with the Toledo *Commercial*.

179.34–36 five poems published in the *Atlantic Monthly*, two of them in the same number: Howells' contributions from mid-1860 to mid-1861 were "Pleasure-Pain" and "Lost Beliefs" (April, pages 468–470, 486), "The Pilot's Story" (September, pages 323–325), "The Old Homestead" (February, page 213), and "Bubbles" (April, page 415).

180.10–11 another story of village life: Howells recounts the same story in "First Impressions of Literary New York," in *Literary Friends and Acquaintance*, and in "Young Contributors and Editors," *Youth's Companion*, 9 May 1901, page 245; part of the story, entitled "A Dream," was published in the *Knickerbocker*, LVIII (August 1861), 146–150. The manuscript, entitled "Geoffrey Winter," is in the Howells Collection at the Houghton Library.

180.18 *Their Wedding Journey*: first serialized in the *Atlantic Monthly*, XXVIII (July–December 1871), and published in book form immediately afterwards.

183.6 a very affected study: the manuscript story about "the mystical Antoine" has not been located.

185.1 J. Q. A. Ward: John Quincy Adams Ward (1830–1910) completed his statue of the "Indian *Hunter*" in 1864; it was exhibited at the Paris Exposition in 1867 and a short time later was the first statue placed in Central Park.

186.1 Thomas D. Jones: Thomas Dow Jones (1811–1881) did complete the marble bust of Chase in 1876; it was placed in the chambers of the U. S. Supreme Court.

186.31   Ada Isaacs Menken: *Adah* Isaacs Menken (1835–1868), whose real name was Dolores Adios Fuertes, was famous for her appearances in states of apparent nudity and for her four marriages, the second to John C. Heenan (1835–1873), who in 1860 fought Tom Sayers, holder of the English belt, in London; the bout ended in a court battle in which both men were finally awarded champion's belts.

187.20   A. P. Russell: Addison Peale Russell (1826–1912), Ohio Secretary of State from 1857 to 1861, financial agent for the State of Ohio in New York City from 1862 to 1868; he published the first edition of *Library Notes* in 1875, and a revised and enlarged second edition in 1879.

188.14   a book of "Ohio Stories": *Stories of Ohio*, 1897.

188.31   in that winter of 1859–60, after Lincoln had been elected: actually election day was 5 November 1860, before the winter of 1860–1861.

192.34   a tattered manuscript: the poem at 193.3–30 is derived from an otherwise unpublished manuscript (in the Howells Collection at the Houghton Library) entitled "Legend of the College."

194.9–10   Forty-seven years we were together here, and then she died: Howells married Elinor Mead on 24 December 1862; she died 6 May 1910, at the age of 73.

196.2   James M. Comly: Comly (1832–1912?) enlisted in the Ohio Volunteers in 1861; he became editor and proprietor of the *Ohio State Journal* in October 1865, was later appointed postmaster of Columbus under Grant in 1870, minister to Hawaii under Hayes from 1877 to 1882, and returned to Ohio to become editor of the Toledo *Commercial*, which he bought with a partner shortly after the ministerial appointment ended.

196.8–9   *Cornhill Magazine*, then so brand new: it was begun in January 1860, and edited by Thackeray from that time to April 1862.

196.9   *Saturday Review*: the English magazine began publication in 1855.

196.10   Thackeray stooping from his Jovian height: Thackeray's blast at the *Superfine Review* appeared in "Roundabout Papers: No. VIII: De Juventute," *Cornhill Magazine*, II (October 1860), 501–512.

200.23–24   the young Patti, now so old: Adelina Patti (1843–1919), Italian operatic soprano and one of the most famous singers of all time, made her second American tour during the 1860–1861 season, and probably appeared in Columbus at that time.

201.3–4   The source of this fragment of poetry has not been identified.

201.25   Wordsworth, "The Solitary Reaper," l. 19; the original reads "For old, unhappy, far-off things . . ."

202.8   John G. Mitchell: John Grant Mitchell (1838–?) was commissioned brigadier-general in 1865 and breveted major-general of the Ohio Volunteers for special gallantry in the battle of Bentonville, North Carolina, 17 March 1865. His wife, Laura Platt Mitchell, was Elinor Mead Howells' cousin.

203.2   "put an antic disposition on": *Hamlet*, I, v, 172.

203.12   I depersonalized them: the poem is probably "For One of the Killed," first published in *Poems* (1873).

203.30   William Dennison: Dennison (1815–1882) was Governor of Ohio from 1860 to 1862, and U. S. Postmaster-General from 1864 to 1866; he may have been an author of the letter signed by prominent Ohio figures petitioning Lincoln for a consulate for Howells (12 March 1861, MS at National Archives).

204.25   Apparently he meant to be editor as well as proprietor:
                on 4 July 1861 Henry D. Cooke dissolved his connec-
                tion with the paper and with his partner, F. W. Hurtt;
                Hurtt then became associated with Dr. I. J. Allen and
                they took control of the *Journal* under the name Hurtt,
                Allen and Company, with Allen becoming editor.

205.7–8   a chapter of *Literary Friends and Acquaintance*: "First
                Impressions of Literary New York."

208.12   Vasari: Giorgio Vasari (1511–1574), Florentine archi-
                tect, painter and writer, most famous for his *Lives of
                the Artists* (1550).

208.14–15   General Worth: William Jenkins Worth (1794–1849),
                second in command to Taylor in the Mexican War;
                he led the storming of the Bishop's Palace in the
                Battle of Monterey and took part in the occupation
                of Mexico City.

208.24   John Rogers groups: works by John Rogers (1829–
                1904), American sculptor famous for small groups il-
                lustrating scenes from the Civil War, country life, and
                other genre subjects.

208.34   before I sailed: Howells left the United States on the
                City of Glasgow on 9 November 1861.

209.4–5   our vice-consul for Cività Vecchia: he has not been
                identified.

211.2–3   the *City of Glasgow* never did roll entirely over: the
                boat did burn to the water's edge without sinking
                on 29 July 1865, but in mid-ocean, not in Cork
                Harbor, as Howells suggests.

211.24–25   he took his place in a sea novel of mine: Mr. Hicks
                of *The Lady of the Aroostook* (1879).

214.18–19   cunninger of fence: an echo of *Twelfth Night*, III, iv,
                321 — "he had beene valiant, and so cunning in fence."

215.18   our consul in Paris: John Bigelow (1817–1911), American author and diplomat, famous for his service in France in preventing official recognition of the Confederacy.

215.23   his vice-consul: Edward Tuck (1842–1930), American banker and philanthropist.

216.25–26   the little Suabian capital: Stuttgart, capital of Würtemberg.

216.26   the resident consul: W. F. Nast, Cincinnati journalist.

219.5–6   a misadventure, which . . . I used a few years afterward: "At the Sign of the Savage," *Atlantic Monthly*, XL (1877), 36–48.

220.4–5   consul at Vienna: Theodore Canisius, Illinois publisher and a personal friend of Lincoln who wrote a popular biography of him in German.

220.25   Colonel Waring: George Edwin Waring (1833–1898), American sanitary engineer, appointed commissioner of street cleaning in New York in 1894.

223.27   my overland journey to Venice ended: Howells arrived there on 7 December 1861.

225.1   my predecessor: J. J. Sprenger. No further information about him has been located.

226.6   Pastorelli: his real name was G. Antonio Tortorini (1805?–?).

226.36   a small city not far from Padua: Tortorini's home was in Monselice.

227.22   sixty scudi: about fifty-seven dollars.

228.8   my exequatur: Howells told the story of his problem
               in this matter in a letter to his friend J. J. Piatt of
               27 January 1862, later printed under the title "Await-
               ing His Exequatur (Returned from the Dead-Letter
               Office)," in *Hesperian Tree: An Annual of the Ohio
               Valley—1903*, a volume edited by Piatt.

228.11   Frezzeria: a shopping area behind St. Mark's Square.

229.13   fifty florins: the equivalent of twenty-five American
               dollars in the currency of the period. Twelve Austrian
               sovereigns (see 229.19 in the text) had this same value.

231.24   *villeggiatura*: Italian—country holiday.

231.24–25   By the time he came back to Venice I had been mar-
               ried: Howells married Elinor Mead on 24 December
               1862.

234.4   Then once again I was in Venice: Howells revisited
               Venice with his family in April 1883.

234.18   this Tito Melema like behavior: Tito Melema is a
               character in George Eliot's *Romola*.

236.2   fifty thousand francs: about ten thousand dollars.

237.19–20   except a friend nearer my own age: Eugenio Brunetta,
               the "Biondini" of "A Young Venetian Friend."

239.8   *condizione civile*: Italian—refined station.

239.21–22   a *commediante*, in the phrase which Pio VII. applied to
               Napoleon: Howells is referring here apparently not
               to fact but to a portion of the French author Vigny's
               Servitude et Grandeur Militaires, where Pope Pius VII is
               described as calling Napoleon this as Napoleon is
               justifying the Pope's crowning him emperor; *com-
               mediante*: Italian—comedian, actor.

240.12 an early sketch: "Tonelli's Marriage," first printed in the *Atlantic Monthly*, XXII (July 1868), 96–110, and collected in *A Fearful Responsibility and Other Stories* (1881).

241.17–18 President of the Venetian republic of 1848: Daniele Manin, elected 22 March 1848.

242.17–18 the great daughter of the great Garcia: Mari Malibran (1808–1836), popular operatic contralto; her father was Manuel del Popolo García (1775–1832), Spanish musician and impresario, the first person to produce opera in Italian in New York and teacher of, among others, his own daughter and Jenny Lind.

242.28 *"Non so spiegarmi"*: Italian—"I can't explain."

243.9 the thing that is not: the expression for falsehood used by the Houyhnhnms in Swift's *Gulliver's Travels*, Book IV.

245.18 left our little one in charge of her uncle the sculptor: Winifred Howells, born 17 December 1863, and Mrs. Howells' brother, Larkin G. Mead, Jr. (1835–1910).

245.25–26 the sculptor and the beautiful Venetian girl who fell in love with each other: Larkin G. Mead, Jr., married Marietta da Benvenuti on 26 February 1866.

246.19–20 the Moody and Sankey revivals: evangelistic tours begun in 1870 by Dwight Moody (1837–1899) and Ira Sankey (1840–1908).

246.29–30 he got leave of absence and returned provisionally: Howells applied for his leave in the spring of 1865, was granted four months on 21 June, and left Venice on 3 July.

249.5 now that she is lost: Winifred Howells died on 3 March 1889.

249.25 *ricapito*: Italian—address, place of call; the more common spelling is *recapito*.

TEXTUAL APPARATUS

Textual Commentary

Years of My Youth

The first and only book edition of *Years of My Youth* (BAL 9843) appeared under the Harper and Brothers imprint in 1916; the first impression carried on the copyright page the printing-date code "F–Q," signifying that the text was printed in June 1916; the second impression carried the letters "K–Q" (October 1916). The book was deposited at the Library of Congress after this second impression, on 7 November 1916. Both impressions bear the note "Published October, 1916" on the copyright page, as does the third impression of the book, printed in October 1917 (printing-date identification "K–R") and containing photographic illustrations of scenes of Howells' youth and an introduction by Clifton Johnson, who had prepared the photographs. Some typographical errors in the two earlier impressions were corrected in the plates for this printing, but no further textual changes were introduced. There were no other impressions of the book, and after these three printings its publication history ended.

The pre-publication development of the text of *Years of My Youth* offers a sharp contrast to this straightforward printing history. Howells' creation of the book was a confusing patchwork process, which began with the writing and rewriting of original material which was then trimmed and further rewritten for use as the set of three essays entitled "Life in an Old-Time State Capital" published in *Harper's Monthly* from September through November 1914. Then Howells apparently took back the copy he had submitted to the magazine, began by reinstating the material the magazine editors had wanted cut out, and then went on to expand it further (this segment coincides generally with pages 57–206 of the present edition). He also prepared several new sections for the book, including an introductory section on the family genealogy and his earliest life (pages 3–38), which he had originally written for *Harper's Monthly* but then decided not to print there, and a survey of his teen-age diary of the 1850's (pages 62–67). Further, he incorporated into the book portions of two reminiscences published some twenty-five years earlier, "Year in a Log-Cabin, A Bit of Autobiography," (pages 39–56 in this text), printed in *Youth's Companion* in 1887, and "The Country Printer" (pages 71–78), which appeared in *Scribner's* in 1893, as well as a poem entitled "The Coming" (pages 171–172) which had first appeared in the *Ohio State Journal* in 1860, while Howells was on the staff of that newspaper.

Howells' sense of the development and full contents of the book seems never to have been completely coherent, and the kinds of printer's copy materials which were apparently used in preparing *Years of My Youth* are evidence of the waning but struggling powers of the craftsman-artist who at the age of seventy-nine still worked to create books out of whatever scraps of memory and history, fragment and fact, he could bring to his aid. What physical evidence remains of his work on the text consists of a portion of the typescript which he had first submitted to *Harper's Monthly* and then reworked for the book. This typescript, prepared for him from an earlier—now missing—manuscript or typescript, he further revised in his own hand and supplemented with additions which he wrote in long-hand or typed himself. The expanded typescript, which became printer's copy for the Harper and Brothers edition of *Years of My Youth*, even contains Harper galley material among its leaves; these galleys had apparently been set from manuscript or typescript submitted at some early stage of planning for the book, and Howells worked them over again and recombined the text with the other typescript material. Such copy as still exists from this complicated process constitutes only the second half of the book, and no information is available which would indicate what happened to the manuscript or typescript from which the early sections of the book were set, or to the marked copies or tearsheets or transcriptions of the reminiscences which Howells seems to have submitted for setting those sections. In addition to the extant portions of the printer's copy typescript, however, certain segments of the material on which Howells continued his pre-publication revision of his text do survive: these include a section of unrevised first Harper book galleys set from the printer's copy typescript, a more extensive section of first galleys of which the unrevised galleys were a duplicate—this set heavily revised in Howells' hand—and the remnants of seven partial stages of page proofs for the book, also revised at different points in Howells' hand.

As a result of the confusing method of preparation of the book and of the incomplete evidence of the process, the choices of copy-texts for *Years of My Youth* have necessarily been made from among the widely different extant forms of the various segments. The genealogical relationships of the extant pre-publication typescript, galley, and proof materials, of the earlier published material, and of the parts of *Years of My Youth* which survive only in the first edition itself, as well as the evidence these provide of authorial attention to substance and form, indicate that in all four different groups of materials constitute the copy-texts. The earliest group in point of time consists of the first printings of the newspaper poem "The Coming" and the two periodical reminiscences, "Year in a Log-Cabin" and "The Country Printer," at least for the sections of these pieces incorporated into the present text; the extant printer's copy typescript material prepared specifically for the book makes up the second, and largest, group; the third consists of those sections of newly prepared pre-publication material—galleys and page proofs—for which no typescript survives; and the fourth the book itself in those sections where no other form is extant. The effective result of the application of editorial effort to the textual materials of *Years of My Youth* is a book substantively different from the original publication in only about thirty readings, but more strikingly variant from it in spelling, punctuation, capitalization, and paragraphing.

The copy-texts selected for each portion of the book, together with a record of all the known forms pertinent to each section and the extent to which these forms coincide with each other, are identified in the table below. The printer's copy typescript and extant pre-publication materials which derive from it are described in A Note on the Manuscripts and Other Pre-Publication Forms of the Texts, pages 310–328. The discussion which follows the table considers essentially the degree of authorial attention evidenced in and among the different groups of copy-texts and the bearing such information has upon the critical text of *Years of My Youth* presented in this edition.

KEY TO SYMBOLS

N1   "The Coming," *Ohio State Journal*, 23 January 1860

R1   "The Coming," *Ohio State Journal*, Centennial Edition, 26 October 1911

S1　"Year in a Log-Cabin, A Bit of Autobiography," *Youth's Companion*, LX (May 1887)

S2　"The Country Printer," *Scribner's*, XIII (May 1893)

M　*My Year in a Log Cabin*, Harper and Brothers, 1893

T　"The Country Printer," *Impressions and Experiences*, Harper and Brothers, 1896

V　"The Country Printer," *Impressions and Experiences*, David Douglas, 1896

W　"The Country Printer," *Impressions and Experiences*, Harper and Brothers, 1909

MSY　117 leaves of printer's copy typescript of *Years of My Youth*

LG　Single galley sheet of *Years of My Youth* numbered 25

UG　41 leaves of unrevised first galleys for *Years of My Youth*

RG　61 leaves of author's revised first galleys for *Years of My Youth*

P1–P7　Seven partial sets of page proofs for *Years of My Youth*

A　*Years of My Youth*, Harper and Brothers, 1916

		Extant states of the text	*Copy-text*
3–39.5	I/¶ It is hard . . . . none as insists.	A	A
39.5–54.28	For my father . . . . I was home-/	S1, M, A	S1
54.28–56.28	sick still. . . . from my mind.	S1, M, LG, A	S1
57–71.6	II/¶ If in a child's . . . . our enterprise.	RG, A	RG
71.7–78.11	¶ In politics . . . . end of a year.	S2, T, V, W, RG, A	S2
78.12–91.27	VII/¶ The printing-office . . . . was shared	RG, A	RG
91.27–109.19	in some tacit way . . . . this outing.	RG, P1, P2, P3, P5, A	RG

110–159.5	III/¶ Throughout . . . . speaking.	MSY, UG, RG, P2, P3, P5, A	MSY
159.6–161.14	¶ I do not know . . . . heaven all blue.	MSY, UG, RG, P2, P3, P5, P7, A	MSY
161.15–162.18	III/¶ Only those . . . . than he could	MSY, UG, RG, P3, P5, P7, A	MSY
162.18–171.31	have saved . . . . "In Memoriam."	MSY, UG, RG, P3, P5, A	MSY
171.32–172.24	The Men . . . . hopeful rhyme.	N1, R1, MSY, UG, RG, P3, P5, A	N1
172.25–189.30	The vision . . . . measures now taken	MSY, UG, RG, P3, P5, A	MSY
189.30–194.27	to effect it . . . . of humanity.	MSY, UG, RG, P3, P5, P6, A	MSY
194.27	It was what	MSY, UG, RG, P3, A	MSY
194.27–198.26	it had been . . . . so dread-/	MSY, UG, RG, P3, P4, A	MSY
198.26	ful to the . . . . who lives, I	MSY, UG, RG, P3, P4, P5, A	MSY

198.26–205.12	was a congeries . . . . well be that	MSY, MSY
		UG, RG,
		P3, P5, P7,
		A
205.13–206.5	as weeping . . . . THE END	UG, RG, UG
		P3, P5, P7,
		A

THE EARLY PERIODICAL PIECES

"The Coming," which Howells delivered before the Ohio Editorial Convention at Tiffin on 18 January 1860 during the period of his employment by the *Ohio State Journal* (see page 171 in the present text), was first printed in the *Journal* on 23 January of that same year, and reprinted in the Centennial Edition of the newspaper on 26 October 1911. No manuscript has been found.

"Year in a Log-Cabin, A Bit of Autobiography," was first printed in *Youth's Companion*, LX (12 May 1887), 213–215. The only other publication of the text before inclusion of the major portion of it in *Years of My Youth* was that of Harper and Brothers: the essay was published under that company's imprint with the title *My Year in a Log Cabin* (BAL 9676) as part of the Harper Black and White Series in 1893, and was deposited in the Library of Congress on 10 October 1893 after a first-impression printing of 4,000 copies.[1] Two reimpressions have been identified, one dated 1902 on the title page and the other bearing only the copyright date 1893. These later impressions are textually identical to the first. No manuscript is known to exist.

Nor is there a manuscript for "The Country Printer." It was first printed in *Scribner's*, XIII (1893), 539–558, and subsequently collected with other essays in *Impressions and Experiences*, which went through three different editions. The first, under the Harper and Brothers imprint (BAL 9706), was published in 1896, and deposited on 25 September of that year after a first-impression printing of 1,500 copies;[2] only one later impression, with the copyright date 1896, has

---

1. For these figures see the Harper "Memorandum Book" for 1892–1894, p. 38. The Harper material is surveyed by Edwin and Virginia Price Barber in "A Description of Old Harper and Brothers Publishing Records Recently Come to Light," *Bulletin of Bibliography*, XXV (1967), 1–6, 29–34, 39–40.

2. Harper "Memorandum Book," 1892–1894, p. 107.

been identified. A second edition, similar to the Harper text in format, was published by David Douglas of Edinburgh; it bears the same title-page date of 1896, and was received for deposit at the British Museum on 6 October 1896. No later impressions have been identified. A third edition, the second by Harper and Brothers, was published in 1909 in the typography of the Library Edition then being prepared by Harper. But it was never published as part of the Library Edition, and does not carry the series title page which distinguishes the items in that group. No later impressions of the third edition are known.[3]

Part of the full 1860 text of "The Coming" is represented in typed form in the extant printer's copy typescript of *Years of My Youth*. This poem typescript, different in physical appearance from the other materials in the typescript, bears the words "Centennial Edition" in the top left corner of the first page. This evidence and its specific textual readings indicate that the typist was working not from the original 1860 version but from the Centennial reprinting of the poem in the *Ohio State Journal* of 26 October 1911; it appeared there on page [33] of a special section entitled "One Hundred Years of National Progress."[4] Although Howells made some holograph changes in this typescript, the fact of his working on a copy clearly intended to reproduce the Centennial text, which was in turn intended to reproduce the 1860 printing, makes his own source for the poem effectively that first printing, and this version has therefore been selected as the copy-text for the section of "The Coming" reprinted in the present edition.

The transmission of the texts of the two periodical essays was

3. "The Country Printer" was also published as a gift book by the Plimpton Press of Norwood, Massachusetts, under the title *The Country Printer* (BAL 9843) in a limited edition of four hundred copies in 1916. The book was prepared with the permission of Harper and Brothers and appears to have been set from a copy of the 1909 Harper edition of *Impressions and Experiences*. This edition is not relevant to the genealogy of "The Country Printer" as it was finally used in *Years of My Youth*, since it does not seem to have been readied under Howells' direct supervision and since it was published too late to have been a source for setting the pertinent sections of the present text.

4. See A Note on the Manuscripts, p. 315, for a description of the typescript material. The full text of the poem had also been reprinted in *The Bookman* in July 1912 (XXXV, 510–514), but spelling and punctuation are significantly altered there. Howells obviously intended to reproduce the original of the poem, and not this modernized version, in *Years of My Youth*.

slightly more complicated. Howells made a few substantive changes between the magazine printing and book publication of "Year in a Log-Cabin," and a good many more between that version and the text as printed in *Years of My Youth*, where it was apparently set from a marked copy, tear sheets, or typed transcription of the 1893 Harper edition. In the case of "The Country Printer," Howells made a limited number of substantive changes between the *Scribner's* printing and the first edition of *Impressions and Experiences*. These changes were preserved in the British Edition, which appears to have been set from some form of that first edition—galleys, proofs, or published Harper text. The later Harper edition was also prepared from some form of the first edition, and it preserved the substantive changes which that edition contained; there is no evidence in this third edition that Howells initiated further revision. He did, however, make a great number of substantive changes between the text of the essay in *Impressions and Experiences* and the text of those sections used in *Years of My Youth*; although it excerpts only a small part of the essay, the text of the present edition bears evidence of having been set from some form of the later Harper edition, probably a marked copy of the published book.[5]

---

5. The following copies of the books spoken of as relevant to the establishment of the text of the present edition, including at least earliest and latest known impressions, have been collated in the preparation of the critical text of *Years of My Youth*: copies of the first impression of *Years of My Youth*, BAL 9841, in Louis J. Budd's collection, in the Howells Edition Center (HE9841.1.1) and in the Public Library of Cincinnati and Hamilton County (B:H86.1, cop. 9) and the Indiana University Library (PS2033.A6); copies of the second impression in the Howells Edition Center (HE9841.2.1, HE9841.2.2); copies of the illustrated impression in the Harvard College (*AC85.H8395 916yc[A]) and Alderman libraries; copies of *My Year in a Log Cabin*, BAL 9676, in the University of California at Santa Barbara (PS2029.M8), Ohio State University (EL140.H859 Myi) and Lilly (PS2029.M9) libraries; a copy of the 1902 impression in the University of Pennsylvania Library (813.H835 My), and of the copyright 1893 impression in the University of California Library (t955.H859 my); copies of the first edition of *Impressions and Experiences*, BAL 9706, first impression, in the Indiana University (PS2029.I3) and Lilly (PS2029.I55 and PS2029.I55, copy 2) libraries; copies of the later impression in the University of Illinois (814.H83i) and University of Texas (814.H839 im 1896r) libraries; copies of the British Edition in the Alderman, University of Texas (814.H839im) and Cambridge University (Misc.7.89.1348) libraries; copies of the later Harper edition, G&A 08–09n, in the collections of Louis J. Budd and Thomas Wortham and in the University of Chicago Library (PS2029.I35 1909); and copies of *The Country Printer*, BAL 9843, in the Indiana University (PS2029.C8), Lilly (PS2029.C8) and Yale

The general evidence of the printing history of the two essays indicates that, although in his work on them Howells did make substantive revisions at the different stages described above, at no time after the first printing of each did he ever attend in any consistent way to the accidentals—the punctuation, spelling, and so on—of his text. Instead, both essays underwent increasing corruption of accidentals through the later phases of publication, even through their use in *Years of My Youth*. The first periodical publications, even though their preparation precedes that of *Years of My Youth* by almost twenty-five years, must therefore be accepted as the copy-texts for those sections of the present edition into which they were incorporated.[6] Despite the fact that Howells' style underwent some change over that long period, this change was by no means so striking as to present problems of consistency in the incorporation of the early essays into the continuous text of *Years of My Youth*. Only when substantive revision demands a change in accidentals, or when copy-text accidentals are clearly in error, have the later texts been drawn upon—and then only because they are convenient sources for readings accepted on the authority of the present editor, not because they have any authority of their own in accidentals.

University (Ix.H847.916C) libraries. The copy of the 1860 *Ohio State Journal*, in which "The Coming" was printed, is that of the Ohio Historical Society, and the copies of all periodicals used in preparing the text of *Years of My Youth* and the later autobiographical essays are those of the Indiana University Library.

6. Since the bulk of "Year in a Log-Cabin" is incorporated into *Years of My Youth*, the Emendations and Rejected Substantives lists include all the material in the original version of that essay. But only a relatively small portion of "The Country Printer"—approximately one-third of the original—was used by Howells in his autobiography, and it thus presents a different textual situation: because the essay maintains an existence of its own as a literary and historical document distinct from *Years of My Youth*, and because the useful emphasis of the textual apparatus should be to detail the history of the text being printed here rather than merely to reproduce associated but not directly relevant materials, the lengthy sections of "The Country Printer" not used in the present edition are not printed in the apparatus. For the convenience of any reader who may wish to examine the material used in *Years of My Youth* in relation to its original context, the following list provides the correspondences between the present text and coincident sections of the printing of the essay in the first edition of *Impressions and Experiences*, Harper and Brothers, 1896 (BAL 9706)—the page and line numbers for the present edition appear before the slash, and the pertinent numbers for the portions of "The Country Printer" with which they coincide appear after it: 71.7–75.30/4.21–14.5, 75.32–77.31/19.17–24.11, 77.32–78.11/26.1–27.6.

The Printer's Copy Typescript and Coincident Texts

The evidence presented by the printer's copy typescript and the surviving pre-publication materials derived from it makes necessary some complex considerations. It is fundamental of course that where this typescript exists, it is accepted as copy-text with all of Howells' revisions considered an integral part of the text. Despite his varying degrees of attention to accidentals during the several phases of his revision and proofreading thereafter, the typescript represents his earliest and fullest attention to the whole of the materials of his creation; it is the form of his text which he released to the publisher.[7] As an indication of the reliability of the typescript copy-text, it must be noted that a major part of it is typescript prepared not by Howells himself but by a typist working from an earlier manuscript (or, more probably, a heavily revised typescript draft), and that therefore the final typescript may contain a number of non-authorial readings. But these readings cannot be identified. The typist reproduced what are known to have been Howells' own preferences for spelling, punctuation and capitalization, at least so far as these can be verified by Howells' own handwriting and by other contemporary manuscript materials. The printer's copy typescript of *Years of My Youth* must therefore be accepted with a recognition of the possibility of indeterminable variants.

The typescript is copy-text for pages 110–205 of the present edition, but even within this section some specific exceptions have been dictated by the nature of the materials incorporated into it. First, comparison of the accidentals in the earlier galley sections which comprise a portion of the final typescript (see A Note on the Manuscripts, pages 313–314) against accidentals in the portions of this same typescript prepared by Howells himself indicates that the galley sections have

---

7. Galley marks and line breaks throughout the printer's copy typescript coincide with line breaks in the galleys of *Years of My Youth*. The same typescript may also have been used in setting portions of the text of "In an Old-Time State Capital" in *Harper's Monthly*. A very few line breaks marked in it coincide with line breaks in the periodical publication. But the extent of the differences between the text of *Years of My Youth* and that of "In an Old-Time State Capital" is so great that extensive revision in proof must be postulated. Further, Howells' own dissatisfaction with the periodical publication and the cutting and molding he had to do to satisfy the requirements of the magazine are clear indication that it has no useful place in the genealogy of *Years of My Youth*; see Howells' letters concerning the periodical publication in the Introduction, pages *xviii–xx*.

been styled to conform with the Harper office practice. Where Howells' usage can be clearly determined, it has been restored in these sections. Moreover, a number of identifiable non-authorial revisions in accidentals throughout the typescript (see A Note on the Manuscripts, pages 317–320) have been rejected outright because of their nature, although a limited number have been accepted as necessary corrections of the copy-text and are recorded in Emendations. Finally, where the partial typescript of Howells' early poem "The Coming" occurs in this material, copy-text is not the typescript version but the 1860 newspaper text from which it ultimately derived.

The evidence provided by the typescript requires one further consideration. Where typescript and galleys set from it coincide, there is proof that the compositor has sometimes mistakenly interpreted Howells' text in setting type. In a number of cases, Howells caught the error in later stages of his reading, and corrected to his original version; in others the erroneous reading remained in the published text; and in still others Howells revised but to a new reading rather than to the original one. Information about his general working methods suggests that he did not meticulously verify the derived text word for word and letter for letter against its source. Instead, his attention was to the text before him only, and his effort was to correct it and establish its consistency as given. Thus, in the case of substantive errors in typesetting, he responded or failed to respond to something he did not write. Where his response resulted in a re-institution of his original reading, the matter is of no consequence; but where he either failed to correct or revised to a new reading, it is of crucial importance: he was reacting to something not his own as if it were his own. With a few exceptions noted in Emendations, the original printer's copy typescript reading has been preserved on the grounds that it most nearly represents Howells' conscious intention.

Pre-Publication Materials Not Coincident with the Typescript; The Book Text

Two other kinds of copy-text material pertinent to *Years of My Youth* are still to be considered: galley material for which no corresponding manuscript or typescript is extant, and portions of the book text for which there is no pre-publication text whatsoever. Where the book text is the only available text there is no choice but to accept it as it stands and to emend it on editorial authority only at those points where it clearly contradicts Howells' own stylistic preferences. Such editorial corrections are recorded in Emendations.[8] The same procedure has been applied to those sections where the first galleys revised by Howells serve as copy-text, but with a further refinement: there appears to have been some attempt to style Howells' text while the galleys were being set and again sometime afterward (during the same period at which Howells was also making substantive revisions). When these stylistic sophistications can be identified, they have been emended on the authority of the present edition. Otherwise, the author's revised first galleys too must be accepted as they stand, with Howells' corrections and those of the publisher's proofreader on them; the revisions made by the proofreader on the galleys themselves are not of a stylistic kind and must be taken as corrections to the now-missing manuscript from which the text was being set. Finally, though they must be accepted as copy-texts for significant portions of the present edition, both galleys and book text lack the more fully satisfactory authority of a manuscript; they have instead the secondary authority of texts which have been unfortunately and irrevocably distorted in the process of their derivation.

GENERAL CONSIDERATIONS IN THE TEXT
OF *Years of My Youth*

As many as the surviving pre-publication stages of the text of *Years of My Youth* are, they do not record all the stages of revision between the earliest extant portion for each part and the text as it was finally published. In addition to apparently non-authorial stylistic changes introduced both in the setting of galleys and later in the preparation of page proofs, there are authorial revisions in set type which are not

---

8. Although the early poetic effort printed on pages 65–67 of the present text is derived essentially from a manuscript of the same poem in his boyhood diary (now in the Howells Collection in the Houghton Library; the text of the poem also appears in the unpublished manuscript-typescript, "The Real Diary of a Boy"— see below, p. 329), the means of its preparation for publication here cannot be determined: the original manuscript is so vastly different in accidentals from the version in *Years of My Youth* that the changes can be accounted for only by postulating a high degree of attention to them on Howells' part—perhaps at some stage after the "Real Diary" text—and not by presuming typing or other transcription errors. For this reason the text as it appears in the book edition has been accepted as copy-text.

represented by Howells' request for them in written revisions occurring throughout these surviving materials. All of the Emendations accepted into those sections where printer's copy typescript and proofs exist, but where the reading of the present edition has as its source the published book text, are revisions for which we have no evidence in Howells' hand; taken together, these readings represent at least one full stage of revision after the latest extant portions of proofs. A limited number of these revisions (those at 99.8, 196.12, 196.14 [twice], 196.18 and 201.33) may not be by Howells, but since they are necessary for clarity they have been accepted. In addition, Howells made three revisions between third and fourth page-proof stages which are not verified by his hand-written correction of P3 (two at 194.30 and one at 194.31). With these exceptions, the galleys and page proofs do record all other authorial revision. Where typescript and proofs do not exist and the revised galleys are the only extant stage before the published book, there may have been one or several stages of revision between them, though no evidence exists which would settle that issue.

These different pre-publication materials also evidence certain other non-authorial revisions, but of corrective rather than stylistic kinds. For that section of the text where the first stage of page proofs (P1) is the next extant form after revised galleys, three such revisions have been accepted (at 96.20, 104.31 and 107.34); where the second page proofs (P2) are the first stage after galleys preserving printer's copy typescript errors made by Howells, nine have been accepted (113.22, 118.11, 119.7, 127.5, 131.14, 135.18, 140.9, 143.36–144.1 and 148.27); where P3 is the first set of proofs after galleys which preserve typescript errors, four have been accepted (at 161.28, 185.17, 192.1 and 206.5). Again, where the second stage of page proofs (P2) presents in set type material added by Howells in the first stage,[9] mistakes occurring in those added sections are corrected by the compositor and the corrections have been accepted: these occur at 100.23 and following in the present text (and are fully recorded in a Textual Note at that point), and also at 111.9, 113.28 and 114.7.

Special technical conventions have been adopted because of the

---

9. See A Note on the Manuscripts and Other Pre-Publication Forms of the Texts, p. 324, for a description of the P1 additions.

number and complexity of the texts involved in the publication history of *Years of My Youth*. First, the Rejected Substantives list contains all readings which did not originate with Howells, even though he may eventually have corrected to the original readings himself. Second, the Emendations list contains all the changes Howells did institute himself, even when after a number of revisions by him the reading finally adopted is identical to that of the copy-text on which the revision is based. Finally, two special methods of dealing with revisions within accepted and rejected long sections of text—both of them explained in the headnote to Emendations—are used to avoid extensive and unnecessary repetition of textual material.

The Later Autobiographical Essays

The texts of "Overland to Venice," "An Old Venetian Friend" and "A Young Venetian Friend," periodical pieces which Howells wrote in anticipation of the second volume of his autobiography, offer none of the complications of *Years of My Youth*. "Overland to Venice," which appeared in *Harper's Monthly* in November 1918 (CXXXVII, 837–845), and "A Young Venetian Friend," which appeared there in May 1919 (CXXXVIII, 827–833), are represented by no extant manuscript and were never reprinted. The magazine versions are thus the copy-texts, and the texts of the present edition are virtually reprints, though typographical errors and nonsense readings have been corrected on editorial authority and identifiable stylistic elements which represent the Harper practice rather than Howells' own have been emended to accord with Howells' usage. The text of "An Old Venetian Friend" is represented not only by the *Harper's Monthly* publication of April 1919 (CXXXVIII, 634–640), but also by a complete manuscript (see A Note on the Manuscripts, pages 329–330, for a complete description of it). Though the manuscript contains a good many errors and was extensively revised, in typescript or proof or both, before publication, it is the nearest Howells came to a coherent combination of substance and form, and it has therefore been accepted as the copy-text for this essay.

General Editorial Policy

No attempt has been made in the present edition to preserve the purely visual appurtenances of the copy-texts: type style, format of part, section and paragraph openings, the spacing of indentations and normalization of italic punctuation.[10] Finally, and most importantly, no effort has been made to correct Howells' historical and factual errors (including his misspelling of certain proper names)—though when these occur they are pointed out in the Notes to the Text (pages 259–291, above). To accept non-authorial corrections of accidentals is necessary to the preparation of a clear and readable text, but to revise beyond that in an important autobiographical document, a testament of the human memory at its best and worst, is to destroy its full personal value, its record of the mind—and art—of W. D. Howells.

D.J.N.

----

10. We have normalized the use of italic punctuation after italic letters. Only question marks and exclamation points are set in italics after italicized letters in our text, and all others in roman; this policy is consistent with the various copy-texts with the exception of the published book text of *Years of My Youth*, in which semicolons and colons are consistently italicized after italicized words.

A Note on the Manuscripts
and Other Pre-Publication Forms of the Texts

I. THE MATERIALS FOR *YEARS OF MY YOUTH*

All pre-publication materials relevant to the text of *Years of My Youth* are in the Howells Collection at the Houghton Library at Harvard University. These materials include a partial typescript, three different sections of galleys, and portions of seven partial stages of page proofs; all of them represent distinct phases in the preparation of the published book text. The bibliographical descriptions of these materials are presented in the following sections; their significance for the establishment of the critical text of *Years of My Youth* is discussed in the Textual Commentary (pages 295–309).

The Printer's Copy Typescript

The extant typescript, which was used as setting copy for the first edition, consists of one hundred and seventeen leaves and coincides generally with parts III and IV of *Years of My Youth* (pages 110–205).[1] The final numbering sequence on the leaves is quite involved and is the result of revision into and around an earlier typescript, of which eighty leaves, originally numbered 17–97 (lacking only the leaf numbered 94) are present in the extant typescript. The final numbering of the full typescript is given in the following list, and with it the original numbering of the earlier typescript leaves where they exist:

---

1. The table on pp. 297–300 in the Textual Commentary offers a comprehensive outline of the parts of *Years of My Youth* represented by the different pre-publication stages of the text and also indicates the extent to which these stages coincide with each other. It should be consulted for all such information about the materials for *Years of My Youth* discussed in this Note on the Manuscripts.

The Numbering of the Printer's Copy Typescript

Final	Original	Final	Original
154		176	33
2 = 154		177	34
155		A177	
2 = 155		178	35
156		179	36
157		180	37
157		181	38
158		182	39
158		183	40
159		184	
160		185	
161		186	
162		183(1)	
163		184(2)	41
164		185(3)	42
165		186(4)	43
166	17	187(5)	44
167	18	186(6)	45
168	19	187(7)	
169	20	2 = 187	
A20 = 169		3 = 187	46
170	21	188	47
171	22	189	48
172	23	190	49
173	24	191	50
168	25	192	51
169	26	193	52
170		194	53
2 = 170	27	195	54
171	28	196	55
172	29	197	56
173	30	198	57
174		199	58
2 = 174	31	200	59
A p.2 = 174		201	60
175	32	202	61

Final	Original	Final	Original
2 = 202		219	78
3 = 202		220	79
4 = 202		221	80
5 = 202		222	81
6 = 202		223	82
7 = 202		224	83
203	62	225	84
204	63	226	85
205	64	227	86
206	65	228	87
A65 = 206		229	88
207	66	230	89
208	67	231	90
209	68	232	91
210	69	233	92
211	70	234	93
212	71	235	–90–
213	72	A235	–89–
214	73	236	–91–
215	74	237	95
216	75	238	96
217	76	238	97
218	77		

Of that earlier typescript, leaves originally numbered 17–43 are on lined 8½ in. × 11 in. paper (although some leaves are shorter, presumably trimmed by Howells to remove portions of the text in revising) watermarked "Merchants Pure Linen," each leaf containing twenty-eight to thirty lines of text in black elite type-face. Leaf 44 of the earlier typescript—187(5) in the final sequence—is on the same kind of paper but contains fourteen full lines of elite type, followed immediately by fifteen full lines of pica type filling out the remainder of the sheet. Leaves 45 through 97, which continue in pica type (twenty-seven to twenty-nine lines per page) are on 8½ in. × 11 in. unlined paper watermarked "BERKSHIRE BOND U.S.A." Despite the changes in type-faces and papers, the whole of this earlier typescript appears to have been prepared by the same typist (not by Howells), since the observance of the right margins in both type sections is generally the same and the format for numbering the pages is continuous as well as identical in placement. The majority of the leaves introduced into and around this original typescript were typed in Howells' distinctive script-face type or written by him in black ink. They consist of sheets of 8 in. × 10½ in. bond typing paper with the watermark "BERKSHIRE VESPER LINEN U.S.A." Some are completely covered with text, some only partially used, and the versos of several continue text from the recto or contain material to be inserted into it. But there are several notable exceptions to this format as well.

Within the first extant section of newly prepared leaves are portions of an earlier set of Harper galleys, on plain pulp paper. The running heads on these galleys, which carry the title "Some Years of My Youth," suggest the text may have been set from manuscript which Howells forwarded to Frederick A. Duneka of Harper and Brothers "for business purposes" sometime after 29 April 1915 but before the submission of the full manuscript on 6 July.[2] Sections of galleys numbered 4 through 8 only are represented in the typescript, and galley 8 contains only twenty-seven—rather than the usual ninety-eight to one hundred and four—lines of type and breaks off in the middle of a word. This may not have been the last line of type prepared in the setting of the earlier galleys, however, since printer's line-break and galley-break marks, beginning with the number 9, continue on the typescript leaf which follows the last of the galley leaves and carry on the sequence through the typescript to the number 15.[3] These galleys are revised in both pencil and ink in Howells' hand.

The original sequence of the material on these galleys cannot be reconstructed with confidence from their arrangement in the typescript, but it can be partially indicated by a description of the leaves which contain them; these are, in the final numbering, 2 = 155, 156,

---

2. See the Introduction, pp. xxi-xxii.

3. In several instances these original galley marks fall on leaves added to the earlier typescript, indicating that Howells had completed the major part of his revision before submitting text to the publisher for typesetting the first time. These galley breaks do not coincide with the divisions in the later galleys set from this typescript, and it is not clear why Howells used only part of these earlier galleys in his final stages of revision. In any case, given the amount of local revision he introduced on the earlier galley sections—and thus presumably on the further portions of the typescript—it was certainly less expensive for the publisher to request a complete resetting rather than line-by-line revisions of the set type in the earlier galleys.

157, 157[*bis*], 163, 164 and 165. Leaf 2 = 155 consists of a full sheet of the bond paper Howells used throughout the added sections, to the bottom half of which is pasted an 8¾-inch length of galley sheet of the usual 8½-inch width of all galleys which are part of the *Years of My Youth* material; this galley section, probably the bottom part of the galley originally numbered 4 (since galley 5 begins the next leaf), contains twenty-eight lines of text. At the bottom of this galley sheet Howells wrote in pencil three and one-half lines of text to be inserted into the galley text above, and below this is pinned an 8½ in. × 2½ in. piece of unlined heavy typing stock, onto which has been typed in blue with revisions in blue pencil a transcription of those lines. The transcription, probably prepared in the publisher's office, is not completely accurate; it is followed by the words "Translation of above." Leaf 156 consists of the top portion of earlier galley 5 with its galley heading, measures 4 inches in length, and contains sixteen lines of type; the bottom of this sheet is pasted over the top half inch of a full sheet of "Vesper Linen" containing text in ink in Howells' hand. The first leaf numbered 157 consists of a 4-inch piece of galley containing twenty-three lines of type pasted over the top 3½ inches of a galley sheet 10½ inches long; the pasted-on section covers only the galley heading, numbered 6, of the larger sheet. The second leaf numbered 157 is a single piece of galley 11 inches long; it has been trimmed at top and bottom, and carries no galley heading. Leaf 163 is a full piece of bond paper carrying at the top four lines of text in Howells' hand; immediately beneath these lines two small sections of galley are pasted on the sheet, one 2 inches long and containing eleven lines of text and the second 6¼ inches long and containing thirty-seven lines of text. Leaf 164 is a full galley sheet, numbered 7, 22 inches long. Leaf 165, the last leaf containing galley material and the last of the leaves in the extant typescript newly introduced at the beginning of the earlier typescript segment, is the full galley sheet numbered 8, 22 inches long but containing only twenty-seven lines of type.

Other leaves in the typescript are also exceptions to the general format. Leaf 2–154 is an 8 in. × 10½ in. sheet of bond paper watermarked "Berkshire Souvenir Bond U.S.A." and contains two lines and a word of text typed in the same pica face used in the major section of leaves of the earlier typescript. The leaf is numbered 7 in type in the upper right-hand corner, but this is over-written in ink with a

"31"; this number is superseded by "2 = 153" and then by the number finally given it, both of these numbers in pencil and centered at the top of the page. Leaf 155 is on the usual bond paper of the newly introduced leaves, but is only about 9½ inches long, the bottom of the leaf having been trimmed. Leaf 160 consists of a full sheet of bond paper, in black ink manuscript; but over the top third of the sheet and the text it contains is pasted a piece of the same paper 4 inches long, with text in the distinctive script-face type of Howells' typewriter. Leaf 166, a renumbering of page 17 of the earlier typescript, contains on its verso nineteen and one-half lines in ink in Howells' hand, followed by eight and one-half lines in the distinctive script-face of his typewriter; pasted over the bottom half inch of the verso of the sheet is a 3 in. × 8 in. piece of bond paper containing nine more typed lines. Leaf 183, originally numbered 40, has been reduced to an 8-inch length by the cutting off of the bottom section of the sheet. Leaf 183(1), the last page of a four-page insertion following leaf 183, has that bottom section of leaf 183 pasted to it. The first leaf and last two leaves of the group numbered 2 = 202 through 7 = 202 are on regular bond paper with text in Howells' hand in black ink, and 7 = 202, containing only three and one-half manuscript lines in ink, has pasted beneath these a three-inch piece of typed text cut from the bottom of leaf 202 (originally numbered 61). Leaves 3 = 202 through 5 = 202 consist of buff bulk paper with text in purple carbon and contain a transcription made by someone other than Howells of the text of his poem "The Coming," probably prepared directly from a clipping of the *Ohio State Journal* reprinting of it in the paper's Centennial Edition on 26 October 1911, which was in turn prepared from the original printing of January 1860.[4] Leaves 235, A235, and 236 are face sheets from a copy of the essay entitled "Life in a State Capital Fifty-Odd Years Ago," where they were originally numbered 90, 89 and 91; the carbon copies of these leaves and of the whole of

---

4. See Textual Commentary, pp. 301 and 305, for a discussion of the choice of copy-text for this poem.

During his preparation of the autobiographical material Howells carried on a correspondence with Theodore T. Frankenberg of the *Journal* staff. In reply to a question from Frankenberg about what of his early material was first published there and what reprinted, Howells said he could tell only by seeing the pieces, and asked Frankenberg to send copies of the material in question. On the Frankenberg correspondence see Introduction, p. xvi, footnote 15.

the rest of this essay are in the Houghton Library.[5] The revisions on the leaves in the present typescript are different from those in the carbon copy, and are presumed to have been made to fit the demands of the present text as Howells prepared it. Leaf A235 of this group of three, however, does not fit into the text in any coherent way.[6] Finally, the parenthetical numbers on leaves 183(1) through 187(7) in the manuscript indicate a pagination sequence provided not by Howells but probably by the reader or compositor as clarification of the sequence of the leaves in this duplicated numerical sequence.[7]

Howells' revisions in this typescript are of different kinds, ranging from the alteration of single words, marks of punctuation, and short phrases to the addition or deletion of full paragraphs and sections and the moving of significant portions of the text. No clear pattern of revision emerges which could establish that it was a consistent and orderly process. No attempt has been made in the present text to offer a full record of these internal alterations; thus cancellations, self-editings, interlinings, careted insertions, and so on which are authorial in origin have been accepted as pre-copy-text alterations, thus integral parts of the copy-text and not listed in the apparatus. Further, no record has been made of doubled punctuation (which occurs approximately forty times in the typescript), since it is obviously the result of Howells' failure to cancel one mark in the process of a substantive revision in which he included this same punctuation or a different one. This policy has been adopted not because such internal evidence is not significant but because the mechanics of transcription have not been adequately developed to meet the needs of the scholar who wishes to base his research on such facsimile reproduction; he must work with the typescript itself or with a well-

---

5. See below, pp. 328–329, for a description of the essay materials.
6. See Emendations, 203.15–16, and the accompanying Textual Note.
7. On the verso of leaf 2–174 Howells pencilled "Days of My Youth/Part I"; on the recto of leaf 175 appear the partially erased notes in another hand "Voucher #17" in pencil and " 'Days of My Youth'/By W. D. Howells—2nd Paper" in black crayon. The possible division of the text at this point and the note concerning the title may be references to the use of this manuscript for "In an Old-Time State Capital," published in three papers in *Harper's Monthly* in 1914 (see Introduction, pp. xviii-xx). But the periodical text is very different from the typescript, and if the text was set from this typescript it was much changed afterward—the division at this point, for example, does not even vaguely coincide with the division of the papers in the magazine. (See also Textual Commentary, p. 304, footnote 7.)

prepared photo-facsimile. The Emendations list does, however, record all false starts and doubled words, since these can be easily identified.

In addition to corrections in pencil and ink in Howells' hand throughout the typescript, there are many other marks: one group consists of compositor's marks in blue and black pencil indicating line- and galley-breaks, but there are also a significant number of black-pencil revisions in the text which appear to have been made by a Harper editor rather than by Howells. Some of these consist of the addition or deletion of punctuation; others are merely "x's" placed above certain words or in the margins of the text, apparently provided by an editor or reader to indicate to the compositor that a different form (presumably that of the Harper and Brothers style of the period) should be substituted for what appears on the page—hyphenated forms for unhyphenated and vice-versa, "gaiety" for "gayety," *-er* endings rather than *-re* in words like "theatre," "centre," and "sombre." There are approximately 250 such "x's" in the extant typescript.

The following list records only those revisions within the typescript which can with relative assurance be identified as non-authorial and which occur within the text lines; the list does not record the occurrence of "x's," since these, although they may have been indications to someone else to alter the text, do not change its essential physical state on the pages themselves. The list records the location of the reading in the present text. Entries prefaced by an asterisk occur within typescript readings cancelled at later stages of revision; the original readings can be found in Emendations at these points. Non-authorial typescript readings which have been accepted into the present text are so identified in Emendations.

Authorial comma deleted by Harper editor after the following words: 123.22 longing; 123.33 silk; 125.2 East; 125.13 out; 125.13 days); 126.27 abeyance; 126.34 two; 127.8 chief; 129.33 well; 131.22 noonings; *133.24–29 guests; 134.9 calls; 134.10 said; 134.15 me; 134.22 Ohio; 134.23 Lincoln; 134.30 administration; 134.34 affair; 139.11 doubt; 139.14 attention; 139.20 *Press*; 139.23 more; 139.29 1859; 139.33 Alleghanies; 141.16 say; 141.20 upon; 142.30 A.; 144.26 risks; 145.7–8 village; 145.9 me; 145.10 me; 145.17 me; 145.28 world; 145.32 me; 145.34 Columbus; 146.1 Broad;

146.13 pall; 146.16 heaven; 149.1 home; 149.17 good;
149.17 then; 149.18 say; 150.8 parties; 150.8 that; 150.13 home;
151.4 cousin; 151.12 tribute; 151.19 friend; 151.29 work;
*152.27 knew; *152.27 post-office; 154.2 Heine;
154.3 magazine; 154.9 author; 154.18 river; 154.24–25 with it;
155.1 Oh; 155.5 years; 155.7 Cincinnati; 155.10 rejected;
155.11 page; 155.27 presence; 155.30 home; 156.12 *Story*;
156.14–15 newspaper; 156.24 inevitably; 156.30 *Faun*;
*157.35–158.4 supper; *158.21 1860; 159.9 poem; 159.12 of;
159.16 *Monthly*; 159.28 should; 159.34 tradition; 159.34 law;
159.35 time; 161.28 invaders; 161.32 Virginia; 162.8 testify;
162.11 life; 162.33 capital; 163.14 in; 163.34 us; 164.21 there;
164.22 day; 164.36 Columbus; 165.1 comrades; 165.19 keepsake;
165.34 S.; 166.22 House; 167.25 excursions; 167.25 lakes;
169.34 me; 170.6 print; 173.16 publisher; 173.27 it; 174.10 man;
174.11 see; 174.25 time; 175.20 him; 176.27 them; 177.30 time;
178.25 River; 179.2 do; 179.20 excitement; 184.26 one;
184.26 time; 188.22 enemies; 188.26 well; 188.26 again;
189.2 nights; 190.12 office; 190.19 war; *190.30 wiser;
190.36 Houses; 191.29 youth; 194.20 control; 195.29 tell of;
*196.3–197.1 politics; *196.3–197.1 *Journal*; 198.11 home;
199.30 began; *200.18 Sumter; 204.1 behalf; 204.3 backing;
204.16 it; 204.27 life; 205.1 arrived.

Comma supplied by Harper editor after the following words:
126.27 editor; 126.36 or; 127.33 literature; 127.34 say was;
133.2 publicly; 133.23 dinner; *133.24–29 courses; 134.3 eyes;
134.5 were; 134.33–34 secretaries; 134.34 Nicolay; 134.34 said;
*135.2 help me; 137.9 divines; 137.11 mine; 137.11 too;
138.13 think; 138.22 who; 138.22 he; 139.14 unbroken;
139.20 York; 141.12 literature; 141.16 of; 142.19 it; 142.19 too;
142.19 that; 143.6 die; 145.8 I; 145.8 too; 145.23 he; 145.23 too;
145.36 High; 145.36 eastward; 148.29 Southerners;
149.20 change; 149.20 any; 150.8 or; 151.7 kindest; *152.27 who;
153.7 youth; *153.10 and; 156.7 has; 156.8 course;
156.34 to-night; *158.25 enemy; 159.2 accident; 160.1 one;
160.16 future; 164.31 poet; 165.3 was; 165.3 doubt; 165.18 title);
165.36 said; 172.33 and; 173.20 books; 173.26 over;
174.22 humble; 175.2 Washington; 175.34 full-bearded;

176.32 arms; 177.31 coming; 177.32 arm; 178.23 Falls;
179.22 deep; 181.20 mainly; 181.20 wholly; 182.25 where;
182.25 before; 182.33 joy; 183.28 correspondent; 186.24 had;
186.24 fact; 188.2 him; 188.22 enemies); 188.28 and; 188.28 us;
189.27 coming; 194.33 now; *196.3–197.1 fine;
*196.3–197.1 eyes; *196.3–197.1 moustache; 198.36 and;
198.36 fact; 199.33 South; 199.34 caste; 203.18 much;
203.19 believe; *204.21 hopeful.

Authorial two-word forms hyphenated by Harper editor:
123.18 police station; 123.30 station house; 123.36 police stations;
134.25 fellow Ohioans.

Authorial *afterwards* changed to *afterward* by Harper editor at 134.6,
134.26–27, *134.30, 144.6, 151.20, *152.27, 159.3, 159.36,
182.12, 183.36, 187.14, *187.25–26, 188.15.

Authorial lower-case forms capitalized by Harper editor:
134.18 president; 134.18 president; 134.21 president;
134.29 president; 134.33 president's; 135.1 president;
*152.27 heaven.

Miscellaneous Harper editorial changes in accidentals:

134.22	governor ship] *changed to* governorship
*135.2	Atlantic Monthly] *italicized*
138.22	allegiance;] *semicolon changed to comma*
157.22	law-students] *hyphen deleted*
163.9	State] *changed to lower-case* s
*173.9	Convention's] *changed to lower-case* c
173.17	"Poems of Two Friends"] *changed to* "*Poems of Two Friends*
173.29	"Romance of a Mummy"] *changed to* "*Romance of a Mummy*"
174.27	regretted] *second* t *deleted*
175.32	Journal] *italicized*
175.33	"My Literary Passions,"] *changed to* "*My Literary Passions*,"
177.22	"Life of Lincoln,"] *changed to* "*Life of Lincoln*,"

179.20   bizarre] *italicized*
*196.3–197.1   meantime] *made two words*

Harper editorial changes in substantives:
127.6   fom] *changed to* from
134.8   Years] *changed to* Year's
134.28   upon] *changed to* upon him
163.14   that] *changed to* the
181.21   grocers] *changed to* grocers'

Galley Number 25 (LG)

In the Howells Collection materials for *Years of My Youth* is a single sheet of glossy white tissue 8¼ in. × 22 in. containing eighty lines of set type and headed "Gal. 25—YEARS OF MY YOUTH—Francis"; the material on it overlaps the last part of the section containing material from "Year in a Log-Cabin."[8] As with all galleys mentioned from this point, this material represents the first extant typeset form of what actually did become the book *Years of My Youth*. There are no revisions in Howells' hand on the sheet, but eight in the hands of others: one in compositor's blue pencil, a "G5"—presumably a galley identification number of some kind—in the top right corner; the notation in black crayon at the end of the set type, "End P[art?]. 1/"; and three division marks and accompanying numbers (63, 64, 65) along the right margin of the type indicating breaks for distributing the galley text into page forms. Since this single galley is on different paper from the other galley materials and contains no authorial revision, it is not clear whether it is to be considered part of the unrevised or the author's revised first galleys (described below); for this reason it has been treated as a separate pre-publication item.

Unrevised First Galleys (UG)

The unrevised first galley material consists of forty-one leaves of plain pulp paper, all approximately 8¼ in. × 23 in., each leaf with a

---

8. Again, refer to the table on pp. 297–300 in the Textual Commentary for a complete record of the correspondence of the various forms of the text.

heading identifying it by galley number (47 through 87), the title "Years of My Youth" (with the exception of galley 47, headed "Some Years of My Youth," galley 73, "Years of My Yout" [sic], and galleys 74, 76, 78 and 87, "Years of Youth"), and the name "Cardwell," identifying the compositor. Each sheet contains between eighty-four and one hundred and thirteen lines of type, with most bearing ninety-five to one hundred. There are no marks in Howells' hand, but printer's corrections, queries, and suggestions appear in black ink in the margins at several points. The galleys and the printer's marks on them are duplicated on matching sections in the author's revised first galleys (see below), although the latter contain additional authorial and non-authorial marks and their physical arrangement has been altered.

Author's First Revised Galleys (RG)

The material referred to throughout the apparatus as the author's revised first galleys consists of sixty-one leaves, generally of single sheets of paper of the same substance and approximate size as the unrevised galleys, carrying in their headings the galley numbers 26 through 87. The material on these leaves represents the greatest bulk of all the pre-publication items, coinciding basically with parts II through IV of the published book. Corrections and revisions occur on the galleys in Howells' hand in black pencil; there are also some editorial marks in black ink, as well as shop marks and instructions in blue pencil and orange crayon. Galley sheets 26 through 46 carry in the heading the name "Josten" as that of the compositor; galleys 26 through 30 carry the title "Some Years of my Youth" (with misspellings at several appearances); galleys 31 through 35, 37 and 38, 40 through 44, and 46 the title "Years of my Youth"; galley 36, "of my Youth"; galley 39, "Days of Youth"; and galley 45, "Years of Youth." This portion of the galleys also contains line divisions and numbers in black ink indicating book-page divisions. These division marks end with galley 46. Galleys 47 through the end are identical in basic format to the unrevised first galleys, of which they are a duplicate. The "Josten" and "Cardwell" sections (as well as the single galley numbered 25 [LG] with the name "Francis") may represent distinct settings of type prepared from different sections of the full typescript at the same time, but this is not certain. Nor are the differences in title on the galleys of much use in determining the specific periods of their preparation, except that they reiterate the repeated transformations through which the title went before publication.[9]

Several exceptions to the single-leaf, single-full-length-sheet format occur in the revised galleys, most but not all of them the result of authorial revision and re-arrangement. Following galley 36 is a single galley sheet, 15 inches long, containing no galley heading, but in blue pencil the number "36½"; the text on this sheet continues galley 36 and is continued on galley 37. Galley 38, only 9¼ inches long and containing nineteen lines of type, is pasted to the front of full-sized galley 39 at the top edge, presumably to keep galley 38 from being misplaced. Galley 46 is 11½ inches in length, contains only thirty-one lines of text, and ends coincidentally with the end of Part II of the present text. Galley 47 consists of a piece of galley sheet "47" 12¼ inches long, under the bottom edge of which is pasted a piece of 8 in. × 6¼ in. paper of the "VESPER LINEN" kind normally used by Howells in revision, with text in black script-face type and corrections in pencil; to the bottom of this in turn is pasted a piece of galley 11¾ inches long, the remainder of galley 47. Galley 48 consists of a 9-inch section of galley headed in type "Gal. 48," to which are pasted two pieces of the same bond typing paper 4¼ inches long, both with text in black script-face type and corrections in pencil, followed by the rest of the original galley 48. Galley 49 consists of the pasting together of a 7¼-inch piece of galley headed with that number, another galley section approximately 3 inches long, a piece of bond paper 2 inches long containing text in script-face type, a galley section 8¼ inches long, a piece of bond paper 2 inches long with two lines of text in black ink, and a galley piece 9½ inches long. There are no galley sheets numbered 50 and 51, the text of these having been distributed to other points within the revised galleys or omitted completely.[10] Galley 52 consists of a piece of galley 10½ inches long with that heading number to which is attached by means of a blank piece of bond paper pasted behind them both a galley sheet 7½ inches long; over the bottom of this in turn is pasted a galley piece 2 inches long with

---

9. See Introduction, pp. xviii-xxii, for pertinent biographical material. External evidence indicates only that the book was probably set in type beginning shortly after 6 July 1915.

10. The placement of the text as the result of this fragmentation of the revised galleys is described in Emendations at those points of the present text where such changes take place, particularly at 121.4 and in the Textual Note there.

the heading "Gal. 50" and another galley piece 15¼ inches in length also pasted to the 7½-inch piece. Galley 62 is 43½ inches long in all and consists of a full-length galley sheet headed with that number, over the bottom of which is pasted a 16¼ inch galley section, under the bottom of which is pasted another galley section 10¼ inches long with the heading "Gal. 51." The galley headed "64" consists of a full-length galley sheet under the bottom edge of which is pasted an 11-inch galley section headed "Gal. 65"—to the top of this double sheet and behind it is pinned an unheaded galley section 11 inches long with the number "65" in pencil in the left-hand margin (the text on this pinned sheet coincides with the beginning of Part IV in the present text, and for that reason may have been cut away from the top half of the full galley sheet which contained it).

Page Proofs (P1–P7)

Among the Howells Collection materials are a number of sheets of page proofs. They represent the stages of preparation of the book text of *Years of My Youth* after author's revised first galleys and before publication. From the evidence of revision in and onto them and the sequence which this revision follows, it appears that these sheets are remnants of seven partial stages of page proofs.[11] All the page-proof materials are on glossy-finish, thin tissue paper, and the majority measure approximately 10 in. × 15 in. (any exceptions will be noted in the specific information below for each proof section). The majority of the sheets also contain four page-length sections of type, with running heads and page numbers, blocked in with black dummy rules. The type is usually arranged on a sheet so that the text reads across the shorter sheet dimension; the page sections are so placed on the sheets that the first page in the sequence is at the upper left quarter, the second at the upper right, the third at the bottom left, and the fourth at the bottom right. Howells' revisions and corrections, when these occur—and not all the stages of proof carry on them evidence of his work—are in black pencil, and printer's corrections, queries, and suggestions are in black ink.

---

11. Except where it appears necessary for clarification, the information given on the table on pp. 297–300 in the Textual Commentary concerning the portions of the final text which these proofs represent and the extent to which they coincide with each other will not be repeated below.

The first segment of page proof (designated hereafter as P1) consists of five such proof sheets in the usual format, with the single exception of the last sheet of the group, which contains only three book pages arranged side by side across the long dimension of the full-sized sheet. The pagination sequence runs from 103 to and including 121. In addition to Howells' corrections and the usual printer's marks, another hand has changed the numbers of pages 115 and following to 114 and so on in black crayon and pencil; presumably this is the work of a compositor compensating for the space being taken in the page forms by changes requested both on the galleys and these and other proofs. The major change in this portion of proof occurs on the full sheet containing the pages numbered 111 through 114; a strip of paper made up of two pieces of Howells' regular bond, containing fifty-four lines of text in black in his script-face type with corrections in pencil and black ink, is attached to the top of the proof, and text on it designated for insertion into the set text.[12] Finally, on the first sheet of this segment is written in Howells' hand "Please send revises"; its occurrence here probably indicates that he received or returned this section as a distinct set.

The second segment of page proof (P2) consists of 22 sheets. The first six contain pages numbered 100–121, with the fourth sheet, full-sized, having only two type-pages, 112 and 113, arranged side-by-side and centered across the long dimension. The next eight sheets contain pages numbered in type 119–150, but these numbers are changed in orange crayon to 122–153. The last eight sheets contain pages numbered in type 154–185. All the sheets contain revisions in pencil by Howells, but taken together they may originally have represented two or more distinct stages of preparation or authorial revision. The first six have a "2" penned in the upper left-hand corner (perhaps meaning second printer's page proofs of that section), and the first sheet has in Howells' hand, "Please return for revision with the same pages. W.D.H." The second, eight-sheet, section has no numbers in the upper left-hand corners and no notation to the printer in Howells' hand about sending revises. The third section of P2, on which the pagination in type continues the sequence in crayon on the second section, also has no handwritten numbering identifying

---

12. See Emendations at 100.2–101.31 and following for a full record of this P1 revision and later changes made in it.

the group, but does have Howells' notation at the top of the first sheet, "Please send revises. W.D.H." These points and the fact that the text on these sheets is continuous suggest P2 was being prepared while Howells was working on P1 and that it was originally sent in sections. The first section, which coincides with P1 almost exactly, contains in type revisions indicated by Howells on P1, and was probably sent after the second section of P2; the changes in pagination on the second section were done by hand because the proofs had already been pulled when P1 with its extensive revisions was returned, necessitating expansion of the pagination; and the page numbers on the third section are set in type because these proofs had not yet been pulled when P1 came back, and were sent a short time later, after the pagination was corrected. In any case, taken together these three sections represent the first proof stage of any kind after P1 or after revised galleys where there is no extant P1. In spite of the intricacy of the pagination, P2 does appear to represent a single stage of revision.

The third segment of extant page proof (P3) consists of 36 leaves, generally of the same format as the rest, with the pages numbered 100–237. Beginning with the page numbered 186, the numbering of the pages is lowered by two in pencil in a hand other than Howells' through page 205, so that the resultant numbering is 184–203. Beginning with page 194, however, this second numbering is raised by one, so that, for example, the original 194, which had been changed to 192, is changed again to 193. This second numbering continues through the earlier one and beyond it to 213, which becomes 212. Pages 214–237 are unchanged. The numbering has no special textual significance, and was probably the compositor's adjustment, as he worked through the proofs, to compensate for the different major and minor revisions being called for by Howells.

There are several exceptions to the general format in P3. The fourth leaf contains only two type-pages, 112 and 113 (identical in numbering and general content to the same material in the same format in P2). The thirty-fourth and thirty-fifth leaves are the two cut-up parts of the sheet originally containing pages 230–233, one consisting of the single page section numbered 231 and the other remaining part of the full sheet with the other three pages. Pasted to the top left edge of leaf thirty-two (pages 222–225; coinciding generally with 192.3–197.24 in the present text) is a slip of unlined paper approximately 8 in. × 3 in. containing in pencil seven lines of text in

Howells' hand for insertion into the set text. The revisions indicated on this slip (and some of those on the cut-up sheet 230–233) are a second stage of revision of the material, made at some point after an earlier group of revisions made by Howells in P3 was set in type. The revision on the slip (which occurs at 194.5–11 in the present text) is probably some form of the reading sent by Howells to his daughter during the preparation of the book, asking her advice in describing his wife.[13] External evidence would thus indicate that Howells had done the first stage of revision on P3 before 30 October 1915, the date of the letter, and that he had completed his later revision within two or three days of that time. The cut-up pieces of pages 230–233 probably went through the two stages of revision at these same periods.[14]

The fourth page-proof segment (P4) consists of a single proof sheet containing pages numbered 219–222. The text on the sheet comprises the stage of the text after that of the same material on P3, with some P3 revisions set in type and corrections in a handwriting other than that of Howells to make the set type agree exactly with his P3 revisions. But in addition to differences from P3 not called for by Howells there (see Textual Commentary, page 307, for a comment on this missing stage of revision) and revisions in Howells' hand on the proof sheet itself, there is attached to the right edge of the sheet a slip 5 in. × 17 in. made up of three sheets of tissue pasted together, containing text typed in pica type with blue ribbon and revised in black ink by Howells, with directions in another hand locating the point of insertion of material into the set text.[15]

The fifth section of page proof (P5) consists of 35 full-sized tissue sheets containing pages numbered 100–234. Sheets thirteen and fourteen are essentially duplicates of each other, both containing pages numbered 146–149 (131.14–134.28 in the present text), except that sheet thirteen, which carries revisions in Howells' hand, also has in another hand the revision of a single word which had been called for by Howells on P3 ("her" for "the" at 134.3 in the present text). Sheet fourteen has this correction set in type, but does not carry any cor-

---

13. See Emendations at 194.5–11 and the accompanying Textual Note.

14. For details see Emendations at 202.9–10 and the accompanying Textual Note.

15. This new material is recorded at 196.3–197.1 in Emendations, and is there further described in a Textual Note.

rection or revision made by Howells in his hand; since it is in all respects like its duplicate before Howells' revision, it is not recorded separately in the apparatus to this text.

All sheets in P5 contain four type-page sections, with the exception of sheet four, which contains only 112 and 113 (the same pages, with the same text, as in P2 and P3); of sheet twenty-one, containing only pages 174 through 176, the upper left quarter section of the sheet filled only with type blanks; and of sheet thirty-five, which contains only 233 and 234—the point at which the book text ends in this set of proofs—set side-by-side across the long dimension of the sheet. The sheet which would have contained pages 221–224 is not present in this set.[16] For the most part P5 contains only printer's corrections in black ink which bring the sheets into agreement with Howells' manuscript revisions on P3. Revisions by Howells on P5 occur at only two points: on sheet thirteen (the first state of pages 146 through 149) several lines have been deleted for replacement by text typed in pica with blue ribbon and revised in Howells' black-ink manuscript on a 1½ in. × 8 in. tissue slip;[17] and on sheet thirty-four (containing pages numbered 229 through 232) are revisions in pencil on the sheet itself.[18]

The sixth segment of proof (P6) consists of a single full-sized sheet containing pages numbered 217 through 220. In type content this sheet is nothing but a duplicate of the sheet containing the same page numbers in P5; but to the lower right edge of the sheet is attached a 2½ in. × 8 in. slip of unlined paper containing a reading in black ink in Howells' hand which is indicated as replacing part of the contents of the set page. This duplicate of the P5 sheet was probably being held by Howells in anticipation of his daughter's response to the material concerning his wife on which he was working in a copy of P3. After finally submitting this P6 revision, Howells made the one further revision described in Emendations, a revision verified by the published text but by no other extant proof stage: the revision is clearly by

---

16. The fact that the text missing here is essentially the same as that which does appear in P4 (exact coincidence is missed by one line of type) but that the numbers of the pages do not coincide may indicate that Howells' revision for P4 was sent to the publisher while the next stage of proofs after P3 was being prepared, and that the printer began to make the P4 revision and held out that particular section of pages from the next extensive set he did send to Howells (P5).

17. See Emendations at 133.24–29 for a record of the revision.

18. See Emendations at 202.9–10 and following and the accompanying Textual Note for details of the relationship of P5 and P7 here.

Howells, since it deals with exactly that point he discussed with his daughter in his 2 November 1915 letter to her.[19]

The last of the extant segments of page proof (P7) consists of four full-sized sheets. The first contains pages numbered 179 through 182, the other three sheets pages 223 through 226, 227 through 230, and 231 and 232 (the end of the book text in this set). Howells' revisions are in black pencil. In the margin of the third sheet is a note in his hand to "See correction on other proofs (p. 229)." The reference is to his revision of the same portion of the text (202.9–10 and following in the present edition) in the page proofs referred to here as P5.

As many and as coincident as these seven sections of proof are, they do not represent all the stages of revision between galleys and published book, either authorial or editorial.[20] Nor is their variety necessarily indicative of many full stages of revision or of long periods of time. After Howells' work on the first galleys, there seem to have been two really full steps in his revision of the text, that represented by his work on P1, P2, and P3, and another some time after that point, represented by his attention to various sections of the extant portions of the proof as well as by revisions verified only in the published text. And the time which elapsed between the various stages of revision of the section concerning his testament to his wife, which carried through four sets of proofs, was only a very few days.

Early Drafts

In addition to the items directly pertinent to the copy-text of *Years of My Youth* there are in the Howells Collection at the Houghton Library two unpublished pieces which, if not as significant textually for a study of the autobiographical materials, are certainly important to the scholar who will want to deal with the fullest genealogical history of Howells' text.

One, the earliest extant piece of essay autobiographical material, is the carbon of a typescript entitled "Life in a State Capital Fifty-Odd Years Ago." It consists of 93 leaves 8½ in. × 11 in. (numbered [1]–6, 8–77, 79–95) prepared by a typist, probably from a manuscript first draft which has not survived, and contains a good deal of black-ink and pencil manuscript revision. But the typescript carbon is quite

---

19. Again, see Emendations at 194.5–11 and the accompanying Textual Note.
20. See Textual Commentary, pp. 306–307.

different in arrangement and content from the text which finally saw print or even from the typescript which Howells submitted to the publisher in preparation of *Years of My Youth*. It cannot be considered by any means fair copy for the later version, since between them seem to lie several major stages of revision, the first of them perhaps a new beginning on the ribbon copy of which this essay version is a carbon. In fact, three leaves of the ribbon copy, coinciding with the pages numbered 89, 90, and 91, appear in the *Years of My Youth* typescript.[21]

The other unpublished piece is a batch of material, not really a complete or coherent text, entitled "The Real Diary of a Boy." This too appears to be a very early draft stage, and consists of 18 leaves of typed text ([1]–18), corrected and at points revised by a hand other than Howells' own in pencil; the carbon copy of page 1 with Howells' revisions in pencil and ink; and 11 more leaves consisting of sheets of 8 in. × 10 in. blue writing paper torn across their width (numbered 2–11, 19) and containing Howells' manuscript hand in black ink. The text of the essay is essentially a running commentary on the boyhood diary of Howells (also in the Harvard Howells Collection), and it quotes from that diary extensively. These fragmentary materials may represent an early stage of the essay Howells submitted to Duneka some time after 31 January 1916 under the title "The Boy and his Diary";[22] after it was refused publication independent of *Years of My Youth* he fit it into the book text itself. But the external evidence of the titles and a comparison of the earlier partial essay with the section concerning his diary in the present text (62.3–67.19) suggest that there is no direct textual relationship between them.

Though neither of these unpublished pieces has been cited directly in the preparation of the present text, both have been used to verify information about Howells' preferences in punctuation, spelling, capitalization, and other such minutiæ of style.

II. THE MANUSCRIPT OF "AN OLD VENETIAN FRIEND" (MSO)

The manuscript of "An Old Venetian Friend," now in the possesion of W. W. Howells, consists of 38 leaves of light blue, unwater-

---

21. See above, pp. 315–316.
22. See the Introduction, p. xxiii.

marked paper, measuring 5 in. × 8 in. These leaves are half pieces of Howells' stationery, which consisted of sheets 10 in. × 8 in. folded in half along the shorter dimension and bearing Howells' printed letter-head centered at the top of the outside recto. The heading "W. D. HOWELLS, 130 WEST 57TH STREET" is present on all the odd-numbered leaves in the manuscript. The text, mostly on the rectos of the leaves, is in Howells' hand in black ink, with revision usually in black ink, but with a limited number of revisions in black pencil. The material appears to have been written straight out, and is free of extensive re-arrangement and renumbering of leaves. Leaves 32 and 35 appear to have originally been numbered 22 and 25, but the text on them is continuous with the adjoining leaves and the original numbers were apparently only errors. In addition to limited local revision of words and phrases, there are four longer cancels of four-and-a-half, seven, ten, and twelve lines. Text for insertion into the recto appears on the versos of leaves 4, 8, 14, 20, and 29. The original title of the essay was "An Old Italian Friend," but this has been changed by Howells in the manuscript.

D.J.N.

Textual Notes

<table>
<tr>
<td>4.4</td>
<td>The "aging" spelling consistently used by Howells in the typescript is restored over the form preferred by his Harper editors at this point, where the published book text is copy-text.</td>
</tr>
<tr>
<td>7.21</td>
<td>The "worshipping" spelling consistently used by Howells in the typescript is restored over the form preferred by his Harper editors; see, for example, 138.19–20 and 150.29 in the present text for examples of Howells' usage.</td>
</tr>
<tr>
<td>8.8</td>
<td>Here and at 26.2 and 29.3–4, where the book edition is copy-text, the hyphenated form "log-cabin" which was Howells' consistent usage both in the earlier periodical essays from which Years of My Youth is drawn and in the extant typescript is restored over the form preferred by his Harper editors.</td>
</tr>
<tr>
<td>10.28</td>
<td>Here and at 10.35, where the published book is copy-text, at 68.1, 92.12 and 103.36, where the author's revised first galleys are copy-text, and at 116.15 and 118.6, where early galley sections are part of the typescript copy-text, the unhyphenated form "antislavery" consistently used by Howells in the typescript is restored over the hyphenated form preferred by his Harper editors.</td>
</tr>
<tr>
<td>11.5</td>
<td>At this point, where the published book is copy-text, at 93.25, 94.32, 103.6 and 104.1, where the revised first galleys are copy-text, and at 116.16, where early galley sections are part of the typescript copy-text,</td>
</tr>
</table>

331

the unhyphenated form "proslavery" consistently used by Howells is restored over the hyphenated form preferred by his Harper editors.

20.33　　Here, where the book edition is copy-text, and at 91.30, where the revised first galleys are copy-text, the "centre" spelling consistently used by Howells is restored over the form preferred by his Harper editors. This same restoration is made at 217.8 in "Overland to Venice," where the *Harper's Monthly* serial publication is copy-text.

22.1　　The word "cometimes" has no identifiable source in slang or dialect, and suggests a typographical error for "sometimes" rather than a neologism.

31.33　　Here and at 32.18 and 35.23, where the published book is copy-text, the "theatre" spelling consistently used by Howells is restored over the form preferred by his Harper editors.

39.5–6　　The section of *Years of My Youth* drawn from the earlier "Year in a Log-Cabin, A Bit of Autobiography," begins here and ends at 56.28; see the Textual Commentary for a discussion of this material.

39.32　　This and all other changes in paragraphing from the periodical version of "Year in a Log-Cabin" in the present text—recorded in the Emendations list— have been accepted as authentic authorial revisions.

42.32　　The reading of the book text of *My Year in a Log Cabin*, though probably not authorial, is preferable because of authorial revision in the present text at 42.30.

47.27　　The only major inconsistency among the various texts drawn upon by Howells in preparing *Years of My Youth* and within the printer's copy typescript itself is the treatment of titles of books, long poems, and newspapers, which are not styled consistently by Howells or his editors. To preserve these irregularities, however, would only be distracting, and so the present edition adopts throughout the italicized form, which is also the form fairly consistently used throughout the Harper book text.

The following list records all instances in which the inconsistent typescript or early serial forms—where these are copy-text—have been regularized (all italicized forms which occur in the text and do not appear on this list or in Emendations, where they may be present for special textual reasons, preserve copy-text readings). In this list the location of the reading in the present text is followed by the symbol of the text which first records the form accepted here, followed by a slash, the symbol for the copy-text at that point, and the copy-text reading:

47.27	M/S1	"Western Adventure,"
47.30	A/S1	"Howe's Collections for the History of Ohio,"
49.29	M/S1	"First Book of History,"
73.6	W/S2	Don Quixote
114.11	P2/MSY	Hiawatha
114.18	P2/MSY	Percy's Reliques
124.10	UG/MSY	Gazette
124.17	UG/MSY	Gazette
124.18	UG/MSY	Herald
124.25	UG/MSY	Gazette
124.34	UG/MSY	Gazette
125.9	UG/MSY	Ohio State Journal
125.14	UG/MSY	Journal's
125.18	UG/MSY	Gazette
154.1	UG/MSY	Atlantic
156.12	UG/MSY	The Pilot's Story
160.6	UG/MSY	"A Modern Instance"
173.29	UG/MSY	"A Romance of a Mummy"

175.7	UG/MSY	"Poems of Two Friends"
175.32	*MSY*/MSY	Journal
175.33	UG/MSY	"My Literary Passions,"
177.22	UG/MSY	"Life of Lincoln"
178.30–31	UG/MSY	*"Literary Friends and Acquaintance"*
179.35	UG/MSY	Atlantic Monthly
180.18	UG/MSY	*"Their Wedding Journey"*
182.8	UG/MSY	Atlantic Monthly
183.28	HE/MSY	*Cincinnati Gazette*
187.15	UG/MSY	*"Library Notes"*,
195.5	UG/MSY	State Journal
196.18	A/P4	Atlantic

51.13   Despite the general authority of the corrections introduced into the book text of *Years of My Youth* in this section, the context demonstrates the fact of error here.

52.22   Both the general authority of the book-text readings in this section and æsthetic quality argue for the acceptance of "whirr" for "whirl."

55.10   The present edition accepts as authorial the change in paragraphing in the single galley numbered 25 (LG), but does not accept the accompanying change of "By-and-by" to an unhyphenated form.

55.13–14   The published book (A) actually reads "deadening; the"—the result of a change in accidentals between the serial and book versions of "Year in a Log-Cabin"; although this reading was preserved in the book edition of *Years of My Youth* it has been rejected in the present text as non-authorial in origin.

60.11   The readings of the author's revised first galleys here and at 60.24–25 and 61.2 are obviously the result of bad type or bad inking of the form from which the proof was pulled.

62.3–67.19   The material derived from the earlier version of the essay "The Real Diary of a Boy" was introduced at this point in the text some time after revised first galleys and before book publication; see A Note on the Manuscripts and Other Pre-Publication Forms of the Text, page 329, for a description of the essay materials.

70.23   The spelling "fulfill" consistently used by Howells in the typescript is restored at this point, where his revised first galleys are copy-text, over the form preferred by his Harper editors.

70.35   The spelling "gayeties" consistently used by Howells in the typescript is restored at this point, where the revised first galleys are copy-text for *Years of My Youth*, over the form preferred by his Harper editors. On the same principle, "gayly" replaces "gaily" at 221.6 in "Overland to Venice," where the *Harper's Monthly* version is copy-text.

71.7   The reading "always," which originated in the text of "The Country Printer" in the second Harper edition of *Impressions and Experiences*, is rejected because the general texture of the alterations from the magazine version and the first two book editions of "The Country Printer" in the second Harper edition argues against its being authorial.

73.1   Although there is some slight justification for accepting the serial reading "slipin' " as meaning "sleighing" (in derivation from the dialectic *slipe*—"to smear; slippery"), the form in the first book edition —"slippin' "—is the more recognizable term for the same thing, and is therefore accepted as preferable, if not authorial, in the present text.

76.12   The present text retains the original copy-text reading here and at 76.13 for want of any satisfactory explanation of the nonsensical readings of the published book text.

96.17   A proofreader's deletion of "that" in revised first galleys (the word was later restored by Howells in P2) is presumed to be a correction to the reading of the now missing manuscript or typescript for this same section and not an independent revision.

96.20   Although probably not by Howells, this revision made some time after the extant revised first galleys and before the first stage of page proofs—in which it is correctly set in type—must be accepted as the only proper spelling of the word. At 161.28 the same word is set correctly in P3 after being misspelled in typescript and galleys.

98.31   Howells' revision to "make" in P1 is indistinct; the revision was not picked up when his revisions were set in type, and Howells duplicated the change in marking P2.

100.2–101.31   The section heading "xiii" was mislocated by the compositor in setting type from Howells' P1 revisions, and was placed between the paragraphs at 100.2–3 in the present text. Howells returned it to its proper place in revising P2.

100.23   The P1 reading is a nonsense repetition uncorrected by Howells in a long typescript addition to the first stage of page proofs. Other errors of the same kind in the typescript, all of them corrected by the compositor in set type in P2, occur at 100.34, 101.8, 101.12, 101.17 and 101.19, and are recorded in Emendations.

101.25   Howells had mistakenly written "do" in the long addition to P1 made at this point. The compositor set it in type for P2 as "don't," but Howells revised to "do not" on those same proofs.

102.4   The proofreader had questioned the revised-galley reading in the margin of the galley sheet, but Howells did not correct it until P1.

111.1   Howells neglected to delete the comma after making the careted insertion of "before, had" above the line in the typescript.

111.3   Emendations: the proofreader questioned the typescript "in" on the first galleys, but Howells did not cancel it until P2; yet it was still present on the P3 pages, where he cancelled it again.

111.3   Rejected Substantives: Howells' revised-galley changes here and at 192.2 are rejected on the grounds that they were apparently prompted by erroneous setting from typescript. Howells sensed the differences from his autograph but did not, characteristically, resolve them with reference to what he had written.

111.22   The nonsense repetitions here and at 111.28 resulted from Howells' interpolation of further material onto the verso of the typescript page.

113.14   The printer's copy at this point consists of galleys inserted into the typescript pages. Since these galleys reflect styling of Howells' now missing manuscript or typescript, his consistent spelling of "sombre" has been restored over the form preferred by his Harper editors.

113.22   Howells neglected to change his typescript period to a comma when inserting a script-face typed section into his revised first galleys here.

115.35   The compositor set Howells' typescript "Capital" as "capital" and his revised-galley "capitol" as "Capitol"; the present reading must be accepted as authorial, however, because in revising P2 Howells changed both capitalization and spelling.

116.19–117.2   Except for the creation in the author's revised first galleys of the last sentence of this emendation ("Even the next . . . tardy surprise.") and the insertion of the section number between what were only separate paragraphs, the rest of this emendation ("If it was . . . . official world.") consists of a typeset section moved from another part of the revised galleys; see Emendations at 121.4 and the accompanying Textual Note.

116.21   The repetition resulted from the pasting of part of a pre-typescript galley to the typescript page.

118.8–120.8   Except for the opening phrase ("In those . . . society"), newly written in the author's revised first galleys, and the replacement of the original words "though I shared in" by "confined to" at 118.9, the remainder of this long emendation consists of a section relocated from a later portion of the revised galleys; see Emendations at 121.4 and the accompanying Textual Note.

118.11   The typescript here consists of part of the pre-typescript galleys, which apparently styled the manuscript from which they were set. The P2 reading may not be authorial, but it is consistent with Howells' normal usage.

118.21–22   Emendation is necessary because of substantive revision following it at 118.22.

118.24   Here as at 113.14 and 118.11 the typescript consists of pre-typescript galleys, which apparently styled the manuscript or typescript from which they were set. The spelling "gayety" consistently used by Howells is therefore restored over the form preferred by his Harper editors.

121.4　　Howells divided a long typescript section into different segments and distributed it to other parts of the
text in his revision of the galleys. The details of the
re-distribution are listed below; the typescript readings internal to these sections and the emendations
made on them are recorded in the apparatus at the
points of relocation:

¶That was a very crucial moment . . . . air.]
moved to 147.3–148.26.
¶I am advancing . . . . them with me./III] *later
cancelled after being moved to 148.26.*
¶If it was once surmised . . . . official world,] *moved
to 116.19–116.34.*
the generalized hospitality . . . . life about me.]
used at 118.9–120.7.

121.36　　Howells accepts the proofreader's marginal suggestion that "it" be inserted to correct the nonsense
reading which had resulted from Howells' revisions
within the printer's copy typescript.

122.28　　As is the case at 113.14, 118.11 and 118.24, the typescript here consists of part of the pre-typescript galleys, which styled the manuscript or typescript from
which they were set. Therefore the unhyphenated
form consistently used by Howells in his typescript
(see 123.18 and 123.36 for examples) is restored over
the hyphenated form preferred by his Harper editors.

123.21　　In spite of the obscuring of the typescript reading in
the setting of the galleys, Howells' revised-galley
emendation is accepted over the original reading on
the grounds that he was revising for reasons of sound
rather than sense.

124.28–29　　The comma supplied after "Reid" in the setting of
the galleys, although not authorial, is accepted in
the present text for the sake of the sense of Howells'
further revision in the revised galleys.

128.3–4   The letter "s" is clearly meant to designate the word "a" to echo the preceding phrase, and is not an uncorrected random letter or false start.

129.7   Howells accepted this stylistic sophistication suggested by the proofreader in the margin of the galleys.

131.4   Here and at 131.5 the forms supplied by the unrevised first galleys are accepted in replacement of the over-styling of the typescript.

131.14   The incorrect typescript punctuation was not set in type in the galleys. A replacement reading, perhaps not authorial, was supplied at some point after the extant revised galleys.

134.3   Though not authorial in origin, the comma must be accepted for the sake of the later substantive revision of the phrase which follows it.

134.8   The addition of "made" here, of "I" at 143.18–19, "my" at 144.14–15, "in" at 152.24, "on" at 158.12, and the replacement of "that" by "the" at 175.18 are all changes suggested by the proofreader in the margins of the first galleys; these changes, however, are followed by question marks to indicate to Howells that the final choice is his—Howells has indicated his acceptance of them by crossing out the question marks and leaving the proofreader's revisions.

135.18   After rearranging the material in Part III at 118.8–120.8 (see Emendations at that point and the accompanying Textual Note) and introducing the section heading "IV" there, Howells had gone on to change the headings following it at 124.3, 127.29 and 131.16 to accord with the addition of that new heading. But he failed to make changes beyond that

point at 135.18 and 140.9, where the correct numbers are presumably supplied by a proofreader. At
143.36–144.1 and following, the problem is further
complicated by errors in the original typescript
numbering: Howells had skipped from "vii" to
"ix" and a compositor or reader noticed the omis-
sion, then caught the further error by correcting the
new number "ix" where Howells had supplied it
in the revised galleys at 148.27. This same kind of
error occurs in Part IV beginning at 175.28, where
Howells had supplied a second "vi" and someone
else supplied a "vii" to replace it; Howells continued the incorrect numbering through the rest of
the text, and it was further corrected, at 178.4,
180.25, 184.7, 188.30 and 197.22. All these readings
are recorded in Emendations.

138.35   The word "verse" ends a sentence in the middle of
the last line of a typescript leaf. "Naturally" begins
the next leaf, but is not indented from the left margin.
Howells' typical practice suggests that he did not
wish to begin a new paragraph at this point.

139.20   Here and at 139.22, 139.34, 155.20 and 155.22
Howells changes the form of "the" before magazine
titles from capitalized italics to lower-case roman in
response to a query in the margins of the revised first
galleys.

143.20   Howells had corrected the first galley reading to his
typescript spelling before rejecting it in turn for
"already."

147.2–148.26   This long section is moved to this point in the revised
galleys from its original place in the typescript; see
Emendations at 121.4 and accompanying Textual
Note.

148.26   A special format has been adopted for the presenta-
           tion of the emendations at this point because of the
           length of the entry. The internal emendations in the
           text finally adopted in the revised galleys ("I am
           advancing . . . . lost limb.") are recorded within the
           transcription of the original typescript copy-text
           reading here, and the emended text can be recon-
           structed from it, so that the full revised-galley read-
           ing with P2 revisions need not be repeated. The
           whole of this long reading was finally rejected in
           revision in P3.

152.27   An unidentified typewriter character appears in the
           place of the second "t" in "contribution" and the
           first "t" in "interests" in the sentence in the rejected
           typescript reading which begins "That part of his
           memoir . . . ." This same character appears in the
           typescript "the" of "the saints" at 139.7 in the
           present text.

157.33   The lower-case "c" in "college" was questioned by
           the editor in the margin of P2 here (and at 191.23
           in P3) and Howells changed it to a capital letter in
           both cases.

159.9–11   The basic text of the P7 reading is already set in type
           in the P7 proofs, indicating that the reading had
           been supplied some time after P5, the last extant
           proof material preceding this section. The reading
           in type in P7, however, is not complete, and a hand
           other than Howells' has made further changes, pre-
           sumably in the process of proofreading, to bring the
           new typesetting into line with the text Howells had
           supplied: a comma is inserted after "say," "verse"
           replaces the typeset "vision," and "poet" replaces
           the word "part" which had appeared in type.

159.18   In making the revision in P7 recorded here, Howells
           neglected to change the comma after "me" to a
           period, a correction probably made thereafter by the
           compositor and verified in the published book text.

160.2   The readings supplied by the compositor in the first galleys here and at 162.6 and 163.12 must be accepted as alternatives to the nonsense readings of the printer's copy typescript.

171.31   The copy-text for Howells' poem, "The Coming," is the 23 January 1860 *Ohio State Journal* printing of it; see Textual Commentary, pages 300–301.

192.30   The forms "esthetic" here and "room-mate" at 192.32 are apparently the result of styling by the publisher of this new section (192.3–194.1) which was introduced some time after P6, the last extant pre-publication text. The forms consistently used by Howells are restored over the forms preferred by his editors. The unhyphenated form "roommate" also replaces the hyphenated one at 210.23 in "Overland to Venice," where the *Harper's Monthly* serial publication is copy-text.

194.5–11   The record of revision in this brief section documents Howells' concern for finding the proper terms to acknowledge the influence of his wife. The sequence of revision is difficult to describe with confidence, because the actual stages of revision do not coincide with the physical states of the various extant pre-publication forms of the text. But the sequence appears to be as follows:

        1. Minor revision of the typescript reading in the author's revised first galleys;
        2. First stage of revision in P3, which bears evidence of two stages of revision—this first revision, recorded in Emendations as P3(1), resulted in the typeset reading in P5;
        3. Howells' use of the P3 pages a second time—the results of which are recorded in Emendations as P3(2)—to prepare a further, tentative revision of the same material;

4. The copying of this second P3 revision, with further minor corrections, onto a slip of paper attached to the P6 proof—P6 was in type content a duplicate of the section of P5 proof bearing the same page numbers;

5. Finally, at some point after P5 and P6 and before publication, the introduction of one further revision which can be observed by a comparison of the reading of the present text (A) with that of P6:

> A   here, and
> P6   in this life;

On 30 October 1915 Howells had written to his daughter Mildred asking help in choosing the right words to describe his wife (MS at Harvard). Upon receiving her reply he wrote again, on 2 November (MS at Harvard):

> I am glad of your hearty approval, which I anticipated by sending in the changed proof yesterday, knowing I could take it back if need be. The reason I wished to say "in this life" was that I felt it right to express my hope, if not belief, of another; but if it seems hypocritical when I get the revise I will cut the words out.

The specific reference to the words "in this life" is probably related to the second P3 reading, which Howells sent to his daughter in some form or other and about which she commented after he had returned P6 with its recopying of the P3 reading. After her reply he made the change in proofs some time after P6 which resulted in the readings of the published text.

194.20–21   Although the stages of revision here are not as complicated as those described in the Textual Note at 194.5–11, they again involve the double use of the P3 proof—recorded in Emendations as P3(1) and P3(2) —to prepare revisions incorporated into the text in set type in P5 and in Howells' handwriting on the proof in P6 respectively.

194.22   See the Textual Note at 194.5–11 for a discussion of the meaning of the symbol P3(2). Howells seems to have tentatively cancelled these words in his second revision of P3 and then rejected the cancellation in transferring the other P3(2) revisions to the P6 proof.

194.25   Again, see the Textual Note at 194.5–11 for an explanation of the symbols P3(1) and P3(2). Apparently Howells made a trial revision in the second stage of his work on P3 and then rejected the sentence entirely in transferring his revisions to P6.

196.3–197.1   A long section typed by Howells and attached to the P4 proofs at this point replaces the printer's copy typescript reading and the revisions made upon it. The fact of Howells' typing explains the nonsense duplications at 196.14, 196.18 (twice) and 196.27, corrected in setting the type for this new material.

196.27–197.1   Here again, as at 148.26 and 192.3–194.1 a special format has been adopted to record the emendations which are made within this section: the last part of the P4 reading consists essentially of the same reading as that of the typescript at 196.3–197.1, with the inclusion of the revised-galley and P3 revisions, from "he kept, on" to "of course intending"; that reading is therefore not repeated in the P4 section of the emendation record but can be reconstructed from the transcription of the original reading given in Emendations at 196.3–197.1.

202.9–10   The peculiar sequence of revision here and at 202.12 (twice), 202.13 (twice), 202.17 and 202.17–19, in which the physical states of the page proofs do not coincide with the actual stages of revision, is another, though slightly less complicated, instance of the special use of the P3 proofs (see Textual Note at 194.5–11). Howells was apparently not satisfied with what he had originally written at these points, but was unable immediately to determine a course of revision. So he cut out of the P3 sheet the quarter containing this particular page section (numbered 231 in P3; coinciding with 202.1–30 in the present text) and returned the rest of P3 with its revisions to the publisher. (Thus P5 and P7 document in type at other points revisions that Howells made on P3 galleys at this stage of revision, but carry the same typeset text as had originally been prepared for the section on this page.) Then he seems to have made some tentative revisions on the P3 page he was holding back (which he did not then transfer to any other set) and to have made final revisions of the same section on P5. But he also seems to have been working on these P5 revisions on one set of proofs while the publisher was preparing P7, and to have been sufficiently satisfied with at least this portion of P5 to leave it as he had now revised it—although he did revise in P7 at other points—writing in the margin of P7 with reference to this particular P5 section, "See correction on other proofs."

203.15–16   The typescript pagination is not clear at this point, as the proofreader also notes in the margin of the galleys. The pagination and texts of the leaves in question are as follows:

> *235 (originally numbered 90)*: easily beat me. I . . . . If in all this
>
> *236 (originally numbered 91)*: I seem to be accusing . . . . volunteer./xiii ¶ It was a question . . . . [*203.17ff. in the present text*]
>
> *A235 (originally numbered 89)*: It did not matter . . . . major-general forced upon him.

There is no indication anywhere on the leaves themselves as to where the material on A235 is to be inserted. Since it duplicates information appearing elsewhere in the full typescript, and since it is, like leaves 235 and 236, a typed sheet for which a carbon copy exists in the "Life in a State Capital Fifty-Odd Years Ago" materials (see A Note on the Manuscripts, pages 315, 328), it may have been left with those two leaves by mistake when Howells introduced them into his *Years of My Youth* typescript. In rechecking the numbering of the final typescript he found this as yet un-renumbered leaf among the other materials, left it where he found it *between* leaves 235 and 236, and numbered it A235 to indicate where it seemed to belong—without examining its contents. The Harper compositor, trying to find some sensible place for it in type, placed the material appearing on A235 between "volunteer." and section heading XIII of leaf 236.

The question of the influence of this erroneous placement upon the general texture of revision of the text and of the stages of revision which finally eliminated it must remain academic. There is no evidence from which to reconstruct the relative æsthetic or psychological authority of other readings. As for the contents of leaf A235 itself, part was cancelled in revised galleys and the rest in P3, but only after local attempts at revision failed to give it satisfactory sense.

203.34–204.2   The compositor probably mistakenly removed this sentence because of the confused state of Howells' revision in the galleys: Howells had first cancelled this and the preceding sentence, then erased the cancellation marks and made only the internal revision indicated at 203.34 in Emendations.

205.7–8   Before revision in Howells' hand in P7, the set type in this set of proofs began "I have told elsewhere . . ."—a different reading from that of the extant stages from typescript through P5. The original P7 reading resulted from revision subsequent to P3 but no longer extant.

210.26   The double *l* forms "travelling" and "traveller" replace the single *l* forms preferred by the *Harper's Monthly* copy-texts here and at 213.32, 215.10, 219.10 and 223.19 ("fellow-travellers") in "Overland to Venice," at 236.4 in "An Old Venetian Friend" (where the *Harper's* spelling is imposed on an authorial revision of the manuscript copy-text), and at 250.11 and 250.19 in "A Young Venetian Friend."

226.9–10   The failure to reproduce Howells' introduction of a new paragraph at this point probably resulted from failure on the part of typist or compositor to recognize the paragraph symbol careted into the manuscript.

229.9   Though the possibility exists that the manuscript "natural" was misread as "national," the latter form is nonetheless the reading demanded by the context.

231.27   The nonsense readings of the manuscript of "An Old Venetian Friend" here and at 231.31–32, 232.32, 234.35 and 235.15 are the result of Howells' incomplete revision of his text.

233.6   The serial spelling "mustache" is rejected in favor of Howells' usual "moustache" in the process of accepting the authorial substantive revision verified by the serial text.

234.19   Here and at 235.11 and 236.35—where Howells had also capitalized the word—Howells' unitalicized form "cauntree" is replaced by the italicized and lower-case form of the serial to make it consistent with the other appearances of the word in manuscript.

Emendations

The following list records all substantive and accidental changes introduced into the several copy-texts for the different parts of *Years of My Youth* (see the table on pages 297–300) and for the autobiographical essays. The reading of the present edition appears to the left of the bracket; the source of that reading, followed by a semicolon, the reading of the copy-text and subsequent texts agreeing with it as well as the variant substantive readings of texts after copy-text and before the reading accepted into the present text appear to the right of the bracket. The list does not record non-authorial revisions of accidentals in texts between copy-text and the reading of the present edition. Readings of texts subsequent to the source of the adopted reading may be presumed to agree with the adopted reading unless recorded in Rejected Substantives.

Within an entry, the curved dash ∼ represents the same word that appears before the bracket and is used in recording punctuation and paragraphing variants. The abbreviation HE indicates emendation made for the first time in the present edition and not found in any of the materials examined in the preparation of this text. If the form adopted here has appeared in an earlier state of the text, that text is cited for historical interest, even though it may have no textual authority. *Om.* means that the reading to the left of the bracket does not appear in the text to the right of the semicolon. The italicized form *MSΥ* indicates a non-authorial reading in the author's typescript of *Years of My Youth*. An asterisk indicates that the reading is discussed in the Textual Notes.

Because of the number and complexity of texts and stages of authorial revision involved in the history of *Years of My Youth*, two further conventions have been adopted. Some local emendations within longer readings have been recorded by being placed in brackets within those readings; the material within a set of brackets is to be interpreted as replacing only the single word which precedes the brackets, and the symbols placed inside the brackets immediately after this material record the texts which contain it. The symbols at the end of the full reading record, as usual, the texts which contain the full general reading. Also, the symbol † is placed before a specific entry to indicate that the reading at that point is part of a longer emendation, recorded in a preceding entry, which includes the section of the present text in which this specific emendation occurs.

The following texts are referred to:

MSY	117 leaves of printer's copy typescript of *Years of My Youth*
MSO	38 leaves of manuscript of "An Old Venetian Friend"
LG	Single galley sheet of *Years of My Youth* numbered 25
UG	41 leaves of unrevised first galleys for *Years of My Youth*
RG	61 leaves of author's revised first galleys for *Years of My Youth*
P1–P7	Seven partial sets of page proofs for *Years of My Youth*
N1	"The Coming," *Ohio State Journal*, 23 January 1860
R1	"The Coming," *Ohio State Journal*, Centennial Edition, 26 October 1911
S1	"Year in a Log-Cabin, A Bit of Autobiography," *Youth's Companion*, LX (May 1887)
S2	"The Country Printer," *Scribner's*, XIII (May 1893)
S3	"Overland to Venice," *Harper's Monthly*, CXXXVII (November 1918)
S4	"An Old Venetian Friend," *Harper's Monthly*, CXXXVIII (April 1919)
S5	"A Young Venetian Friend," *Harper's Monthly*, CXXXVIII (May 1919)
M	*My Year in a Log Cabin*, Harper and Brothers, 1893
T	"The Country Printer," *Impressions and Experiences*, Harper and Brothers, 1896
V	"The Country Printer," *Impressions and Experiences*, David Douglas, 1896
W	"The Country Printer," *Impressions and Experiences*, Harper and Brothers, 1909
A	*Years of My Youth*, Harper and Brothers, 1916

YEARS OF MY YOUTH

*4.4	aging] HE; ageing A
4.17	iridescent] HE; iridiscent A
5.21	called] HE; call A
*7.21	worshipping] HE; worshiping A
*8.8	log-cabins] HE; log cabins A
*10.28	antislavery] HE; anti-slavery A
*11.5	proslavery] HE; pro-slavery A
*20.33	centre] HE; center A
*22.1	sometimes] HE; cometimes A
*31.33	theatre] HE; theater A
*39.5–6	For my father, whose boyhood had been] A; 1/¶ In the fall of the year 1850 my father removed with his family from the city of D——, where we had been living, to a property on the Little Miami River, to take charge of a saw-mill and grist-mill, and superintend the [their M] never-accomplished transformation of [om. M] the [om. M] latter [om. M] into a [om. M] paper-mill [paper-mills M]. The property belonged to his brothers—physicians and druggists—who were to follow later, when they had disposed of their business in town. My father left a disastrous newspaper enterprise behind him, when he came out to apply his mechanical taste and his knowledge of farming to the care of their place. Early in the century his parents had brought him to Ohio from Wales, and his boyhood was S1, M
39.7	it] A; and for him it S1, M
39.9	many] A; forty S1, M
39.9	matter-of-fact] M; matter-of fact S1
39.10	brick.] A; brick. ¶ He had a passion for nature as tender and genuine, and as deeply moralized as that of the English poets, by whom it had been nourished; and he had [om. M] taught us children all that he felt for the woods and fields and open skies; all our walks had led into them and under them. S1, M

39.12	in] A; in such S1, M
39.13	at the mills] A; on the property S1, M
39.14	which we made] A; in which we took up S1, M
39.18	at the time] A; thirty years ago S1; forty years ago M
39.20	poor-white] A; *om.* S1, M
39.25	the family] A; we S1, M
39.32	remember, had] A; remember it, was not without S1, M
*39.32	qualities. He] A; ∼. ¶ ∼ S1, M
39.33	from] A; bought at S1, M
39.34	people] A; the persons S1, M
39.35	publishers] A; publisher S1, M
40.3	heroine.] A; heroine. I really suppose that a cheap wall paper could have been got for the same money, though it might not have seemed so economical. ¶ I am not sure that the use of the newspapers was not a tributary reminiscence of my father's pioneer life; I cannot remember that it excited any comment in the neighbors, who were frank with their opinions of everything else we did. But it does not greatly matter; the newspapers hid the walls and the stains with which our old Virginian predecessor, who had the habit of chewing tobacco in bed, had ineffaceably streaked the plastering near the head of his couch. S1, M
40.8–9	true backwoods] A; the true pioneer S1, M
40.9	but] A; but had been neatly S1, M
40.10	was] A; was solidly S1, M
40.11	stone. Within] A; ∼. ¶ ∼ S1, M
40.11–12	desired] A; asked for S1, M
40.19	tasted] A; tasted with the appetite of tired youth S1, M
40.20	of] A; of the camp and S1, M
40.20	juices.] A; juices. ¶ I suppose it took a day or two to put the improvements which I have mentioned upon the cabin, but I am not certain. S1, M
40.22	sense.] A; sense. Once I remember waking, and seeing the man who was always the youngest of his

boys sitting upright on his bed. ¶ "What are you doing?" I asked. ¶ "Oh, resting!" he answered; and that gave us one of the heaven-blessed laughs with which we could blow away almost any cloud of care or pain./II. S1, M

40.26	left easily accessible in] A; packed in easily accessible S1, M
40.26	barrels. There] A; barrels. ¶ There yet S1, M
40.29	ours] A; her S1, M
40.30	autumnal] A; beautiful autumnal S1, M
40.31	panoplied] A; well panoplied S1; all panoplied M
40.32	books and authors] A; poems and histories S1, M
40.34	Shakespeare. But] A; Shakespeare, on—

"The glory that was Greece,
And the grandeur that was Rome."

¶ But S1, M

40.35	thoughts—] M; ~, S1
41.5	it. The] A; ~. ¶ ~ S1, M
41.6	up] A; up under those sycamores S1, M
41.8	to stay.] A; stay. I do not know just how it is with a boy's world now, but at that time it was a very dangerous world. It was full of ghosts, for one thing, and it abounded in Indians on the war-path, and amateurs of kidnapping and murder of all sorts. S1, M
41.9–10	compel; you] A; compel. You S1, M
41.10	when] A; with whom S1, M
41.11	with him] A; *om.* S1, M
41.16	replied. We] A; ~. ¶ ~ S1, M
41.20	had] A; had apparently S1, M
41.20–21	sympathy. When] A; ~. ¶ ~ S1, M
41.21	the other side of]A; *om.* S1, M
41.23	turned] A; turned again S1, M
41.28–29	say. ¶ I] A; say./III. ¶ I S1, M
41.30	father] A; father humorously S1, M
41.33	found. One] A; ~. ¶ ~ S1, M
41.34	as] A; as I believe the S1, M
41.36	"Baby."] M; baby. S1
42.3	travels. Then] A; ~. ¶ ~ S1, M

42.4　　　　　which] A; which, I think, came from one of the
　　　　　　　　saw-mill hands, and which S1, M
42.14　　　　　was] A; I believe that it was S1, M
42.29　　　　　safety. We] A; ∼. ¶ ∼ S1, M
42.30　　　　　they] A; it never came to that. They S1, M
*42.32　　　　it;] M; ∼, S1
42.33–34　　　families. ¶ We] A; families. Some of their nests we
　　　　　　　　found, notably one under the smoke-house, where
　　　　　　　　the adventurous boy who discovered it was at-
　　　　　　　　tacked in the dark by its owner, and bitten in the
　　　　　　　　nose, to the natural gratification of those who had
　　　　　　　　urged him to the enterprise. But he brought away
　　　　　　　　some of the eggs, and we had them fried, and I
　　　　　　　　know nothing that conveys a vivider idea of in-
　　　　　　　　exhaustible abundance than a fried goose-egg./IV.
　　　　　　　　¶ The geese were not much profit—they had to be
　　　　　　　　sold, finally, for little or nothing—but their soft
　　　　　　　　and woolly goslings were a great pleasure to all the
　　　　　　　　children, who were plunged in grief when the
　　　　　　　　miller's sow made a foray among them. ¶ This was
　　　　　　　　a fierce and predatory animal that was in some sort
　　　　　　　　a neighborhood terror. She made her lair in the
　　　　　　　　reeds by the riverside, breaking out a perfect circle,
　　　　　　　　which she kept against all comers, especially boys,
　　　　　　　　till her young were born. Then she returned to her
　　　　　　　　sty near the miller's house, convenient to the young
　　　　　　　　turkeys, chickens and goslings, leading forth her
　　　　　　　　brood in a savage defiance which no one dared to
　　　　　　　　front, except the miller, who did so with a shot-gun,
　　　　　　　　at times, when her depredations became outra-
　　　　　　　　geous. Wherever she appeared, the children ran
　　　　　　　　screaming, and the boldest boy was glad of the top
　　　　　　　　rail of a fence. ¶ She was, in fact, a wild beast, but
　　　　　　　　our own pigs were very social creatures. We S1, M
42.34　　　　　pigs from our old Virginian predecessors,] A; of
　　　　　　　　them, I believe, from the old Virginians whom we
　　　　　　　　had succeeded in the cabin, S1, M
43.1　　　　　but,] A; and S1, M
43.5　　　　　stones. All] A; ∼. ¶ ∼ S1, M

43.8   boys] A; children, and more particularly boys, S1,
        M
43.13   from] A; of S1, M
43.16   IX] A; V S1, M
43.26   it?" We] A; it?" Usually he had not hit it, though
        now and then our murderous young blood was
        stirred by the death agonies of some of the poor
        creatures whose destruction boys exult in. ¶ We
        S1, M
43.28   to death] M; out of their pain S1
43.32   of] A; of all S1, M
44.4   woods-pastures] A; wood-pastures S1, M
44.10   blossoms. I] A; ~. ¶ ~ S1, M
44.18   air-tops.] A; air-tops. I hope we came away with-
        out any of them. ¶ The only one I ever killed was a
        black squirrel which fell from aloft, and lodged
        near the first crotch of a tall elm. The younger
        brother, who followed me as I followed my elder,
        climbed up to get the squirrel, but when he
        mounted into the crotch, he found himself with his
        back tight against the main branch, and unable
        either to go up or come down. It was a terrible mo-
        ment, which we deplored with many tears and vain
        cries for help. ¶ It was no longer a question of get-
        ting the dead squirrel, but the live boy to the
        ground. It appeared to me that to make a rope fast
        to the limb, and then have him slip down, hand
        over hand, was the best way; only, we had no rope,
        and I could not have got it to him, if we had. I pro-
        posed going for help, but my brother could [would
        M] not consent to be left alone; and, in fact, I could
        not bear the thought of leaving him perched up
        there, however securely, fifty feet from the earth.
        I might have climbed up and pulled [pull M] him
        out, but we decided that this would only be swifter
        destruction. ¶ I really cannot tell how he contrived
        to free himself, or why he is not in that tree to this
        day. The squirrel is. S1, M
44.21   only] A; again but S1, M

44.23   When] A; After S1, M
44.25   for] A; to find S1, M
44.26   we found them] M; found S1
44.27   a] A; the S1, M
44.27   mother] M; mothers S1
44.28   her] M; their S1
44.28   brood] M; broods S1
44.32   charmed] A; charmed just S1, M
45.9   concerning] A; in respect to S1, M
45.21   water.] A; water./vi. ¶ The winter, which was so sore a trial for my mother in the log-cabin, and was not, perhaps, such a poetic rapture for my father as he had hoped, was a long delight to their children. S1, M
45.32–33   historical romance] A; romantic picturesqueness S1, M
45.36–46.1   corn grated . . . in] A; corn, grated to meal, when just out of S1, M
46.14–15   floor. When we were once] A; floor. ¶ Once S1, M
46.20   floor.] A; floor. I should not like to step out of bed into a snow-wreath in the morning, now; but then I was glad to do it, and, so far from thinking that or anything in our life a hardship, I counted it all joy. S1, M
46.28   Night." There] A; ~." ¶ ~ S1, M
46.29   but these] A; which I must have read also, but I remember only these, that S1, M
46.30   fitfully] A; seriously S1, M
46.34   boy's] A; small-boy's S1, M
47.1   of] A; in S1, M
47.1   many. By this time] A; many. ¶ We had always worked, and S1, M
47.1   axes] A; axes now S1, M
47.5   inroad] A; havoc S1, M
47.10   scarcely] A; barely S1, M
47.14–15   so easily. ¶ They] A; delightfully./vii. ¶ They S1, M
47.17   had] A; had all S1, M
47.21   It was] A; Yet no atoll in the far Pacific could

have been more satisfactory to us. It was low and
Sɪ, M

47.22   half] A; was half Sɪ, M

47.24   darts] A; spears and darts Sɪ, M

47.24–25   fights. The] A; ~. ¶ ~ Sɪ, M

*47.27   *Western Adventure,*] M; "Western Adventure," Sɪ

47.29   life.] A; life. I have wondered often since, who wrote
or compiled that book; we had printed it ourselves
in D., from the stereotype plates of some temporary
publisher whose name is quite lost to me. Sɪ, M

47.32   life] A; own life Sɪ, M

48.4   spirit] A; spirits Sɪ, M

48.5   from] A; with Sɪ, M

48.8   the Indian chief] A; *om.* Sɪ, M

48.10   x] A; vɪɪɪ Sɪ, M

48.17   sod. But] A; sod. I have no recollection of really
enjoying any of the visionary red-cores and white-
cores which had furnished us a Barmecide feast
when we planted their seed, and so I suppose none
of them grew. ¶ But Sɪ, M

48.19   them] A; their slopes Sɪ, M

48.27–28   house, and for this we were now] A; house. The
frame had been raised, as the custom of that country still was, in a frolic of the neighbors, to whom
unlimited coffee and a boiled ham had been served
in requital of their civility, and now we were Sɪ, M

48.29   We] A; To do this we Sɪ, M

48.32   fire. The] A; fire. ¶ This Sɪ, M

48.32–33   often took] A; never took less than three or four
boys, and often Sɪ, M

48.33   neighborhood] A; ~, Sɪ, M

48.33   turn] A; turn and change Sɪ, M

48.34   It] A; The summer of Southern Ohio is surely no
joke, and it Sɪ, M

49.2   spitted] A; whose ears we spitted Sɪ, M

49.3   stove;] M; ~ ; Sɪ

49.4   time. But] A; ~. ¶ ~ Sɪ, M

49.6   reduced] A; reduced almost Sɪ, M

49.7

river. We] A; river. In those days one went in swimming (we did not say bathing) four or five times a day with advantage and refreshment; anything more than that was, perhaps, thought unwholesome. ¶ We S1, M

49.12–25

We believed .... heaped.] A; *om.* S1; We believed .... heaped. Sometimes we saw a muskrat smoothly swimming to or from his hole, and making a long straight line through the water, and lusted for his blood; but he always chose the times for these excursions when we had not our trusty smooth-bore with us, and we stoned him in vain. ¶ I have spoken of the freshets which sometimes inundated our island; but these were never very serious. They fertilized it with the loam they brought down from richer lands above, and they strewed its low shores with stranded drift. But there were so many dams on the river that no freshet could gather furious head upon it; at the worst, it could back up upon us the slack water from the mill-dam below us. Once this took place in such degree that our wheels stood still in their flooded tubs. This was a truly tremendous time. The event appears in the retrospect to have covered many days; I dare say it covered a half-day at most. M

†49.17

us] A; me M

†49.17

We] A; The truth is, we M

†49.19

year. There] A; ~. ¶ ~ M

†49.21

begun and] A; begun, M

49.27

passed] A; passes S1, M

49.27

our] A; that S1, M

49.31

helplessly] A; hopelessly S1, M

49.35

might] A; might often S1, M

50.1

winter.] A; winter. ¶ There were not many boys in our neighborhood, and we brothers had to make the most of one another's company. S1, M

50.1

while] A; while in the winter S1, M

50.7–8

oaks. ¶ Our] A; oaks./IX. ¶ We had a poor fellow named B——, for our saw-miller, whose sad for-

tunes are vividly associated with the loveliness of
the early summer in my mind. He was a hapless,
harmless, kindly creature, and he had passed most
of his manhood in a sort of peonage to a rich, neighboring farmer whom he was hopelessly in debt to,
so that I suppose it was like the gift of freedom to
him when he came into our employ; but his happiness did not last long. ¶ Within a month or two, he
was seized with a flux that carried him off after a
few days, and then began to attack his family. He
had half-a-dozen children, and they all died, except one boy, who was left with his foolish, simple
mother. My oldest brother had helped nurse them,
and had watched with them, and seen them die,
and it fell to me to go to the next village, one
morning, and buy linen to make the last two of
their shrouds. I mounted the italic-footed mare,
bare-backed, as usual, with my legs going to sleep
on either side of her, but my brain wildly awake,
and set out through the beautiful morning, turned
lurid and ghastly by the errand on which I was
bent. ¶ When I came back, with that linen in my
hand, it was as if I were accompanied by troops of
sheeted dead, from whom that italic-footed nightmare could not be persuaded to escape by any sawing of her mouth, or any thumping of her sides by
[with M] my bare heels. ¶ I am astonished now
that this terror should have been so transient. The
little ones were laid with their father and their
brothers and sisters in the unfenced graveyard on
the top of our hill, where the pigs foraged for acorns
above their heads in the fall, and then my sun shone
again. So did the sun of the surviving B——s. The
mother turned her household goods into ready
money, and with this and the wages due her husband, bought a changeable silk dress for herself
and an oil-cloth cap for her son, and equipped in
these splendors, the two set off up the road toward
the town of X——, gay, light-hearted in their desti-

tution, and consoled after the bereavement of a
single week./x. ¶ Our S1, M

50.8   slowly. The] A; slowly. There were various delays
          and some difficulties, but it was all intensely inter-
          esting, and we watched its growth with eyes that
          hardly left it night or day. Life in the S1, M

50.9   summer, and we] A; summer; we were all impa-
          tient to be out of it. We S1, M

50.12   it.] A; it. We were to have a parlor, a dining-room,
          and a library; there were to be three chambers for
          the family and a spare room; after six months in the
          log-cabin, we could hardly have imagined it, if we
          had not seen these divisions actually made by the
          studding. ¶ In that region, there is no soft wood.
          S1, M

50.15–16 color. It] A; color [~. M] In this, neither the car-
          penter nor any of the neighbors could think with
          him; the local ideal was brick for a house, and if
          not that, then white paint and green blinds, and
          always two front doors; but my father had his way,
          and our home was fashioned according to his plans.
          ¶ It S1, M

50.21   little] A; pitiful little S1, M

50.21–22 two miles away] A; where I went to buy those
          shrouds S1, M

50.23   memories] A; impressions S1, M

50.26   her. Now] A; her. What her pleasures were, I can
          scarcely imagine. She was cut off from church-
          going because we were Swedenborgians; short of
          Cincinnati, sixty miles away, there was no worship
          of our faith, and the local preaching was not edify-
          ing, theologically or intellectually. ¶ Now S1, M

50.29   for her] A; *om.* S1, M

50.31   *Heavenly Arcana*] A; heavenly Arcana S1; Heavenly
          Arcana M

51.5   a] A; the swift S1, M

51.6   again. It] A; ~. ¶ ~ S1, M

51.11   with] A; and S1, M

51.12–52.3 awe. ¶ I . . . . hopes./xI] A; awe; and life was rich

unspeakably./xɪ Sɪ; awe; and life was rich unspeakably. ¶ I . . . . hopes./xɪ M

†51.15   nights, and] A; nights when my brother used to
row across the river to the cabin of the B——s,
where the poor man and his children lay dying in
turn, and I wondered and shuddered at his courage; but M

†51.15   of these nights] A; night M
†51.16   memory. My] A; ∼. ¶ ∼ M
†51.19   after twilight] A; into the night M
†51.21   stood] A; stand M
†51.22   grew] A; grows M
†51.23   them. We] A; ∼. ¶ ∼ M
†51.25   densely] A; closely M
52.8   sibilance] A; sibilance ordinarily Sɪ, M
52.8   by day] A; *om.* Sɪ, M
52.15   tawny] A; golden Sɪ, M
*52.22   whirr] A; whirl Sɪ, M
52.22   millstones] A; burrs Sɪ, M
53.5   shrill] A; long Sɪ, M
53.5   lament. The] A; ∼. ¶ ∼ Sɪ, M
53.8–9   lumber. ¶ It] A; lumber. How we should have
lived through all these complicated mechanical
perils I cannot very well imagine now; but there is
a special providence that watches over boys, and
appoints the greater number of them to grow up in
spite of their environment. ¶ Nothing was ever
drowned in those swift and sullen races, except our
spool-pig, as they call the invalid titman of the herd
in that region; though once one of the grist-miller's
children came near giving a touch of tragedy to
their waters. He fell into the race just above the
saw-mill gate, and was eddying round into the rush
upon its wheel, when I caught him by his long,
yellow hair, and pulled him out. His mother came
rushing from her door, at the outcry we had all set
up, and perceiving him safe, immediately fell upon
him in merited chastisement. No notice, then or
thereafter, was taken of his preserver, by either of

his parents; but I was not the less a hero in my own
eyes./XII. ¶ I cannot remember now whether it
S1, M

53.9   early] A; early spring after our first winter in the
log-cabin, or in the early S1, M

53.9   winter] A; winter, which found us still there, S1, M

53.10   these] A; these vain S1, M

53.11   X——,] A; X——. I was, though so young, a good
compositor, swift and clean, and S1, M

53.13   hand. There] A; hand, there S1, M

53.14   myself but] A; myself that S1, M

53.17   throat] A; throat, and blinded me with tears S1, M

53.25   which] A; that S1, M

53.30   I] A; All the time, I S1, M

53.32   how] A; how at every moment S1, M

53.33   and I] A; I S1, M

53.34   among them] A; there S1, M

54.4   desolation. The] A; ~. ¶ ~ S1, M

54.21   a like] A; this S1, M

54.23–24   kindly circumstance]A; various circumstances S1,
M

54.24   Dayton] A; D—— S1, M

54.24–25   my young uncle] A; one of my uncles was still living, and he S1, M

54.26   the town] A; D—— S1, M

54.27   but for all] A; who stood to me for all that was at
once naturally and conventionally refined, a type
of gracious loveliness and worldly splendor. ¶ They
had an only child, to whom her cousin's presence
in the house was a constant joy. Over them all hung
the shadow of fragile health, and I look back at
them through the halo of their early death; but
the remembrance cannot make them kinder than
they really were. With all S1, M

54.36   thirst.] LG; thirst. ¶ Sometimes I left the table,
and ran out for a burst of tears behind the house;
every night after dark, I cried there alone. S1, M

55.2   when I returned from my work] LG; when, returning from work, S1, M

55.3	and found] A; I found S1, M, LG
*55.10	home. By-and-by] LG; home. ¶ By-and-by S1, M
55.13	decaying tops of the girdled trees in] A; tops of S1, M, LG
*55.13–14	deadening.] A; deadening.* [Footnote in S1, M, LG:] *The trees girdled, and left to die and decay, standing. S1, M, LG
55.18	Sometimes] LG; Presently S1, M
55.20	low] LG; soft, low S1, M
55.21	I] LG; and I S1, M
55.22	peace, and the] LG; peace. The S1, M
55.23	death. At] LG; ~. ¶ ~ S1, M
56.1	through] LG; through all S1, M
56.2	freshly] LG; om. S1, M
56.3	if] LG; freshly as if S1, M
56.20	boys,] LG; boys, on S1, M
56.25	him] LG; this animal S1, M
56.27	journey] LG; time S1, M
56.28	mind.] LG; mind./XIII ¶ I had not seen the old place for thirty years, when four years ago I found myself in the pretty little town of X——, which had once appeared so lordly and so proud to my poor rustic eyes,—with a vacant half-day on my hands. I hired a buggy and a boy, and had him drive me down to that point on the river where our Mills, at least, used to be. ¶ The road was all strange to me, and when I reached my destination that was stranger still. All [om. M] the [om. M] natural [om. M] features [om. M] were [om. M] there, [om. M] but [om. M] the [The M] timber had been cut from the hill and island, and where the stately hickories had once towered and the sycamores drooped, there was now a bald knob, and a sterile tract of sand, good hardly for the grazing of the few cows that cropped its scanty herbage. They were both very much smaller; the hill was not the mountain it had seemed; the island no longer rivaled the proportions of England. ¶ The grist-mill, whose gray bulk had kept so large a place in my memory, was

sadly dwarfed, and in its decrepitude it had canted backwards, and seemed tottering to its fall. I explored it from wheel-pit to cooling-floor; there was not an Indian in it; but ah, what ghosts! ghosts of the living and the dead; my brothers', my playmates', my own! At last, it was really haunted. I think no touch of repair had been put upon it, or upon the old saw-mill, either, in [on M] whose roof the shingles had all curled up like the feathers of a frizzly chicken in the rains and suns of those thirty summers past. The head-race, once a type of silent, sullen power, now crept feebly to its work; even the water seemed to have grown old, and anything might have battled successfully with the currents where the spool-pig was drowned, and the miller's boy was carried so near his death. ¶ I had with me for company the [om. M] miller's [om. M] boy [om. M] again, [om. M] but [om. M] now [om. M] the boy of the present miller, who silently followed me about, and answered my questions as he could. The epoch of our possession was as remote and as unstoried to him as that of the Mound-Builders. A small frame house, exactly the size and shape of our log-cabin, occupied its site, and he had never even heard that any other house had ever stood there. The "new house," shingled and weatherboarded with black-walnut, had bleached to a silvery gray, and had no longer a trace of its rich brown. He let me go into it, and wander about at will. It was very little, and the small rooms were very low. It was plastered now; it was even papered; but it was not half so fine as it used to be. ¶ I asked him if there was a graveyard on top of the hill, and he said, yes; an old one; and we went up together to look at it, with its stones all fallen, or sunken away, and no memory of the simple, harmless man and his little children whom I had seen laid there, going down with each into the dust, in terror and desolation of spirit. His widow probably no longer wears dresses of changeable silk; and where is the orphan boy in the oil-cloth cap? In Congress, for all I know. ¶ I looked across the bare island to where their cabin had stood, and my eyes might as well have sought the cities of the plain. The boy at my elbow could not make out why the gray-mustached, middle-aged man should care, and when I attempted to tell him that I had once been a boy of his age there, and that this place had been my home, the boy of whom I have here written so freely seemed so much less a part of me than the boy to whom I spoke, that, upon the whole, I had rather a sense of imposing upon my listener. [listener./ THE END M] S1, M

57.9	is impossible. His] A; must result in caricature. Important or unimportant, his RG
58.3–4	despotisms] A; depotisms RG
*60.11	little] A; i tle RG
60.20	us across] A; across us RG
60.22	as] A; to us RG
60.24–25	amiable] A; amia RG
61.2	upon] A; u on RG
*62.3–67.19	In *My Literary Passions* . . . . his soul into them, too.] A; *om.* RG
69.6	but] A; and RG
69.11	so few and so trivial events] A; of few events and so trivial RG
69.12	primarily] A; primiarly RG
69.13	while] A; when RG
*70.23	fulfill] HE; fulfil RG, A
*70.35	gayeties] HE; gaieties RG, A
71.17	States.] RG; States. With the removal of the press to the county-seat there was a hope that this field could [would V] be widened, till every Freesoil voter became a subscriber. It did not fall out so; even of those who subscribed in the ardor of their political sympathies, many never paid; but our list was nevertheless handsomely increased, and numbered fifteen or sixteen hundred. I do not

know how it may be now, but then most country papers had a list of four or five hundred subscribers; a few had a thousand, a very few twelve hundred, and these were fairly decimated by delinquents. We were so flown with hope that I remember there was serious talk of risking the loss of the delinquents on our list by exacting payment in advance; but the measure was thought too bold, and we compromised by demanding two dollars a year for the paper, and taking a dollar and a half if paid in advance. Twenty-five years later my brother, who had followed my father in the business, discovered that a man who never meant to pay for his paper would as lief owe two dollars a [*om.* T-W] year [*om.* T-W] for [*om.* T-W] it [*om.* T-W] as any less sum, and he at last risked the loss of the delinquents by requiring advance payment; it was an heroic venture, but it was perhaps time to make it. S2, T-W

71.35   there now, but half a century] RG; there, though there is still so little that by any city scale it would seem comically little, pathetically little; but forty years S2, T-W

72.1   us] RG; *om.* S2, T-W

72.3   our] RG; the S2, T-W

72.5   even] RG; *om.* S2, T-W

72.11–12   case, placed] RG; case; the inking rollers had to be thawed before they could be used on the press, and if the current of the editor's soul had not been the most genial that ever flowed in this rough world, it must have been congealed at its source. The cases of type had to be placed very S2, T-W

72.12   window] RG; windows S2, T-W

72.12–13   but getting] A; and they got S2, T-W; and got RG

72.15   made many] A; passed the time in S2, T-W, RG

72.16   severe] RG; very cold S2, T-W

72.17   they] RG; it S2, T-W

72.18   again.] RG; again. The man at the press-wheel was then the enviable man; those who handled the chill damp sheets of paper were no more fortunate than the compositors. [compositors./ɪɪ T-W] S2, T-W

72.27 comfortable] RG; luxurious S2, T-W

72.30 fierce;] RG; fierce; and the lake winds have a malice sharper than the saltest gales of the North Shore of Massachusetts. S2, T-W

*73.1 slippin'] T; slipin' S2

73.7 now] RG; then S2, T-W

73.7 intending] RG; preparing S2, T-W

73.8 The] RG; This S2, T-W

73.9 it was] T; *om.* S2

73.9 it that] T; it, S2

73.15 v] RG; ɪɪɪ S2, T-W

73.18 they] RG; these S2, T-W

73.18 for] RG; to S2, T-W

73.20 singularly] RG; singularly well S2, T-W

75.19 many years after] RG; not long ago S2, T-W

75.20 the] A; his S2, T-W, RG

75.31 vɪ] RG; v S2, T-W

76.7 interests] RG; interest S2, T-W

76.13 were] RG; were apt to be S2, T-W

76.23 virtues.] RG; virtues. They formed in that day a leaven of right thinking and feeling which was to leaven the whole lump of the otherwise proslavery or indifferent State; and I suppose that outside of the antislavery circles of Boston, there was no-where in the country a population so resolute and so intelligent in its political opinions. S2, T-W

76.30 been.] RG; been. A belief in the saving efficacy of spirit phenomena still exists among them, but not, I fancy, at all in the former measure, when nearly every household had its medium, and the tables that tipped outnumbered the tables that did not tip. The old New York *Tribune*, which was circu-lated in the county [country T-W] almost as widely as our own paper, had deeply schooled the people in the economics of Horace Greeley, and they were ready for any sort of millennium, religious or industrial, that should arrive, while they looked very wisely after the main chance in the meantime. S2, T-W

76.33   They] RG; In spite of the English superstition to the contrary, the average American is not very curious, if one may judge from his reticence in the presence of things strange enough to excite question; and if our craft surprised these witnesses they rarely confessed it. ¶ They S2, T-W

77.5   hitched] A; tied S2, T-W, RG

77.8   Fate] RG; But fate S2, T-W

77.11   our] RG; the S2, T-W

77.14   in, and] RG; in. There were several of these who were readers, and they S2, T-W

77.16   Shakespeare. But it] RG; Shakespeare. ¶ It S2, T-W

77.19   almost] A; easily S2, T-W, RG

77.19   convertible.] RG; convertible; and I have seen our printers engaged in hand-to-hand combats with column-rules, two up and two down, quite like the real bouts on the stage. S2, T-W

77.21–22   irreverent. Part] RG; irreverent, even on the lips of law-students bathing themselves in the fiery spirit of Tom Paine. He was willing to meet anyone in debate of moral, religious, or political questions, and the wildest-haired Comeouter [Comeouters W], the most ruthless sceptic, the most credulous spiritualist, found him ready to take them seriously, even when it was hard not to take them in joke. ¶ It was part S2, T-W

77.22   was] RG; om. S2, T-W

77.23   with] RG; with another kind of frequenter: S2, T-W

77.25   such a] RG; the S2, T-W

77.33   just] RG; full S2, T-W

77.35   thrice the present type-setting] T; three times the composition S2

77.36   In that] RG; At the present day the country printer buys of a city agency his paper already printed on one side, and he gets it for the cost of the blank paper, the agency finding its account in the advertisements it puts in. Besides this patent inside, as it is called, the printer buys stereotyped selections of other agencies, which offer him almost as wide a range of matter as the exchange newspapers he used to choose from. The few columns left for local gossip and general news, and for whatever editorial comment he cares to make on passing events, can be easily filled up by two compositors. But in my S2, T-W

78.7	boys] RG; men S2, T-W
78.9	done; but] RG; done, and S2, T-W
78.9	such] T; such a brief S2
78.10	type;] RG; type. They were then paid by the thousand ems, S2, T-W
78.14	largely] A; entirely RG
78.25	confidence] A; constancy RG
82.3	intention] A; attention RG
82.3	climb] A; climbed RG
83.34	serial] A; continued RG
83.34	romance] A; romance of real life, RG
83.34	a succession of] A; *om.* RG
84.9–10	followed] A; always went RG
84.13	in their] A; their mirth, RG
85.1	brothers.] A; brothers. Our tempers were quick, and the strife was often running from words to blows in swift sequence. RG
85.2	and guardian angel] A; *om.* RG
85.3	anxious] A; anxious, indignant RG
85.5	part] A; part this was unjust; RG
85.6	pressure] A; accusations and reproaches RG
85.7–8	as blows . . . children,] A; and blows not at all hard RG
85.9	blows] A; blows and hard the words RG
85.11–12	He would . . . he would] A; His favorite procedure, after ascertaining the fact of the offense, was to RG
85.13	If the] A; The RG
85.13	denied,] A; denied, and then RG

85.15	remained] A; remained for us RG
86.4	out] A; *om.* RG
86.9	joking from any but him. She] A; it at her cost. She implicitly RG
86.9	him] A; my brother RG
86.13	slight] A; scorn RG
86.13	gate] A; gates RG
86.14–23	milk-pails. That was . . . . which long afterward] A; milk-pails; we did not spare even the County Treasurer in our slight. I do not remember who milked our own cow; I did not carry my studies so far as to learn how, and I suspect that my mother herself did, her girls being too little. She had some Pennsylvania-German superstitions, which she did not really believe in, and she was anxious at certain signs and omens; in most things I think she was rather German than Irish. As for my brother's humor, there was a peculiar touch of it in the praise which RG
86.31	share] A; part RG
87.11	metres] A; forms RG
88.20	gramophones] HE; gramaphones RG, A
89.28	first] A; *om.* RG
89.33	Yet] A; But RG
90.2	but] A; but it RG
90.2	begun] A; gone RG
90.19	vivid and ample] A; ample and vivid RG
92.1	disputes] A; dispute RG, P1–P3, P5
92.3	soul,] P3; ~ RG, P1–P2
92.3	doubted] P2; denied RG, P1
92.4	second] P3; other RG, P1–P2
92.13–15	Among . . . religion;] A; It is not too much to say that among the young people there was a tone of mockery [flippancy P1–P2] for [in P1–P2] religious things; RG, P1–P2; Among many of the young people of the village the prevalent tone was irreverent to scoffing in matters of religion; P3, P5
93.10–11	was given to a different muse] P1; had been vowed to literature RG

93.18	fully] P1 ; fully already RG
94.9	especial] P3; peculiar RG, P1–P2
94.22–24	as a . . . Ohio] A; or that I held him in peculiar honor for representing the State of Ohio in the United States Senate RG, P1–P3, P5
94.31	where] A; when RG, P1–P3, P5
94.33	Probably] P1 ; Naturally RG
94.33	would] P1 ; might RG
94.34	and] P1 ; but RG
95.9	overstated] P2; exaggerated RG, P1
95.9	struggle] A; study RG, P1–P3, P5
95.19	much] P1 ; something RG
96.5	bore] P1 ; brought RG
96.7	Venice,] P1 ; ~ RG
*96.17	that] P2; *om.* RG, P1
*96.20	forbore] P1 ; forebore RG
97.1	fine] A; great RG, P1–P3, P5
97.4	Gettysburg] P3; ~ , RG, P1–P2
98.1	after due family counsel] P3; by him and by my elder brother RG; by him after due council brother P1 ; by him, after due council P2
98.12	pay] P1 ; give RG
98.22	would] P2; could not RG, P1
98.22	best] P2; better RG, P1
*98.31	make] P1 ; give RG
99.6	pastures] A; pasture RG, P1–P3, P5
99.8	1852] A; 1858 RG, P1–P3, P5
99.11	half the sky was often hidden] A; the skies were often clouded RG, P1–P3, P5
99.23	much] P2; *om.* RG, P1
99.30–31	this she was practically] P1 ; a sort, of course she was RG
99.31	now the] P3; now that RG, P1–P2
99.33–34	the purchase was as much waste as] P1 ; it is a worse waste than RG
99.34	We were in fact always paying] P1 ; Of course we paid RG
99.35	notes] P1 ; purchase money RG
99.36	the money to meet] P1 ; *om.* RG

100.1	I am glad] P2; at least RG, P1
*100.2–101.31	owned. ¶ In . . . . years./XIII ¶ I do] P1; owned. ¶ I do RG
*†100.23	me] P2; me me P1
†100.26	these matters] P2; this matter P1
†100.33	no] A; little P1–P3, P5
†100.34	publisher] P2; publish/lisher P1
†100.34	incur] P2; incur all P1
†100.35	my] A; my little P1–P3, P5
†101.4	more] A; a little P1–P3, P5
†101.8	maturing of] P2; maturing P1
†101.12	younger] P2; younger one P1
†101.17	above] P2; a/above P1
†101.19	induced,] P2; ~ P1
†101.19	neighboring] P3; surrounding P1–P2
†101.20	were growing] A; had grown P1–P3, P5
†101.22	Not only the] A; The P1–P3, P5
†101.24	but] A; and P1–P3, P5
*†101.25	do not] P2; do P1
101.31–32	of his newspaper] P1; *om.* RG
102.3–4	the light of] P1; *om.* RG
*102.4	knowledge] P1; knowledge threw upon it RG
102.9	still groping] A; and I groped RG, P1–P3, P5
102.21	preference] P1; preferences RG
102.26	perhaps why I am] A; why I am perhaps RG, P1–P3, P5
102.27	thin air] A; the reader's skull RG, P1–P3, P5
102.35	in] P1; of RG
103.6	struggle] A; combat RG, P1–P3, P5
103.29	trouble] P2; harm RG, P1
103.31	quarterlies,] P3; ~ ; RG, P1–P2
103.32	them;] P3; ~ , RG, P1–P2
103.32	I did no] P2; no RG, P1
103.32	with them] P2; was done RG, P1
103.35	were] P2; were even RG, P1
104.16–17	desired] A; reserved RG, P1–P3, P5
104.26	The] A; Somehow the RG, P1–P3, P5
104.27	seemed to comport] A; comported RG, P1–P3, P5
104.31	constituents] P1; constitutents RG

105.9	men,] A; ∼. RG, P1–P3, P5
105.11	he bent] A; probably he felt that he was stooping RG, P1–P3, P5
105.11	Westerner] A; Westerner he honored RG, P1–P3, P5
105.15	xiv] P1; xiii RG
105.32	tastes,] A; ∼ RG, P1–P3, P5
106.25	as for] P1; as RG
107.3	poetry] A; beauty RG, P1–P3, P5
107.6	fun we all] A; pleasure we RG, P1–P3, P5
107.16	a] P1; *om.* RG
107.34	saw] P1; say RG
108.21	giving,] P1; ∼ RG
108.24	from] P2; upon RG, P1
108.27	that] P1; that now RG
108.27	already] P1; *om.* RG
109.5	and] P2; but RG, P1
109.10	distinct longing] P2; the longing to return RG, P1
110.1	his later] UG; later his MSY
110.10	ashamed.] RG; ashamed of being so. It is best for him to own the fact, but if he cannot do this in season, he may do it out of season and so may be of use to other youth who will probably in their turn be like him. MSY, UG
110.10–11	too unsparing in his memories] RG; unjust to himself MSY, UG
110.13	fiction,] UG; ∼ MSY
110.21–22	If I cannot . . . idealize it,] P2; With all but my elder brother [∼, RG] among those old enough to idealize it, Columbus had become MSY, UG, RG
110.23	which] P3; which MSY, UG, RG; whither P2
110.24	kind] P2; good MSY, UG, RG
110.24	enough,] P3; ∼. MSY, UG, RG, P2
110.24–25	I am certain that my] P2; My MSY, UG, RG
*111.1	winter] UG; ∼, MSY
111.2	my heart] P2; our hearts MSY, UG, RG
*111.3	me] P2; me in MSY, UG, RG
111.6	still saw] A; visioned MSY, UG, RG, P2–P3, P5

111.8–20	What I can . . . . labors. ¶ In like manner I am belatedly sensible] P2; I am certain MSY, UG; What I can . . . . labors, perhaps the highest pleasure, I now realize, of her duteous, devoted life. ¶ In like manner I am belatedly sensible RG
†111.9	was] P2; uas RG
*111.22	as] UG; As as MSY
111.24	his] RG; the MSY, UG
111.25	face the proudest down] P3; "put an antic disposition on," MSY, UG, RG, P2
111.28	dancing,] UG; dancing, dancing MSY
111.29	of improving in it] P2; *om.* MSY, UG; of improving it RG
111.30	me.] RG; me of improving it.; MSY, UG
111.31	go to] RG; to go MSY, UG
111.32	buy"—] UG; ~, — MSY
112.6	earnest] P3; careful MSY, UG, RG, P2
112.24	important] RG; impressive MSY, UG
112.29	vividest] RG; greatest MSY, UG
112.34–35	Columbus. ¶ Not] RG; ~. ~ MSY, UG
112.36	finest] RG; finest and largest MSY, UG
113.2	finish] RG; finish throughout MSY, UG
*113.14	sombre] HE; somber MSY, UG, RG, P2–P3, P5, A
113.19–20	week. ¶ I] RG; week. They did not realize the vision of worldly splendor forecast for me by the title-page of that piece of sheet music at home, and I MSY, UG
113.20	not] RG; not even MSY, UG
*113.22	them,] P2; ~. MSY, UG, RG
113.22–114.8	but the world . . . . polite learning] RG; What I had courage for was the conquest of the whole field of literature which I was attempting then MSY, UG
†113.28	whisper] P2; uhisper RG
†114.4	be,] P2; ~ RG
†114.7	was] P2; uas RG
114.9	now went] P2; went MSY, UG; went now RG
114.10	even] RG; *om.* MSY, UG
114.18	read] RG; then read MSY, UG
114.18–19	that winter] RG; *om.* MSY, UG

114.27	cultivated gentlemen] P2; scholars MSY, UG, RG
114.27	they] RG; themselves to MSY, UG
114.29	II] RG; *om.* MSY, UG
114.30	letters] RG; letters after that MSY, UG
114.32–33	for my convenience as a reporter] RG; *om.* MSY, UG
115.1	so] P2; *om.* MSY, UG, RG
115.4	them] P2; us MSY, UG, RG
115.14	Capitol] P2; capital MSY, UG, RG
115.23	These] P2; They MSY, UG, RG
115.25	but] RG; and MSY, UG
115.27	them] RG; it MSY, UG
115.35	being of,] RG; ~ ~ MSY, UG
115.35	in,] RG; ~ MSY, UG
*115.35	capital] P2; Capital MSY; capital UG; capitol RG
116.8	indeed] P3; really MSY, UG, RG, P2
116.10	comparatively] RG; relatively MSY, UG
*116.19–117.2	Law. If it was once surmised . . . . one another./III ¶ The winter . . . official world. Even the next . . . tardy surprise. There] RG; Law. ¶ There MSY, UG
*†116.21	believe] UG; believe believe MSY
†116.22	political] P2; sovereign MSY, UG, RG
†116.34	world.] RG; ~, MSY, UG
117.6	far] RG; far in that brave time MSY, UG
117.11	shared] RG; shared in MSY, UG
117.17	came] RG; came (so incredibly soon) MSY, UG
117.22	noble,] P3; noble and MSY, UG, RG, P2
117.22–23	head. ¶ But] RG; ~ ~ MSY; ~. ~ UG
117.26	once lunched] P2; lunched one day MSY, UG, RG
117.29	valued] RG; respected MSY, UG
*118.8–120.8	In those . . . society was confined to the generalized hospitality of the large . . . . life about me./IV] RG; II MSY, UG
†118.11	Houses] UG; House MSY
*†118.11	legislature] P2; Legislature MSY, UG, RG
†118.21	if] RG; but MSY, UG
*†118.21–22	dancing,] UG; ~ MSY

†118.22   but] RG; for I not only danced badly, but I knew nobody to dance with, if I had ever had the desperate courage to try. But MSY, UG

†118.24   yet] RG; but MSY, UG

*†118.24   gayety] HE; gaiety MSY, UG, RG, P2–P3, P5, A

†118.24   unimpaired] UG; unimparied MSY

†118.34   assembled] RG; summoned MSY, UG

†119.7   gentle] RG; kind MSY, UG

†119.7   antithesis] P2; anthithesis MSY, UG, RG

†119.13   distinction,] RG; distinction, of brilliant original powers, MSY, UG

†119.16   a member] RG; one of the members MSY, UG

†119.22   in Greece alone] RG; only in Greece MSY, UG

†119.25   present] RG; actual MSY, UG

120.10   my] RG; a MSY, UG

120.20   be,] RG; ~ MSY, UG

120.29   surreptitiously,] UG; ~ MSY

120.31   I am since aware,] RG; one now realizes MSY, UG

*121.4   reporter.] RG; reporter. ¶ That was a very crucial moment . . . . air. ¶ I am advancing . . . . them with me./III ¶ If it was once surmised . . . . official world, though I shared in the generalized hospitality . . . . life about me. MSY, UG

121.5   as they went on from day to day] RG; had now MSY, UG

121.7   gave] RG; made MSY, UG

121.9   meant the] UG; meant the the MSY

121.11   as their legislative correspondent] RG; om. MSY, UG

121.13   from] RG; of MSY, UG

121.13   made] RG; came to make MSY, UG

121.19   really] A; quite MSY, UG, RG, P2–P3, P5

*121.36   it has] RG; has MSY, UG

122.10   force] P2; body MSY, UG, RG

*122.28   police stations] HE; police-stations MSY, UG, RG, P2–P3, P5

122.30   capitol] RG; capital MSY, UG

122.36   restaurant,] P2; restaurant, where I ate too much, chiefly to pass away the time, and MSY, UG, RG

123.15	heart.] RG; heart! I was not fit even to make MSY, UG
123.18	me] RG; me once MSY, UG
*123.21	money-chance] RG; well-moneyed chance MSY; well-money chance UG
123.22	longing] *MSY*; ~, MSY
123.24	outside] UG; ouside MSY
123.30	all] P2; *om.* MSY, UG, RG
123.31	been] P2; been all MSY, UG, RG
123.33	once] RG; *om.* MSY, UG
123.33	silk] *MSY*; ~, MSY
123.34	enchanting] RG; agreeable MSY, UG
124.3	v] RG; iv MSY, UG
124.16	asked] RG; applied MSY, UG
124.17	I] RG; When I MSY, UG
124.17	and] RG; *om.* MSY, UG
124.19	sexagenarian] RG; sexagenarian pessimist whose dancing was my admiration MSY, UG
124.19	returned] RG; returned triumphing MSY, UG
124.21	my labors] RG; the triumph MSY, UG
124.22	broke] RG; broke again MSY, UG
124.25	at his suggestion] RG; by his interest MSY, UG
*124.28–29	Reid, in the retrospect] RG; Reid [~, UG] and I remember him MSY, UG
125.23	that] P2; *om.* MSY, UG, RG
125.25	more congenial] P2; nobler MSY, UG, RG
127.5	*États*] P2; *Etats* MSY, UG, RG
127.6	York,"] UG; ~", MSY
127.6	from] *MSY*; fom MSY
127.24	using] RG; using not MSY, UG
127.29	vi] RG; v MSY, UG
127.34	say was,] *MSY*; ~ ~ MSY
128.2	He] P2; Journalism was then of a different ideal from journalism now, and he MSY, UG, RG
*128.3–4	a mocking] UG; s mocking MSY
128.5	contemporaries] UG; contempraries MSY
128.5–6	contemporaries] UG; contempraries MSY
128.10	a] RG; some MSY, UG
128.11	deprecation.] UG; ~, MSY

128.13	undeniably] P2; an undeniably MSY, UG, RG
128.19	acquit] RG; aquit MSY, UG
128.23	American] RG; Republican MSY, UG
128.25	R.] UG; R MSY
128.26–27	to do his memory such honor as I may] P3; to offer my tribute to his memory MSY, UG, RG; to to do his memory such honor as I may P2
128.35	far more constant] P2; constant if not his favorite MSY, UG, RG
*129.7	in his writing] RG; writing MSY, UG
129.21	with] UG; wuth MSY
129.26	Reed's] P2; his MSY, UG, RG
129.27	passion] P3; ~, MSY, UG, RG, P2
130.5	slovenly] P2; slovenly, easy MSY, UG, RG
130.13–14	journalism] RG; newspaper work MSY, UG
131.1	somewhere] RG; sometimes MSY, UG
*131.4	"The Lady of Lyons"] UG; *The Lady of Lyons* MSY
131.5	"The Daughter of the Regiment"] UG; *The Daughter of the Regiment,* MSY
*131.14	situation,] P2; ~; MSY; ~ UG, RG
131.16	VII] RG; VI MSY, UG
131.17	presently] RG; now MSY, UG
131.18	felt] RG; felt in every detail of it MSY, UG
131.19	though] RG; *om.* MSY, UG
131.20	the work] RG; my work MSY, UG
131.23–24	composing-room,] RG; composing-room MSY, UG
132.4	it.] UG; ~, MSY
133.2	publicly,] *MSY*; ~ MSY
133.24–29	with a formality . . . . society.] P5; in courses for the first time in my unworldly experience, after the novel fashion we [*om.* P2–P3] then called Russian. The meat was carved at the side-board by a shining black butler and brought to the guests, instead of being set before the host to be apportioned, as it would elsewhere have been in Columbus [~. UG, RG, P2–P3] MSY, UG, RG, P2–P3
134.3	her] P3; the MSY, UG, RG, P2
*134.3	eyes,] *MSY*; ~ MSY

134.3	were] P3; she had MSY, UG, RG, P2
134.8	Year's and] *MSY*; Years and MSY
*134.8	made] RG; *om.* MSY, UG
134.22	governorship] *MSY*; governor ship MSY
134.28	upon him] *MSY*; upon MSY
134.30	likewise became] A; became afterwards MSY, UG, RG, P2–P3, P5
135.2	best.] P2; best; but he was not the only statesman who hid his beneficence from me, and left me openly to the literary ardor of those most [*om.* RG] efficient young friends who had no reason to help me but my poems in the Atlantic Monthly, and such promise as they gave of my doing better if I had the chance of completer leisure and fairer opportunity than a junior journalist's work could give me. MSY, UG, RG
135.4	I] UG; him I MSY
135.10	not] RG; *om.* MSY, UG
135.16–17	Democrats] RG; Democrats themselves MSY, UG
*135.18	viii] P2; vi MSY, UG; vii RG
135.24	often] P2; always MSY, UG, RG
136.13–14	still bulking] RG; bulking still MSY, UG
136.17	known] P2; succinctly known MSY, UG, RG
136.18	only] P2; *om.* MSY, UG, RG
136.25	party] RG; party oftenest and MSY, UG
137.3	reluctantly] RG; reluctantly and, I suppose, unacceptably MSY, UG
137.3	I,] RG; ~ MSY, UG
137.12	found.] UG; ~ MSY
137.18	which] P2; that MSY, UG, RG
137.25	foibles] A; follies MSY, UG, RG, P2–P3, P5
138.13	think,] *MSY*; ~ MSY
138.18	was] UG; were MSY
138.26	own] P2; confess MSY, UG, RG
138.27	mostly] P3; always MSY, UG, RG, P2
138.33	chiefly] P3; mostly MSY; most UG; mostly RG, P2
139.3	was] RG; was very MSY, UG
139.4	repenting] P2; repenting of MSY, UG, RG
139.6	than] UG; that MSY

139.6	most] P2; any MSY, UG, RG
139.13	seventy-ninth] P2; seventy-eigth MSY; seventy-eighth UG, RG
139.17	those] RG; the MSY, UG
*139.20	the *Saturday Press*] RG; *The Saturday Press* MSY, UG
139.20	York,] *MSY*; ~ MSY
139.23	more] *MSY*; ~, MSY
139.33	Alleghanies] *MSY*; ~, MSY
140.4	and] P2; but MSY, UG, RG
140.4	was able] P2; forebore MSY, UG, RG
140.7	most of] RG; *om.* MSY, UG
140.9	ix] P2; vii MSY, UG, RG
141.16	of,] *MSY*; ~ MSY
141.18	loved not] RG; loved MSY, UG
141.21	saying] RG; answering MSY, UG
141.30	once been] RG; been once MSY, UG
141.34	not] RG; no more MSY, UG
141.35	play] RG; play than I could dance MSY, UG
141.36	So,] P3; So MSY, UG; But RG, P2
143.3	spirit.] RG; spirit. The talk was one night of that journalist senior of mine, whom I was always celebrating, and she hinted some playful doubt of the importance I ascribed to journalists in a world crowded with other greatness. "Oh, but," our hostess mocked, "perhaps *you* will marry a newspaper man yourself some day," and "No", the lovely guest mocked back, "I hope I shall marry something more substantial". MSY, UG
143.6	glad] RG; blithe MSY, UG
143.7	hearts] P3; grief MSY, UG, RG, P2
143.17	mansions] P2; dwellings MSY, UG, RG
143.18	which] P2; these MSY, UG, RG
143.18–19	I somehow] RG; somehow MSY, UG
*143.20	already] RG; then MSY; than UG
143.21–22	from often being there] RG; *om.* MSY, UG
143.23	then,] RG; then, from often being there, MSY, UG
143.24	glimmer] RG; light MSY, UG
143.26	the glad] P2; that glad MSY, UG, RG
143.26	other days] P2; the past MSY, UG, RG

143.27	and with] P2; and MSY, UG, RG
143.27–28	Common and] P2; Common with MSY, UG, RG
143.28	then] RG; *om.* MSY, UG
143.28	elms, with] P2; elms, and MSY, UG, RG
143.28	just] RG; then MSY, UG
143.29	flower, with] RG; flower, with all MSY, UG
143.29	stately] P2; handsome MSY, UG, RG
143.31	business,] UG; ∼ MSY
143.31	with] RG; *om.* MSY, UG
143.35	manifold] P2; many MSY, UG, RG
143.35	transformations,—the] P3; transformations, and in the light of the moment that MSY, UG; transformations—in the light of that moment the RG; transformations that moment the P2
143.36	past is] P2; past is MSY, UG; past RG
143.36–144.1	again./x] P2; again. But till the sea shall give up its dead, the secret of the fate which has [was to RG] darkened [darken RG] that [the RG] bright day shall remain in its keeping./IX [VIII UG, RG] MSY, UG, RG
144.14–15	or my] RG; or MSY, UG
144.15	father,] UG; ∼ MSY
144.19	befriend] P2; witness MSY, UG, RG
144.19	came] RG; came close MSY, UG
145.27	it] P3; I MSY, UG, RG, P2
146.19	singing] P2; dancing MSY, UG, RG
147.1–2	labyrinth] UG; labarynth MSY
*147.2–148.26	realizing it. ¶ That was a very crucial moment . . . . air.] RG; realizing it. MSY, UG
†147.3	but] RG; and MSY, UG
†147.3–4	had come . . . before] RG; came MSY, UG
†147.10	an] RG; *om.* MSY, UG
†147.16	humanity.] UG; ∼ MSY
†147.17	disaster] P2; vain disaster MSY, UG, RG
†147.18	and] RG; but MSY, UG
†147.29–30	States. ¶ There is a] RG; States. ¶ All this has been lately very interestingly by the Rev. Washington Gladden whom I could wish to have touched

on a curious legend which I would perhaps be
wiser to leave untouched. ¶ The MSY, UG

†147.31   probability] RG; probability is MSY, UG

†147.35   Swayne] RG; Justice Swayne MSY, UG

†148.1   for] UG; for of MSY

†148.4   nice] UG; ~, MSY

†148.9   so] RG; too MSY, UG

†148.12   easily] RG; imaginably MSY, UG

†148.19   jurist,] RG; jurist, for he was a great jurist, MSY, UG

†148.20   darkling in the next room, not unkindly,] RG; darkling, not unkindly, in the next room, MSY, UG

†148.21   That] RG; It MSY, UG

†148.24   city, and] RG; city. MSY, UG

†148.26   rarefied] UG; raritfied MSY

*†148.26   air.] P3; air. ¶ I am advancing here very [om. RG, P2] far [quite RG, P2] out of the order of events, and it is an even later time that I anticipate in speaking of the Swayne house seated in among its lawns and gardens at [of UG, RG, P2] the end of State Street, and apt to be glowing with the lights of social mirth on winter nights, and sounding with

"The delight of happy laughter"

from its porches in the summer twilights [twilight UG, RG, P2]; for the Swaynes were of Maryland origin and had the charm of the cordial Southern manners. The eldest son of the house was a young man different from all the others I knew in a marked religiousness of mind, and a certain purity of ideal in conduct. In the [om. UG, RG, P2] the civic unrest which became the Civil War, he took a leading part in the direction of public feeling, especially among our younger citizens; [citizens; and RG, P2] he was of the first to go into the war. He was of the last to suffer from it, when after the peace had come to the main armies a wandering shot found him out in a skirmish fought in ignorance of Lee's surrender and made him a life-long cripple. I felt peculiarly the pathos of this fate, always so bravely borne, when I saw him last, and we stood together, two middle-aged men, at some academic festivity in New Haven, talking of the Columbus times when we were both so young, and [while RG, P2] he rested himself against the wall from the fatigue and perhaps the pain of his lost limb. ¶ I like to think, indeed, of all that gentle, family, and I would not ignore in these trivial, fond records the invitation so astonishingly made me by the father to become the tutor of his two younger sons. He had heard of an approaching lapse of the editorial functions which I had then so gladly and proudly exercised for three or four years, and he proposed this recourse to me, in that overestimate of my and [om. UG, RG, P1, P2] qualifications which as I have boasted, three great universities afterwards shared. It was all very long ago, but I feel yet the delicate thoughtfulness which saved me then from any shame in declaring my utter unfitness for the work offered me. This is the place as well as another to recognize the [om. UG] the difference between my experience and that of many others whose lives I have read. Those others seem so often to have suffered from events unequal to their merits, whereas if I had any complaint to make against fortune it must be for a certain precipitancy in her to seek out some desert in me to crown with her favor; and I think mine has been the commoner fate. If I have made no secret of my earlier struggles for self-advancement, I feel the more bound to declare that when I had once found the way to it, I never wanted the help which I am equally bound to declare I never asked. Fortune has hurried to meet me, indeed, and has put me to the shame of confessing my unfitness for the kindnesses she would do me. More than once I have had to take my gratitude in both hands and vow myself, in return for this, to a helpfulness in like cases towards others, or at least such helpfulness as I could not decently avoid. The hands that have been outstretched to me on my way have long since fallen to dust, but all the more for that do I feel bound to remember them in this record even at the cost of seeming to ask too much of the reader in asking him to remember some of them with me./III MSY, UG, [RG, P2]; I am advancing . . . . lost limb. RG, P2

148.27　　　xI] P2; *om.* MSY, UG; IX RG

148.28　　　of that time] RG; *om.* MSY, UG

148.30　　　derivatively] UG; derivitively MSY

149.16　　　hundred-thousandths] RG; hundredths MSY, UG

149.30　　　a journalist] A; an editor MSY, UG, RG, P2–P3, P5

149.35　　　keep as] P2; keep so MSY, UG, RG

150.16　　　were.] RG; were./x MSY; were./IX UG

151.6　　　equals.] UG; ~, MSY

151.7　　　but the] UG; but the the MSY

151.9　　　when, as] RG; when MSY, UG

151.10　　　know,] RG; know that MSY, UG

151.25　　　the faith] RG; our faith, MSY, UG

152.1　　　refused] RG; *om.* MSY, UG

152.1–2　　　and more explicitly] P2; though still tacitly MSY, UG, RG

152.2　　　the theory] RG; refused the theory MSY, UG

152.7　　　paler] A; dilute MSY, UG, RG, P2–P3, P5

152.15　　　could] A; would MSY, UG, RG, P2–P3, P5

152.24　　　than in] RG; than MSY, UG

152.24–25　　　was not expected to pay] A; never paid MSY, UG, RG, P2–P3, P5

*152.27　　　it.] A; it. ¶ I could then almost have renounced Conway forever. [forever, but RG, P2–P3, P5] I was destined to meet him, and to grow into a greater liking for him which I now find to [*om.* RG, P2–P3, P5] be [*om.* RG, P2–P3, P5] a lasting affection. Most memorable of all my after meetings with him was that most tragical meeting in Venice when he came down [*om.* RG, P2–P3, P5] to be our guest

after an episode which he thought destined to work
his expulsion from human society. With more than
the common instinct for truth he had a gift of in-
accuracy almost unexcelled, but in his memoirs he
has told with rare obedience to the facts how, on his
first coming to London in 1862, he offered on behalf of his antislavery friends in the North to bring
our Civil War, then in a most hopeless hour, to a
close if the friends of slavery in the South would
consent to its abolition in the interest of Confederate independence. He addressed this amazing proposition, which he had no authority whatever to
make, to the Confederate Commissioner Mason,
who with his associate Slidell, had just then been
restored to English keeping after we had taken
them from a British ship on their way to Europe,
and Mason asked nothing better than to lead Conway on, and then give their correspondence to the
London Times. There was of course nothing for Conway's antislavery friends at home but utterly to
disclaim his imaginative diplomacy, and it was
while he was waiting this awful, inevitable fate that
he came [was RG, P2–P3, P5] to [with RG, P2–P3,
P5] us in Venice after vainly trying for consolation
from the tomb of Shakespeare at Stratford-on-
Avon, where, as he told us, he had sat brooding
upon the famous epitaph, with the wish that nobody [somebody RG, P2–P3, P5] would move *his*
bones. We comforted him as we could, and upon
the whole he had no bad time; and when the blow
came it was by no means the killing stroke he had
foreboded. A man of good intents is not suffered in
the order of providence to destroy himself by even
the most deplorable error, and all [*om.* P2–P3, P5]
Conway'r [Conway's UG, RG, P2–P3, P5] intents
were good throughout a life which could not always
fulfill them. He survived the fate which he had pro-
voked and lived to preach for twenty years at Fins-
bury Chapel, in the midst of those inalienable Eng-

lish friendships which cling so fast where once they
have been given. ¶ Years [om. RG, P2–P3, P5]
afterwards [Later, RG, P2–P3, P5] when I was
on my way home from [from my post at RG, P2–
P3, P5] Venice I saw him in London, where he
took me to lunch at the house of a radical member
of Parliament whose face, when [om. RG, P2–
P3, P5] we [om. RG, P2–P3, P5] met [om. RG,
P2–P3, P5] him, [om. RG, P2–P3, P5] I can still
see [see as it looked RG, P2–P3, P5] over the
shoulder of Conway clasping him in a loving
embrace in his version of the usual nonchalant national greeting. "I suppose you know Conway?"
the face said for sole comment; but who really
knew Conway? In a certain way the whole world
kneu [knew UG, RG, P2–P3, P5] Conway, and I
hope will some day know him better as a singular
[signal RG, P2–P3, P5] element of the strange psy-
chology of the antislavery agitation: [agitation: as
RG, P2–P3, P5] the fervid young Virginian thinking himself out of his ancestral Methodism into
Unitarianism of the widest latitude, and out of the
tradition of a leading Virginian family with [and
RG, P2–P3, P5] its infatuation for slavery, and
then living to lead his father's slaves out of the
bonds in which he had been bound with them; and
then living longer yet to paint the impossible conditions he had helped to destroy as something not
so impossible as one might have imagined them.
That part of his memoir is perhaps the most valuable part of it, or is at least his most voluable [valu-
able UG, RG, P2–P3, P5] contribution [contribu-
tion to UG, RG, P2–P3, P5] the philosophy of the
whole terrible matter; but there was a phase of
Conway's more intimate life which appealed to me
there in Venice beyond in [om. UG, RG, P2–P3,
P5] anything in our common political interests or
my compassion for him in what he thought his mor-
tal strait. "Oh," he would say, again and again,

"if my wife had been with me, I never should have done it! I knew, as soon as my letter to Mason had slipped from my fingers into the post-office, what a mistake it was, but *she* would have known it from the first, and she never would have let me make it." Long after that, when we were both elderly men, and that had befallen him which is the greatest sorrow that Heaven can send upon a man, I went to pity him for the loss of this inestimable wife. He spoke vaguely and wanderingly, as a man stunned by such a blow must speak, and then somehow we touched upon the hope of their meeting again. "We talked of that," he said, "but she would not let me build upon it, as if it were something that did not matter, or was something that could not shape our lives. 'There is [*om.* UG, RG] nothing but duty,' she would say, "*nothing but duty*." MSY, UG, RG, P2–P3, P5

153.3	autobiographer] UG; autobiograher MSY
153.7	youth,] *MSY*; ~ MSY
153.10	has] A; has been mostly [most UG] selfish, and if not otherwise sinful, has MSY, UG; has been mostly selfish, and has RG, P2–P3, P5
153.10–11	which he would not much rather forget] A; to his credit MSY, UG, RG, P2–P3, P5
153.11	own] UG; oun MSY
153.11–12	behalf, or . . . past] A; behalf it will be too late to recall the often ignoble and foolish past MSY, UG, RG, P2–P3, P5
154.13	overrunning] UG; overruning MSY
154.14	"Evangeline,"] UG; *Evangeline* MSY
154.14–15	"Andromeda,"] UG; *Andromeda*, MSY
154.15	Goethe's "Hermann and Dorothea,"] P2; *Goethe's Herman* and *Dorothea*, MSY; Goethe's "Herman" and Dorothea," UG, RG
154.15	while] P3; but MSY, UG, RG, P2
154.18	steamboat,] P2; ~ MSY, UG, RG
154.34	screech] UG; screach MSY
155.7	Monthly] P3; Casket MSY, UG, RG, P2

155.13	papers.] UG; ~ MSY
155.31	fitfully] RG; irregularly MSY, UG
155.34	party;] UG; ~,; MSY
156.2	outdoors] A; *om.* MSY, UG, RG, P2–P3, P5
156.2–3	presciently] A; more intelligently MSY, UG, RG, P2–P3, P5
156.3	calls] A; calls and parties MSY, UG; parties RG, P2–P3, P5
156.9	much] A; *om.* MSY, UG, RG, P2–P3, P5
156.12	the *Atlantic*] RG; *the Atlantic* MSY, UG
156.17	observation] P2; observance MSY, UG, RG
157.1	half the night away, for all I know] P2; for all I know, half the night away MSY, UG; half the night away for all I know RG
157.3	were] UG; was MSY
157.9	in] A; on MSY, UG, RG, P2–P3, P5
157.14	come] P2; come out of that MSY, UG, RG
157.17	millennium. I] RG; millenium. ¶ I MSY; millennium. ¶ I UG
157.24	in a] A; in a strange, MSY, UG, RG, P2–P3, P5
157.29–31	like, who . . . room.] A; like. MSY, UG, RG, P2–P3, P5
*157.33	College] P2; college MSY, UG, RG
157.35–158.4	noontime, when . . . . fortune] A; noontime; after the [*om.* P3, P5] early [*om.* P3, P5] dark when I passed the college [College P2–P3, P5] on my way home to [from P3, P5] supper [work P3, P5], I found it best [well P3, P5] to run [rum UG] at the top of my speed, and thus often [*om.* P3, P5] saved myself from being overtaken by the spectres which would naturally pursue a nervous boy of [*om.* RG, P2–P3, P5] thirteen [*om.* RG, P2–P3, P5] from the dissecting-room. Now I dwelt within the awful precincts of the college, [College, P2–P3, P5] and for all I knew of its whereabouts I lodged in the dissecting-room itself, which with the other rooms was given up to such moneyed youth MSY, UG, RG, P2–P3, P5
158.5	table] P2; board MSY, UG, RG

158.12   than on] RG; than MSY, UG

158.14   accessible] UG; accesible MSY

158.17   never] P2; not MSY, UG, RG

158.19   to whose] RG; whose MSY, UG

158.20   praise] RG; tribute MSY, UG

158.21   1860] RG; 1830 MSY, UG

158.25   is. The management] P3; is. Our jokes did not spare any of our number, and they especially visited one who had the idiosyncrasy of repeating whatever was said to him, and who could be played upon to indefinite repetition by saying the [the same RG, P2] thing over again to [*om.* RG, P2] him [*om.* RG, P2]. It was apparently from some defect in his make-up equivalent to stuttering, but he was a good fellow, and no one was his enemy though many continued his tormentors till he lost a wager to one of us, and paid it with a champagne supper to the whole companionship. This was a riot of such make as none of us had imagined before, and remained both unrivaled [unexampled RG, P2] and unexampled [unrivaled RG, P2], through the whole era of my stay in the College. ¶ The management MSY, UG, RG, P2

158.30   immediately] P2; temporarily MSY, UG, RG

158.32   attaching] P2; attached MSY, UG, RG

158.36   legend was] A; story ran MSY, UG, RG, P2–P3, P5

159.1   when] A; that MSY, UG, RG, P2–P3, P5

159.2   accident,] *MSY*; ~ MSY

159.2   her, she] A; her. She MSY, UG, RG, P2–P3, P5

159.3   not speak] RG; not speak for years MSY, UG

159.3   after] P2; with MSY, UG, RG

159.4   stress] P2; strain MSY, UG, RG

159.4   away] UG; auay MSY

*159.9–11   say, but I . . . be.] P7; say now, but perhaps it was the prose figure of the heroine, whom in those days I should have required to be young and beautiful. MSY, UG, RG, P2–P3, P5

*159.18   me.] A; me, if we had not been of such different
           schools, he [Fullerton RG, P2–P3, P5] writing like
           Browning, and I like Heine. MSY, UG, RG, P2–
           P3, P5; me, P7

159.19   a] P7; om. MSY, UG, RG, P2–P3, P5

159.20   I should like to believe] P7; om. MSY, UG, RG,
           P2–P3, P5

159.25   shy] P7; proud MSY, UG, RG, P2–P3, P5

159.27   at] RG; at my MSY, UG

*160.2   that] UG; om. MSY

160.10   effectively] P2; perfectly MSY, UG, RG

160.16   future,] *MSY*; ~ MSY

160.17   young] P2; young men MSY, UG, RG

160.25–27 joke. ¶ We Collegians . . . . in society] P3; joke. A
           blithe young Irish bank clerk was of every nightly
           company of ours, though he was not of our college
           companionship, and he could make the jokes which
           required nothing but our young good will to enjoy.
           He could walk the middle of the unpaved street,
           and kick the powder that covered it inches deep in
           the Columbis [Columbus UG, RG, P2] summer
           and kill us with laughter by saying, "Dust, dust,
           how dost thou?" Or if he had not that inspiration
           or the like, he could hold us rapt by his threat of
           offering himself to one of the proudest and prettiest
           of the girls we knew. On a certain night he shook
           hands with us all round, saying, "Now fellows, I
           am going to pop, and if I fail, you won't see me
           again for two weeks." But whether he popped or
           not, we never knew. We did not see him again till
           one of us looked him up in his room, and found him
           rejoicing in his rejection, if it was his rejection, or
           still part of his joke. Before the Civil War came he
           transferred his practice of finance to a little city in
           Alabama, and we heard no more of him except
           that when the fighting began he took the Confed-
           erate side, and after the war went back to Ireland,
           where I think he died; so many have [om. P2] died,
           [om. P2] of that companionship of ours [ours have

died P2]. ¶ He was of no politics, but the rest of us were Republicans, more radical or less, as nearly all the people we knew were. There were two young men who MSY, UG, RG, P2

160.36   soon;] P3; soon. Once talking of it with a philosophical young Scotchman, very unlike that blithe, [~ RG, P2] young Irishman in everything but being a bank clerk, we conjectured that it would not [*om.* RG, P2] disappear in about two hundred years from that year of 1859. We were not very precise; a little more; a little less; but about two hundred years, we thought; and though we felt it a long time to wait, we made up our minds to wait. He was going back to Edinburgh soon; MSY, UG, RG, P2

161.24   some] P3; many MSY, UG, RG
161.28   forbore] P3; forebore MSY, UG, RG
162.2   dignity] RG; serenity MSY, UG
162.6   up] UG; up in MSY
162.9   bad] UG; bed MSY
162.21   than] UG; then MSY
162.22   wrongs] A; crimes MSY, UG, RG, P3, P5
162.34–35   family; and . . . respect for] A; family, who showed me as a cherished relic a penknife which had belonged to MSY, UG, RG, P3, P5
163.12   of most] UG; of most most MSY
163.12   penetrating, most amusing] UG; ~ ~ ~, MSY
164.32   was] RG; had MSY, UG
164.32   grotesquely] RG; grotesquely been MSY, UG
165.14   and] RG; and so MSY, UG
165.31   Canada. While] RG; Canada; while MSY, UG
165.35   tendency,] RG; ~. MSY, UG
165.36   Yes] RG; "Yes MSY, UG
165.36   his motive] P3; he MSY, UG, RG
166.1   been] P3; heard his motive MSY, UG, RG
166.1   construed.] RG; ~." MSY, UG
166.2–3   I am . . . me] A; perhaps the other world looked at it differently MSY, UG, RG, P3, P5
166.18   eternal] UG; enternal MSY

167.5	them] UG; thrm MSY
167.6	held] P3; *om.* MSY, UG, RG
167.6	another] P3; another no end MSY, UG, RG
167.7	such as in] A; of MSY, UG, RG, P3, P5
167.8	brings the summer] A; when the summer comes MSY, UG, RG, P3, P5
167.17	tropics;] RG; ~, MSY, UG
168.11	can recollect] P3; recollect ever MSY, UG, RG
168.13	clean] RG; clear MSY, UG
169.6	temperate] UG; tenperate MSY
169.15–16	expected. ¶ There] A; ~. ~ MSY, UG, RG, P3, P5
169.16	heat] A; heat of the early July night MSY, UG, RG, P3, P5
169.16–17	at some . . . had taken] A; I took MSY, UG, RG, P3, P5
169.26	trees,] UG; ~ ; MSY
169.35	a Cincinnati journalist] RG; the editor of a Cincinnati paper MSY, UG
170.3	coverlet,] RG; ~ MSY, UG
170.3	meek] A; shy MSY, UG, RG, P3, P5
170.11	experiences,] RG; experiences, and MSY, UG
171.8	time, but] RG; time, and that the payment became the basis of a new engagement with him. But MSY, UG
171.11	wabbled] A; wobbled MSY, UG, RG, P3, P5
171.15	as many] P3; thousands of MSY, UG, RG
171.29	a] RG; a poetic MSY, UG
171.31	been] RG; used them MSY, UG
171.31	with] RG; in MSY, UG
*171.31	"In Memoriam."] RG; "*In Memoriam*"./

As in some morning twilight dim,
   Men see a wide, disordered train
   Move vague and large along the plain,
Like a procession of [in MSY, UG] a dream—

Till, shining through the somber pines
   That frown beneath the mountain-brows
   Hoar with world-old, eternal snows,
The sun strikes wide in crimson lines,

And, here and there, amid the stir,—
   Unlitten, [~ MSY, UG] men of meaner frame,—
   Smites the steel warrior into flame,
From burning helm to gleaming spur;—

We see, in all the dawns of Time,
   The unknown many of the past,
   Obscurely noisy, darkly vast,—
And shining out of these sublime,

The men whose great souls caught the sun
   On mails of proof and arms of might,
   Riding to battle from the night
Of years where nothing has been done:

The Martyrs, that in heathen-lands
   Have wrestled with all shapes of death,
   (The quick soul strength to wasting breath,)
And won the victory from his hands;

The Prophets, that in speech have stood,
   And preached the Right, and shown the Truth,
   Launching rebuke, and sparing ruth,
Amid the furious multitude;

The Champions, that with sword and lance,
   And iron hands and mighty blows,
   Have struggled with the people's foes,
And conquered, in forlorn advance. N1, R1, MSY, UG

172.1	these,] RG; ~; N1, R1, MSY, UG
172.24	rhyme!] MSY; ~. N1, R1
172.25	me now,] RG; me, with the lines in print before me, MSY, UG
172.27	journalists] A; newspaper men MSY, UG, RG, P3, P5
172.27	forecast] RG; vision MSY, UG
172.28	coming] RG; future MSY, UG
172.28	newspaper man] A; journalist MSY, UG, RG, P3, P5
172.31	In this case] A; If he does MSY, UG, RG, P3, P5
173.1	over-generous] RG; generous MSY, UG
173.2	recall] RG; recall now MSY, UG
173.3	no doubt] RG; I suppose MSY, UG

173.7–8   fearful] RG; doubtful MSY, UG

173.9   could, but] RG; could, and I had my reward in seeing my poem, as it appears printed as part of the Convention's proceedings in our paper. But MSY, UG

173.10   cannot] RG; cannot exactly MSY, UG

173.10   own] RG; *om.* MSY, UG

173.11   from the] RG; from that MSY, UG

173.14   was] RG; I was MSY, UG

173.16   publisher] *MSY*; ~, MSY

173.17   *Poems of Two Friends*] UG; "Poems of Two Friends" MSY; *"Poems of Two Friends MSY*

173.21   handle] UG; handls MSY

173.32   life of Abraham Lincoln, printed with his speeches] A; "Life and Speeches of Abraham Lincoln", printed MSY, UG, RG, P3, P5

173.33   life and speeches of Hannibal Hamlin,] A; "Life and Speeches of Hannibal Hamlin", MSY, UG, RG, P3, P5

174.5   by name] RG; *om.* MSY, UG

174.5   himself] RG; himself by name MSY, UG

174.9   though] RG; though even now MSY, UG

174.10   might] RG; might very well MSY, UG

174.11   see,] RG; see, at all MSY, UG

174.11   world] RG; world even MSY, UG

174.12   was to] RG; was MSY, UG

174.13   knew,] RG; ~ MSY, UG

174.16   reality was] RG; reality MSY, UG

174.35   must,] RG; ~ MSY, UG

175.13   to him for] P3; to him for MSY, UG; for to him RG

175.18   the burdens] RG; that burdens MSY, UG

175.25   those] RG; these MSY, UG

175.28   vii] UG; vi MSY

175.29–30   most worthy of] A; not unworthy MSY, UG, RG, P3, P5

175.34   handsome face] A; handsome face MSY, UG, RG; attractive face P3, P5

176.1   reading] RG; giving MSY, UG

176.1   win] P3; turn MSY, UG, RG

176.26	those] A; these MSY, UG, RG, P3, P5
177.2	left the] RG; left MSY, UG
177.6	solemn] RG; serious MSY, UG
177.16	those] RG; these MSY, UG
177.17	are] P3; were MSY, UG, RG
177.18–19	horse-stealing." ¶ Once] RG; horse-stealing." Once MSY, UG
177.30–31	(when . . . Hayes,)] RG; ~ . . . ~, MSY, UG
178.4	viii] UG; vii MSY
178.6	*Life of Lincoln*] P3; life of Lincoln MSY, UG; Life of Lincoln RG
178.8	always] RG; always everywhere MSY, UG
178.10–11	of my money,] P3; on account MSY, UG, RG
178.15	my] RG; my graphic MSY, UG
178.22	saw] RG; did see MSY, UG
178.24	them] RG; it MSY, UG
178.24–25	the Cincinnati *Gazette*] RG; a Cincinnati paper MSY, UG
178.25	saw] RG; did see MSY, UG
178.33	still] RG; even MSY, UG
179.5	yet] RG; still MSY, UG
179.13	so] RG; very MSY, UG
180.7	all-but-mortal] UG; all-but mortal MSY
180.16	its] RG; *om.* MSY, UG
180.16	the] RG; the only MSY, UG
180.16	best] RG; *om.* MSY, UG
180.25	ix] UG; viii MSY
181.11	northern] A; southern MSY, UG, RG, P3, P5
181.12	with the] RG; with MSY, UG
181.13	cannot say] RG; do not know MSY, UG
181.16	wide] A; ample MSY, UG, RG, P3, P5
181.21	grocers'] *MSY*; grocers MSY
181.24	carriage,] RG; ~ MSY, UG
181.24	breakfast,] RG; ~ MSY, UG
181.25	among] P3; along with MSY, UG, RG
181.30	On] RG; After MSY, UG
182.7	"The Pilot's Story"] UG; The Pilot's Story MSY
182.9	Lincoln] RG; Lincoln on MSY, UG
182.9	on] RG; *om.* MSY, UG

182.14	poetry] P3; literature MSY, UG, RG
182.29	rejected, or protested,] RG; ~ ~ ~ MSY, UG
182.33	night] RG; feast MSY, UG
184.7	x] UG; IX MSY
184.17	ambitions] A; ideals MSY, UG, RG, P3, P5
184.18	ideals] A; ambitions MSY, UG, RG, P3, P5
184.34	great] RG; *om.* MSY, UG
185.2	a statue] RG; his statue MSY, UG
185.5	Indian-Fighter] RG; Indian Fighter MSY, UG
185.9	and] RG; but MSY, UG
185.17	Columbus,] P3; ~ MSY, UG, RG
186.2	jealous] RG; prejudiced MSY, UG
186.10	many such] A; a good many MSY, UG, RG, P3, P5
186.35–36	for a moment she made] P3; she made for a moment MSY, UG, RG
187.12	thoughtfulness] A; thoughtfulness of me MSY, UG, RG, P3, P5
187.13–14	still feel. ¶ This] A; am glad still to feel. He MSY, UG, RG, P3, P5
187.21	first, and] A; first and when MSY, UG, RG, P3, P5
187.23	of] A; to MSY, UG, RG, P3, P5
187.23	Cincinnati] A; *Cincinnati* MSY, UG, RG, P3, P5
187.23	*Gazette*;] A; *Gazette*, MSY, UG, RG, P3, P5
187.25–26	After the war] A; Afterwards MSY, UG, RG, P3, P5
187.27	a] RG; the MSY, UG
187.29	six] A; five MSY, UG, RG, P3, P5
188.26	out] A; about MSY, UG, RG, P3, P5
188.30	XI] UG; x MSY
189.3	This] RG; That MSY, UG
189.6	practical] RG; serious MSY, UG
189.19–20	all. ¶ I] RG; ~. ~ MSY, UG
189.21	felt it] RG; did MSY, UG
189.23	an entire] RG; a whole MSY, UG
189.32	North] RG; whole North MSY, UG
189.35	some] A; many MSY, UG, RG, P3, P5–P6
190.26–27	censorship;] RG; censureship; and MSY, UG

190.30	wiser now] RG; now wiser MSY, UG
191.18	exacted] RG; inflicted on me MSY, UG
191.19	absolutely] RG; entirely MSY, UG
191.22	alluring] A; attractive MSY, UG, RG, P3, P5–P6
191.24	lodged,] UG; ~ ; MSY
191.24	ward] A; theatre MSY, UG, RG, P3, P5–P6
191.28	place] A; room MSY, UG, RG, P3, P5–P6
191.29	such] RG; those MSY, UG
192.1	young men,] P3; ~, ~ MSY, UG, RG
192.3	oysters] A; incomparable oysters MSY, UG, RG, P3, P5–P6
192.3–194.1	Ambos. ¶ It is strange . . . . the air.' "/xii] A; Ambos. Of the incidents one distinguishes itself above the others as characteristic of all life in its blending of tragic and comic. In the midst of our mirth on a certain evening theer [there UG, RG, P3, P5–P6] came a cry of "*Dead?*" and then a confused tumult of voices with the rumor of a swoon; and it seemed that one of the young girls had got word from home that a sister had suddenly died of heart disease. Everybody was quickly persuaded of the fact except a [*om.* UG, RG, P3, P5–P6] the father of a child which he had left with its mother in their rooms on an upper floor; he was decided [sure RG, P3, P5–P6] that it was his child which had died, and he had to be pulled and pushed upstairs by all the friends who could get about him, and the child roused from its sleep to convince him by its indignant wails that it was still living. The dances were not late affairs, but while the evening lasted it was full of the joy which has now gone out of the world, if it ever was really in it. MSY, UG; Ambos. The dances were not . . . really in it. Of the incidents . . . . still living. RG, P3, P5–P6
*†192.30	æsthetic] HE; esthetic A
†192.32	roommate] HE; room-mate A
*194.5–11	the next year, and . . . . seem as if] A; within the year, and forty-seven years we lived together; then she died and left me to the loss which only eternity

can repair. [repair. ¶ RG] It [But it RG] did not
seem, [seem, then RG] that gayest winter in the
world, that MSY, UG, RG; within the year, and
forty-seven years we lived together; then she died;
but it did not seem, that gayest winter in the world,
that P3(1), P5; the next year, and with her unerring artistic taste and conscience she became my
constant impulse toward reality and sincerity in
my work. She was the first to blame and the first to
praise, as she was the first to read, what I wrote.
Forty-seven years we were together in this life; then
she died; but in that gayest time when we met, it
did not seem as if P3(2); the next year, and she
became with her unerring artistic taste and conscience my constant impulse toward reality and
sincerity in my work. She was the first to blame
and the first to praise, as she was the first to read
what I wrote. Forty-seven years we were together
in this life; then she died. But in that gayest time
when we met it did not seem as if P6

194.12   radiant. Though] A; beautiful, though MSY, UG,
            RG; beautiful. Though P3, P5–P6

194.12   was] RG; was then MSY, UG

194.13   soon, few] P3; soon. Few MSY, UG, RG

194.14   would] P6; would ever MSY, UG, RG, P3, P5

*194.20–21 majority.] P3(2), P6; majority. When they could
            no longer control the majority in the North they
            were potent to control the majority in the South.
            MSY, UG, RG, P3(1), P5

194.21   brook] P6; brook any MSY, UG, RG, P3, P5

*194.25   good.] P6; good. The situation was without par-
            allel in the history of the world. MSY, UG, RG,
            P3(1), P5; The situation was without parallel in
            history. P3(2)

194.26   they were] RG; it was MSY, UG

194.28   them] P3; it MSY, UG, RG

194.30   they] P3; it MSY, UG, RG

194.30   all;] P4; all; and that was why and how the war
            came; MSY, UG, RG, P3

194.30   never] P4; never suffer control; it could never
               MSY, UG, RG, P3
194.31   hardly] P4; not MSY, UG, RG, P3
195.18   some] RG; even some MSY, UG
195.19   may] A; will MSY, UG, RG, P3-P4
195.26   record and reveal] RG; reveal and record MSY,
               UG
195.28–29   entirety. ¶ At] RG; ~. ~ MSY, UG
195.34   remained] UG; ramained MSY
196.1–3   ours who . . . journalist.] RG; ours; MSY, UG
†196.2   Comly] A; Comley RG, P3-P4
*196.3–197.1   Of all the friends . . . . of course a potential] P4;
               and [om. P3] it [It P3] appears to me now that I had
               nothing temperamental in common with him, but
               I did not like him the less for that, and apparently
               he liked me in spite of our difference. We read many
               of the same books, but he was not such a multifari-
               ous reader as I, and in obedience to his legalist
               instincts he was of more conservative politics. It
               does not seem to me that we talked much of politics,
               or of the events that were hurrying the nation toward
               the Civil War. Mostly we talked of the [the young
               P3] girls we knew, studying [om. P3] their char-
               acters and charms and qualities, as is the custom of
               young men in all times and places. He was no great
               talker, and much of our walking must have been
               done without talking, but he could sing the sweetest
               tenor, and his voice was always lifted at the houses
               where there was singing. Though I cannot say
               what his attraction was for me, or why he should
               have tolerated me, perhaps he divined that with
               some despicable qualities [traits P3] I was not
               meanly grudging of certain [om. RG, P3] things
               in which grudging was meanest. ¶ [no ¶ RG, P3]
               In after years he sought at times to do me friendly
               offices when he thought I needed them, and when
               he succeeded to the control of the *Journal*, he kept,
               on terms of his own, the tradition of Reed, which
               Price and I had continued after our fashion. In the

meantime he had fought through the war with such
gallantry and efficiency that he came out of it a
brigadier-general. But his Viking frame harbored
an enemy deadlier than the common foe, and after
years of newspaper work, when he was sent minister
to Hawaii, he died there of tuberculosis. I say Viking, because with his tall, strong [straight P3] figure, his fine regular features, his blue eyes and his
moustache thin and ashen blonde [blond P3], he
looked the sort of Norseman we see in picture at
the prow of raven-beaked boats, and I can well
imagine how he won in battle the distinction which
was not a difference in Ohio, where generals so
abounded from the war. We must sometimes have
talked about the books we were reading, that is to
say the novels, though very seldom about public
events, which is the stranger, or the less strange
because, a student of law, he was of course intending MSY, UG, RG, P3

†196.12	Comly] A; Comley P4
†196.14	reader] A; rea/reader P4
†196.14	and not] A; as I, or P4
†196.17	other, yet I had] A; other except P4
†196.18	of] A; o/of P4
†196.18	in] A; in/in P4
†196.21–24	The conceit . . . urging how] A; He did not ex- plicitly require an explanation, but I felt that it was due to the kindness between us that I should make him realize how most P4
†196.25–26	situation . . . . but] A; conception was, and P4
†196.27	breath] A; b/breath P4
†196.27	relief] A; satisfaction P4
*†196.27–197.1	perfectly he . . . . potential] A; this truth sufficed. The walks that we took together might in all have encircled the globe, but our talks were not nearly so long. Up and down the far-stretching streets there uas little to distract our thoughts from our- selves, but our cons/sciousness supersensed the young girls behind the windows of the familiar

houses beyond the pleasant lawns and gardens, and no doubt we talked of these, and the wonder of their looks and words, their wit and their wisdom and their beauty, as in every time and place young men have talked of young girls; but I have an abidin/ing impression that much of our walking was done without any talking whatever; apparently it was enough for us to be walking together. ¶ I cannot think now why in most things he should have tolerated me, but perhaps he divined that I was always at least willing to be the great and fine things I was always dreaming of being. When in after years he succeeded to the control of our newspaper he kept, on . . . . of course intending P4

197.2	day.] RG; day. But mainly as young men always we talked of the girls we knew. MSY, UG
197.3–21	He was . . . . few years later.] A; *om.* MSY, UG, RG, P3–P4
197.22	xiii] UG; xii MSY
197.30	this] RG; that MSY, UG
198.4	flattering] P3; successful MSY, UG, RG
198.5	was] RG; was to be MSY, UG
198.22–23	it better] A; one's suffering MSY, UG, RG, P3–P4
199.3–4	telegraphic] RG; telegraph MSY, UG
199.5	company] UG; conpany MSY
199.9	character] UG; sharacter MSY
199.13	that the] RG; that MSY, UG
199.19	been of] RG; been MSY, UG
200.15	story] A; epic MSY, UG, RG, P3, P5, P7
200.18	Sumter,] P3; ~, — MSY, UG, RG
200.32–33	Instantly the] RG; The MSY, UG
200.33	was] RG; was instantly MSY, UG
201.14	man, and the] RG; man. The MSY, UG
201.24	smoke-rolled] RG; rolled MSY, UG
201.33	my] RG; my greatest and last remaining MSY, UG
201.33	Comly,] A; *om.* MSY, UG; Comley, RG, P3, P5, P7
201.33–34	had been one of the earliest, and] A; destined to come out one of the many Ohio generals, MSY, UG, RG, P3, P5, P7

202.1	he gave] A; gave MSY, UG, RG, P3, P5, P7
202.2	helplessly] A; *om.* MSY, UG, RG, P3, P5, P7
202.8	John G. Mitchell] RG; he MSY, UG
*202.9–10	to which . . . distinction.] P5; which he did not care to exchange for the brevet of major-general later forced upon him. MSY, UG, RG, P3(1), P7; to receive later the brevet of major-general. P3(2)
202.12	group;] P5; group; he lived somewhere apart, MSY, UG, RG, P3(1), P7; group; he was not of that till the last winter of my Columbus years, but P3(2)
202.12	familiarly] P5; intimately MSY, UG, RG, P3(1), P7; *om.* P3(2)
202.13	friendship] P5; more than sisterhood MSY, UG, RG, P3(1), P7; sisterhood P3(2)
202.13	become] P5; doubled life for us as MSY, UG, RG, P3(1), P7; *om.* P3(2)
202.14	rapt] RG; tireless MSY, UG
202.15	put] RG; write MSY, UG
202.17	forms] P5; afterward became MSY, UG, RG, P3(1), P7; has become P3(2)
202.17–19	history. No . . . told.] A; history: lost, unless she who survives him should [may RG, P7] have devotedly, as she alone could adequately have set them down. MSY, UG, RG, P7; history: P3; history. No stories of that life which I have read have seemed to me so frank, so full, so real, so Tolstoyan as those he told. P5
202.20	Our] A; The MSY, UG, RG, P3, P5, P7
202.23	and the] RG; and of the MSY, UG
202.24	bunks] P3; ~, MSY, UG, RG
202.25	many] RG; *om.* MSY, UG
203.2	oftentimes] A; sometimes MSY, UG, RG, P3, P5, P7
*203.15–16	year./XIV] P3; year. ¶ With varying accesses of irresolution I still thought of volunteering, and one night, as Price and I sat waiting for the latest dispatches, I was in question so extreme that I said to my fellow-editor, "Price, if you will volunteer,

I will." "Well," he answered, "I *won't*," and that, for such reason as it had, seemed to close the question. If in all this I seem to be accusing myself, it is only partially an appearance; I am also excusing the innumerable majority of my contemporaries who also failed also to volunteer. ¶ It did not matter that no one seemed to expect me to volunteer, and when a blithe young step-cousin came down to be [the UG] capital from the northwestern corner of the State, with a company for the three years' service got together under his captaincy, and offered me his confident hope of a lieutenancy I was not tempted, though I had no illusions about war. I wrote home upon that very vague tender of a lieutenancy in an unaccepted company that I was considering it; but again I wrote: "It is a sad fact that after the war has been fought out the government must treat upon the basis of disunion at last. I don't see how the war could have been avoided, but it is not the less a stupid and foolish war on that account; war is always stupid and foolish." Again I wrote: "Everything is in an uproar here, and the war feeling is on the increase, if possible. There has been a sort of calm to-day in the city, but down at the camp the troops are drilling, and the blind and mad devil of war is spreading himself generally. The volunteers seem to be in very good spirits and to look upon campaigning as a frolic." It will appear that I was no great prophet or philosopher, but a very frank observer. Only two or three of the friends who had formed our College group went to the war; one of these was my greatest friend of all, the young Viking, whom I found officer of the day at the camp; he gave me what time he could, but he was preoccupied, and the whole world I had known was estranged. One morning I remember meeting another friend, coming down the State House steps, and smiling joyfully; he was a law student, and he had just been made adjutant of a newly accepted regiment. Almost immediately afterward he was changed to the line, and at the end of the war, having fought its last important battle, he came out with the rank of brigadier-general, which he did not care to exchange for that brevet major-general forced upon him./xiii [xv UG] MSY, UG; year./xv ¶ It did not matter that no one seemed to expect me to volunteer, and when a lively young step cousin came down to the capital from the northwestern corner of the State, with a company for the three years' service got together under his captaincy, and offered me his confident hope of a lieutenancy, I was tempted, though I had no illusions about war. I wrote home upon that very vague tender of a lieutenancy in an unaccepted company that I was considering it, but again I wrote: "It is a sad fact that after the war has been fought out the government must treat upon the basis of disunion at last." It will appear from this that I was no great prophet or philosopher, if a very frank observer. ¶ But with varying accesses of irresolution I still thought of volunteering, and one night, as Price and I sat waiting for the latest despatches, I was in question so extreme that I said to my fellow-editor, "Price, if you will volunteer, *I* will." "Well," he answered, "I *won't*," and that, for such reason as it was, seemed to close the question. If in all this I seem to be accusing myself, it is only partially an appearance; I am also excusing the innumerable majority of my contemporaries who also failed to volunteer. RG

203.18	already] A; *om.* MSY, UG, RG, P3, P5, P7
203.20	desire] A; ambition MSY, UG, RG, P3, P5, P7
203.23	of] UG; if MSY
203.30–31	Postmaster General] RG; Secretary of the Interior MSY, UG
203.34	Treasury.] RG; Treasury, and MSY, UG
204.21	Meanwhile] P7; Our chief, whom I shall always remember with affection, was in his escape from

the *State Journal* and its adversity of the optimistic belief that the fees came to something between twelve and fifteen hundred dollars. But still I somehow feared, and I sent my friend Piatt, then conveniently a clerk in the Treasury Department, and begged him to go to the State Department, and if possible verify this bright belief of my chief, who was no doubt so [*om.* RG, P3, P5] glad not to have me fall to the ground when he must withdraw the high horse from under me. Piatt learned that the fees at Rome were between three and five hundred a year; and again I had my hesitations. Yet I had always heard that Italy was a very cheap country, and I suppose I thought vaguely that I could eke out my pay by writing and selling my stuff to the newspapers and magazines, I think The Atlantic, for the most part. Besides, there was nothing else, and I could not part with even so poor a certainty as three or five hundred a year. There was nobody in Columbus then who had traveled abroad except one lady whom I happened not to know, but whom I was hospitably taken to see by a lady who did know her. She had not only been in Rome, but had lived there a whole winter, and she was enthusiastic. She said that for five hundred dollars a year in Rome you could live like a prince, and I went home rich for a night of golden dreams. I do not know quite how or why I should have wakened to doubt in the morning; Price was still hopeful as he had always been, but more and more it seemed to me that the cost of living at Rome would bear looking into; meanwhile MSY, UG, RG, P3, P5

204.30	inevitable.] P3; inevitable. I cannot remember that I was now [*om.* RG] very heavy hearted. MSY, UG, RG
204.31	Columbus,"] UG; ~", MSY
204.36	world.] P3; world./xiv MSY, UG, RG
*205.7-8	has been told . . . rehearsed] P7; I need not tell MSY, UG, RG, P3, P5

205.15	of the] A; of UG, RG, P3, P5, P7
205.30	fate] RG; "fate shears" UG
205.35	train] P7; *om.* UG, RG, P3, P5
205.35	mounted] P7; mounted into UG, RG, P3, P5
206.1–2	offer his memory this vow] A; render him this tribute UG; make his memory this offer RG, P3, P5, P7
206.3	somewhen] RG; somewhere UG
206.4	were] A; were so UG, RG, P3, P5, P7
206.4	so] A; *om.* UG, RG, P3, P5, P7
206.5	THE END] P3; End UG, RG

"OVERLAND TO VENICE"

*210.26	travelling] HE; traveling S3
222.8	pass] HE; pass it S3

"AN OLD VENETIAN FRIEND"

225.4–7	I was . . . misgivings] S4; It was partly to my own fault for I had reported myself to the police on my arrival as a journalist by profession, and had naturally roused the anxiety of the authorities MSO
225.9	the Austrian] S4; their MSO
225.11–12	hottest; . . . wait. ¶ In] S4; hottest. In MSO
225.13–14	Demonstration, as . . . resistance,] S4; Demostration MSO
225.15	might have] S4; justly MSO
225.16	imperial] S4; goatee MSO
225.21–22	once. We presently] S4; once; we MSO
225.22	comrades,] S4; ~ MSO
225.23	fifty-six] S4; fifty six MSO
226.7	That] S4; Pastorelli MSO
226.11	were the] S4; were MSO
226.11–13	race, which . . . sincere. We] S4; race. It seems to me that we MSO
226.14	largely] S4; *om.* MSO
226.14	company] S4; society largely MSO
226.16	lived] S4; been MSO
226.19	I think] S4; *om.* MSO
226.20	largely] S4; partly MSO

226.20	there] S4; *om.* MSO
226.21	Dictionary, which, if he did not find] S4; Dictionary there. He seemed to think this MSO
226.22	he owned] S4; and he said MSO
226.22	read] S4; read it MSO
226.24	I] S4; I myself MSO
226.27	Bible?] S4; ~, MSO
226.28	not] S4; *om.* MSO
226.33–34	Protestantism. ¶ He] S4; ~. ~ MSO
226.35	"country"] S4; ~ MSO
226.35	*cauntree*] S4; cauntree MSO
226.36	city] S4; town MSO
227.2	now] S4; then MSO
227.2	Venice,] S4; ~ MSO
227.3	town] S4; *patria* MSO
227.5	was] S4; went MSO
227.5	in] S4; in as MSO
227.7	mostly] S4; *om.* MSO
227.7	I] S4; We MSO
227.8	believe] S4; think MSO
227.9	with the] S4; with any MSO
227.12–13	others. ¶ I] S4; ~. ~ MSO
227.16	believe] S4; think MSO
227.17	middle class, but] S4; bourgeois, and though MSO
227.18–21	enough to . . . . for he] S4; enough, and he had long before he died, a title from the Pope, he did not pay His Holiness too much money for it, and did not overvalue it. He MSO
227.29	a] S4; *om.* MSO
227.30	which] S4; and it MSO
227.31	merely] S4; only MSO
227.32	the consul] S4; him MSO
228.8	and even] S4; but if my acquaintance Pastorelli promptly attached himself to me on the terms of constant friendship that he might practice his English gratis I must own it a fit judgment. Even MSO
228.11	a] S4; that MSO
228.12	Pastorelli] S4; friend MSO
228.16–17	which . . . office,] S4; *om.* MSO

228.17	otherwise below] S4; unworthy MSO
228.19	presently,] S4; ~ MSO
228.21	inquiring] S4; indignant MSO
228.22–23	shobby!" ¶ In] S4; ~ !" ~ MSO
228.25	had] S4; had eager MSO
228.26	me] S4; to MSO
228.26	eagle.] S4; eagle and me. Even after MSO
228.27	*exequatur*, but] S4; *exequatur* I MSO
228.29	salary, when] S4; salary. MSO
228.31	want!"] S4; ~ ." MSO
228.33	"Listen!"] S4; "*Senta !* Listen!" MSO
229.3	life] S4; life in Italy and Spain MSO
229.4	personally] S4; indeed MSO
229.6	after] S4; when MSO
229.6	them] S4; it MSO
229.8	fact] S4; experience MSO
*229.9	national] S4; natural MSO
229.9	him.] S4; him; and MSO
229.11	it; but] S4; it. But MSO
229.15	withholding] S4; witholding MSO
229.17	Listen] S4; *Senta* MSO
229.22	money-changer's] S4; money-changers MSO
229.26	entirely] S4; pretty well MSO
229.31	said that] S4; *om.* MSO
229.32	money-changer's] S4; money changers MSO
229.34	I] S4; I believe that I MSO
229.34	them] S4; them, somehow, MSO
229.35	days] S4; days the MSO
229.35–36	at Venice] S4; *om.* MSO
229.36	drafts,] S4; ~ MSO
229.36	not] S4; not merely MSO
230.1	doubt] S4; distrust MSO
230.4	left] S4; had left MSO
230.5	obliged] S4; made MSO
230.6	to] S4; *om.* MSO
230.7	I] S4; He was a very firm though a very looking, skull-capped, spectacled and slippered old German, with pale hands which he rubbed softly together and I MSO

230.8	to] S4; to the MSO
230.11	this] S4; that MSO
230.13	not,] S4; ~ MSO
230.15–17	in . . . . Pastorelli] S4; Pastorelli. He MSO
230.20	cafés] S4; cafés of MSO
230.23	modest] S4; *om.* MSO
230.24–25	*Youth, or Giovinotto*] S4; or *Giovinotto* youths MSO
230.25	us] S4; *om.* MSO
230.27	sponge-cake drops] S4; sponge-drops MSO
230.29	gentle] S4; kindly MSO
230.31	ought] S4; was MSO
230.31	to have been] S4; *om.* MSO
230.32	possible] HE; I could MSO; possibly S4
231.6	draught, but] S4; dose, for MSO
231.7	over] S4; over me MSO
231.11	have drugged] S4; provisionally drug MSO
231.12	must have] S4; *om.* MSO
231.13	suffocation] S4; suffocation with them MSO
231.18	opportunity] S4; which seems MSO
231.18	races] S4; peoples MSO
231.18	these] S4; these was MSO
231.21	such a] S4; a very MSO
231.25	my] S4; my dear young MSO
*231.27	him in my letters to her] S4; him -ness MSO
231.28	familiarity] S4; familiarity at once MSO
231.29	no] S4; *om.* MSO
231.31–32	boy, . . . him,] S4; boy with him, last school years, MSO
231.33	call upon us. Long after] S4; make his calls, but it was a some time before MSO
231.34	passed] S4; wore away. When it passed as much as it ever could MSO
231.34	town] S4; cauntree MSO
231.35	was going to pass the summer] S4; had gone to live the year round MSO
231.36–232.1	life, and we imagined] S4; life; it was as if he had imagined it out of an Unabridged Dictionary of Anglosaxon civilization, and we perceived MSO
232.2	an] S4; *om.* MSO

232.3   as] S4; *om.* MSO
232.6   than] S4; *om.* MSO
232.16   icy cold] S4; to an icy coldness MSO
232.18   provided] S4; provid- MSO
232.19   for] S4; *om.* MSO
232.21   our] S4; the MSO
232.22   but] S4; but which MSO
232.23   loathing] S4; loathing for MSO
232.27   then] S4; *om.* MSO
232.30   for] S4; *om.* MSO
232.30   persons] S4; people MSO
232.32   This] S4; It this MSO
232.36   taken] S4; taken from our society MSO
233.4   town] S4; cauntree MSO
233.4   *podestà* or mayor] S4; mayor or syndic MSO
233.4   place] S4; town MSO
*233.6   to a moustache] HE; to moustaches MSO; to a
               mustache S4
233.6   *Austriacante*] S4; Austricante MSO
233.7   walks] S4; walks about the place MSO
233.7   abruptly] S4; abrupt-/abruptly MSO
233.14   after a moment] S4; then MSO
233.18   They] S4; There MSO
233.24   found] S4; did find MSO
233.24   myself] S4; *om.* MSO
233.29   then] S4; *om.* MSO
233.31   partly] S4; *om.* MSO
233.34   Giustiniani] S4; Giustinian MSO
233.34-35   Canal . . . . was] S4; Canal, and I can only once
               distinctly visualize found him one day in our parlor
               perspiring after his walk from the Piazza and wip-
               ing his forehead while he panted out that it was
               thirty degrees of heat. He meant thirty degrees
               Reaumur, and I never could get the degrees of
               that thermometer into those of our familiar Fahr-
               enheit so as feel their extremes fitly; but I still see
               Pastorelli sitting there wiping his forehead, and
               suffering from the sun which beat upon the shutters
               of our balconies and distilled the rosin through

their green paint. But after that there is an interval
of weeks and months in Venice in which there is
no sight of him, and then MSO

234.1	so] S4; *om.* MSO
234.3	we . . . than] S4; heard nothing as MSO
234.5	him,] S4; him. Perhaps I did not ask very insist- ently, MSO
234.9	eighty,] S4; eighty, and I do not feel it such super- annuation; MSO
234.15	painful,] S4; ~ MSO
234.18	Melema] S4; Malemma MSO
*234.19	*cauntree*] S4; cauntree MSO
234.21	weeks;] S4; weeks, and MSO
234.28	In] S4; I had kept my writing a secret from my wiser self, but now I had to own what I had done. "But we are all packed, and we must be at Verona day after tomorrow, and we can't go to see him. But we must!" "But we can't," I reasoned, and I urged all the fact of all the arrangements we had made I prevailed against my wish and hers, and in MSO
234.28	him] S4; Pastorelli MSO
234.29–30	him; we . . . and] S4; him while MSO
234.32	explained] S4; explained and explained MSO
234.33–34	have been wishing] S4; am trying MSO
234.35	waste the little] S4; waste that little that MSO
235.3	had come] S4; came MSO
235.12	friend. Perhaps] S4; ~. ¶ ~ MSO
235.15	a] S4; a a MSO
235.15	money] S4; mony MSO
235.17	my] S4; *om.* MSO
235.17	humiliation] S4; shame MSO
235.17–18	atonement. When] S4; ~. ¶ ~ MSO
235.18	*timonella*] S4; timonella MSO
235.20	in the gallery] S4; *om.* MSO
235.22	young] S4; *om.* MSO
235.23	Howells] S4; H. MSO
235.23	called] S4; called out MSO
235.25	had come] S4; was there MSO

235.29	otherwise imperfectly] S4; *om.* MSO
235.30	his deep-brimmed] S4; the deep MSO
235.30	and] S4; and the MSO
235.30	suit] S4; suit which he was wearing MSO
235.33	get] S4; himself MSO
235.35	beautiful] S4; *om.* MSO
235.35	villa] S4; villa which MSO
235.36	town;] S4; Cauntree; and MSO
236.4	travelling] HE; able to travel MSO; traveling S4
236.6	always] S4; and always MSO
236.7	entreaty] S4; invitation MSO
236.8	He] S4; When he seemed tired he MSO
236.13	Liver*pull*] S4; Liver-*pull* MSO
236.18	them, but since] S4; him. Since MSO
236.20	he made] S4; he had made MSO
236.21	we] S4; he MSO
236.21	came] S4; came in MSO
236.23	how] S4; *om.* MSO
236.29	swimming] S4; dimming MSO
236.32	most] S4; most ancient and MSO
236.36	this] S4; that MSO
237.3	first] S4; *om.* MSO
237.5	Latin peoples] S4; Spanish-speaking people MSO
237.6	the enthusiasm which endeared] S4; his enthusiasm for MSO
237.7	to him] S4; *om.* MSO
237.9	our] S4; our own MSO
237.11	*italianissimi*] S4; Italianissimistic MSO
237.12	than] S4; *om.* MSO
237.14	Venetians] S4; Venetians of his sex MSO
237.16	Liver*pull*] S4; Liverrpull MSO
237.17	Venetians] S4; Venitians MSO
237.18	clergymen] S4; churchmen MSO
237.19	except] S4; exccept MSO
237.21	language] S4; languages MSO
237.23	when] S4; for MSO
237.25	somehow] S4; ~, MSO
237.27	as I] S4; as I as I MSO
237.31	justify,] S4; ~ MSO

237.32   that] S4; that there MSO

, "A Young Venetian Friend"

246.8–9   beginning,] HE; ~ S5
247.5   but in] HE; but it S5

Rejected Substantives

The following list records all substantive variants subsequent to the reading accepted at each point in the present edition which have been rejected as non-authorial. The reading of the present edition appears to the left of the bracket; the source of that reading, followed by a semicolon, the subsequent variant reading or readings and their sources appear to the right of the bracket. The reading of any unlisted text, antecedent or subsequent, other than copy-text, which is extant for that portion of the present text (see the table on pages 297–300) may be presumed to agree with the reading to the left of the bracket unless recorded in Emendations. If the authority for the present reading is other than the copy-text for that section, the copy-text reading is recorded in Emendations. The curved dash ∼ represents the same word that appears before the bracket and is used in recording punctuation and paragraphing variants. *Om.* means that the reading to the left of the bracket does not appear in the text cited to the right of the semicolon. The italicized form *MSY* indicates a non-authorial reading in the author's manuscript of *Years of My Youth*. An asterisk indicates that the reading is discussed in the Textual Notes.

The following texts are referred to:

MSY   117 leaves of printer's copy typescript of *Years of My Youth*

MSO   38 leaves of manuscript of "An Old Venetian Friend"

LG   Single galley sheet of *Years of My Youth* numbered 25

UG   41 leaves of unrevised first galleys for *Years of My Youth*

RG   61 leaves of author's revised first galleys for *Years of My Youth*

P1–P7   Seven partial sets of page proofs for *Years of My Youth*

N1   "The Coming," *Ohio State Journal*, 23 January 1860

R1   "The Coming," *Ohio State Journal*, Centennial Edition, 26 October 1911

S1   "Year in a Log-Cabin, A Bit of Autobiography," *Youth's Companion*, LX (May 1887)

S2   "The Country Printer," *Scribner's*, XIII (May 1893)
S3   "Overland to Venice," *Harper's Monthly*, CXXXVII (November 1918)
S4   "An Old Venetian Friend," *Harper's Monthly*, CXXXVIII (April 1919)
S5   "A Young Venetian Friend," *Harper's Monthly*, CXXXVIII (May 1919)
M   *My Year in a Log Cabin*, Harper and Brothers, 1893
T   "The Country Printer," *Impressions and Experiences*, Harper and Brothers, 1896
V   "The Country Printer," *Impressions and Experiences*, David Douglas, 1896
W   "The Country Printer," *Impressions and Experiences*, Harper and Brothers, 1909
A   *Years of My Youth*, Harper and Brothers, 1916

YEARS OF MY YOUTH

39.25	to] S1; of M
40.12	pioneering] S1; pioneer M, A
40.16	made] S1; made a M, A
41.23	Subose] S1; Suboss A
41.25	at] S1; in M, A
42.28	alarm] S1; alarum A
43.8	barbarous] S1; barbaric M, A
43.25	others] S1; other M
45.18	sounded] S1; bounded M, A
48.23	now if I were] S1; if I were now M, A
*51.13	effect] M; effort A
53.6	pits] S1; pit A
53.19	older] S1; elder A
55.23	crossed the] S1; crossed a M
*71.7	already] S2; always W, RG, A
73.23	seemed] S2; seem T-W, RG, A
75.33	self-respectful] S2; self-respecting T-W, RG, A
76.5	very] S2; *om.* T-W, RG, A
*76.12	around him,] S2; him, about A
76.13	about] S2; around A
76.28	had] S2; *om.* T-W, RG, A
78.9	journeymen] S2; journeyman V

93.18	fully] P1; fully already P2-P3, P5, A
101.32	his] P1; the P2–P3, P5, A
110	III] MSY; PART III UG
*111.3	a State Capital] MSY; State capital UG; a capital RG, P2–P3, P5, A
111.8	of. What] RG; ∼. ¶ ∼ P2–P3, P5, A
111.29	in] P2; *om.* P3, P5, A
111.33	experience] MSY; experiences UG, RG, P2–P3, P5, A
114.32	as any] MSY; an any UG, RG
115.24	well-warmed] MSY; well-armed UG
116.33	1856–7] MSY; 1856–57 UG, RG, P2–P3, P5, A
121.33	lived. He] MSY; ∼. ¶ ∼ UG, RG, P2–P3, P5, A
123.12	censorious] MSY; conscious UG, RG, P2–P3, P5, A
123.32	graduation] MSY; graduating UG, RG, P2–P3, P5, A
124.19	and] MSY; and I UG, RG, P2–P3, P5, A
125.6	these] MSY; those UG, RG, P2–P3, P5, A
127.30	tacitly] MSY; tactily UG, RG
129.26	Reed] MSY; *om.* P2
130.13–14	journalism. He] MSY; ∼. ¶ ∼ UG
131.12	either with] MSY; with either UG, RG, P2–P3, P5, A
136.20–21	odorless] MSY; ordorless UG, RG
138.23	Swedenborgian] MSY; Swendenborgian UG, RG
*138.35	verse. Naturally] MSY; ∼. ¶ ∼ UG, RG, P2–P3, P5, A
143.11	sea. But] MSY; ∼. ¶ ∼ UG, RG, P2-P3, P5, A
143.28	uncaterpillared] MSY; underpillared UG
143.32	Bullfinch] MSY; Bellfinch UG
143.36	full] MSY; all UG, RG, P2–P3, P5, A
147.36–148.1	juridical] MSY; judicial UG, RG, P2–P3, P5, A
148.11	where] MSY; when UG, RG, P2–P3, P5, A
148.15	at least once] MSY; once at least UG, RG, P2–P3, P5, A
152.10	me] MSY; us UG
153.6	by] MSY; of UG, RG
154.33	word] MSY; work UG, RG
155.7	Fellows'] MSY; Fellow's UG, RG, P2–P3, P5, A
155.33	usage] MSY; usages UG, RG, P2–P3, P5
156.29	those] MSY; these UG, RG

158.6	experience] MSY; experiences UG
158.7	conjecture] MSY; conjucture UG
158.25	is] MSY; it UG
160.13	rate] MSY; right UG, RG
160.34	or disorder] MSY; *om.* UG, RG, P2–P3, P5, P7, A
162.10	Oswald] MSY; Oswalf UG
162.25	understood] MSY; stood UG
163.14	for that] MSY; for the *MSY*
172.24–25	rhyme!/The] MSY; ~. ¶ ~ UG, RG, P3, P5, A
172.33	ideals] MSY; idols UG
173.12–13	poem. ¶ I] MSY; ~. ~ UG, RG, P3, P5, A
177.22	Lamon's] MSY; Laoon's UG
178.5	book's] MSY; books UG, RG
178.7	forestalled] MSY; forestalle UG
181.28	citizen] MSY; a citizen UG
185.27	sculpture] MSY; sculptor UG
185.29	capitol] MSY; capital UG, RG, P3, P5, A
189.26	national] MSY; personal UG, RG, P3, P5
189.26	resources] MSY; recourses UG
190.16	but] MSY; *om.* UG, RG, P3, P5–P6, A
190.28	on much] MSY; on as much A
191.1	its] MSY; it A
191.12–13	done. ¶ Their] MSY; done./xi ¶ Their UG, RG; done./xii ¶ Their P3, P5–P6
192.2	home from the dance] MSY; from the dance UG; to their homes RG, P3, P5–P6, A
*194.22	they brooked no self-question of it;] MSY; *om.* P3(2)
194.27	It] MSY; If A
195.22	battle] MSY; bottle UG
201.20	of their] MSY; of the UG, RG, P3, P5, P7, A
202.10	play] MSY; played UG
*203.34–204.2	I had heard . . . not know.] MSY; *om.* P3, P5, P7, A
204.33–34	overweening] MSY; everweening UG, RG
206.2	somewhere we] UG; we somewhere P3, P5, P7, A

"An Old Venetian Friend"

*226.9–10	pseudonym. ¶ The] MSO; ~. ~ S4
227.6	N——] MSO; N——'s S4
232.22	so] MSO; *om.* S4

Word-Division

List A records compounds or possible compounds hyphenated at the
end of the line in the copy-text for each portion of the present edition
(or in readings after copy-text if authoritative) and resolved as hyphenated or one word as listed below. If the words occur elsewhere
in the copy-texts or if Howells' manuscripts of this period fairly consistently followed one practice respecting the particular compound
or possible compound, the resolution was made on that basis. Otherwise his *Harper's* or other periodical texts of this period were used as
guides, as were contemporary unpublished materials. List B is a guide
to transcription of compounds or possible compounds hyphenated at
the end of the line in the present text: compounds recorded here
should be transcribed as given; words divided at the end of the line
and not listed should be transcribed as one word.

LIST A

4.29	clergyman
5.9	-grandfather
9.5	*Downfall*
10.35	grandfather
14.20	grandmother
23.13	antislavery
23.25	over-proud
23.33–34	preoccupied
24.19	printing-office
25.11	homesick
25.13	beef-steak
26.28	passenger-boats
29.27	cabin-boys
30.12	three-days'
30.31	mis-shapen
33.33	Sunday-evening
34.12	circus-rehearsals
35.10	simple-hearted
35.26	water-works
36.17	wide-spread
39.12	clap-boarded
40.20	wildwood
41.18	saw-mill
41.21	tail-race
41.34	hide-bound
42.24	disoccupation
43.5	housewifely
43.29	weak-minded
46.5	self-sugared
47.6	saw-logs
49.12	snapping-turtles
49.23	pearl-disease

418

49.24	muskrats	117.8–9	tobacco-smoked
51.34	childhood	117.26–27	beer-saloons
52.7	tub-wheels	125.27	newspaper
54.29	log-cabin	129.3	self-sufficing
55.15	half-way	135.12	over-imagined
55.18	log-cabin	145.34	twenty-three
58.25	newspaper	149.7	Northwestern
62.30	typesetting	149.22	sky-scraping
63.3	sitting-room	151.4	stepdaughters
64.29	printer-boy	152.4	ever-widening
67.29	half-holidays	160.23	one-o'clock
67.33	homesick	162.32	twenty-five
68.26	book-room	167.5	thick-lashed
70.31	county-seat	174.17	backwoods
71.12	outnumber	174.21	underlay
72.19	office-building	179.17	northwestern
73.25	publication-day	182.26	half-dozens
74.10	hand-press	182.27	spirit-lamps
75.30	make-up	187.28	cannon-shot
77.18	printing-office	191.30	childhood
79.21	snake-bite	192.36	self-mocking
82.13–14	sixteen-bladed	197.11	brigadier-general
87.26–27	blackberry-patch	201.23–24	windrows
88.12	poverty-stricken	205.23	midnight
88.26	half-dazed	209.21	outspeeded
93.32	canal-digger	209.25	vice-consul
94.19	old-fashioned	210.4	first-cabin
95.7	single-handed	211.29	smoking-room
95.22	printing-office	214.32	omnibus-
95.26	overweight	215.1	spring-bottoms
98.18	printing-business	216.10	eating-rooms
98.30	half-soled	218.7	schoolmaster
99.17	fellow-villagers	218.16	schoolmaster
100.6–7	newspaper	218.19	schoolmaster
102.11–12	text-books	220.8	apartment-houses
103.28	newspaper	220.23	overnight
108.31–32	shamefacedly	223.10	misadventures
112.16	plank-road	223.19	fellow-travellers
113.9	armchairs	225.23	twenty-four

236.30	straightforward	73.22	county-seat
237.18	clergymen	74.6	power-press
244.28–29	summer-evening	74.8	hand-press
		74.16	second-hand
	LIST B	78.1	boy-apprentice
		88.10	apprentice-girls
11.17	blue-eyed	91.33	-and-book
15.30	simple-heartedly	91.35	organ-builder
22.12	Sunday-school	92.7	sleigh-rides
23.31	corn-meal	92.35	dry-goods
26.19	-the-River	102.11	text-books
27.30	down-stream	117.8	tobacco-smoked
29.3	log-cabins	117.15	gold-plate
29.6	coast-born	117.26	beer-saloons
29.13	pilot-house	118.18	old-fashioned
31.20	tri-weekly	118.26	smooth-shaven
32.14	street-fighting	131.23	composing-room
36.9	printing-office	146.34	law-abiding
37.14	fellow-apprentice	147.15	right-minded
42.12	iron-weeds	149.15	ninety-nine
42.25	brick-yard	149.18	over-muchness
45.12	-a-day	150.35	old-world
46.27	ever-beautiful	155.2	self-denial
47.31	battle-ground	164.15	news-editor's
49.2	red-hot	180.19	travel-adventure
49.12	water-snakes	181.1	book-store
49.30	weak-kneed	181.10	old-fashioned
50.3	log-hut	185.5	hunting-shirt
51.24	long-fallen	202.8	brigadier-general
53.5	saw-dust	208.21	sword-hilts
55.23	tail-race	215.10	second-class
63.28	shirt-bosoms	216.13	second-class
64.5	printing-office	222.26	self-respect
69.22	dissecting-room	242.8	self-respectful
70.16	printing-business	244.15	wooden-heeled
71.22	saw-mills	244.28	summer-evening